The Social and Political Life of Latin American Infrastructures

The Social and Political Life of Latin American Infrastructures

Edited by Jonathan Alderman and Geoff Goodwin

SCHOOL OF
ADVANCED STUDY
UNIVERSITY
OF LONDON

University of London Press
Centre for Latin American and Caribbean Studies,
Institute of Modern Languages Research,
School of Advanced Study,
University of London, 2022

British Library Cataloguing-in-Publication Data
A catalogue record for this publication is available from the British Library

This book is also available online at http://humanities-digital-library.org.

ISBN:
978-1-908857-95-8 (paperback edition)
978-1-908857-97-2 (.epub edition)
978-1-908857-98-9 (.pdf edition)

DOI: 10.14296/gljm4371

Cover image: Skyline of São Paulo in the haze of the dawn, Brazil, South America. Jose Luis Stephens/Shutterstock.com.

Centre for Latin American and Caribbean Studies
Institute of Modern Languages Research
School of Advanced Study
University of London
Senate House
London WC1E 7HU

Contents

Notes on contributors

Jonathan Alderman is currently a Postdoctoral Fellow at LMU Munich, and has previously been a Stipendiary Fellow at the Institute of Latin American Studies, University of London. He has a PhD in Social Anthropology from the University of St Andrews, an MA in Latin American Studies from the Institute for the Study of the Americas, University of London, and a BA in Philosophy from the University of Essex. His work explores subject formation in the US–Mexico borderland and in Andean Bolivia, and how the relationships between people and the state and the landscape in the Andes are mediated through infrastructure and ritual.

Ursula Balderson is currently working on a project about labour responses to climate change at the Centre for Employment Relations Innovation and Change at the University of Leeds. Prior to this she completed a postdoctoral project at the University of Cambridge. She is an interdisciplinary social scientist whose work considers the socio-political and emotional dimensions of infrastructure projects and how work and workers will be affected by the transition to a greener economy. She obtained her PhD from Newcastle University.

Sarah Bennison is a Research Fellow at the University of St Andrews, where she has worked since 2017. Her interdisciplinary Andeanist research interests include water customs, customary law, khipus and community texts. With a primary interest in Peru, she specialises in irrigation rituals of the Huarochirí province (Lima) from the early colonial era to the current day. She graduated from Newcastle University in 2016 with a PhD in Iberian and Latin American studies funded by the Arts and Humanities Research Council. Her first book, *The Entablo Manuscript: Water Rituals and Khipu Boards of San Pedro de Casta, Peru*, will be published by University of Texas Press in 2023.

Julie Dayot has a background in Economics (from the École Normale Supérieure of Cachan) and after seven months of travel across South America – where she first encountered mining conflicts in the midst of protests in Cajamarca, Peru – she decided to apply for an MPhil in Development Studies at the University of Oxford. Her MPhil research brought her back to Latin America, and the Ecuadorian Amazon, where she analysed the dilemmas between 'difference' and 'equality' faced by the Quichua inhabitants of the Lower Napo River – where oil extraction projects come with environmental impacts, but also a 'social compensation' in the domains of health, education and basic services. Based on an eight-month second period of fieldwork in the Lower Napo River of the Ecuadorian Amazon, her PhD thesis is an ethnographic investigation of the acceptance of an oil extraction project by the Quichua communities of the Lower Napo River.

Nicole Fadellin is visiting faculty in the John Martinson Honors College at Purdue University. She has previously worked as a curator for the National Library of Peru, the Peruvian Ministry of Culture, and the House of Peruvian Literature. Her research focuses on the relationship between infrastructure studies and Latin American literary studies. She has examined the promise of infrastructure in contemporary Caribbean literature, and her next project explores cultural representations of energy infrastructure in the wake of the Cold War. She holds a PhD in Spanish from the University of Wisconsin-Madison.

Yuri Gama is currently a Latin American History PhD candidate, and an Instructor at University of Massachusetts Amherst. With a master's degree in Liberal Studies and a bachelor's degree in Social Sciences, his ongoing dissertation examines the urban history of Northeast Brazil between 1890 and 1990. Analysing urban planning, industrialisation, and development, his research unveils the intersection of affordable housing, citizenship and nation building while dissecting authorities and elites ideas and practices. Yuri's writings can be found in English and Portuguese on open-access and paywalled mediums such as Planning Perspectives, H-LatAm, and the Urban History Association website. Yuri has experience in oral history and public engagement, producing community-related journalistic and sociological content. Sharing his research and teachings, Yuri has been on podcasts, community radio shows, and published in blogs and ebooks. With experience in archival research and fieldwork, he has presented his research in Brazil, the United States and the UK.

Geoff Goodwin is a Lecturer in Global Political Economy at the University of Leeds. He previously taught at the London School of Economics, University of Oxford and University College London, and was a Research Associate at FLACSO-Quito. His interdisciplinary research focuses on land, water, infrastructure and activism in Ecuador and Colombia. He also recently started investigating water history, politics and infrastructure in London. He holds a PhD in Political Economy (University College London) and MA in Economics (University of Leeds).

Valeria Guarneros-Meza has a PhD in Public Policy. Her research focuses on the relationships between public management processes and citizen/community participation in contexts of local securitisation, informality and extractivism.

Her research has been published in international and interdisciplinary journals such as *Public Administration*, *International Journal of Urban and Regional Research* and *Latin American Perspectives*.

Penny Harvey is Professor of Social Anthropology at the University of Manchester. Her research has focused on infrastructures of social change, the material and social relations of modern statecraft, knowledge practices and the politics of value. She has conducted long-term ethnographic research in Peru looking at civic infrastructures projects including road construction, sanitation, and waste management systems. She co-founded the Beam network for social research on nuclear science and is currently engaged in the ethnographic study of nuclear infrastructures in the UK.

Sam Rumé is a doctoral candidate in Social Anthropology at the University of Manchester. He holds a BA in Social and Cultural Anthropology from the University of Aix-Marseille and an MA in Anthropology and Ethnography from the University of Barcelona. Having undertaken extensive fieldwork in Cuenca, Ecuador, in 2017–18 and 2020–21, his research focuses on the politics of urban change and sustainability, mobilities and infrastructures from a Latin American perspective.

Marcela Torres-Wong has a PhD in Political Science from the American University in Washington DC, a master's degree in Anthropology from the Pontificia Universidad Católica del Peru, and a law degree from the same university. Her research areas include socio-environmental conflicts, extractive industries, indigenous movements, and participatory institutions in Bolivia, Peru, and Mexico. Since 2017 she has served as a professor at the Latin American Faculty of Social Science (FLACSO-Mexico). Before that she served as an Indigenous rights lawyer for Indigenous organisations in the Peruvian Amazon. Her research has been funded by prestigious institutions such as the Inter-American Foundation and the Tinker Foundation, both based in Washington DC, as well as the National Center for Scientific Research in Paris (CNRS). She has carried out fieldwork in the Amazon basin in Peru and Bolivia, El Chaco in Bolivia, and Oaxaca, Chiapas, Tabasco, Mérida and San Luis Potosí in Mexico.

Diego Valdivieso received his PhD in Social Anthropology from the University of Manchester. Currently, he is a postdoctoral researcher at the Campus Villarrica of the Pontifical Catholic University of Chile and the Centre for Intercultural and Indigenous Research. Diego's work explores local configurations of the state, illustrated by the Chilean case, through the analysis of the everyday practices and experiences of state officials charged with the implementation of (rural) development programmes

Nicolás Valenzuela-Levi works as Assistant Professor at the Universidad Técnica Federico Santa María, Chile, teaching and doing research on issues of territorial studies and urban planning at the Department of Architecture. He obtained the Architecture and Master in Urban Development degrees from the Pontificia Universidad Católica de Chile, and the MPhil in Development Studies and PhD in Land Economy from the University of Cambridge. His work concentrates on the link between urban infrastructure and inequalities, using the lens of institutional political economy and environmental sciences. He has published his work on sectors such as transport, telecommunications and waste management, including case studies such as Santiago de Chile, Medellin, London and Barcelona. As part of his non-academic work, he was appointed to the board of directors of the Metro de Santiago for the 2022–24 period.

Dr Clara Voyvodic Casabó is a Senior Research Fellow at the University of Bristol in the Department of Sociology, Politics, and International Studies. She holds a PhD in International Relations from the University of Oxford. Her research focuses on the impact of armed conflict, organised crime and development on local order, focusing on Colombia. She has also taught Politics, International Relations, International Security and Conflict, History of the Cold War and the World Wars, State Crime and Terrorism, and Political Philosophy.

List of figures

Acknowledgements

This book stems from a one-day workshop held at the Institute of Latin American Studies, University of London, on 20 September 2019. Most of the contributors to this book participated in the event and the chapters included in this book are based on their workshop papers. We would like to thank Linda Newson and Olga Jiménez for helping to organize the event and Miranda Sheild Johansson and Patrick O'Hare for chairing panels and contributing to the workshop. We are indebted to Penny Harvey for her encouragement and support throughout this project and for her terrific foreword to this book. Two external reviewers provided excellent comments and suggestions on a complete draft of the book manuscript, which helped us make significant improvements to the volume. Everyone at University of London Press has been kind, attentive, and patient throughout the writing and publication process. We would particularly like to thank Robert Davies for his fantastic work pulling together the manuscript. We are also grateful to the SFB1369 at Ludwig Maximilian University and the German Research Foundation (DFG, Deutsche Forschungsgemeinschaft) for supporting the book project and to Eugena Koci for compiling the index. Finally, we would like to thank the contributing authors for making this book a reality. We have heard horror stories about compiling edited collections, but our experience has been precisely the opposite!

Foreword

Penny Harvey

Doreen Massey opened her influential book *For Space* by suggesting that 'it could be productive to think about space differently' (2005, p. 1). She was looking for a way to reformulate political questions in ways that would lend more weight to relational understandings of the world. More than anything she wanted to contribute to existing debates about how things could be otherwise, by demonstrating that there were always alternatives, despite the sensation that the contemporary trajectories of global systems, capitalist aspirations, and entrenched identities seemed to be both dominant and inevitable. She set the scene for this discussion by describing one formative moment of encounter in what would become the unfolding history of 'Latin America'. In November 1519, Hernán Cortés and his small army caught sight of the immense city of Tenochtitlán for the first time. She suggests that the Aztec leader, Moctezuma, had forebodings about the arrival of the Spanish army. The direction from which the strangers were approaching, coupled with calendrical alignments of diverse cosmological indicators, indicated a particular quality of time and space, and a potential fragility to what might otherwise have appeared as a solid position of power and authority. The Spanish forces were moved by an altogether different understanding of space as a continuous territory over which they could move, a surface on which they could act to impose their own, rightful future.

Massey had less to say about how this early modern European understanding of time and space prevailed. She was more interested in its limitations, and particularly in the consequences of its impoverished spatial imagination. The politics that she championed demanded a move away from thinking of space as a homogeneous surface and argued for the importance of conceptualising space as a site of encounter, a relational phenomenon where multiple trajectories confront and/or accommodate each other, hence the challenge to think about space differently, a challenge that has been taken up in many quarters over the following years. One of those ways has been to put infrastructures centre stage. So, what exactly has a focus on infrastructures brought to the table?

One key contribution has been to highlight the work of the material relations that underpin surface effects. Put simply, a focus on infrastructures is a focus on the otherwise mundane or hidden work involved in creating that sense of continuous space or surface that Massey wanted to challenge. Infrastructures are the mechanisms by which a seamless connectivity is achieved and stabilised.

Close empirical study of infrastructural systems has also drawn attention to how the achievement of continuity is premised on choices and channels that exclude alternatives. The intrinsic political life of any infrastructure refers to these choices, the interests they serve, and the struggles they provoke. An empirical focus on infrastructures also disrupts the primacy of surfaces, the assumptions of linear temporalities, or homogenous agency. Infrastructures rely on other conceptual bridges (notions of interface and alignment come into play), and gaps (hence the importance of leakage, repair, and decay). Instability, interruptions, and fragility are highlighted by the effort required to maintain the experience of seamless connectivity and flow. The tensions between engineered design and improvisation becomes highly visible as soon as any specific infrastructural project is followed or investigated from close-up. Equally the limits of human agency are also continually revealed by the hubris of the modern aspiration to control and contain wider environmental forces.

All these issues have clear political valence as we enter the third decade of the twenty-first century. The infrastructures and circulations of an industrialised global economy have produced a glittering array of technological possibilities alongside massive challenges, social inequalities, unspeakable human suffering, and the mass extinction of many other-than human life forms. Brutal conflicts over mineral resources, over territory, political autonomy, and financial accumulation, coupled with the effects of climate change have provoked the displacement of human populations, as migrants and refugees search for a modicum of stability from which to build a life worth living. Latin America is no stranger to such movements.

In the light of these arguments, it is strange to recall that it was less than a decade ago that Hannah Knox and I were still discussing whether or not to present our ethnography of roads in Peru as a book about 'infrastructure' (Harvey and Knox, 2015). At the time, the foundational work on infrastructures was written by those working on communications technologies (Bowker and Star, 1999; Edwards, 2007, 2009, 2010; Star, 1999; Star and Ruhleder, 1996) and the concept of 'network' was more commonly debated by theorists of connectivity and circulation. However, in time 'infrastructure' proved to be a more grounded, more flexible, and more overtly political concept than the network. The focus it provided generated an ongoing stream of fascinating empirical research across the social sciences and humanities. The 'infrastructure' concept captured something of the anticipation and the promise of material transformation. It also pointed to the tangible often obdurate presence that prompted researchers to explore failed and abandoned experiments and to think about previous histories of future making, alongside those that continue to be generated today. Furthermore, as this collection clearly demonstrates, infrastructures are not limited to a notion of networked connectivity. On the contrary, the connectivity that infrastructures produce is intermittent, compromised, and partial in its distribution. Infrastructures are designed to constrain and channel movement but also routinely expand, extend, and leak not least because they provoke responses in and from the world they seek to order and constrain. And in the process, they consistently pose fresh questions and novel sites from which to consider the politics of material relations – whether in unnoticed everyday spaces, or in dramatic corporate and state-sponsored constructions, in the archive, the media, or in bureaucratic practices.

This collection clearly acknowledges the multivalence of engineered infrastructures, and the capacity of these material forms to exceed the purposes for which they were designed. Thus, we find an echo of Massey's call to think differently about space, and to show how and why infrastructures emerge as sites of political action. Designed to deliver a seamless flow, these systems become obvious targets for those seeking to disrupt the complacency of an unexamined status quo. As I write, the 'Insulate Britain' movement is taking radical action to block one of the UK's main motorways, the M25 that was built to enable the circulation of traffic around the Greater London area. The activists are seeking to draw attention to the causes and effects of climate change. Their challenge is to a government, and to voters, who argue that it is criminal to cause misery to motorists and/or to disrupt the workings of the economy, but who show little concern to the misery of those whose lives and livelihoods have been decimated by climate change. Their aim is to disrupt the complacency of space as surface, to show what it feels like to live in a space of disruption, and to pose the question of priorities, to ask what matters, and who it matters to. It is precisely because of the enabling function of infrastructural systems, and the simultaneity of connectivity and disconnection that infrastructures afford, that the politics of space can turn so quickly to a struggle over the grounds for life itself.

Thus, despite the continuing enthusiasm for infrastructural solutions to all manner of human difficulties, there is no sense in which such solutions have any intrinsic emancipatory quality. On the contrary, the weaponisation of infrastructural systems has been grasped with alacrity not only by protest groups but also by powerful state and corporate actors. Eyal Weizman's classic work on the politics of Israel's architecture of occupation (Weizman, 2007, 2017) reminds us of the centrality of infrastructural systems to the politics of territorial containment and control. These strategies of containment do not emerge from an impoverished spatial imagination. On the contrary they embrace the ambiguities and uncertainties of continuity and disruption, of visibility and invisibility, and of open-ended relational space. Wars are fought strategically, and in these circumstances the infrastructures that sustain life will always become key sites of vulnerability. Attacks on roads and bridges, on food and water supplies, on shelter and communications have always shaped human conflicts. The surprising element of Weizman's study (2007) was his elaboration of the extent to which the Israeli army was strategically mobilising the work of Deleuze and Guattari, thinking with Massey about how to move beyond the surface, open to the possibilities of material elasticity, understanding the importance of infrastructures, of the sub-surface, of the air, of the possibilities of moving through space in unexpected ways. The confrontations of both war and protest are experimental in the sense that they emerge from the search to find new and surprising geometries of space, new possibilities for surveillance and attack. Contemporary warfare does not necessarily involve face-to-face combat. But this is not to in any way diminish the importance of the huge investments made by those who work tirelessly to bring more liveable worlds into being (Escobar, 2018). Here again infrastructures come to the fore, in the architectures of collaboration and mutual commitment, and in the materialisation of the aesthetic and affective possibilities of living otherwise. The excitement of thinking through the politics of infrastructures lies squarely in these spaces of possibility – the acts of inclusion and exclusion that make for both life and death, the need for connection and for autonomy, the strategies and counterstrategies for containment and disruption. Infrastructures thus not only create the grounds of possibility for specific forms and ways of life but also for the expansive connections that both sustain and potentially undermine very diverse ways of being. Liveable worlds must constantly be made and remade, always adjusting and confronting possibilities that others, often distant and anonymous others, put in place.

What then of the notion of Latin American infrastructures? If infrastructures are the many different and often conflicting material conditions of possibility for multiple life forms, and forms of life, through what lens do they acquire a regional, or even local identity or significance? The question brings me back to the significance of this collection of essays that works with the recognition of infrastructures as *both* open-ended systems of connectivity and circulation *and* as identifiable assemblages that affect lives in particular ways, in specific times and places. The empirical questions that infrastructures pose always include both the identification of connections and circulations that are supported, and those that are curtailed or closed off. Thus, we can ask about the intended effects of specific designs, and the responses that these designs elicit over time. But such questions can only be answered with reference to specified encounters.

The editors have identified three key themes that emerged across the diverse case studies presented here: nation, state, and citizenship; development, promise, and progress; disappointment, failure, and decay. These themes clearly point to sites of powerful intersection and encounter that justify a regional focus. At the same time, the chapters also reflect more localised regional sensibilities and a clear awareness of the overarching effects of the histories of imperial politics from Europe, the USA, the Soviet Union, and most recently from China. These intersections conjure a sense of encounter that both re-creates and threatens the relevance of any specific regional political agency. These shifting scales of association return me to my starting point, this time via the work of Mol and Law (1994) and their interest in the contrasting social topologies that structured responses to the incidence of anaemia caused by malnutrition. Working, for sake of example, with the spatial entities of 'Africa' and 'the Netherlands' Mol and Law were interested in the different relational assumptions embedded in three contrasting figures: regional clusters, networks of stable relations, and what they refer to as 'fluid spatiality' where contingency, mutation, and variation come to the fore. There are clear resonances here with our current experience of the coronavirus pandemic and the politics of space. In December 2021, a new variant of the virus, omicron, threatens human populations. Many different possible infrastructures of contagion are considered as points of vulnerability, including regions, networks, and fluid spatialities. Thus, we find whole 'regions' identified as dangerous. From the perspective of the UK government, it is currently the African nations that are designated as the most hazardous, and travel to and from this region is curtailed. These acts of spatial generalisation have taken many different shapes over the past two years. Several months ago, it was Latin America. More locally in the UK itself, some regions of the country were locked down, while others were encouraged to stay open. While the regional confinements come and go, all are asked to be attentive to their social networks, the proximity of interpersonal encounters is also regulated in public spaces. The precautions are imposed as infrastructures for health (masks, vaccines, hygiene, proximities, ventilation, etc.), that in turn create new challenges of isolation, of mistrust, of unevenly distributed regulation, etc. In practice the agile mutations of the virus demonstrate a far more fluid spatiality, its own infrastructures of mutability not yet clear enough to those who work to limit its capacity to spread.

Perhaps more important than anything at the current moment is the need to search for a diplomatic awareness of the positioning of others. Again, the empirical chapters in this collection are instructive because they were researched in close relationship to people actively looking for ways to produce or imagine liveable conditions for engaging uncertain futures. It is in such spaces that even the most spectacular of infrastructural initiatives becomes mundane, ultimately the assemblage is no more (and no less) than what it can and does deliver in the everyday. At the same time, as numerous writers have taught us, the everyday is made in the shadow of previous encounters. The specific ways in which prior events registered and affected people's lives resonate and form the ground of future possibilities.

References

Bowker, G. and S.L. Star (1999) *Sorting Things Out: Classification and its Consequences* (Cambridge, MA: MIT Press).

Edwards, P.N. (2010) *A Vast Machine: Computer Models, Climate Data, and the Politics of Global Warming* (Cambridge, MA: MIT Press).

Edwards, P.N. et al. (2007) *Understanding Infrastructure: Dynamics, Tensions, and Design* (Ann Arbor, MI: Deep Blue).

Edwards, P.N. et al. (2009) 'Introduction: an agenda for infrastructure studies', *Journal of the Association for Information Systems*, 10 (5): 6.

Escobar, A. (2018) *Designs for the Pluriverse: Radical Interdependence, Autonomy, and the Making of Worlds* (Durham, NC: Duke University Press).

Harvey, P. and H. Knox (2015) *Roads: An Anthropology of Infrastructure and Expertise* (Ithaca, NY: Cornell University Press).

Mol, A. and J. Law. (1994) 'Regions, networks and fluids: anaemia and social topology', *Social Studies of Science*, 24 (4): 641–71.

Massey, D. (2005) *For Space*. (London: Sage Publications).

Star, S.L. (1999) 'The ethnography of infrastructure', *American Behavioral Scientist* 43(3): 377–91.

Star, S.L. and K. Ruhleder (1996) 'Steps toward an ecology of infrastructure: design and access for large information spaces', *Information Systems Research*, 7 (1): 111–34.

Weizman, E. (2007) *Hollow Land: Israel's Architecture of Occupation* (New York: Verso Books).

Weizman, E. (2017) *Forensic Architecture: Violence at the Threshold of Detectability* (New York: Zone Books).

Introduction: infrastructure as relational and experimental process

Jonathan Alderman and Geoff Goodwin

Introduction[1]

In early October 2019, thousands of Ecuadorians took to the streets to protest against the IMF-sponsored austerity politics of the Moreno government. The trigger for the protest was the sudden removal of fuel subsidies, which reduced the cost of transport and the price of essential goods. In Quito, the capital, members of indigenous, student, transport, teacher and labour movements flooded the narrow streets and expansive plazas of the *centro histórico* and occupied public spaces throughout the city. Elsewhere in the Andes, indigenous protesters blocked the Panamericana, the undulating highway that connects Ecuador to Colombia in the north, and Peru in the south. Boulders, rocks, trees, and tyres were strewn across the road at strategic points to regulate the circulation of people, goods, and vehicles. Meanwhile, thousands of indigenous peoples from across the Andes marched along the Panamericana to Quito, before occupying El Arbolito park; close to the National Assembly – a symbolic site of state power. Faced with escalating state repression, indigenous protesters sought refuge in the Casa de la Cultura, a glittering modernist building constructed in the 1940s to promote cultural activity and forge national identity. Inside, drawing on long-established practices, the protesters formed their own assembly to deliberate and strategise. The scale and intensity of the protests forced the Moreno government to backdown, reinstate the fuel subsidies, and enter into dialogue with representatives of social movements. Yet the protest came at terrible human cost, with state violence leaving at least eleven protesters dead and thousands more injured.

Similar scenes unfolded across Latin America in late 2019 as waves of protests brought the decade to a tumultuous close. The causes, sites, and tactics of these

1 We are indebted to Hanne Cottyn, Adriana Massidda and Marlit Rosolowsky for providing feedback and guidance on this chapter. Several of the contributing authors also read and commented on this chapter, leading to significant improvements. We remain responsible for any errors and omissions.

J. Alderman and G. Goodwin, 'Introduction: infrastructure as relational and experimental process' in *The Social and Political Life of Latin American Infrastructures*, ed. J. Alderman and G. Goodwin (London, 2022), pp. 1–26. License: CC BY-NC-ND 4.0.

mobilisations were multiple, as were the actors involved. Yet they revealed a crucial point: the centrality of infrastructure to the social and political life of Latin America. Taking this as a point of departure, this volume analyses the social and political dimensions of a wide range of Latin American infrastructures, from a crumbling nuclear plant in Cuba to a sparkling tram network in Ecuador. In doing so, it makes a unique contribution to the cross-disciplinary infrastructure literature and the multidisciplinary field of Latin American studies. In this introductory chapter, we tie together the main empirical and theoretical threads of the book and weave them into this literature. We identify three core themes that cut across the volume and connect it to the existing scholarship: i) *nation, state, citizenship* ii) *development, promise, progress*, and iii) *disappointment, failure, decay*. We argue that insights related to these three broad themes provide support for conceptualising infrastructure as a relational and experimental process. Our conceptual approach builds explicitly on the working definition of infrastructures elaborated by Harvey et al. (2017, p. 5): 'material assemblages that generate effects and structure social relations, either through engineered (i.e. planned and purposefully crafted) or non-engineered (i.e. unplanned and emergent) activities'. Hence, infrastructures have relational and experimental qualities and are better understood as open-ended processes rather than static and stable configurations. This suggests analytical attention should not only be paid to the plans, designs, and materiality of infrastructures but also to the diverse effects and relations they generate. Conceptualising infrastructure as a relational and experimental process therefore draws attention to the temporal and historical dimensions of infrastructure. While this book focuses on infrastructures in the 20th and 21st centuries, we situate them within a longer historical arc, including the period of colonial-capitalist expansion, which commenced in Latin America in the late 15th and early 16th centuries. Thus, Latin American infrastructures are connected to long-run historical processes of accumulation, commodification, and colonialism and these processes weigh heavily on contemporary dynamics. Infrastructures have also been at the centre of resistance to these processes, including socialist struggles to challenge global capitalist structures and relations and indigenous efforts to resist colonial-capitalist development. The chapters in this volume provide important new insights into these issues and demonstrate the analytical value of exploring social and political change through infrastructure.

In the remainder of this introduction, we further explicate the conceptual case for viewing infrastructure as a relational and experimental process, before considering the specificity of Latin American infrastructures, and discussing the book's three core themes in greater detail: i) *nation, state, citizenship* ii) *development, promise, progress*, and iii) *disappointment, failure, decay*. The chapter concludes by signalling the wider contributions this volume makes to Latin American studies scholarship.

Infrastructure as relational and experimental process

The wave of protests that swept across Latin America at the end of the 2010s indicates the relational and experimental nature of infrastructure. Roads, for example, are not only used to circulate and connect but also to disrupt and immobilise. Blocking roads offers protesters the opportunity to derail daily life, bring visibility to their struggles, and interrupt processes of commodification and accumulation. Dependence on markets for the provisioning of essential goods makes Latin American towns and cities particularly vulnerable to blockades. Roads connect urban consumers to national and international markets and help stack the shelves of shops and supermarkets. While their role in this process often goes unnoticed, during protests they are thrust into the forefront of everyday life and their operation (or lack thereof) becomes an urgent social and political concern. Blockades therefore not only bring visibility to the grievances and demands of protesters but also to the social and political life of Latin American infrastructures (Star, 1999; Anand, 2020; Colven, 2020).

The visibility of infrastructure relates to its unpredictability and rebelliousness. Rather than evolving along the paths envisioned by politicians, engineers, and planners, infrastructures often travel in surprising directions and generate unexpected social, political, and environmental effects (Harvey 2017 et al.; Anand, 2017; Gupta, 2018; Goodwin, 2018). Multiple factors explain this. First, infrastructures are not only made by planners and engineers but also by the people who use and occupy them. Hence, there are always 'non-engineered' and 'emergent' dimensions to infrastructure that politicians, engineers, and planners cannot fully control (Harvey et al., 2017, pp. 13–14). Take, for example, public plazas, one of the defining features of Latin American towns and cities. Built to promote civic engagement and religious obedience, protesters routinely use them to contest citizenship and challenge religious authorities. Equally, the steps of a private bank might be constructed to allow access to customers and employees and convey a sense of security and prestige, but they are also sporadically used by skateboarders, who hurl along them, shattering the orderly visions of corporate planners in the process. Infrastructures are therefore contested spaces where different meanings and practices collide and interact. The unpredictability of infrastructure is accentuated by its recursive or dialectic qualities: infrastructure generates economic, social, political, and ecological effects, which feed back to reconfigure infrastructure in a continuous cycle of undetermined change (Harvey, 2017 et al.). The complex web of relations that are established through infrastructures are impossible to predetermine, being 'subject to experimentation' (Harvey et al., 2017, p. 12; see also, Anand, 2017; Gupta, 2018). This cautions against drawing simple lines between cause and effect, especially since infrastructural effects are not spatially or temporally bounded.

This process can bring into being 'new practical ontologies' or 'new configurations of the world' (Jensen and Morita, 2017, p. 618; see also Barua, 2021). Infrastructures thereby have the potential to reconfigure what is regarded as 'natural' or 'social' in a particular setting. Indeed, Escobar (2017) argues that ontology is inherent in the design process: 'every tool or technology is ontological in the sense that, however humbly or minutely, it inaugurates a set of rituals, ways of doing, and modes of being', thus 'in designing tools, we (humans) design the conditions for our existence and, in turn the conditions of our designing. We design tools and these tools design us back' (Escobar, 2017, p. 110; see also Stengers, 2010). This draws critical attention to the actors involved in the design of infrastructure and their epistemological, ontological, and ideological proclivities (Harvey and Knox, 2015; Appel et al., 2018; Bear, 2020). Much infrastructure in Latin America, for example, is based on dualist modernist ontologies which dichotomise 'nature' and 'society', and infrastructures designed along these lines promote this separation. This can create tensions when infrastructures are introduced in settings where divergent ontologies (co)exist. Thus, infrastructures are a key domain of ontological and pluriversal politics (de la Cadena, 2010, 2015; Bennison, 2016; Escobar, 2017, 2020; Tym, 2020).

Conceptualising infrastructures as seditious and experimental draws attention to infrastructural cracks and splinters (Graham and Marvin, 2001). While gaps within and between Latin American infrastructures have always been evident (e.g. Bennett, 1998; Swyngedouw, 1997), they have expanded and multiplied since the early 1980s as public investment has declined and private firms have taken a more central role in funding and operating infrastructure (World Bank, 1994; Wilson, 2004; Harvey et al., 2017; Appel et al., 2018). Headline figures indicate this general trend: public infrastructure investment in Latin America dropped from 3 per cent of GDP in the early 1980s to less than 1 per cent in the early 2000s, while private investment increased from 0.5 per cent to 1.5 per cent during the same period (CEPAL 2016, p. 5).[2] This downward trend in public investment was reversed in the late 2000s as some Latin American governments took advantage of favourable economic conditions to restore or construct infrastructure. This proved short-lived, however, as the end of the commodity boom, the Odebrecht corruption scandal, and increased economic and political instability negatively impacted public infrastructure investment across the region.[3]

2 Infrastructure investment in Latin America lags behind most other regions in the world. See Calderón and Servén (2011) and CEPAL (2016) for historical and comparative data.

3 Odebrecht was a Brazilian construction firm that paid bribes to politicians and bureaucrats in exchange for lucrative infrastructure contracts. The scandal swept across Latin America in the 2010s, resulting in the imprisonment of several high-ranking politicians and bureaucrats and contributing to the decline or weakening of incumbent presidents and governments. See Durand (2019).

The splintering of Latin American infrastructure since the 1980s has been associated with deterioration, as public services and infrastructures have been run down or transferred to private firms to manage (Appel et al., 2018). Heightened reliance on the private sector has increased space for multinational corporations to develop and operate Latin American infrastructure, while financialisation has converted it into a 'global asset class' (Bear, 2020; see also Loftus et al., 2019; Pryke and Allen, 2019).[4] Infrastructure therefore not only supports the circulation and expansion of capital *within* Latin America but also the flow of capital *out* of Latin America. In doing so, it can cement global centre-periphery structures and relations (Prebisch, 1950; dos Santos, 1970). While global neoliberal restructuring has facilitated outflows of capital from Latin America (Harvey 2003), this has been a prominent feature of capitalism for centuries, as Galeano's famous metaphor of the 'open veins' of Latin America graphically depicts (Galeano, 1973/1997). Yet, as we have already suggested, infrastructure does not always bolster capitalist relations and processes, and, as the recent wave of protests in Latin America have shown, it can also be used to subvert accumulation and commodification and support non-capitalist practices and relations (Bravo Díaz, 2020; Humeres, 2021 see also Juris, 2012; von Schnitzler, 2016; Khalili, 2021).

The recent plundering of Latin American infrastructure for profit has reduced the amount of funds available for its maintenance and development. However, the fragmentation and erosion of Latin American infrastructures and the neoliberal restructuring of capitalist states have also created opportunities for rural and urban communities to take greater collective control of infrastructures and reconfigure political relations and practices (Goodwin, 2019, 2021). Hence, cracks within and between infrastructure can sometimes be generative (Harvey et al., 2017). The absence of infrastructure can also have interesting political effects. Roads are potent protest infrastructures in the Andes partly because of the lack of alternative transport infrastructure. In Ecuador and Bolivia, for example, national train networks, which were central to post-independence nation-building in both countries, deteriorated in the 1970s and 1980s, ultimately making towns and cities more reliant on roads for supplies of essential items and hence more vulnerable to blockades. The lack or collapse of infrastructure, as Butler (2016) notes, is also frequently a source of protest and resistance as people mobilise collectively to improve their living conditions. Thus, infrastructural absence and degradation can shape political relations and practices in unexpected ways (Anand et al., 2018; Budds et al., 2020).

The experimental nature of infrastructure and the diverse relations and effects it generates reveals infrastructure as a process, not a temporally bounded static configuration. Gupta (2018) notes that the mainstream view of

4 Public-private partnerships (PPPs) have played a key role in the integration of Latin American infrastructures into global processes of financialisation, especially since the North Atlantic financial crisis in 2007–8. See Bayliss and Van Waeyenberge (2018) and Chauvet et al. (2020).

infrastructure as starting with planning and ending with inauguration fails to capture the temporality and complexity of infrastructure. The fact that much infrastructure is never officially inaugurated further unsettles such linear views of infrastructure development. Indeed, according to Carse and Kneas (2019, p. 9), 'planned, blocked, delayed or abandoned projects are ubiquitous – the norm, rather than the exception'. Infrastructure, then, is never really finished and is effectively 'always in-the-making' (Silva-Novoa Sánchez et al., 2019). Once an irrigation network is built, for example, new relations and practices emerge which feedback to modify the network in a continuous dialectical process of change. The various material components of the system – canals, pipes, dams, levers, pumps, switches – require maintenance and, ultimately, replacement. This requires mobilising labour, finance, materials, and knowledge and some form of collective organisation and decision-making (Boelens and Vos, 2014; Anand, 2020). The periodic maintenance and replacement of irrigation infrastructure is accompanied by micro, barely perceptible, modifications that peasants and farmers make to the network to improve or alter the distribution of water, keeping check with changing hydrological and climatic conditions, which themselves are in a constant state of flux. Irrigation infrastructure is therefore reshaped through individual and collective human actions at different scales and temporalities. To add to this complexity, it is also modified by non-human forms of agency (Strang, 2016; Harvey et al., 2017; see also Scarborough, 2014). Water corrodes and buffets canals, pipes, and dams, while the plants and animals that surround and penetrate the network reshape it in multiple ways (Anand, 2017; see also Jensen, 2017; Barua, 2021). Hence, infrastructures are constantly evolving and their effects ripple through human and non-human worlds.

The specificity of Latin American infrastructures

Viewing infrastructure as culturally and environmentally embedded implies that the same material assemblages will generate diverse effects and relations and take alternative meanings in different settings (Pfaffenberger, 1992). This is especially true in Latin America, one of the most socially and geographically diverse regions in the world (Allmark, 1997). Yet there are some common factors that have shaped Latin American infrastructures and distinguished them from infrastructures elsewhere in the world. In this section, we discuss factors related to three broad and overlapping themes – i) *colonialism/imperialism* ii) *economy/society* and iii) *environment/space.*

First, the timing and pattern of European colonialism left a significant mark on Latin American infrastructures. New technologies, rationalities, and ontologies were introduced from the 15th and 16th centuries as the region was slowly and unevenly incorporated into European empires. The uneven pattern of colonialism and the widespread resistance of indigenous peoples ensured that existing technologies, rationalities, and ontologies were not extinguished. Indigenous infrastructures, including elaborate irrigation systems constructed by the Aztec, Maya, Huari, Tiahuanaco, and Inca empires, provided the foundation for infrastructures developed during the period of European colonial rule, and continue to underpin much infrastructure today (Galeano 1973/1997; Sherbondy, 1993; Scarborough, 1994; Harvey and Knox, 2015). Foreign intervention continued after most Latin American countries gained independence in the early 19th century as imperial powers, especially Britain and the United States, vied for political-economic control of the region. British influence was particularly strong in the 19th century as British capital, engineers, and machinery poured into Latin America and reconfigured the region's infrastructure (Stone, 1968; Errázuriz and Giucci, 2016; Guajardo Soto, 2021, 2022). Meanwhile, viewing Latin America as its 'backyard', US politicians, planners, and bureaucracies were especially active in restructuring Latin American societies and environments through infrastructure in the 20th century, with the Panama Canal perhaps the most striking example (Carse, 2014; Villanueva, 2020).[5] The Cold War, which had distinct Latin American characteristics (Booth, 2021), left a huge infrastructural footprint in the region (Chastain and Lorek, 2020), not least through investment and programmes linked to the Alliance for Progress (Rabe, 1999). Soviet involvement in the development of Latin American infrastructure was much less prominent during the Cold War, but still left its mark, not least in Cuba (Blasier, 2002). More recently, China has become a central actor in infrastructure development in Latin America, including financing and constructing multiple mining, oil, transport, and energy infrastructures in the Andes and Amazon (Chauvet et al., 2020). The intervention of Western European and North American powers in Latin America has left enduring epistemological and ontological legacies as 'cognitive empires' have shaped how infrastructures have been demanded, conceived, and received (Santos, 2018; see also Quijano, 2008; Rivera Cusicanqui, 2010/2020). Hence, Latin America's long and diverse histories of colonialism and imperialism continue to weigh heavily on the region's infrastructures. However, as recent scholarship has shown (e.g. Thurner, 2019; Chastain and Lorek, 2020), Latin America has not been a passive receiver of foreign science and expertise, but has actively contributed to the development of global knowledge related to technology and infrastructure. Thus, Latin America is an important epistemic site and this is reflected in its infrastructures.

5 Construction of what became known as the Panama Canal was started by French engineers in the late 19th century and completed by US firms in the early 20th century. This followed the separation of Panama from Colombia, a move that successive US governments actively supported. The construction of the canal was largely undertaken by workers from the Caribbean, who suffered terrible working and living conditions. The canal was opened in 1914 and has been one of the most important commercial waterways in the world ever since. See Campling and Colás (2021) for a global perspective.

Second, Latin America's early incorporation into the capitalist world economy through colonialism involved constructing the infrastructures required to produce and export minerals, fuels, and agriculture (Galeano, 1973/1997). These historical infrastructures, which underpinned early capitalist development in Europe, continue to dissect and configure Latin American societies, while more recent infrastructures have deepened the insertion of Latin American countries into global production and distribution networks, including those for illicit commodities, like cocaine (Grisaffi, 2019; Gutiérrez and Ciro, 2022). Dependency on the export of primary goods, which remains the defining macro feature of most Latin American economies, imbues the region's infrastructure with greater uncertainty and instability as public and private investment are closely linked to volatile cycles in world commodity markets (Acosta, 2009; Svampa, 2012). Specialisation in primary export production and the enduring legacies of colonialism have contributed to making Latin America the most unequal region in the world (Sánchez-Ancochea, 2020), with huge disparities in income and wealth reflected in infrastructures that often segregate and exclude rather than unite and include. Gaping class differences overlap and intersect with entrenched racial and ethnic inequalities and discrimination and Latin American infrastructure can both cement and alter class and race relations. These processes have deep historical roots in Latin America. For example, following the Toledan reforms that forcibly moved indigenous populations from their communities in the late 16th century, colonial towns were constructed as infrastructures of governance that organised space along racial divisions that endure today. Ethnic and racial diversity has also brought vibrancy to Latin American infrastructure as indigenous peoples and Afro Latinos have drawn on ancestral traditions to refashion and forge infrastructures (Escobar, 2020).

Third, Latin American environments and geographies are highly diverse, presenting multiple challenges to designers and users of infrastructure (Allmark, 1997; Coletta and Raftopoulos, 2016). This contributes to the incompleteness, fragmentation, and decay of infrastructures in the region. At the same time, infrastructures have reconfigured and pummelled Latin American ecosystems, from mangroves dotted along the Pacific coast to *páramos* perched high in the Andes. Indigenous peoples have often been the most severely impacted by the restructuring of habitats and environments through infrastructure, especially in the Amazonian region, which has seen massive socio-environmental destruction since the early 20th century, in particular (Orta-Martínez and Finer, 2010; Bebbington et al., 2020; Ioris, 2021). In these cases, infrastructures have often been a form of 'slow violence' as the socio-environmental damage that they generate has emerged gradually, sometimes, barely detectably (Nixon, 2011). Meanwhile, urbanisation has unfolded at breakneck speed across Latin America since the early 20th century and swathes of agricultural and pastoral land have been converted into towns and cities, transforming built and natural environments and human-nature relations in the process. Viewed as engines of development, cities have increasingly been seen to represent Latin America's future(s) and infrastructures have been planned and constructed to attempt to realise these modernising visions. Spatial inequalities have deepened as Latin American states have prioritised urban over rural infrastructures and populations. Water has been redirected to quench the thirst of ever-expanding urban populations (Swyngedouw, 1997), while mega-dams have been constructed to bring electricity to towns and cities (Purcell, 2020). The diverse Latin American cities that have emerged out of these processes are sites of vibrancy and hope, on the one hand, and poverty and segregation, on the other. The 'auto-construction' of low-income neighbourhoods has created space for the emergence of new political practices and relations, while the development of high-income gated communities has generated new forms of exclusion and inequality (Amin, 2014; Maclean, 2015; Zeiderman, 2016; Perry, 2016; Geraghty and Massidda, 2019; Massidda, 2018, 2021; Gyger, 2019; Boulos, 2021). Today, over 80 per cent of Latin Americans are estimated to live in urban areas, making the region one of the most urbanised in the world.

In diverse ways, the chapters in this volume show how the above factors have shaped Latin American infrastructures and given them distinct characteristics. In the following sections, we outline the three broad themes that cut across the book and literature – i) *nation, state, citizenship* ii) *development, promise, progress* iii) *disappointment, failure, decay* – and explain how the chapters further advance understanding of these issues.

Nation, state, citizenship

Infrastructure is frequently a state project (Scott 1998), though as we shall see across several chapters in this book, the lines between state, public, private, community, national, and international infrastructure are often blurred. Demand for infrastructure often originates from below, from citizens themselves; however, it is generally the state that has the resources and expertise to coordinate and construct large infrastructure projects, even if the construction itself is often undertaken by private companies and/or infrastructure users (Holston, 2008; Deavila Pertuz, 2019; Gyger, 2019; Goodwin, 2019, 2021). Infrastructure therefore mediates relations between states and citizens, and acts as a tool of governmentality, enabling states to act on citizens, shaping them in particular ways (Foucault, 2008; Larkin, 2018, p. 182). Indeed, infrastructure has been described as a 'technology of liberal rule' (Appel et al., 2018, p. 4). Liberalism applies supposedly universal principles to treat citizens as equals. However, in the real world, the decisions made by governments professing 'liberal' values do not depart from a neutral value-less position, where decisions are made behind a 'veil of ignorance' free of personal and collective prejudices (Rawls, 1999), as the so-called communitarian critics of liberal philosopher

John Rawls rightly point out (Mulhall and Swift, 1992). Liberal governance always guarantees equal citizenship, liberty, and access to goods under the preconditions set from the epistemological perspective of the more powerful. The outcome is highly differentiated forms of citizenship in which different classes and groups have different levels of rights and privileges (Larson, 2004; Holston, 2008; Lazar, 2013; Nuijten, 2013; Anand, 2017).

This is particularly evident in Latin America, where state formation has been heavily influenced by European colonisation. Indeed, it could be argued that 'Latin American states were co-produced along with infrastructure' (Velho and Ureta, 2019, p. 430) that was originally designed to exploit native resources but leave none of the profits with native people. While Latin American states obtained independence from their respective colonisers in the 19th century, they became what Quijano has called 'independent states of colonial societies', marked by persisting internal colonialism, or 'coloniality' (Quijano, 2008, p. 123), developing alongside and through infrastructural construction. Socially, many Latin American states contain large indigenous populations. Politically, however, indigenous demands, epistemologies and ontologies have been largely ignored by Latin American states. Even in Bolivia, where Evo Morales is widely perceived to have been the country's first indigenous president when he was elected in 2005, and where one of the slogans of his government's programmes *vivir bien* was based on indigenous notions of living well within rural Andean communities, proposals for infrastructure construction led to high-profile conflicts between the state and indigenous peoples. One source of tension in these struggles was the right of indigenous peoples to be consulted over state projects that infringed their collective rights, which is enshrined in International Labour Organization (ILO) Convention 169. The efforts of indigenous communities and movements to use consultations as a tool to influence the design and implementation of large-scale infrastructure projects in Bolivia were frustrated by the centralised decision-making processes of the Morales governments. While the conditions for the failures of the 20th-century high-modernist schemes that Scott (1998) documents were not present in 21st-century Bolivia, large-scale infrastructure projects under Morales were infused with a similar 'muscle-bound' belief in scientific knowledge and linear progress (see also Escobar, 2010; Hope, 2021).

Hence, 200 years after independence, 'capitalist Euro modernity' is still taken as the model for the design of much Latin American infrastructure (Escobar, 2020). The contributors to this volume shine new light on this issue. In Sam Rumé's chapter, for example, we see that in Ecuador, another country where indigenous epistemologies and ontologies have been explicitly projected through state discourse in the form of *buen vivir* or *sumak kawsay* (Martínez Novo, 2014), a new tram network whose original motivation included the reproduction of a heritage aesthetic evolved into one explicitly modelled on modern European transportation, of propelling citizens in the Andean city of

Cuenca towards a European modernity. The dominance of Eurocentric best practices in the design and construction of the tram network, which finally started operating in 2020, leads him to ask whether the advances imagined by the tramway could be seen as perpetuating 'colonial cultures of planning'.

Through studying infrastructures, we can glimpse the political rationality behind them (Larkin, 2013, p. 328). The values of the dominant culture are reproduced by engineers and architects and embedded in the infrastructure that people use; in order to access and take advantage of this infrastructure its users often reproduce the dominant values themselves (Bourdieu and Wacquant, 1992; Foucault, 2008). In her chapter, Julie Dayot shows how values evolve among an indigenous community in the Ecuadorian Amazon when the municipality charges the inhabitants for access to water through a new drinking water plant, which was part of a compensation package the community agreed with oil companies operating in their territory. Valeria Guarneros-Meza and Marcela Torres-Wong illustrate in their chapter that infrastructure linked to extractive industries has disciplining and biopolitical dimensions, with local authorities and mining firms in Mexico using practices and discourses that promoted highly circumscribed forms of participation and citizenship. Meanwhile, in the chapter by Yuri Gama we see how the rationalities of 20th-century Brazilian politicians, bureaucrats, and planners were instilled in state housing projects and new forms of citizenship and living were promoted through this infrastructure.

Gama's analysis of housing in Natal, Brazil shows it is not only Latin American governments that have attempted to forge modern Latin American subjects through infrastructure. Planners, engineers, architects, politicians, and bureaucrats from the United States were heavily involved in the construction of this housing, especially through the Alliance for Progress, launched in 1961 by the Kennedy government to counter the spread of communism in Latin America (see also Healey, 2020). Housing in Natal not only provided a habitat for workers but also promoted economic rationality and financial discipline, helping to embed capitalist relations and practices. The Soviet Union was not absent from this process of subject-making during the Cold War, as the chapter by Nicole Fadellin demonstrates. Her analysis of literary and theatrical representations of a nuclear energy plant in Cuba shows how Fidel Castro drew on Russian technology, knowledge, labour, and finance to cultivate modern revolutionary subjects.

Cuba's nuclear dream – which took shape through the so-called 'Project of the Century' – shows infrastructure has a 'state effect' (Harvey, 2005), giving the state form and proximity through its material visibility. The separation of the form from its function in this manner gives infrastructure what Larkin (2013, p. 329) calls a 'poetic quality', through which the state represents itself to its citizens. The poetics of infrastructure mean that a state's effects are intimately related to its affects. This is because 'any social project that is not imposed by force alone must be affective in order to be effective' (Mazzarella, 2009, p. 299; see also Amin, 2014; von Schnitzler, 2016). Indeed, the state and infrastructure are often conflated and the regard in which citizens hold the state is shaped by the mediating force of infrastructure. The longing for infrastructure such as roads 'is intimately connected to the perilous state of contemporary provision' (Harvey, 2018, p. 82), and this is often felt as state neglect or abandonment. Ursula Balderson's chapter shows a desire for water infrastructure in Mataquita, Peru, experienced as emotional suffering, to emerge out of, and stored within, intertwined desires for infrastructure and rights as citizens. Here intangible aspects of the social environment influenced the design of water infrastructure at the site. Or, as Diego Valdivieso shows in his ethnographic study in Quehui Island, Chile, citizens demand the greater presence of an absent state and this presence is felt through the construction of a new municipal building and other infrastructures.

The case of Quehui Island shows that infrastructures are key to building and maintaining Latin American nations and make visible 'the oscillating margins of the state' (Harvey, 2014, p. 281; see also Hetherington and Campbell, 2014). Infrastructure provision can be a useful governmental strategy in areas where the territorial reach of the state is in doubt or being challenged. In her chapter, Clara Voyvodic argues that in Colombia infrastructure has been weaponised as a means to assert territorial authority by both the state and armed rebel groups. By constructing infrastructure projects, the state provides something that armed groups often cannot. Hence, infrastructure has been used as a counter-insurgency and state-consolidation strategy in Colombia. However, groups like the *Fuerzas Armadas Revolucionarias de Colombia* (FARC) have been able to assert their own authority by subverting, capturing and, modifying state infrastructures. Thus, while the construction and operation of infrastructure demonstrates the power of the state, the only response of non-state armed groups is not to destroy it. In fact, Voyvodic's analysis shows that these infrastructures can support the application of authority and power of armed groups who use them to challenge the state's monopoly on violence (see also Peñaranda Currie et al., 2021). She also demonstrates that the relationship between the state and non-state armed groups can be complementary, with paramilitary organisations aligned to the government heavily involved in the protection and development of state infrastructures in Colombia.

Development, promise, progress

One of the most powerful characteristics of infrastructure is its potential to transform time and space: 'Once we conceptualize infrastructures not just in term of the different places that they connect, but as spatiotemporal projects – as chronotopes – then we can open up new ways of thinking about the temporality and spatiality of infrastructure' (Appel et al., 2018, p. 17). The promise of infrastructure lies in its power to transform, acting in the present as a (perhaps literal) bridge to the future. Infrastructure often creates a sense of modernity (Larkin, 2013, p. 337), which itself has the power to transform its users into modern citizens. Indeed, it is precisely to project themselves and their citizens as advanced and modern that many nation states build infrastructure, rather than necessarily to meet a felt need (Appel et al., 2018, p. 19). Efforts to shape the present and future through infrastructure are therefore never politically neutral. Rather, as Gupta (2018, p. 66) argues: 'Infrastructures are important because the future they bring about always favours one set of political actors over others.'

When viewing state-sponsored infrastructures as chrono-political projects, it is significant that in the Latin American context infrastructure projects are tightly bound to the notion of 'development' (Escobar, 1995/2012; Hetherington, 2014; Harvey et al., 2017; Purcell, 2020). Since the late 20th century, as previously noted, Latin American societies have become increasingly urban, but even as rural to urban migration has increased, social inequalities remain rooted in coloniality (Quijano, 2008). Peri-urban and rural dwellers, who are often indigenous, are still commonly projected as civilisationally inferior and backward by their urban middle- and upper-class counterparts (Alderman, 2022). Infrastructure projects as development are bound with chrono-political objectives to modernise citizens living at the periphery of the state by creating the 'material, social, and ideational conditions that configure lifeworlds' (Harvey, 2014, p. 283). Escobar (2003, p. 61) argues that the effect of development can therefore be to alienate those being developed from their own social reality. Several chapters in this book highlight this as a real concern among many people directly affected by infrastructure construction. Yet they also show that infrastructures are sometimes welcomed precisely for their transformative, modernising qualities. We see in Dayot's chapter, for example, that while most community members refuse to pay for water supplied through a new water plant, they all embrace the new infrastructure, and no one wants to go back to drinking water from the river, which has been heavily polluted through oil production and upstream activities. Her chapter shows that infrastructure is not only necessary to support capitalist development but also to make human life possible in the wake of the socio-environmental destruction it generates.

Contributors to this volume also show that Latin Americans excluded from modernising infrastructure do not passively wait for the state or private firms to incorporate them. In Nicolás Valenzuela-Levi's chapter, for example, we see how Chileans who lack internet coverage in Santiago have found innovative ways to connect to the network and develop digitised relations and practices, despite being abandoned by multinational corporations and state regulators. The response of residents living in low-income neighbourhoods to being excluded from internet services is to subvert the capitalist logic of private enterprise through innovative collective initiatives, which share internet around the neighbourhood (see also Humeres, 2021). New subjectivities have emerged through this collective process, creating space for alternative forms of political action in the city.

While state-sponsored infrastructure often has modernising, future-oriented, perspectives, it can project backward as well as forward and political conflicts can emerge over how to (re)construct the past as well as the future (de Sousa Santos, 2019). In Rumé's chapter we see that the tram in Cuenca, Ecuador, took on several temporal identities from 'picturesque heritage object' to 'cutting edge technology', with each identity projecting alternative visions of the past and future. His analysis shows that Cuenca itself had to be reconfigured in order to meet the requirements of the tram; that is, through its tram design, the city, a UNESCO World Heritage Site, was forced to redesign itself. This involved the destruction of historic stone brick roads, which stoked tensions as some *cuencanos* felt the history of their city was being swept aside to make way for the modern tram network. Delays in constructing the tram network added further chrono-political tensions as for several years Cuenca was stuck in a chaotic liminal state between its past and future.

Community-constructed and managed infrastructure also has the potential to connect the present with the past. Larkin (2013, p. 329) argues that infrastructures, as 'objects that create the grounds on which other objects operate' are not just things, but 'also the relation between things'. This can extend, as Sarah Bennison shows in her ethno-historical analysis in Peru, to relationships between the 'living' and the 'dead'. In her chapter, we see how ancestors communicate with living community members on the correct way of performing irrigation canal maintenance rituals through *khipus*, knotted record-keeping instruments, which are rooted in Andean pre-colonial history. Indeed, the ancestors are themselves understood as the owners of the canals. The engagement of the youth with urban centres through road infrastructure, constructed in the 1920s, and the migration of many, had knock-on effects for the maintenance of community-constructed infrastructure, the irrigation canals. It also had profound implications for the identity of the community of San Pedro de Casta (Huarochirí, Lima) itself, whose relations with canal-dwelling ancestors are maintained and expressed through the canal-cleaning ritual. Considering the infrastructure in her case study as a 'temporal intermediary', Bennison cautions us to consider the fact that 'infrastructures do not only function to communicate and transport goods or information between people, but also with non-human and/or formerly human actors'. Infrastructure therefore not only has the capacity to bring life (biopolitics – Foucault, 2008) or accelerate death (necropolitics – Mbembe, 2019) but to disrupt relations between the living and the dead and alter the practices and subjectivities embedded in these relations.

How affected communities relate to infrastructure may be determined by their collective identities, forged through history, as the above case illustrates. Infrastructure is shown to distort the relationship between two communities at the centre of the chapter by Guarneros-Meza and Torres-Wong. The right to decide whether mining should take place overlaps with a territorial dispute. How each community responds to the mine is in direct proportion to their own historical and spatial identities. One community owed its very existence to the discovery of a mine in 1776; meanwhile, its neighbour's anti-mining stance drew on traditions of indigenous decision-making, hybridised with state-institutions.

This shows that what constitutes progress for some might represent deterioration for others. Infrastructure can have the effect of squeezing space and pushing together people previously kept apart. When a *teleférico* (cable car) was built connecting the middle-class areas of the *zona sur* of the city of La Paz with the popular neighbourhoods of the city of El Alto above, the residents of some of La Paz's most expensive and exclusive neighbourhoods were horrified to find that this led to spaces such as the local multiplex cinema being 'invaded' by working-class Aymaras from the city above (Maclean, 2018). Hence, class and race relations and discrimination sometimes undermine the promise of infrastructure to connect and unite people, especially in highly unequal and spatially segregated Latin American cities.

Disappointment, failure, decay

Promises often go unfulfilled. And a promise made, once broken, can lead to greater disappointment than if it had never been made at all. Infrastructures may fail or break down either due to internal disruption or because of a breakdown between the infrastructure and the domain of relations it is supposed to sustain, or that are required to sustain it. In fact, the complexity and fragility of infrastructure means that it might be best to think of it as functioning 'against the odds' (Harvey et al., 2017, p. 12). However, as Velho and Ureta (2019, p. 433) point out, disrepair does not necessarily mean that infrastructure is moribund, because a great deal of Latin American infrastructure effectively exists 'in a state of *partial* disrepair and *partial* functionality'.

In Fadellin's chapter, the 'Cuban nuclear dream', which was becoming physically realised through the Nuclear City, inhabited by engineers who had devoted their lives to the project, comes to a halt because of circumstances beyond the control of the actors directly involved: the fall of the Berlin Wall and collapse of the Soviet Union. When the dream of being thrust forward into the future by nuclear power becomes unrealisable, those living in the Nuclear City are left instead in suspended animation. Dreams of progress and development were replaced by decay as crumbling nuclear infrastructure reflected a growing sense of economic crisis and political impasse. Ruination became 'a lived condition' (Velho and Ureta, 2019, p. 436, see also Gupta, 2018).

In Rumé's chapter, promise turns not just to disappointment but to apprehension and preoccupation as it becomes clear that it is not possible to create the tram in Cuenca, Ecuador according to the original specifications envisaged. In this case, the (long-term) temporality of infrastructure collides with the (short-term) temporality of the political. The projections for the design and functioning of the tram seemed to fit electoral objectives, projecting voters' desires into an imagined reality. However, when the form of infrastructural reality is revealed as different from that promised this had consequences for the relationship between the governing and the governed. Rumé argues that the state 'is seen through the same processual lens as its infrastructure projects. The uncertainty of the outcomes of infrastructure projects thus goes hand in hand with the uncertainty of the state effect, a failing infrastructure being likely to expose the flaws of the responsible entities and thereby damage their relationship with those to be governed'.

The disappointment of infrastructure can also be experienced through a longing unfulfilled. The islanders of Quehui, Chile, experience the distant state through an idealised projection, as caring, and yet paradoxically also as neglectful and inconvenient. This is because of the fundamental role played by intermittent mobility infrastructure over many years. Valdivieso suggests that a change in the affective relationship occurs when state presence becomes more permanent on the island, through the construction of municipal offices.

The members of the communities in the Peruvian Andes at the heart of Balderson's chapter also experienced disappointment through their negotiations with the Canadian mining company, Barrick Gold. Their collective efforts to overcome water scarcity through the construction of water storage reservoirs were frustrated by the firm's refusal to recognise the problems caused by its operations and the water rights of the communities. Balderson recounts: 'The community wanted as much water storage capacity to be built as possible partly to alleviate the water crisis but also as the material presence of reservoirs in the village served as visible indicators of the community's social worth.' Yet the mining firm refused to cede to the community's demands, proposing to build one reservoir instead of five, despite the considerable income it was generating from the mine and ruination of the environment (see also Damonte et al, 2022).

In the above case, the community's own labour power was used to construct the infrastructure that emerged out of the dispute. Collective labour power of Latin American communities has not only been mobilised to overcome disappointment but also to prevent failure and decay and build alternative futures (Holston, 2008; Amin, 2014; Massidda, 2018, 2021). In Ecuador, for example, the collective labour practice, the *minga*, has played a pivotal role in maintaining and repairing hydraulic infrastructure, especially in rural Andean communities (Boelens and Vos, 2014; Goodwin 2019, 2021; Manosalvas et al., 2021). New relations and subjectivities have emerged through these diverse processes, showing that the limitations and fragility of infrastructure can be generative as well as disruptive.

Conclusion

In this introductory chapter, we have argued that infrastructure can be fruitfully understood as a relational and experimental process. The authors included in this volume approach infrastructure from distinct theoretical and methodological perspectives but their analysis offers broad support for this conceptual approach and provides important new insights into the cross-disciplinary infrastructure scholarship. We have identified three themes that connect the chapters to this literature: i) *nation, state, citizenship* ii) *development, promise, progress* iii) *disappointment, failure, decay*.

In shining new light on these issues, the book also provides new perspectives on Latin American history, society, and politics. The three themes that we have identified cross-cut Latin America, revealing certain specificities in the relationship that Latin Americans have with infrastructure and with their states through infrastructure. To understand the social and political life of Latin American infrastructures we must consider infrastructure's historical role as a tool of colonial-capitalist states, first to facilitate extraction of local resources, often out of the continent altogether, to very little benefit of local populations, and second as a method of reshaping societies and environments, creating highly differentiated forms of citizenship, and forging nation states. These legacies continue to weigh heavily on Latin America, and infrastructure remains at the heart of contested processes of capitalist development across the region.

In Latin American societies, which are marked by deep racial and ethnic division and considerable social and class stratification, state infrastructure projects often, if certainly not always, reinforce existing inequalities. Projects designed to propel local populations forward into the future inevitably follow designs of the more powerful in society, resulting in Latin American development reproducing the visions of elites, politicians, and bureaucrats, that often take their cue from North America and Western Europe, rather than a vision from below of what Latin American infrastructure should look like and the purposes it should serve. The conversion of infrastructure into a global asset class through financialisation has strengthened these tendencies as much infrastructure today is primarily designed to meet the needs of international investors instead of infrastructure users.

Yet infrastructures have not only served the interests of states and capital, they have also provided a foundation for Latin Americans to contest capitalist development and forge new forms of citizenship and politics. Infrastructures always produce excess, something that is not captured in the designs and visions of politicians, planners, and engineers, but emerges once infrastructures come into contact with the human and non-human world, generating diverse effects, which extend across space and time. The protests that erupted across Latin America as the 2010s drew to a close show that the social and political life of infrastructures take unexpected twists and turns and these are only likely to multiply as Latin American societies step into the unknown of their post-pandemic futures.

References

Acosta, A. (2009) *La maldición de la abundancia* (Quito: Abya-Yala).

Alderman, J. (2022) '"City thinking": rural urbanisation and mobility in Andean Bolivia'. *Bulletin of Latin American Research*, 41 (1): 21–46.

Allmark, T. (1997) 'Environment and society in Latin America', in M. Redclift and G. Woodgate (eds.), *The International Handbook of Environmental Sociology* (Cheltenham: Edward Elgar), pp. 390–402.

Amin, A. (2014) 'Lively infrastructure', *Theory, Culture and Society,* 31 (7/8): 137–61.

Anand, N. (2017) *Hydraulic City: Water and the Infrastructures of Citizenship in Mumbai* (Durham, NC and London: Duke University Press).

Anand, N. (2020) 'After breakdown: invisibility and the labour of infrastructure maintenance', *Economic and Political Weekly,* LV (51): 52–6.

Appel, H., Anand, N., and Gupta, A. (2018) 'Introduction: temporality, politics, and the promise of Infrastructure', in N. Anand, A. Gupta, and H. Appel (eds.), *The Promise of Infrastructure.* (Durham, NC and London: Duke University Press), pp. 1–38.

Barua, M. (2021) 'Infrastructure and non-human life: a wider ontology', *Progress in Human Geography,* early view.

Bayliss, K. and E. Van Waeyenberge (2018) 'Unpacking the public private partnership revival', *The Journal of Development Studies*, 54 (4): 577–93.

Bear, L. (2020) 'Speculations on infrastructure: from colonial public works to a post-colonial global asset class on the Indian railways 1840–2017', *Economy and Society*, 49 (1): 45–70.

Bebbington, A. et al. (2020) 'Priorities for governing large-scale infrastructure in the tropics', *PNAS,* 117 (36): 21829-21833.

Bennett, V. (1998). 'Housewives, urban protest and water policy in Monterrey, Mexico', *International Journal of Water Resources Development,* 14 (4): 48–497.

Bennison, S. (2016) 'Who are the children of pariacaca? Exploring identity through narratives of water and landscape in Huarochirí, Peru' (unpublished doctoral thesis, Newcastle University).

Blasier, C. (2002) 'Soviet impacts on Latin America', *Russian History,* 29 (2/4): 481–97.

Boelens, R. and J. Vos (2014) 'Legal pluralism, hydraulic property creation and sustainability: the materialized nature of water rights in user-managed systems', *Current Opinion in Environmental Sustainability,* 11: 55–62.

Booth, W. (2021) 'Rethinking Latin America's Cold War', *The Historical Journal,* 64 (4): 1128–50.

Boulos, G. (2021) 'Struggles of the roofless', *New Left Review,* 130: 6–23.

Bourdieu, P. and L. Wacquant (1992) *An Invitation to Reflexive Sociology* (Cambridge and Malden, MA: Polity).

Bravo Díaz, A. (2021) '"Sumak Kawsay is harmful for all of us" oil roads and well-being among the Waorani in Ecuadorian Amazonia', *Latin American Perspectives,* 28 (3): 51–68.

Budds, J., K. Ramakrishnan, and K. O'Reilly (2020) 'Between decay and repair: embodied experiences of infrastructure's materiality', *EPE: Nature and Space,* early view.

Butler, J. (2016) 'Rethinking vulnerability and resistance', in J. Butler et al. (eds.), *Vulnerability in Resistance* (London and Durham, NC: Duke University Press).

Calderón, C. and L. Servén (2011) 'Infrastructure in Latin America in Ocampo', in J.A. and J. Ros (eds.), *The Oxford Handbook of Latin American Economics* (Oxford and New York: Oxford University Press).

Campling, L. and A. Colás (2021) *Capitalism and the Sea* (London: Verso).

Carse, A. (2014) *Beyond the Big Ditch: Politics, Ecology, and Infrastructure at the Panama Canal* (Cambridge, MA: MIT Press).

Carse, A. and D. Kneas (2019) 'Unbuilt and unfinished: the temporalities of infrastructure', *Environment and Society: Advances in Research,* 10: 9–28.

CEPAL (2016) 'Latin America's infrastructure investment situation and challenges', *FAL Bulletin,* 347 (3): 1–17.

Chastain A.B. and T.W. Lorek (2020) *Itineraries of Expertise: Science, Technology and the Environment in Latin America's Long Cold War,* Pittsburgh: University of Pittsburgh Press.

Chauvet, P. et al. (2020) 'China: current and potential role in infrastructure investment in Latin America', *CEPAL International Trade Series,* 144: 1–69.

Coletta, M. and M. Raftopoulos (2016) *Provincialising Nature: Multidisciplinary Approaches to the Politics of the Environment in Latin America* (London: Institute of Latin American Studies).

Colven, E. (2020) 'Subterranean infrastructures in a sinking city: the politics of visibility in Jakarta', *Critical Asian Studies,* 52 (3): 311–31.

Damonte, G., A. Ulloa, A. Quiroga, and A. López (2022) 'La apuesta por la infraestructura: inversión pública y la reproducción de la escasez hídrica en contextos de gran minería en Perú y Colombia', *Estudios Atacameños,* 68: 1–32.

Deavila Pertuz, O. (2019) 'Community action, the informal city and popular politics in Cartagena (Colombia) during the National Front, 1958–74', in N.H.D. Gerathy and A.L. Massidda (eds.), *Creative Spaces: Urban Culture and Marginality in Latin America* (London: University of London Press).

de la Cadena, M. (2010) 'Indigenous cosmopolitics in the Andes: conceptual reflections beyond "Politics"', *Cultural Anthropology,* 25 (2): 334–70.

de la Cadena, M. (2015) *Earth Beings: Ecologies of Practice Across Andean Worlds* (Durham, NC: Duke University Press).

de Sousa Santos, A.A. (2019) *The Politics of Memory: Urban Cultural Heritage in Brazil* (Lanham, MD: Rowman & Littlefield Publishers).

dos Santos, T. (1970) 'The structure of dependence', *American Economic Review,* 60 (2): 231–36.

Durand, F. (2019) 'The Odebrecht Tsunami', NACLA Report on the Americas, 51 (2): 146–52.

Errázuriz, T. and G. Giucci (2016) 'The ambiguities of progress: cultural appropriation of electric trams in the Southern Cone, 1890–1950 (Chile, Argentina, Uruguay and Brazil)', *Icon,* 22: 55–77.

Escobar, A. (1995/2012) *Encountering Development: The Making and Unmaking of the Third World.* (Princeton: Princeton University Press), pp. vii–xii and 102–53).

Escobar, A. (2003) 'Mundos y conocimientos de otro modo: el programa de investigación de modernidad/colonialidad latinoamericano', *Tabula Rasa,* 1: 51–86.

Escobar, A. (2010) 'Latin America at a crossroads: alternative modernizations, post-liberalism or post-development?' *Cultural Studies,* 24 (1): 1–65.

Escobar, A. (2017) *Designs for the Pluriverse: Radical Interdependence, Autonomy, and the Making of Worlds* (Durham, NC and London: Duke University Press).

Escobar, A. (2020) *Pluriversal Politics* (Durham, NC and London: Duke University Press).

Foucault, M. (2008) *The Birth of Biopolitics: Lectures at the College de France 1978–79* (London and New York: Palgrave Macmillan).

Galeano, E. (1973/1997) *The Open Veins of Latin America* (New York: Monthly Review Press).

Gerathy, N.H.D. and A.L. Massidda (eds.) (2019) *Creative Spaces: Urban Culture and Marginality in Latin America* (London: University of London Press).

Goodwin, G. (2018) 'Water, infrastructure and power: contention and resistance in postcolonial cities of the south', *Development and Change,* 49 (6): 1616–30.

Goodwin, G. (2019) 'The problem and promise of coproduction: politics, history, and autonomy', *World Development,* 122: 501–13.

Goodwin, G. (2021) 'Cerca del río y lejos del agua: water, autonomy, and hope in the Ecuadorian Andes', in A. Ioris (ed.), *Environment and Development: Challenges, Policies and Practices* (Basingstoke: Palgrave Macmillan) pp. 225–52.

Graham, S. and S. Marvin (2001) *Splintering Urbanism: Networked Infrastructures, Technological Mobilities and the Urban Condition* (London and New York: Routledge).

Grisaffi, T. (2019) *Coca Yes, Cocaine No: How Bolivia's Coca Growers Reshaped Democracy*, Durham, NC and London: Duke University Press.

Guajardo Soto, G. (2021) 'Tecnología, poder e infraestructura ferroviaria en la conformación urbana de la Ciudad de México, ca. 1870–1960', *Quaderns d'història de l'enginyeria,* XIX: 1–31.

Guajardo Soto, G. (2022) 'Las infrastructuras y los transportes', in M. Llorca-Jaña and R. Miller (eds.), *Historia económica de Chile desde la Independencia* (Santiago: RIL editores) pp. 557–605.

Gutiérrez, J.A. and E. Ciro (2022) 'Tillyian process without a Tillyian effect: criminalised economies and state-building in the Colombian conflict', *Journal of Political Power*, early view.

Gupta, A. (2018) 'The future in ruins: thoughts on the temporality of infrastructure', in N. Anand, A. Gupta, and H. Appel (eds.), *The Promise of Infrastructure* (Durham, NC and London: Duke University Press), pp. 62–79.

Gyger, H. (2019) *Improvised Cities: Architecture, Urbanization and Innovation in Peru* (Pittsburgh: Pittsburgh University Press).

Harvey, D. (2003) *The New Imperialism* (Oxford: Oxford University Press).

Harvey, P. (2005) 'The materiality of state effects', in C.N. Krohn-Hansen (ed.), *State Formation: Anthropological Perspectives* (London: Pluto Press), pp. 123–41.

Harvey, P. (2018) 'Infrastructures in and out of time: the promise of roads in contemporary Peru', in N. Anand, A. Gupta, and H. Appel (eds.), *The Promise of Infrastructure* (Durham, NC and London: Duke University Press), pp. 80–101.

Harvey, P. (2014) 'Infrastructures of the frontier in Latin America', *The Journal of Latin American and Caribbean Anthropology,* 19 (2): 280–3.

Harvey, P. and H. Knox (2015) *Roads: An Anthropology of Infrastructure and Expertise* (Ithaca, NY: Cornell University Press).

Harvey, P., C.B. Jensen, and A. Morita (2017) 'Introduction: infrastructural complications', in P. Harvey, C.B. Jensen, and A. Morita (eds.), *Infrastructures and Social Complexity: A Companion* (London: Routledge), pp. 1–22.

Healey, M. (2020) 'Planning, politics and praxis at Colombia's inter-American housing lab, 1951–1966', in A.B. Chastain and T.W. Lorek (eds.), *Itineraries of Expertise: Science, Technology and the Environment in Latin America's Long Cold War* (Pittsburgh: University of Pittsburgh Press), pp. 199–216.

Hetherington, K. (2014) 'Waiting for the surveyor: development promises and the temporality of infrastructure', *The Journal of Latin American and Caribbean Anthropology*, 19 (2): 195–211.

Hetherington, K. and J.M. Campbell (2014) 'Nature, infrastructure, and the state: rethinking development in Latin America', *The Journal of Latin American and Caribbean Anthropology,* 19 (2): 191–4.

Holston, J. (2008) *Insurgent Citizenship: Disjunctions of Democracy and Modernity in Brazil* (Princeton, NJ: Princeton University Press).

Hope, J. (2021) 'Driving development in the Amazon: extending infrastructural citizenship with political ecology in Bolivia', *EPE: Nature and Space*, early view.

Humeres, M. (2021) 'Colgados: el hurto de la energia electrica como resistencia a la noción de usuario racional-economico en Chile (1980–86)', *ARBOR Ciencia,* 197–801: 1–13.

Ioris, A. (ed.) (2021) *Environment and Development: Challenges, Policies and Practices* (Basingstoke: Palgrave Macmillan).

Jensen, C.B. (2017). 'Multinatural infrastructure: Phonm Pen sewage', in P. Harvey, C.B. Jensen, and A. Morita (eds.), *Infrastructures and Social Complexity: A Companion* (London: Routledge) pp. 227–41.

Jensen, C.B. and A. Morita (2017) 'Introduction: infrastructures as ontological experiments', *Ethnos: Journal of Anthropology,* 82 (4): 615–26.

Juris, J. S. (2012) 'Reflections on #Occupy Everywhere: social media, public space, and emerging logics of aggregation', *American Ethnologist,* 39 (2): 259–79.

Khalili, I. (2021) 'Apocalyptic infrastructures', *Noema*, 23 March.

Larkin, B. (2013) 'The politics and poetics of infrastructure', *Annual Review of Anthropology,* 42: 327–43.

Larkin, B. (2018) 'Promising forms: the political aesthetics of infrastructure', in N. Anand, A. Gupta, and H. Appel (eds.), *The Promise of Infrastructure* (Durham, NC and London: Duke University Press).

Larson, B. (2004) *Trials of Nation Making: Liberalism, Race, and Ethnicity in the Andes, 1810–1910.* (Cambridge; Cambridge University Press).

Lazar, S. (2013) *The Anthropology of Citizenship: A Reader* (London: John Wiley).

Loftus, A., H. March, and T. Purcell (2019) 'The political economy of water infrastructure: an introduction to financialization', *WIREs Water,* 6 (1): 1–7.

Maclean, K. (2015) *Social Urbanism and the Politics of Violence: The Medellín Miracle* (Basingstoke: Palgrave Macmillan).

Maclean, K. (2018) 'Envisioning gender, indigeneity and urban change: the case of La Paz, Bolivia', *Gender, Place & Culture,* 25 (5): 711–26.

Manosalvas, R. et al. (2021) 'Contractual reciprocity and the re-making of community hydrosocial territories: the case of La Chimba in the Ecuadorian Páramos', *Water* 13, early view.

Martínez Novo, C. (2014) 'Managing diversity in postneoliberal Ecuador', *Journal of Latin American and Caribbean Anthropology*, 19 (1): 103–25.

Massidda, A.L. (2018) 'Utopian visions for Buenos Aires shantytowns: collective imaginaries of housing rights, upgrading and eviction (1956–2013)', *Bulletin of Latin American Research* 37 (2): 144–59.

Massidda, A.L. (2021) 'Shantytowns, housing and state order: the plan de emergencia in 1950s Argentina', *Planning Perspectives*, 36 (2): 215–36.

Mbembe, A. (2019) *Necropolitics* (Durham, NC and London: Duke University Press).

Mazzarella, W. (2009) 'Affect: What is it good for?', in S. Dube (ed.), *Enchantments of Modernity: Empire, Nation, Globalization* (London: Routledge).

Mulhall, S. and A. Swift (1992) *Liberals and Communitarians* (Oxford: Blackwell).

Nixon, R. (2011) *Slow Violence and the Environmentalism of the Poor* (Cambridge, MA: Harvard University Press).

Nuijten, M. (2013) 'The perversity of the "citizenship game": slum-upgrading in the urban periphery of Recife, Brazil', *Critique of Anthropology,* 33 (1): 8–25.

Orta-Martínez, M. and M. Finer (2010) 'Oil frontiers and indigenous resistance in the Peruvian Amazon', *Ecological Economics,* 70(2): 207–18.

Peñarranda Curie, I. S. Otero-Bahamon, and S. Uribe (2021) 'What is the state made of? Coca, roads, and the materiality of state formation in the frontier', *World Development* 141, early view.

Perry, K.K. (2016) 'Geographies of power: Black women mobilizing intersectionality in Brazil', *Meridians,* 14 (1): 94–120.

Pfaffenberger, B. (1992) 'Social anthropology of technology', *Annual Review of Anthropology,* 21: 491–516.

Prebisch, R. (1950) *The Economic Development of Latin America and its Principal Problems* (New York: United Nations).

Purcell, T. (2020) 'Dams and hydroelectricity: circulation of knowledge and technological imaginaries in South America, 1945–1970', in A.B. Chastain and T.W Lorek (eds.), *Itineraries of Expertise: Science, Technology and the Environment in Latin America's Long Cold War* (Pittsburgh: University of Pittsburgh Press), pp. 217–36.

Pryke, M. and J. Allen (2019) 'Financialising urban water infrastructure: extracting local value, distributing value globally', *Urban Studies* 56 (7): 1326–46.

Quijano, A. (2008) 'Coloniality of power, eurocentrism, and social classification', in M. Moraña, E. Dussel, and C.A. Jáuregui (ed.), *Coloniality at Large: Latin America and the Postcolonial Debate* (Durham, NC and London: Duke University Press).

Rabe, S. (1999) *The Most Dangerous Area in the World: John F. Kennedy Confronts Communist Revolution in Latin America* (Chapel Hill: University of North Carolina Press).

Rawls, J. (1999) *A Theory of Justice* (Cambridge, MA: Harvard University Press).

Rivera Cusicanqui, S. (2010/2020) *Ch'ixinakax utxiwa: On Practices and Discourses of Decolonization* (London: Polity Press).

Sánchez-Ancochea, D. (2020) *The Costs of Inequality in Latin America: Lessons and Warnings for the Rest of the World* (London: I.B. Tauris/Bloomsbury).

Santos, B.D.S. (2018) *The End of the Cognitive Empire: The Coming of Age of Epistemologies of the South* (Durham, NC and London: Duke University Press).

Scarborough, V.L. (1994) 'Water management as a function of locational and appropriational movements and the case of the classic Maya of Tikal', in C.M. Duncan and D.W. Tandy (eds.), *From Political Economy to Anthropology: Situating Economic Life in Past Societies* (Montreal and New York: Black Rose Books), pp. 105–119.

Scarborough, V.L. (2014) 'Does water have agency? Does it need to?', *Archaeological Dialogues,* 21 (2): 133–50.

Scott, J. (1998) *Seeing Like a State* (New Haven, CT: Yale University Press).

Sherbondy, J.E. (1993) 'Water and Power: the role of irrigation districts in the transition from Inca to Spanish Cuzco', in W.P. Mitchell and D. Guilet (eds.), *Irrigation at High Altitudes: The Social Organization of Water Control Systems in the Andes* (Washington, DC: Society for Latin American Anthropology and The American Anthropological Association).

Silva-Novoa Sanchez, L.M., J.S. Kemerink-Seyoum, and M. Zwarteveen (2019) 'Water infrastructure always in-the-making: distributing water and authority through the water supply network in Moamba, Mozambique', *Water,* 11 (9): 1–17.

Star, S.L. (1999) 'The ethnography of infrastructure', *American Behavioural Scientist,* 43 (3): 377–91.

Stengers, I. (2010). *Cosmopolitics* (Minnesota: University of Minnesota Press).

Stone, I. (1968) 'British long-term investment in Latin America, 1865–1913', *The Business History Review,* 42 (3): 311–39.

Strang, V. (2014) 'Fluid consistencies. Material relationality in human engagements with water', *Archaeological Dialogues,* 21 (2): 133–50.

Strang, V. (2016) 'Infrastructural relations: water, political power and the rise of a new "despotic regime"', *Water Alternatives,* 9 (2): 292–318.

Svampa, M. (2012) 'Resource extractivism and alternatives: Latin American perspectives on development', *Journal Fur Entwicklungspolitik,* 3: 43–73.

Swyngedouw, E. (1997) 'Power, nature, and the city. The conquest of water and the political ecology of urbanization in Guayaquil, Ecuador: 1880–1990', *Environment and Planning A: Economy and Space*, 29: 311–32.

Thurner, M. (ed.) (2019) *The First Wave of Decolonization* (London and New York: Routledge).

Tym, C. (2020) 'Tsunki only see the fish as their hens in certain rivers: situating the politics of Shuar ontology in the Ecuadorian intercultural state', *The Journal of Latin American and Caribbean Anthropology*, 25 (2): 199–217.

Velho, R. and S. Ureta (2019) 'Frail modernities: Latin American infrastructures between repair and ruination', *Tapuya: Latin American Science, Technology and Society*, 2 (1): 428–41.

Villanueva, M.E. (2020) 'Third worldism and the Panama Canal', in T.C. Field, S. Krepp, and V. Patina (eds.), *Latin America and the Global Cold War* (Chapel Hill: University of North Carolina Press), pp. 343–66.

von Schnitzler, A. (2016) *Democracy's Infrastructure: Techno-politics and Protest after Apartheid* (Princeton and Oxford: Princeton University Press).

Wilson, F. (2004) 'Towards a political economy of roads: experiences from Peru', *Development and Change*, 35 (3): 525–46.

World Bank (1994) *World Development Report: Infrastructure for Development* (Washington DC: World Bank).

Zeiderman, A. (2016) *Endangered City: The Politics of Security and Risk in Bogotá* (Durham and London: Duke University Press).

1. Dreams of an anchored state: mobility infrastructure and state presence in Quehui Island, Chile

Diego Valdivieso

> Little by little we are meeting the expectations that the neighbours invest in our management [said the mayor during an interview outside the new municipal building on Quehui Island]. People are seeing that we comply, that we keep our word (...) the important thing is that today the neighbours, without the need to travel to the municipality, will have the possibility of coming to this small municipality that is here in Quehui to request aid from the different municipal departments from right here, from the island, without the need to go to the city [Castro]. We want to decentralise our management, and we are succeeding. (...) We want no neighbour to be left behind. The islands today are growing at a level of development that Castro has always had (...) we are proud because we feel that with this investment we are not only decentralising, but also improving municipal care in remote areas of our district. (Radio Chiloé, 16 November 2018)

On a sunny day in mid-November 2018 the mayor of Castro, the capital city of the Chiloé Archipelago in southern Chile, visited Quehui Island to inaugurate a municipal building. After years of waiting, unfulfilled promises, and several disappointments, the construction of one of the projects most coveted by the islanders was finally concluded. Following an approximate investment of 75 million pesos (approximately £73,000), the promise of a direct and prompt connection with the municipality and its various services and agencies was finally being materialised. A future without depending entirely on water-mobility infrastructure such as ferries and motorboats to access municipal services became more and more possible every day. The dream of what I address as an 'anchored state' (as opposed to a state that depends on water-mobility infrastructure) was coming true.

However, rather than addressing the degree of fulfilment of this promise, this chapter discusses the material and affective conditions that generate the dream or longing tied to this promised state infrastructure. To bring this objective to fruition, I build on 12 months of continuous ethnographic fieldwork I conducted

D. Valdivieso, 'Dreams of an anchored state: mobility infrastructure and state presence in Quehui Island, Chile' in *The Social and Political Life of Latin American Infrastructures*, ed. J. Alderman and G. Goodwin (London, 2022), pp. 27–50.

during 2016–17 when the construction of the building was still a promise and the mayor had not yet visited the island to lay the foundation stone. Throughout that year, and within the scope of my doctoral research, I accompanied state officials who implemented the Programa de Desarrollo Territorial Indígena (PDTI) [Indigenous Territorial Development Programme], a state-led development programme focused on indigenous farmers, in the Chiloé Archipelago, seeking to explore the neoliberal state and how it can be studied through an analysis of the work of state actors at local level. By conducting participant observation, I gained access to the everyday activities of the 'extension teams' charged with the execution of the programme in Castro district. The team was composed of one coordinator, Jorge, and two technicians, Bruno and Renato. All of them had degrees in agriculture-related subjects.

Bruno and Renato are *Chilotes*[1] and were born and raised in the proximities of Castro. Jorge, on the other hand, comes from a family of self-made *estancieros* [landowners in Patagonia] in the southernmost region of the country. His family was originally from Chiloé, and when he moved to the main island of the archipelago those family connections were still there. The three officials were raised primarily in the countryside, where they worked along with their families and actively participated in taking care of the crops and livestock that provided the means of support or additional income for their households. While Jorge and Bruno identified themselves as Chilotes, Renato identified himself as a Williche, the name of the original inhabitants of the archipelago,[2] and proudly carried an indigenous surname that is regarded as an ethnic marker in the Chilean context. Their approach to farmers, and how they were perceived by them, was informed – and to a certain extent legitimised – by their shared territorial belonging, their upbringing moulded by a rural and peasant life, and the formal and informal education to which they were exposed.

Among their daily activities, the officials should offer regular technical advice and support to farmers participating in the programme. To achieve the improvement or continuity of their production systems and/or development of new endeavours and/or businesses in their territories, officials must carry out several visits to the users, distribute internal resources, capture and relocate external resources, transform these resources into projects (e.g. delivery of greenhouses, solar panels, motor pumps, and walking tractors), and arrange and coordinate labour training, workshops, and tours to view successful or different agricultural experiences.

These practices, in line with agricultural extension goals (transfer of technology, knowledge and advice), would take place in the rural sectors covered by the programme – beyond their office in the city. However, most of the farmers

1 Chilote is the demonym used to refer to people from the archipelago of Chiloé.

2 The Williche (willi [south]; che [people] are identified as the southern Mapuche (mapu [land]; che [people]), and the Chilean state has traditionally addressed them as a sub-group of this larger indigenous group.

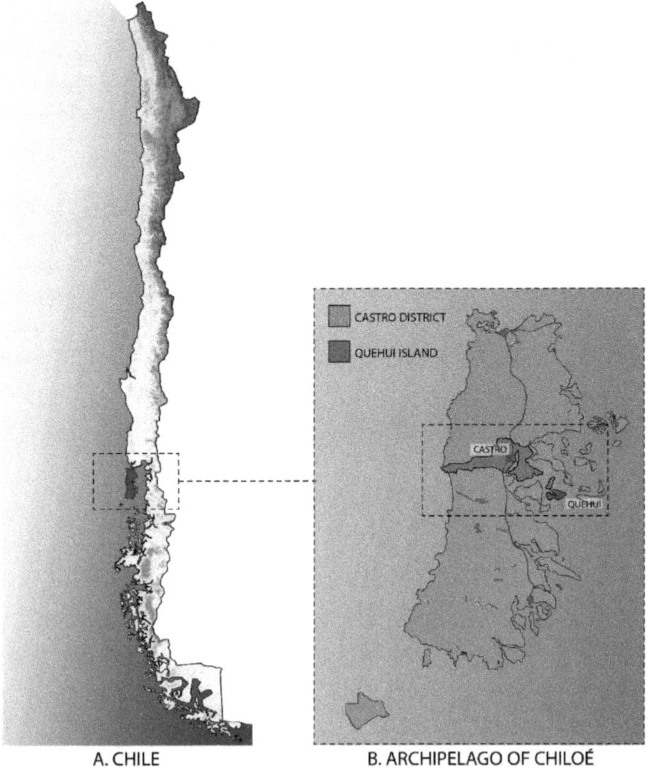

Figure 1.1 Chile, Lakes Region, and Chiloé Archipelago. Provided by Tamara Salinas-Cohn based on (A) www.curriculumnacional.cl; (B) www.gobernacionchiloe.gov.cl/geografia

participating in Castro's PDTI did not work and live in the rural areas surrounding the city, but mainly on one of the two islands under the administration of the municipality: Quehui Island, a ferry and motorboat dependent island, and one of the over 40 islands that compose the Chiloé Archipelago (see Figure 1.1).

The connectivity of Quehui Island, either with the main island of Chiloé (where the city of Castro is located) or with other nearby islands, strictly depends on water-mobility infrastructure, an assemblage of fixed and mobile infrastructure such as ferries, motorboats, timetables, piers, and routes. Both islanders and visitors must take state-subsidised ferries and/or publicly or privately owned motorboats. There are different routes to the island (see Figure 1.2) and the journey time varies depending on the option chosen. For example, the route between Castro and Quehui Island takes about two hours if one opts for the daily ferry service. Hence, motorboats, which allow for more flexibility and faster transport, are a preferred means of travel, a vital infrastructure in the everyday lives of the inhabitants of ferry dependent islands, and their

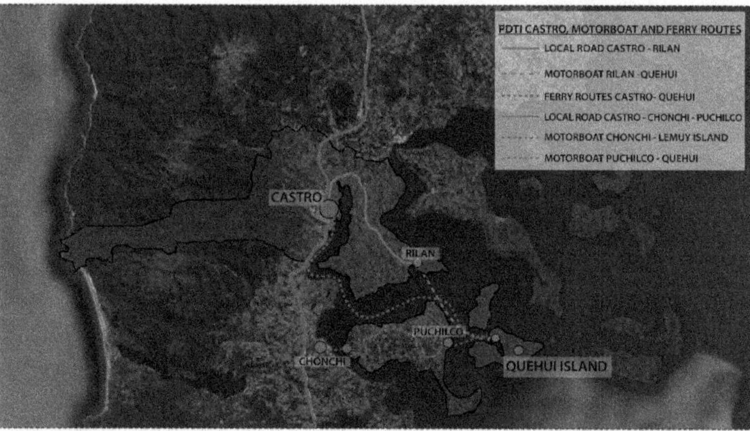

Figure 1.2 The usual routes from Castro to Quehui Island. Provided by Tamara Salinas-Cohn based on Google Earth

presence is fundamental to the archipelago's land and seascape. In the Chiloé Archipelago, it is almost impossible to imagine a panorama without one of these means of transportation, operational or abandoned, anchored in the bay or stranded on the beach.

Research bringing together mobility, island or archipelagic studies, and infrastructure is mainly focused on means of travel, socio-technical assemblages, and everyday strategies of the inhabitants of boat-dependent islands (Christensen and Mertz, 2010; Christensen and Gough, 2012; Vannini, 2011, 2012). Following the non-representational approach employed by Vannini, the work carried out by Lazo (2017), and Lazo and Carvajal (2018a, 2018b) in Chiloé on socio-technical assemblages and embodied experiences, is also a clear example of the preponderance of research focused on how everyday water mobility, the absence of fixed links with the mainland, and lack of permanent state infrastructure are a central aspect of the ways of life of those dwelling on islands.

Taking this realisation as a starting point, this chapter brings a new angle to this type of research. I aim to show how mobility is a key dimension of how islanders experience the state, in practical and affective terms, and how these experiences inform the longing for an anchored/present state on Quehui.

Drawing on my experiences moving back and forth between Castro and Quehui Island accompanying officials in charge of the PDTI in this area, I reflect on the ambivalent affective registers produced when water mobility acts as a central enabler, or inhibiter, of islanders' interactions with the state. Furthermore, I illustrate how – regardless of other forms of state presence on the island – these recurrent, but sporadic, interactions with state actors in charge of delivering welfare policies give rise to narratives of a neglectful state, placing tension upon the different guises that the state takes on in local contexts.

State effects and state affects

Based on Mitchell (1999), Trouillot (2001), and Harvey's (2005) work on state effects, this chapter addresses the role played by water-mobility infrastructure and the aspirations about anchored infrastructure on the affective and material dimension of the state being produced in the interactions between state officials and the islanders. To do this, I bring together ethnographic examples that challenge the idea of the state as a reified, freestanding actor. Following Mitchell (1999), due to the blurred boundary between society and the state, it would not be possible to consider the state as a bounded object or entity. Because of this, he suggests – and I agree – that the state can only be addressed as a complex set of practices and techniques involved in the continuous reproduction of its artificial differentiation from society.

Adding to this approach, but with a focus on how this process is produced and represented, Gupta (2012) allocates the responsibility for this distinction to the routinised practices of state agencies and representations created and mobilised by state officials. For him, the solidity of 'the state' cannot resist the detailed scrutiny of ethnography if we approach it as a highly complex arrangement of institutions with multiple functions, modes of operation, diversified levels, agencies and bureaus, and locations, pulling in different directions. In a similar fashion, and also influenced by the work of Mitchell and Troulliot, Aretxaga (2003, p. 398) argues that 'the state as phenomenological reality is produced through discourses and practices of power, produced in local encounters at the everyday level'. This recognition of the 'everyday' as a space for state practice is also highlighted by Harvey (2005) when she affirms that the state, often regarded as an absent social agent or abstraction, appears in a concrete way in people's lives, entangled in mundane sociality through the materiality of its effects.

Based on the aforementioned, and following Trouillot's argument, the state's lack of empirical boundaries and 'institutional fixity' (Gupta's 'complex array') leaves room for an ethnographic strategy that would 'focus on the multiple sites in which state processes and practices are recognized through their effects' (Trouillot, 2001, pp. 126–7). Rather than residing mainly in its institutions, the materiality of the state depends on the iteration of these effects. Therefore, the question here is how the effects are created, and what it takes to create and maintain the distinction between state and society that has been made 'real' through the effort entailed in specific practices. Taking this into consideration, my focus here is on those performing the state or enacting its authority in a local setting, and on those who, through intermittent interactions with these state actors, encounter these state effects on a daily basis. In this way, the following sections will give an account of how the state is present in Quehui Island through practices and procedures that produce (material) state effects that resonate in the affective register and representations of the state, emerging from the interaction between front-line state officials and the islanders.

In Mazzarella's (2009, p. 299) terms, 'any social project that is not imposed through force alone has to be affective in order to be effective'. In a similar vein, Woodward (2014) argues that state effects are complementary to state affects. While the former tend to be described as seemingly unificatory practices involved in the production of state unity and coherence, the latter perform as the 'differential' accompaniment of these effects, emerging from contingent encounters and relations between state actors and 'those who are enrolled in affective relations with the state' (Woodward, 2016). What I want to extract from this line of argument is the complementarity between effects and affects. In this way, and following Laszczkowski and Reeves (2015), although state affects can be seen as the differential emotional responses fostered by the material consequences of state effects, they should not be addressed only as an epiphenomenon of political life. Here, I argue that this approach is an invitation to understand how the state is enacted and experienced, in affective and effective terms, when different technologies, actors, and aspirations come into play in a local setting.

In this way, the state is not only understood as the accumulation of practices and procedures that reproduce its 'ghost-like' bounded image at the local level, 'but as thriving in embodied, affective resonances within and between persons and things' (Laszczkowski and Reeves, 2015, p. 10). As such, considering the differential emotional responses that can take place in the everyday and intermittent encounters between islanders and state actors, the affective register invoked can adopt a variety of forms such as complaints (e.g. feelings of being neglected) and aspirations (e.g. the desire for a regular presence of the 'caring state').

Taking all this into account, this chapter aims to explore motorboats and mobility infrastructure as a technology of everyday reproductions of state presence, in its different guises, to examine the contradictory affective effects of state presence – or lack thereof – and the aspirations or dreams being informed by these state effects and affects. In this vein, and following the argument of von Schnitzler (2016), attention to infrastructure – and its politics – allow us to explore the forms that the political takes beyond its most common settings and practices. Infrastructure, she argues, is an enabler of techno-political relationships and connections with the state and plays a central role in the constitution of affective capacities.

The intermittent state

The PDTI extension team travels frequently (once or twice a week) to Quehui, using whatever option is available. These regular visits take place because most users of the programme (130 of 148) live and carry out their daily activities – agriculture, cattle, fishing, seaweed harvesting, and handicrafts – on the island. For one year, I witnessed how the team used diverse routes and transport options in order to reach Quehui's pier. Large ferries transporting refuse vehicles for the islanders' rubbish, small, subsidised ferries (foot passengers only) which connect the island with Castro daily, rented speedboats, old motorboats, big ones, and small ones were all employed according to multiple variables. For example, the team's monthly budget, availability of motorboats which may be accompanying them, the number of state or local-government departments involved, available time, and weather conditions, among other factors, are potentially involved in how the island is reached.

The team's presence on the island was mediated by two relevant aspects: weather conditions and accessible motorboats. Beyond these issues, and leaving aside schoolteachers and school administrative staff, healthcare professionals, and technicians,[3] they are by far the state/local-government officials who spend the most time on this island. Because of this, for many islanders, they constitute the state's most visible representatives. If they cannot travel (a situation which is quite common in the autumn and winter, and not unusual during the spring and summer) due to Castro's harbour[4] being closed because of strong winds and heavy rain, the presence of the state/local government is noticeably reduced or, according to a large number of islanders, absent.

When visiting the island, the PDTI officials often fulfilled tasks outside their contractual obligations. Owing to their advanced knowledge about this territory, and due to their regular visits, their role expanded beyond being mere technicians in charge of an agricultural extension programme. On the contrary, they would have to act as information brokers, guides for authorities visiting the island, a point of connection between other programmes and the islanders, escorts for external professionals running labour training courses, and as evaluators or executors of engineering projects, among others. Although they are on the bottom rung of the government and municipality organisational structure, as front-line state officials, the extension team is directly responsible for the dissemination of messages to the inhabitants of the island. They

3 In Chile, a technician is someone who has obtained a degree via the technical higher education system (as opposed to professionals who hold university degrees). Technical education is generally characterised by dedicating more time to job-specific and competence-based training, reducing the time spent, for example, on academic skills.

4 The maritime authority provides daily information about the state of the harbours throughout the country. Depending on weather conditions, it determines harbour closure, whether restrictions apply for certain types of vessels, or if the harbour is open for routine activities.

participate in the production of, and in the interactions and encounters through which, the power and meaning of the state are constantly being negotiated.

In territories such as Quehui, these encounters are determined by the absence of fixed state infrastructure and are mediated by the possibilities of the functioning of transport infrastructure: motorboats and ferries. Consequently, the role of PDTI officials as state actors, those who through their practices and interactions produce state effects, depends on matters that transcend their will and possibilities for action. Owing to this context, the state's presence, on Quehui Island at least when it concerns its 'caring face' based on the delivery of welfare policies, is regarded as ambivalent and sometimes unpredictable; it is intermittent.

In physics, specifically in the field of dynamical systems, intermittence is understood as 'a regime with long-lived nearly periodic laminar phases interrupted by turbulent bursts. This regime results from the collision of stable and unstable periodic cycles' (Pikovsky, 1983, p. L109). I argue that the narratives around the state that the islanders convey, and the experiences of front-line officials embodying the state's authority on the island, follow the patterns of this regime. Both the daily activities of the islanders and officials are characterised by a laminar rhythm – organised and smooth – interrupted by the sporadic interactions that mobility, and the infrastructure that enables or prevents it, renders effective.

Following Navaro-Yashin (2002, p. 135) the state obtains its power not only through its ideological enforcement carried out by institutions such as the army and the education system, but also through 'quotidian, and seemingly spontaneous, events and occasions'. Thus, different state effects, and how people experience them, produce different state representations. Owing to the islanders' interactions with actors representing diverse state agencies, the state is seen as having different roles, responsibilities, and features, and, thus, diverse representations and affective registers emerge. In Quehui, the guises assumed by the state are mainly informed by its sporadic and sometimes unpredictable presence.

Along the same lines as Navaro-Yashin, Obeid's work shows how people would attribute different 'faces' to the state: the oppressive and neglectful face, and the ideal one, 'the face that incorporates its citizens, listens to their problems and provides services that will develop the town' (Obeid, 2010, p. 343). In their imagination, this face of the state, the one focused on giving rather than taking, exists elsewhere. Closer to Quehui, Goudsmit's (2006) work with indigenous people in Bolivia, reflects on the analytical and practical consequences of similar scalar perceptions. The indigenous peasants direct their aspirations towards the benevolent and caring state imagined as the national government – again, elsewhere – and their frustrations towards the local government. Both Obeid and Goudsmit illustrate how people attribute different faces to the state depending on who they recognise as someone performing state-like practices.

In both cases, to experience the caring face of the state you have to move away from its local expressions.

The images of the state that are being produced and are circulating in Quehui, to a greater or lesser extent, follow this same logic, but with the exception that both faces, or guises, appear intermittently, although, due to the persistent possibility of its inconvenience, the punishing state is experienced as more present than absent. Pinker and Harvey's (2015) work on a railway project in the Sacred Valley in Peru shows how the affective force of the state sometimes emerges in the fluctuating movement between its ambivalent presence and absence. Likewise, but as a physical presence rather than a virtual force, the affective registers being elicited in Quehui are products of this same ambivalence. The image of both the caring guise of the state (embodied by officials in charge of delivering welfare programmes) and its inconvenient one (law enforcement) moving back and forth between Castro and the island, without the islanders being able to influence this flow, leaves the islanders with the feeling that the state, although always in an ambivalent way, is more absent than present. In experiencing this intermittence, and regardless of the state workers based on the island, the islanders convey and mobilise narratives about being neglected. Therefore, both 'faces' of the state, due to their intermittency, are combined together in what I identify as the locus of this kind of affective dissatisfaction – the 'neglectful state'.

The guises of the state in Quehui Island

Ester, a short and corpulent woman, sat across from me on the other side of the woodstove, warming her strong hands and short fingers, removing some of the soil trapped under her nails after her morning's work in her *huerta* (garden). She was wearing a thick woollen jumper and a muddy pair of white wellingtons. 'A *matecito*?'[5], she offered me with friendly eyes and a faint smile, before lifting the hot teapot on the stove and pouring some water into the *mate*. 'Sorry for delaying our meeting, but for me, it is really complicated to leave my chores. I am *sola* [an expression indicating that someone – usually a woman – has no children or spouse], and I have to take care of my animals, my potatoes, my vegetables, and most importantly, I am taking care of my aunt', she added, looking towards a closed door in the corner of the room. 'She is very old and now she is bedbound because of a tumour on her leg. I have to be there, helping her and doing everything for her every day. Supposedly a nurse or someone from the municipality is coming to see her soon, but you know how things are. If they come to the island they come for a short time, and they want to leave soon.' In a resigned tone, she finished, saying, 'We will have to keep waiting.'

5 A herbal infusion that is prepared in a container – also called a mate – which is drunk through a straw usually made of metal.

I had arrived at Quehui's main pier the previous evening using the state-subsidised ferry service. My plan was to meet the PDTI officials after conducting a couple of interviews (one of them with Ester), but they had not been able to travel that morning because one of the municipality's motorboats had not left Rilán (a small village located on the peninsula opposite Castro with a 'usable' – but somewhat deteriorated – jetty). The maritime authority had indicated that the harbour was open, but the forecast suggested that during the afternoon the weather would get worse. This risk motivated some municipal officials to convince the motorboat's manager to cancel the trip to the island. Regardless of whether some islanders had already approached the Rural Emergency Centre or the pier in Los Ángeles, waiting for an official who would bring them information, documents, or would deliver public goods, like so many other times, the officials never came. Although the harbour was open and navigation to the island was possible, and despite the waiting islanders who planned their day according to the activities programmed by the officials coming from Castro, the motorboat never reached the island's main pier.

These kinds of recurrent events enabled the emergence of narratives that questioned the presence of the state on the island. Owing to the role played by sea-related activities in their daily lives (fishing, shellfish and seaweed harvesting, transport, among others), many of the islanders are aware of the conditions of navigation. Therefore, they have the knowledge to decide if officials representing different public services (from the municipality or central government) are unable to travel to the island due to structural causes (i.e. weather conditions) or what they perceive as a lack of commitment. Therefore, this context is not only informed by officials not going to the island but also the affective responses that their intermittent presence produces.

The temporal dimension that this intermittence brings with it resonates with Auyero's (2011) work on the micro-relations between state officials and the urban poor in Buenos Aires, Argentina. His ethnographic account illustrates how the urban poor is politically subordinated by the state via the normalisation of the waiting process. Like the urban poor in one of the largest cities in Latin America, the inhabitants of Quehui Island are used to waiting for the 'attention' of the state. However, unlike Auyero's informants, the islanders' wait on the island, is mediated by other factors such as climate and access to water-mobility infrastructure. Similarly, the waiting does not occur in the presence of state agents, but in their absence.

I visited the island frequently during my year of fieldwork to identify the institutions, front-line workers, and individuals with local authority performing state-like practices: dealing with local affairs, implementing public policies, and delivering public goods. In this sense, the perception of the inhabitants of the island that they are in a continuous state of neglect on the part of the local and central government seems to be paradoxical. However, as an ethnographic dichotomy, the presence/absence of the state can be understood as an affective response that describes the relationship of the islanders with wider structures of power in emotional terms, due to their feeling of being historically and currently excluded from national dynamics (Rasmussen, 2015) such as economic progress, development, and connectivity.

On the island, there is state infrastructure (i.e. state schools and a small clinic), and a workforce, mostly residing on the island during their working days, hired by institutions under the administration of the local government of Castro, with resources coming from state institutions such as the Ministries of Health, Agriculture, Defence, Education, the Home Office, and Social Development. Although all these services provide resources and create spaces for their officials to visit the island, public infrastructure located on this territory is still scarce, and mainly focused on providing health and education services. Nevertheless, even though there are schools, an emergency health centre, and front-line workers on the island, islanders frequently affirmed that the Chilean state had historically abandoned them and that this situation has not changed much. They experience the intermittency of the state when waiting for public officials who do not come, or when they see them hurrying to take the motorboat back to Castro to avoid getting 'stuck' on the island. Therefore, in a territory such as Quehui, narratives surrounding the idea of state neglect, or its frequent absence, are relatively common.

The inhabitants of Quehui are aware of, and participate in, state-like activities, and interact with front-line officials in charge of delivering public services. Although the mayor and the municipal council's visit to the island – assuming state-like capacities to deal with local affairs such as healthcare and connectivity – was not a common occurrence, the presence of doctors, among other public servants, and the existence of public infrastructure and services in the territory, exposes the gap between the affective and subjective dimension of the state (imaginaries) and its material effects.

Public infrastructure on the island primarily supports education and healthcare initiatives. Both services are administered and operated by the Corporación Municipal de Castro [Municipal Corporation of Castro] which operates under the local government using resources from the Ministries of Education and Health (Marcel, 1996).

On the one hand, the existence of state schools in Quehui provides a regular state presence (at least during the school year), materialised in its buildings and its staff – teachers and administrative personnel who mostly come from Castro and its surroundings, and who, in most cases, only reside on the island on working days. In addition, at the time of my fieldwork, a doctor was living on the island and he was responsible for the Posta de Salud Rural de Quehui [Rural Emergency Clinic of Quehui], two paramedics worked rotating shifts, and a 'rural team' consisting of a doctor, nurse, nutritionist, paramedical technician, psychologist, midwife, social worker, administrative staff, and a dentist carried out what they call *rondas médicas* (medical rounds) once a week. The medical round supposedly takes place every Tuesday, but due to the port being closed or because the head of the medical team (sometimes influenced by another team member) considers that the weather could deteriorate during the day, their presence on the island is not as regular as the islanders would wish.

Since July 2017, the Dirección de Desarrollo Comunitario (DIDECO, Community Development Management) from the municipality has been renting a motorboat to enable front-line officials in charge of different governmental programmes to travel to Quehui and Chelín (a small island a short distance from Quehui also administered by the Municipality of Castro). Every Thursday (weather permitting) a group of no more than ten officials gather on a jetty close to Castro, waiting for the rented motorboat to cross to the islands to carry out their field tasks.

Other forms of state presence could be found in the, often unexpected, visits by officers from the Armada [the navy], Polícia de Investigaciones [detectives], and Carabineros [the police]. The presence of officials from these institutions in Quehui is an uncomfortable one. On the one hand, several islanders with whom I talked about police officers or navy officers visiting the island told me that they thought that their tasks focused on prevention and control were essential to the islanders' feelings of safety and peace. On the other hand, I realised that most of their daily commercial activities take place under the radar of these law enforcers. Thus, an ambivalent feeling emerges when those state actors disembark in some areas of the island, or when they are seen on the sea routes used by the islanders.

It is quite common to encounter a navy speedboat circulating between the smaller islands, the ramps, and Castro, undertaking routine inspection tasks. While sailing in the area they may stop motorboats to check if their documents and registration are up to date, or they may be patrolling in order to stop, any illegal *flete* (a paid informal service that allows movement through the archipelago without depending on the daily subsidised ferries) or transactions happening at sea (principally black-market oil and unofficial seafood or cattle trading).

Unofficial trading is exemplified by what happened on a cold and rainy morning when the daily ferry to Castro did not arrive, and its horn did not announce its imminent departure. After a couple of minutes talking to some frustrated islanders who would have to wait a day to be able to travel to the city and undertake their errands, I returned to Camilo's inn, where I was staying. I needed to get to Castro somehow. I asked Camilo and Jacinta, his wife, if they knew any motorboat owner who would take me to Puchilco, a settlement on Lemuy Island a journey of approximately 30 minutes from Los Ángeles – the main village on Quehui. I knew that if I could get to Puchilco, I could go by taxi to Puqueldón (the main town on Lemuy), I could then take a direct bus to Castro. 'I think Pedro is the best option', said Camilo, looking for the number on his old cell phone. 'He is one of the only ones that does *fletes* even in this weather.' A couple of hours after I called him, Pedro's brown and white motorboat entered the bay and moored at an old jetty. Just as I was about to board the motorboat he shouted, calling for my attention, and indicating a navy speedboat entering the bay. 'We can't leave until they are gone', he told me as he approached me at the base of the jetty. 'Don't worry; it shouldn't take too long.' When I asked him why we could not start our journey, he explained to me that, as with most of the motorboats in the area, neither the papers nor the registration of the boat were up to date. After a couple of detectives had taken some statements in the village in relation to a boating accident at night, the navy speedboat finally left the main pier. Even though they were no longer visible, Pedro was still worried. 'They could be waiting near the island', he said, while calling a friend who would be able to see from his window if the speedboat was moving away from the island's coast. He hung up smiling, 'Let's go! They are already gone.'

Pedro and the other motorboat owners operating in this area are usually islanders who see owning a boat as an opportunity to complement their traditional sources of income (agriculture or fishing) or choose this occupation as their main source of livelihood. In order to get this extra income and because there is a demand for a transport service that operates rapidly and outside the schedule established by the state-sponsored ferry system, motorboat owners could provide *flete* services on a daily basis despite the risk of being caught by those who embody state law enforcement. In doing so, they enable the movement of people, cattle, seaweed, seafood, building materials, gas canisters, and fuel between the nearby islands. Because they work without the required permits and they are often involved in trading products of dubious origin or moving products defined by the authority as dangerous (i.e. fuel and gas), they operate outside the law and are always on the lookout, hoping that a naval speedboat would not appear on the horizon.

In a similar vein, islanders who own cars or motorcycles would prefer that the Carabineros did not visit the island unless necessary. The presence of the Carabineros in these smaller islands is usually sporadic and in response to some unexpected incident. They travel to the islands when someone makes a complaint or to investigate a criminal incident that has occurred during their absence. In these processes, they take statements and identify those responsible for the illicit actions denounced by witnesses or victims. However, they sometimes travel to these territories for the purposes of prevention and control. These visits often include handing out tickets and fines for expired driving licences, unregistered cars, bad driving practices, and traffic offences. In my travels around the island, I witnessed how people who saw their green and white motorboat would call someone on the island to warn them: 'Van los verdes' (the greens – because of the colour of their uniforms – are going).

Considering that the state and the local government were present through schoolteachers and administrative staff, doctors and paramedics, frequent visits of the medical team, police officers, naval officers, and other front-line officials implementing localised programmes, we need a wider and more open understanding of the state to do something about this feeling of neglect. This comprehensive idea of the state rests, as I have already stated, on a particular attention to the everyday interactions and the differential emotional responses emerging from the relationship between the islanders and front-line state actors at the local level. However, in this case, the paradoxical tension between state neglect and state presence is specifically maintained by the fundamental role played by mobility infrastructure, such as motorboats and ferries, in a context characterised by the absence of fixed links, difficult access (and departure), and limited permanent state infrastructure.

As Merriman and Jones (2017) and Obeid (2010, 2015) contend, affect is not unidirectional, and bodies might react (be affected) differently to encounters with the state. Based on this differential effect, the presence (or intermittence) of the state in Quehui takes on different guises depending on the type of state actor visiting the island, the frequency of these visits, the nature of the services delivered, and how this delivery is carried out. All of this is mediated and determined by access to, and the feasibility of using, mobility infrastructure. As I will discuss further in the next sections, regardless of the intermittent presence of the state, islanders convey narratives and experience practices that actualise the idea of a neglectful state. Because they feel abandoned, they express a longing for the stable presence of the good and caring state (i.e. welfare programmes) and emphasise the inconveniences produced by the presence of the punitive state. These narratives make visible the ambivalence and uncertainty that interactions with 'the state', not as a coherent entity but as a flexible and dispersed configuration, may produce (Pinker and Harvey, 2015). In this vein, the state can be the locus of conflicting emotions and feelings that express desires for connection and disconnection on their own terms (Jansen, 2014; Laszczkowski and Reeves, 2015).

As technical means to connect and/or disconnect places, mobility infrastructure seems to be particularly effective in the articulation of materiality, affect, and feelings. Because these technologies allow or resist the movement of bodies, they also enable the circulation and emergence of affective relations informed and produced by different 'emotions, feelings and memories' (Merriman and Jones, 2017). I suggest that when these mobility infrastructures are involved in the movement of state actors, controlled by state regulations, or when they reveal relations of state presence/absence in a particular territory, the state emerges as an (imagined) body capable of affect towards other bodies. Because other bodies have the capability of being affected to different degrees (or not being affected at all), the imagined state might produce contradictory and concomitant affects that could be expressed as desire or contempt for it (Obeid, 2015).

Mobility infrastructure and the affective register

The dynamic image of the state produced in this territory allows islanders to perceive front-line state officials as state actors with state-like capacities. Hence, if they are not on the island, and therefore the islanders do not interact with them, the emergent idea of the state produced in their everyday practices validates the narratives regarding the neglectful state. However, this 'affective register' is also informed by the entanglement of three elements that play a vital role in the daily life of the islanders: the complex nature of archipelagic formations, the southern weather, and access to and availability of mobility infrastructure.

Added to the complexity of finding a motorboat, crossing to Quehui is difficult when the southern weather shows its temperament. As the chief of the PDTI team once described, activities reliant on sea transport in the south of Chile not only imply the dangers of moving through troubled waters, but also the possibility of not being able to get to or leave the island. According to a report provided by the Port Captaincy of Castro, the local navy office in charge of updating, notifying, and imposing the closure or opening of local harbours based on information provided by the Meteorological Service of the Chilean Navy, during two periods in 2016 and 2017, out of a total of 445 days, 145 (approximately 33 per cent) were categorised as 'variable' (port closed for small boats[6] outside the bay, and sometimes inside too), 'bad weather' (harbour closed for small boats outside and inside the bay), or 'storm' (totally closed). These categories, along with the dangers of sailing in these weather conditions and other issues such as breakdowns, define and determine the possibilities for action by motorboat owners and *patrones* (a position similar to that of captain, but for fishing, passenger or merchant boats under 3,000 GT – Gross Tonnage), and therefore the intermittence of the state's perceived presence on the island.

Weather, and the naval regulations that it activates, frequently immobilises motorboats, drawing our attention to how these technologies of mobility affect the movement of bodies (Christensen and Gough, 2012) and the consequences of these (im)mobilities on local supply and state presence/absence. In the same way, infrastructural breakdown highlights the centrality of maintenance and repair, which continuously allows or prevents connection, movement, and flow (Graham and Thrift, 2007). Whatever the case, the presence of unestablished links in this area of the archipelago highlights the importance of water-mobility infrastructure (Vannini, 2011), which normally resides in a naturalised background as something banal and unexceptional (Edwards, 2003). Hence, one of the ways in which the desire to overcome the inconveniences and obstacles posed by relying on water-mobility infrastructure (taming the uncertainties of availability, maintenance, and weather), is by channelling it through claims for fixed, or what I call 'anchored', infrastructure placed in these challenging territories.

6 Under 50 GT (Gross Tonnage) (tonnage charge allowed by the features of the boat).

Every Friday, a group of schoolteachers would do whatever they could to leave Quehui and join their families and friends in Castro. They jointly organised the rental of a motorboat which, depending on weather conditions, would take them by different routes to their destination. They would assemble in the shelter (a wooden structure with a room and a large, covered terrace, overlooking the pier and the estuary) on the main pier. Now protected from the cold, rain, and wind, they would chat while they waited for the motorboat, and some of them bought food and drinks from the yellow local store opposite this building. Together they boarded the motorboat and then set course for Castro (or another destination that would allow them to reach the city after finding land-based public or private passenger transport services).

A local motorboat owner provided this *flete* service. His old white and brown motorboat, always travelling at the minimum possible speed to reduce fuel expenses, allowed him and his passengers to reach a pier or jetty with accessible roads to Castro. He was also well known for being one of the few motorboat owners who would set sail even under weather conditions that would stop others travelling, or at least make them think twice about the possible outcome of such a reckless practice. 'Always in a hurry to leave', Iris once told me. She was an old woman who owned and managed the local store opposite the pier. On that occasion, I was buying some sweets while the motorboat with the teachers aboard was leaving the bay. 'As if they were going to catch something', she added with her distinct cynicism and bitterness, looking towards the motorboat almost disappearing into the landscape. With that last statement, Iris implied that they were running away from the possibility of catching a disease: they were escaping, leaving the islanders, with their sickness, behind.

But they were not the only municipal or state workers departing that day. Like them, and like every Friday, the doctor living on the island would use the *ambulancha* (a pun resembling the word *ambulancia* – ambulance – which comes from ambu – ambulance, and *lancha* – motorboat) to leave and spend the weekend in the city. On that particular day, the PDTI officials and I were also waiting for our lift to the main island. After the conversation with Iris, and with some sweets in my pocket to share with the team, we waited for the *flete* service provided by another available motorboat owner to leave Quehui and reach our homes and families. On an ordinary weekend, only the paramedics would remain on the island, working alongside the islanders and providing care services. From the perspective of the inhabitants of the island, those left behind, the intermittence of the state becomes a reality through their affective registers. You could almost feel the sentiment of abandonment rising and floating in the air, while some islanders gathered near the pier, smoking cigarettes, sharing beers and a crate of wine, and watching the motorboats departing.

Taking into account the differential affects produced by these events, different feelings and emotions arise. One of those, frequently elicited by the islanders when talking about 'the state', was expressed as a feeling of abandonment. Seeing the officials doing everything in their power to leave the island has a strong affective resonance in some islanders who subsequently circulate narratives fuelled by these experiences and notions of 'relatively immutable historic relations' (Merriman and Jones, 2017). 'It has always been like this', Marta said to me. She had worked as a schoolteacher on the island for almost 40 years. Now retired and settled in a large old house, she offered accommodation to tourists, workers carrying out seasonal tasks (i.e. repairing the roads), and state officials needing to spend a couple of nights on the island. 'They used to come less often because everything was harder back then [referring to connectivity], but now they leave as soon as they can', she added.

Marta's stories about working as a rural schoolteacher in the past, where everything involved a greater effort due to the lack of both infrastructure and state aid, historically informs the affective register that she expresses in the present. However, what was striking in her narrative is that she herself was hired by the state as a schoolteacher, and had to carry out state-like practices. As Wilson (2000) argues, establishing schools in peripheral territories was, and could still be considered as, a technique of government that instantiates the state. Nonetheless – and also informed by her condition of being originally from a town on the main island and, therefore, having lived in a territory with better connectivity – her narrative expressed her capacity to be affected by intermittent relations with state institutions and front-line workers. Regardless of having been a state actor, her time on the island and having lived under other conditions, living on an island dependent on sea transport with difficult access, enhances the image of the neglectful state.

Feelings such as a longing for the caring state (welfare and care programmes), the inconvenience of the forceful state (the police and the navy), and the feelings emerging due to the intermittent presence of front-line state workers arriving and departing, may arise at the same time. These affective registers are intertwined in paradoxical and concomitant ways, and are always historically (by memories and narratives) and situationally informed. However, this entanglement should not be addressed as an irrelevant or meaningless occurrence, but as an example of the intricacies of the affective contingencies circulating around the images of the state.

Anchoring the state

The intermittent presence of the state is experienced as a dynamic mobility of individuals (front-line workers) and infrastructure (motorboats and ferries) going back and forth. Islanders are used to seasonality and predictable changes. The everyday life of those involved in agricultural or sea-related activities depends on knowing how to interpret the wind and the tide. At the end of winter and the beginning of spring, they plant potato seeds. The first freeze of the autumn activates the garlic seed. The northern wind brings rain and the southern wind sun, and low tide allows them to collect shellfish and seaweed. Everything seems to be foreseeable and their experiences provide them with the means to anticipate possible events and to plan their daily, monthly, or seasonal activities based on this knowledge.

One sunny summer afternoon, the farmers stopped baling hay after looking up at the sky. The wind had changed course, anticipating the arrival of a storm. The humidity would rot the unprotected bales scattered on the field, making it clear – at least for those who knew how to read the signs – that they would need to find different work because rain would fall the next day. For an outsider, like me, watching them abandon their activities seemed, at first, a whimsical practice. Because they saw what I could not – that the rain was coming – what they were doing became futile and the next day's activities were already structured by conditions to come. However, this form of planning frequently became impractical when used to anticipate if a programme meeting would, or would not, take place the next day. The islanders would gather outside the local neighbourhood association building waiting for the arrival of the front-line state official who had summoned them until they received a call cancelling the activity, giving excuses, and asking for their understanding. Resignedly, they would say goodbye to each other before going back to their suspended activities. Oxymoronically, islanders experience some interactions with 'the state' as a constant intermittence.

Yet the relationship between the islanders and state actors and institutions not only takes place on the island. There are myriad motives for people from Quehui to travel to the main island, specifically to Castro such as to stocking up with provisions, visiting friends and family, sporadic work commitments, leisure and entertainment, medical appointments, among others. However, one of the main reasons for leaving the island could be regarded as a consequence of procedures required by some state or local-government agencies to gain access, or remain in, different welfare programmes such as the PDTI. Every now and then, the users or beneficiaries of a state programme would have to travel to Castro and face some sort of bureaucracy, and often the outcome of these journeys was futile. This created a situation in which they must once again devote an entire day to take care of their unresolved issues, without any guarantee that they would achieve their goal this time.

In the context of an interview, Renato, a PDTI official, analysed how these journeys to the city could be a source of frustration for the islanders:

> (…) people schedule their trips, and because almost everyone has to take care of animals, they would frequently come [to Castro] just for the day. When they come to deal with some paperwork, sometimes they fail because of lack of time. They get frustrated and, because of that, they postpone it (…). They feel frustrated by the ferry times, which are very limited. They would arrive at 9.30 am, they would get to the municipal office at 10 am, and there would already be a large queue. At 1 pm they

> would be hungry, because by 12 or 1 they have still not been attended to, and they might realise that they require 50 more documents, so, eventually, they would just leave.

In order to face the distinctive and non-commensurable rhythms of the weather, state presence, and municipal office procedures, the Castro local authority started the construction of a municipal building on the island in mid-2017. Although for some islanders and state officials the fulfilment of this promise will not bring anything new to the relationship between the local government and the local population, a significant number of the islanders have high expectations of the possible consequences for their everyday interactions with bureaucracy. For this last group, anchoring the state on the island would provide a direct connection to front-line officials working in a local office, therefore making trips to the main island somewhat avoidable and, thus, less frequent.

Marcelo, one of the islanders who most openly demonstrated his enthusiasm about the construction of a local office expressed the following:

> (…) today people go to Castro to do paperwork ... I will give you an example, for [the Ministry of] National Assets, and they spend all their day in the office because there is an immense flow of people, and people go there all day, and they do not even have lunch. Having that office here [in Quehui], we would not have to go to Castro. We could have an Environmental Health Office too, a Tourism Office, a Social Department office so that people could go with their concerns, to see how they can help you. On our island, there are also many needs that have to be satisfied. Some people do not have work, and there are elderly people who are entirely dependent on the state [approx. £120 per month], so having an office on the island would be a tremendous benefit to people in those circumstances.

Sharing photographs of the building under construction, the mayor of Castro publicly commented on his Facebook page: 'With "works" [his quotation marks] we respond to the dreams of our neighbours (…).' Several months later, he, accompanied by a couple of councillors, visited the island and inaugurated the building. On that occasion, he commented: 'the important thing is that today, the residents of the islands can perform all kinds of procedures in this small municipality without having to travel to Castro. We want to decentralise our management, and we are achieving it' (Chaparro, 2018).

Based on Renato, Marcelo, and the mayor's accounts, the construction of the local municipal office ties together the promises made by the local government and aspirations coming from the islanders. Throughout the mayor's election period that took place in 2016, the final part of which coincided with my fieldwork, the current mayor of Castro, who was born and has family in Chelín Island, sought to directly address the feelings of abandonment that islanders frequently suffer from and with which he, as an islander, was familiar. During the mayor's visits to the island in which he addressed the construction of the municipal delegation, he generally used the tense of infrastructure – the future perfect (Hetherington, 2017). 'We will have solved that problem when the building is ready', I heard the mayor tell a neighbour who complained about having to travel to Castro every time a state-sponsored social programme asked him for a document issued by a public service. By referring to an action that will be completed between now and some point in the future he was giving shape to an anticipatory state: through the materiality of this infrastructural intervention, he was able to link the islanders' past and present notions of the neglectful state with their aspirations of connection and state presence.

Thereby, the local office on Quehui Island, regardless of its actual effects after its official opening, is the result of a specifiable lack resonating through the affective narratives mobilised by the islanders. Harvey (2017) affirms that, as specific interventions that operate through the articulation of identifiable gaps and calculable outcomes, development projects carry a moral charge of an improved future. In this vein, projects such as roads or bridges carry the promise of enhanced connectivity, directly addressing 'a sense of physical isolation or disconnection'. Likewise, and because it falls within the category of development projects, the new municipal building generates similar expectations by gathering aspirations and promises around facilitating access to public services and, therefore, improving the quality of life of the island's inhabitants.

Throughout the chapter, I have argued that mobility, and the infrastructures that enable and disable it, play an essential role in how Quehui islanders experience the state, in practical and affective terms. This final section expands the argument, showing how an 'anchored' state infrastructure can be involved in the reconfiguration of a relationship rendered as intermittent or inconvenient. By tackling the state as 'set of practices and processes and their effects' (Trouillot, 2001), and considering that we cannot separate its abstract manifestation from its material presence, both the front-line officials visiting and the building (and the staff who will work in it) acting as a decentralised municipality, produce state effects. In this case, the decentralised municipality acts in opposition to the affective and practical consequences of depending on motorboats, by rendering the state stable, reducing its intermittence, and anchoring its 'ideal face' or caring guise. On the other hand, its uncomfortable and enforcing face continues to be present due to, paradoxically, the constant threat posed by its intermittence.

Conclusion

In a territory defined by its physical separation, mobility is, of course, essential. Following Baldacchino's (2016, p. 6) definition, archipelagos are 'fluid cultural processes, sites of abstract and material relations of movement and rest, dependent on changing conditions of articulation or connection'. State effects are not impervious to these flows and changes. On the contrary, these effects, and their ability to affect, are the consequence of these processes.

Throughout this chapter, I presented evidence to argue that state officials' visits and activities, especially in areas that are difficult to access, inform affective registers about the presence/absence of the Chilean state. This 'intermittency' is subject to external phenomena such as access to, and the feasibility of using, mobility infrastructure. I illustrated how this infrastructure plays an essential role in how Quehui islanders experience the state, in practical and affective terms, and in the emergence of aspirations related to reducing this intermittence by anchoring its caring face through fixed infrastructure. As Rumé (2022) demonstrates in this volume, infrastructural constructions, in this case a municipality building on the island, affect 'infrastructured practices' of dwelling and mobility. All this together produces and puts into circulation divergent narratives in terms of the manifestations of the state that the islanders long for (its caring guise enacted in the delivery of public services), or are unwilling to accept (its neglectful face, that is the product of its intermittence, and its inconvenient actualisations embodied by law-enforcement officials).

The promise to anchor the state by reducing the role played by water mobility in allowing or hindering the interactions between islanders and state actors draws attention to the shifting affective and material effects being produced by the state and intermittent mobility infrastructures in isolated territories. In this way, my focus on infrastructure, its affective dimensions and material effects, has allowed me to expose the dynamic processes involved in the enactments and unmarked boundaries of the state in local settings. Infrastructure provides a physical medium for state actors to travel and for state practices to be enacted, but it does not set up a clear and fixed line to define it as a discrete and coherent entity. On the contrary, its dynamic and permeable nature comes to light when confronted with its everyday actualisations and the effects that these generate in the process.

References

Aretxaga, B. (2003) 'Maddening states', *Annual Review of Anthropology*, 32 (1): 393–410.

Auyero, J. (2011) 'Patients of the state: an ethnographic account of poor people's waiting', *Latin American Research Review*, 46 (1): 5–29.

Baldacchino, G. (2016) 'More than island tourism: branding, marketing and logistics in archipelago tourist destination', in G. Baldacchino (ed.), *Archipelago Tourism: Policies and Practices* (Oxford and New York: Routledge), pp. 1–18.

Chaparro, L. (2018) 'Alcalde Juan Eduardo Vera inauguró delegación municipal de las islas Quehui y Chelín', *Diario Chiloé*, 16 November

2018, <https://www.diariochiloe.cl/noticia/actualidad/2018/11/alcalde-juan-eduardo-vera-inauguro-delegacion-municipal-de-las-islas-quehui-y-chelin> (accessed 22 February 2019).

Christensen, A.E. and K.V. Gough (2012) 'Island mobilities: spatial and social mobility on Ontong Java, Solomon Islands', *Geografisk Tidsskrift-Danish Journal of Geography*, 112 (1): 52–62.

Christensen, A.E. and O. Mertz (2010) 'Researching Pacific island livelihoods: mobility, natural resource management and nissology', *Asia Pacific Viewpoint*, 51 (3): 278–287.

Edwards, P.N. (2003) 'Infrastructure and modernity: force, time, and social organization in the history of sociotechnical systems', in T.J. Misa, P. Brey, and A. Feenberg (eds.), *Modernity and Technology* (Cambridge, MA: MIT Press), pp. 185–225.

Goudsmit, I.A. (2006) 'Praying for government: peasant disengagement from the Bolivian State', *Bulletin of Latin American Research*, 25 (2): 200–19.

Graham, S. and N. Thrift (2007) 'Out of order: understanding repair and maintenance', *Theory, Culture & Society*, 24 (3): 1–25.

Gupta, A. (2012) *Red Tape: Bureaucracy, Structural Violence, and Poverty in India* (Durham, NC: Duke University Press).

Harvey, P. (2005) 'The materiality of state-effects: an ethnography of a road in the Peruvian Andes', in K.G. Nustad and C. Krohn-Hansen (eds.), *State Formation: Anthropological Perspective* (London and Ann Arbor, MI: Pluto Press), pp. 123–41.

Harvey, P. (2017) 'Containment and disruption: the illicit economies of infrastructural investment', in P. Harvey, C.B. Jensen, and A. Morita (eds.), *Infrastructures and Social Complexity: A Companion* (Oxford and New York: Routledge), pp. 51–63.

Hetherington, K. (2017) 'Surveying the future perfect: Anthropology, development and the promise of infrastructure', in P. Harvey, C. B. Jensen, and A. Morita (eds.), *Infrastructures and Social Complexity: A Companion* (Oxford and New York: Routledge), pp. 40–50.

Jansen, S. (2014) 'Hope for/against the state: gridding in a besieged Sarajevo suburb', *Ethnos*, 79 (2): 238–60.

Laszczkowski, M. and M. Reeves (2015) 'Introduction. Affective states – entanglements, suspensions, suspicions', *Social Analysis*, 59 (4): 1–14.

Lazo, A. (2017) 'Las constelaciones de la movilidad y el género en un archipiélago en transformación. El caso de Chiloé en el sur austral de Chile', in G. Cozzi and P. Velázquez (eds.), *Desigualdad de género y configuraciones espaciales* (Ciudad de México: Universidad Nacional

Autónoma de México Centro de Investigaciones y Estudios de Género), pp. 337–54.

Lazo, A. and D. Carvajal (2018a) 'Habitando la movilidad: el viaje en lancha, los objetos y la experiencia de la movilidad en el archipiélago de Quinchao, Chiloé (Chile)', *Revista Austral de Ciencias Sociales*, 33: 89–102.

Lazo, A. and D. Carvajal (2018b) 'La movilidad y el habitar chilote. Cambios, rupturas y continuidades en las prácticas de movilidad cotidiana de los habitantes del archipiélago de Chiloé, en el sur austral de Chile', *Chungará (Arica)*, 50 (1): 145–54.

Marcel, M. (1996) 'Descentralización y desarrollo: la experiencia Chilena', in G. Ranis (ed.), *Hacia un crecimiento moderno. Ensayos en honor de Carlos Díaz-Alejandro* (Washington, DC: Banco Interamericano de Desarrollo), pp. 85–131.

Mazzarella, W. (2009) Affect: what is good for?, in S. Dube (ed.), *Enchantments of Modernity: Empire, Nation, Globalization* (Abingdon: Routledge), pp. 291–309.

Merriman, P. and R. Jones (2017) 'Nations, materialities and affects', *Progress in Human Geography*, 41 (5): 600–17.

Mitchell, T. (1999) 'Society, economy, and the state effect', in G. Steinmetz (ed.), *State/Culture: State Formation after the Cultural Turn* (New York and London: Cornell University Press), pp. 76–97.

Navaro-Yashin, Y. (2002) *Faces of the State: Secularism and Public Life in Turkey* (Princeton, NJ: Princeton University Press).

Obeid, M. (2010) 'Searching for the "ideal face of the state" in a Lebanese border town', *Journal of the Royal Anthropological Institute*, 16 (2): 330–46.

Obeid, M. (2015) '"States of aspiration": anthropology and new questions for the Middle East', in S. Altorki (ed.), *A Companion to the Anthropology of the Middle East* (Hoboken, NJ: John Wiley & Sons).

Pikovsky, A. (1983) 'A new type of intermittent transition to chaos', *Journal of Physics A*, 16: L109–L12.

Pinker, A. and P. Harvey (2015) 'Negotiating uncertainty. Neo-liberal statecraft in contemporary Peru', *Social Analysis*, 59 (4): 15–31.

Rasmussen, M.B. (2015) *Andean Waterways: Resource Politics in Highland Peru* (Seattle and London: University of Washington Press).

Rumé, S. (2022) 'The contradictions of sustainability: discourse, planning and the tramway in Cuenca, Ecuador', in J. Alderman and G. Goodwin (eds.), *The Social and Political Life of Latin American Infrastructure* (London: University of London Press).

von Schnitzler, A. (2016) *Democracy's Infrastructure: Techno-Politics and Protest after Apartheid*, reprint ed. (Princeton, NJ: Princeton University Press).

Trouillot, M.R. (2001) 'The anthropology of the state in the age of globalization: close encounters of the deceptive kind', *Current Anthropology*, 42 (1): 125–38.

Vannini, P. (2011) 'Constellations of (in-)convenience: disentangling the assemblages of Canada's west coast island mobilities', *Social & Cultural Geography*, 12 (5): 471–92.

Vannini, P. (2012) 'In time, out of time rhythmanalyzing ferry mobilities', *Time & Society*, 21 (2): 241–69.

Wilson, F. (2000), Representing the state? School and teacher in post-Sendero Peru', *Bulletin of Latin American Research*, 19 (1): 1–16.

Woodward, K. (2014) 'Affect, state theory, and the politics of confusion', *Political Geography*, 41: 21–31.

Woodward, K. (2016) State reason and state affect. *Political Geography*, 51: 89–91.

2. 'They want to change us by charging us': drinking water provision and water conflict in the Ecuadorian Amazon

Julie Dayot

From oil conflicts to drinking water provision

The literature on extractivism has focused on conflict and the main theories of oil conflicts come from political ecology. Two frameworks, notably, have emerged to study the conflicts arising between indigenous people, on the one hand, and extractive activities on the other. Known as ecological and cultural distribution conflicts and developed by Martínez-Alier (2002) and Escobar (2008) respectively, they postulate that indigenous people, because of their ecological and cultural 'difference' (Escobar, 2008) – a special attachment to the environment as a provider of livelihood or cultural identity – oppose oil extraction projects which threaten these environments. The two frameworks were influential in the study of Latin American indigenous movements (Schlosberg and Carruthers, 2010). They are particularly suitable for the Amazonian context where, according to Rival, 'the forest constitutes the infrastructure people need' (Venkatesan et al., 2018, p. 47) and 'counter-narratives articulated around notions of incommensurability tend to prevail' (Venkatesan et al., 2018, p. 14). Water, and notably the struggles for the preservation and control over traditional and natural sources of water, is central to those accounts (Jiménez et al., 2014; Dangl, 2007 for Bolivia), which often highlight the different values (and valuation) of water (rivers notably) in relation to indigenous people's cosmologies (see for instance Boelens et al., 2014). In some instances, 'difference' is not only analysed as ecological and cultural but also 'ontological' (de la Cadena, 2019)[1] – a point where political ecology becomes 'political ontology' (Blaser, 2014). In that respect, water is also

1 According to Blaser, when we treat difference as 'ontological' rather than 'cultural', we acknowledge the existence of 'multiple realities or worlds' rather than just 'multiple perspectives or cultural representations' of one unique 'reality or world out there' – which he calls the 'modernist ontological assumption' (2014, p. 4).

J. Dayot, '"They want to change us by charging us": drinking water provision and water conflict in the Ecuadorian Amazon' in *The Social and Political Life of Latin American Infrastructures*, ed. J. Alderman and G. Goodwin (London, 2022), pp. 51–77.

central to what has come to be known as the 'ontological turn' in anthropology (see for instance Wilson and Inkster, 2018).

In Ecuador, against this background, the various agreements found between indigenous people and large extractive companies operating in their territories have become the focus of increased ethnographic attention in the recent years.[2] For the authors trying to make sense of indigenous people's decisions to accept an oil extraction project in their territories (see for instance Fontaine, 2004; Reider and Wasserstrom, 2013; Sabin, 1998), the focus is no longer on 'difference' but on the diversity of indigenous people's claims[3] and notably the material needs of communities at the local level – in the Amazon region in particular, marked by poverty (Perreault, 2001; Perreault, 2003) and the historical absence of the state (Bustamante, 2007; Juteau, 2012; Muratorio, 1991). Those needs are contrasted with the potential benefits brought by large oil companies to their territories. Interestingly, such benefits often come in the form of basic services, and (drinking) water (provision) is also central to such accounts – in territories where the pollution (of the rivers in particular) is sometimes already a daily reality, as well as a long-standing issue, unaddressed by the state. In such cases, infrastructure tends to be demanded and celebrated – as is more common in the literature on infrastructure[4] than in the Amazonian literature. Typically missing from such accounts, however, is an investigation of the challenges associated with the provision of basic services, drinking water in particular, to indigenous communities with different worldviews and practices. This has to do, more broadly, with the question of indigenous people's 'difference' in their quest for 'equality'[5] (Escobar, 2006). This is not only true of Ecuador: as highlighted by Jiménez et al., 'compared to the challenges and conflicts around competing water uses and water resources management, there is far less attention paid in the literature to the challenges related to the provision of water services to indigenous populations' (2014, p. 284).[6] One of such challenges has to do with payment for water services – an understudied aspect of the already scarce literature on basic services provision in indigenous territories (Jiménez et al., 2014).

2 They have been analysed by Becerra, Paichard, Sturma, and Maurice (2013); Fontaine (2009); Guzmán-Gallegos (2012); Haley (2004); Juteau-Martineau et al. (2014); O'Connor (1994); Orta-Martínez and Finer (2010); Rival (1998); Rival (2017); Sawyer (2004); Valdivia (2005); Vallejo (2014); Ziegler-Otero and Ziegler-Otero (2006).

3 Which are not only ecological and cultural, but also economic, social, political, and ethical (Fontaine, 2004).

4 See for instance Hetherington for infrastructure as 'a promise' of 'development, civilization, or simply progress' (2014, p. 197), and Harvey (2018) on 'the promise of roads' in 'the promise of infrastructure'.

5 Escobar defines 'equality' as the ability not to be treated as hierarchically inferior. The concepts of 'difference' and 'equality', however, are not given a fixed content *a priori*.

6 This is based on a review of 185 papers 'focusing on indigenous population and ethnic minorities in relation to water, sanitation and hygiene' (Jiménez et al., 2014, p. 279).

The present chapter analyses a conflict between the municipality and the inhabitants of Samona, a Quichua community of the Napo River in the Ecuadorian Amazon, revolving around the monthly payment which comes with the provision of drinking water to their community as part of the 'social compensation' from oil extraction. It tells a story of infrastructure as celebrated, yet potentially disruptive, which will ultimately result in a non-conflictive, yet problematic situation, with 'equality' being granted at the expense of 'difference' and where 'difference' is, as in Neale and Vincent, taken as fluid, contextual, and pragmatic – 'a category invoked in manifold settings whose meaning is always contingently articulated' (2017, p. 433) – but also heterogeneous (Cepek, 2016) and multidimensional. By analysing the claims of the inhabitants around the drinking water service, which reveal clashes of worldviews with the municipality and a certain conception of 'difference', the chapter describes how 'difference' is reshaped, influenced, and reframed in the search for 'equality' (and equal access to the drinking water). It identifies some of the questions that arise in the search for infrastructure compromises which would be able to incorporate 'difference', and ultimately highlights the importance of investigating those cases where infrastructure is desired, necessary, and demanded by the communities.

Research context and methods

This research was conducted during the second mandate of President Correa (2013–17), a period which arguably marks a narrative shift at the governmental level, from 'difference' to 'equality' – as the 'social compensation' became institutionalised by the state following the failure of the Yasuní-ITT initiative (2007–13).

Launched by the Correa government in 2007 with the stated goal of mitigating climate change (Rival, 2012), the initiative proposed to leave 20 per cent of the country's oil reserves permanently underground in the Ishpingo-Tambococha-Tiputini (ITT) fields of the Yasuní National Park (YNP), in exchange for a monetary compensation from the international community. The park of 982,000 hectares, created in 1979 and declared 'Man and Biosphere Reserve' by UNESCO in 1989, is home to indigenous people (Finer et al., 2008) and an example of biodiversity in the Amazon (Bass et al., 2010). The initiative thus also aimed to protect its biodiversity, and the rights of the different indigenous groups living in it (Finer et al., 2010). In a country where oil extraction represented 56.8 per cent of the total exports (Banco Central del Ecuador, 2013), the initiative arguably made an unprecedented step towards the recognition of the incommensurability between economic development and the rights of nature and indigenous people. Such recognition was further anchored in the 2008 constitution, which not only forbids extractive activities in protected areas (Finer et al., 2009) but also gives rights to nature.[7]

After the failure of the initiative, however, Correa's discourse shifted towards a new extractive compromise, emphasising the need for oil extraction to finance poverty alleviation (Acosta, Gudynas, Martínez, and Vogel, 2009; Barrientos, Gideon, and Molyneux, 2008; Bebbington, 2009), education, and health (Aanestad, 2011; Reygadas and Filgueira, 2010). To meet the new rhetoric, the state nationalised the oil industry (Juteau-Martineau et al., 2014): the Law of Hydrocarbons, reformed in 2010, modifies the status of oil contracts with multinational companies from participative contracts to contracts of services to increase the revenue of the state (Cevallos, 2014). In line with the 2008 constitution – which gives rights to prior consent[8] to the local communities, as well as participation in the benefits and indemnities for the social, cultural, and environmental impacts of extractive projects (Simbaña, 2012) – a complex scheme of economic and social redistribution was implemented at the local level. This arguably marked a rupture with 40 years of unregulated and uncompensated oil development, in the Amazon region in particular – where the history of oil development is widely recognised as 'one of massive ecological and social disruption' (Finer et al., 2008, p. 178).[9]

Oil extraction was finally allowed in the ITT fields of the YNP in 2013 – in direct contradiction with the 2008 Constitution. The abandonment of the initiative also meant the launch of the 11th round[10] of oil extraction in the country, in the context of which 30 agreements of social investments were signed with community leaders and local governments (Vallejo, 2014). While the end of the initiative marked a rupture between Correa and the national indigenous movement (Bebbington, 2009, 2012; Jameson, 2011; Lalander and Peralta, 2012), which had supported him in the 2006 presidential election, indigenous communities at the local level responded favourably to one of the first processes of prior consultation ever held in the country (Vallejo, 2014). In the ITT fields, the process was carried out in 2013 among the different

7 Accepted in 2008 by more than 64 per cent of the Ecuadorian electorate (Lalander and Peralta, 2012), it was considered the most radical constitutional text in the world, along with Bolivia's, in relation to the provision of legal protection of nature (Lalander and Peralta, 2012). It was also said to represent 'significant and dramatic gains for indigenous aspirations' (Becker, 2011, p. 57).

8 The right to prior consent was already in the 1998 constitution but its application was subordinated to another law which was never passed (Simbaña, 2012). Article 1 of the 2008 Constitution states that all the rights of the constitution are directly applicable.

9 For the environmental, social, and cultural impacts of oil extraction in the Amazon see Beristain, Páez Rovira, and Fernández (2009); Bissardon et al. (2013); Finer et al. (2008); Hurtig and San Sebastián (2002); Jochnick et al. (1994); Juteau-Martineau et al. (2014); Kimerling (1990); Larrea (2017); Orta-Martínez and Finer (2010); Paichard (2012); Sabin (1998); San Sebastián and Hurtig (2004); Sawyer (2004).

10 The 11th round consists of 21 blocks in total, in Pastaza, Morona-Santiago, Napo, and Orellana, including the ITT block (Vallejo, 2014).

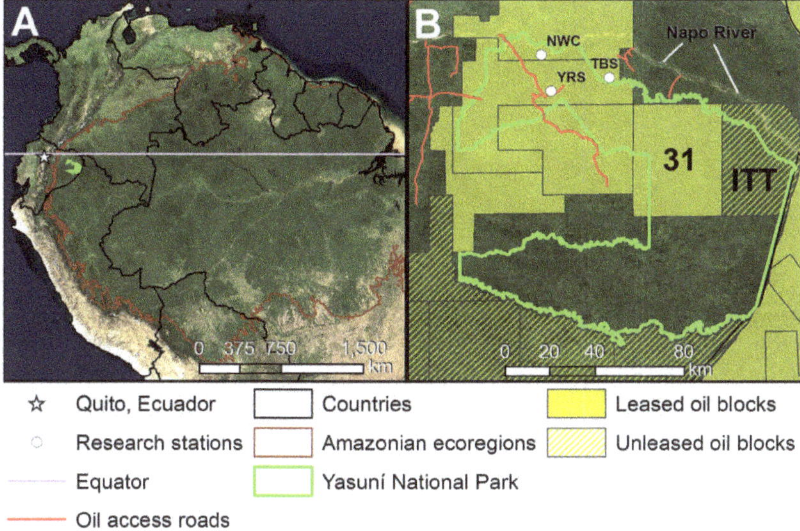

Figure 2.1 Oil blocks 31 and 43 (ITT) along the Napo River and inside he Yasuní National Park. Source: Bass et al. (2010). CC BY 4.0

Quichua communities living inside the block, and the first barrels were extracted in March 2016.

Figure 2.1 shows the overlaps between both the ITT block and block 31, the YNP and the Napo River along which 16 Quichua communities have settled since the 1920s.

I travelled to the Ecuadorian Amazon in August 2016 for an eight-month period of fieldwork, as part of my doctoral research which investigated oil decisions among the Quichua inhabitants of the lower Napo River. I first travelled to Samona – a two-hour canoe trip from Tiputini[11] further up the Napo River – in September 2016, to give English classes to the children of the community school.[12] Samona overlaps block 31,[13] another (and older) oil

11 Tiputini is the village of 500 inhabitants surrounded by the Quichua communities of the lower Napo River and the ITT block overlapping them.

12 It would be more accurate to say I was 'sent' to Samona by Juan Carlos, a councillor from the municipality who offered the president of Samona my services as an English teacher for the children of the community – a mission I accepted, as I was curious to discover a setting where oil extraction had already been present for 16 years. What at first felt like a less-than-ideal place and moment to make progress in my research – oil extraction was no longer a topic of conversation among the inhabitants – would eventually become an ideal setting to make sense of what happens once the 'social compensation' has been provided to the communities. The shift happened as I let go of my focus on oil to investigate the only issue the inhabitants were interested in discussing, and which would increasingly capture my interest: the conflict around the payment for the drinking water.

13 See Figure 2.1.

block, in operation since 2000. It was thus ahead in the oil extraction process compared to the communities of the lower Napo River (overlapping the ITT block where oil extraction had only started a few months before). As I explain in more detail below, while the communities of the ITT block were in the process of negotiating the benefits with the oil company, Samona had already received such benefits – the drinking water plant in particular (Figure 2.2).

I discovered the conflict during my first day in the community, where an exceptional *asamblea*[14] had been organised to discuss it with the *municipio* [municipality]. I would spend my next three visits to Samona, between October and December 2016, investigating the claims of the inhabitants and observing the unfolding of the conflict – while hanging out with them in the centre of the community, playing football with the women, attending the different gatherings which happened while I was there (*asambleas, mingas*,[15] and other celebrations) and occasionally conducting formal interviews with the inhabitants and oil workers. The rest of the chapter is the result of such investigation. It also draws on my interviews and conversations with the inhabitants of Tiputini and the communities of the lower part of the river, as well as with different actors from the municipality, whom I observed (and sometimes followed) in their attempt to make sense of the claims of the inhabitants (and find solutions to the conflict). The chapter finally uses the analysis of official documents from the municipality.

Oil extraction and the drinking water plant

I first met Jaime Salazar, grandchild of Vicente Salazar (who gave his name to the community he first arrived in), during a 'tour of the communities' with the municipality[16] at the end of October (2016). After complaining about the ongoing disappearance of the Quichua culture, he described in great detail the changing needs in the communities, and the reasons why their inhabitants need basic services that they did not need before. According to him, living without those basic services equates to living in poverty. 'I don't like it when people come to say that here, everything's good, and that we need to continue living like that', he told me. 'The *indígena* too has the right to progress'. 'What is really important is to reach progress without losing our culture', he concluded.

I was given the opportunity to witness the practical challenges associated with such an ideal during subsequent journeys to Samona, a Quichua community of

14 Monthly gathering between the *socios* of the community to discuss different matters. A *socio* is a member of the community who is over 18 years of age.

15 Monthly gathering between the *socios* of the community to carry out communitarian work (agricultural, cleaning, building, etc.).

16 Jaime works for the municipality in Tiputini.

115 *socios,* the first community in the *ribera*[17] to ask for, and obtain, drinking water from state oil company Petroamazonas (PAM).

'The plan for drinking water comes from the compensation. I'll tell you the story,' Saul, the president of the community, explains, as I interview him in the centre of the community during my second stay in Samona in October 2016.[18] Petrobras, a Brazilian oil firm, arrived in the *ribera* in 2000 to carry the seismic study in oil block 31, which overlaps the territory of Samona. After three years of negotiations, the community and the firm came to an agreement regarding social compensation. Drinking water was part of the agreement, together with a computing centre, a communal house, electricity network, and a retaining wall along the river. There were also grants for the students, and some health-related benefits. The agreement was finally signed in 2005.

Need and desire

The inhabitants recall with a lot of pride their idea of demanding the drinking water from the oil company. Marcia, a Quichua woman, *socia* of the community and teacher in the community school, remembers, 'it was decided during an *asamblea.* We started asking, "what do we need?" because we were going to receive some money'. Saul insists that 'it was our idea, nobody trained us'. 'I was the promoter of that idea', he adds proudly, 'but everyone agreed. We are the only community with drinking water.' And Paul, a *mestizo* and a sociologist working for PAM's department of communitarian relations, similarly recalls that 'in Samona, there were two to three people with this strong idea (...). And the community asked this. So we did it.'

Before the water plant was built, people would drink the water from the Napo River, which is both polluted[19] and the source of various health issues. They had access to *agua entubada* (piped water) only in the centre, where the standpipe was located – as it is the case in most communities of the *ribera.* While Marcia considers that she does not 'have the knowledge to say if that [piped] water was good or not, Inocencio, an elderly, Quichua man and *socio* of the community, remembers that '[before], the water was dirty'. For Marcia, 'this is a good decision from the *asamblea.*' 'For health', she adds. (...) 'Of course we are happy to have this water now in our houses!'

17 Another name given to the Napo River and communities which surround it.

18 The following summary comes almost exclusively from Saul.

19 While the extent of such pollution is not known with accuracy – because of the absence of 'technical studies' (conversation with a technician in the health centre) – it is common knowledge among the communities. According to the *plan de manejo* of Vicente Salazar – a document produced and edited every year by the Provincial Council – the river is polluted because of different contaminants which are frequently discharged in the upper part of the river, such as *aguas negras* [black water], and pollution related to oil extraction, agriculture, and livestock. It is most often assigned by the inhabitants to oil extraction projects further up the river.

Saul concludes, 'people are happy [about the drinking water]. Only about the payment they are unhappy.'

Involvement of the municipio

The project was delayed as Petrobras left in 2007, due to a change in the Ecuadorian law requiring strategic activities such as oil extraction to be carried out by state-owned companies. 'And they left us like this', Saul goes on, 'without any construction work done. Only the written agreement'. In 2008, the oil field was handed over to state company PAM. 'As a public firm, they didn't have the same possibilities. They removed the matter of the grants, the building of classrooms and of a health centre.' And in 2009, after two years of negotiations, the community finally reached an agreement with PAM, 'with the same five constructions' including the water plant. But the US$900,000 project, too expensive for the public firm, required the involvement of the municipality, which in 2013 added US$450,000 to the US$520,000 invested by the community with the money from the social compensation – as confirmed by the mayor. 'And now they gave us the drinking water', Saul concludes. The plant was finally built in the centre of the community in 2014, through a *convenio*[20] between Petroamazonas and the *municipio*.

From June 2015 onwards, the *municipio* was in charge of the service (water provision) and maintenance of the plant. They started charging the inhabitants monthly and according to their consumption. Katy, a Quichua woman from San Roque (further up the river, near Coca) married to a *socio* of the community, is responsible for the maintenance of the plant in the community. She also controls the water meters once a month. She explains to me – while showing me her office inside of the plant, 'The plant started to work in January 2015 (…) but the municipality just started being in charge last June [2015], and I started my job too.' While the cost for standard consumption (less than 15 cubic meters) used to be US$2,[21] 'the mayor came to *socializar*[22] in August 2015 that the cost would rise to $2.70, and later $3.70'.[23] The municipality justifies the reform (resulting in an increase in the price, which had not changed since 2004) by a 'technical study' underlining the rising costs, as well as the improved quality of the service, 'it's also increased because the water is now

20 A *convenio* in this context is an agreement between the company and the local administration whereby both parties will finance the infrastructure, which will be built by the company and later managed by the municipality.

21 US$1, plus US$1 of administration.

22 There is no good English translation for the Spanish word *socializar*. It means to inform and explain at the same time and is often used by the communities and local governments to talk about state 'projects' being offered to indigenous people or carried out in indigenous territories. I sometimes translate it as 'socialise'.

23 Both amounts include the US$1 administration fee.

drinkable, not just *entubada*', the mayor tells me. 'And the people accepted. But they didn't pay then.'

The water conflict

In July 2015, three months after the service started, many families had not paid anything yet. 'They were asking for exoneration', the mayor explains. The municipality decided to exonerate the inhabitants for three months – and the mayor, in his own words, 'put [his] own salary into that', which meant they would have to pay from August 2015. 'But they did not, and the conflict went on.'

From January 2016 onwards, the monthly cost for standard consumption increased to US$3.70 as previously announced by the mayor. However, 'a year and a half later, only five people are paying for the water', Katy summarises. According to official documents from the municipality, the 81 households in the community benefiting from the service had accumulated a debt of US$3946 to the municipality during the first 11 months of operation (since August 2015), and only four households had paid all their bills in July 2016. More than half of them (44 households) had accumulated 10 or 11 months of bills since the beginning – meaning they had either never paid or paid only for one month of water consumption.

The water for free

During our first interview, Saùl, the president of Samona, tells me, 'The people are not going to pay. They are not going to pay even a cent. This is why, it seems, the mayor is upset. He didn't come to the meeting on the 2nd [of October – when an exceptional *asamblea* was planned between the community and the municipality to discuss the conflict]'.

During my first stay in Samona, it was very clear that the inhabitants wanted the water for free. They were not short of arguments.

The plant and the water are ours

First, there was a great deal of confusion and misunderstanding surrounding questions of rights and competence, the role of the oil firm, the ownership of the social compensation – and the question of who is responsible for paying, in a context where the community had put their own money into the construction of the plant, which is, as a basic service, a competence of the municipality to provide, and comes as a compensation from oil extraction, which pollutes the river. For Saul, 'The municipality can't do anything. The plant and the water are ours.'

Money from the compensation

While the municipality was charging the community 'only the operative and maintenance costs', most inhabitants seemed to think they were being charged

Figure 2.2 The water plant in Samona. Source: González Toro (2017, p. 136). Photo: Patricia González Toro[24]

to repay the plant – which was unfair, in their view, since they had put what they considered to be their own money – the money given by the oil company as part of the 'social compensation' – into the construction of the plant. 'This is our money', Roque Andy, a Quichua man, *socio* of the community, tells me. 'If it was the municipality's money', he adds, 'we would have been happy to pay.' 'Maybe after two years of exoneration though'. He was also under the impression that 'if PAM had done the project it would have been free'. Instead, 'the municipality did it, with the money from the community, and now they are charging the community'. For Ángel, a young Quichua man, *socio* and secretary of the community, this is how the conflict started, 'From then on, the people (...) started thinking: how come we need to pay if the plant is ours? This is where the conflict comes from.'

The municipality had put half the money too – as the mayor and vice mayor reminded me countless times, 'They say the money is theirs!' the vice mayor exclaims. 'Sure it's theirs, but with the 500,000 they could not have afforded a plant like this one. It's one of the best which exists.'

Water as a right and competency of the municipio

Marcia was aware of the involvement of the *municipio*, and thought such involvement was the reason for the monthly payment. In a conversation, she told me, 'The water, let's see. It's from Petroamazonas. Or Petrobras, I am not sure. Then, they let it to the municipality, because it's their competency. The municipality said they put their part. This is why they are charging us for the service'. 'But', she exclaims, it's a basic service, it's a right, it's not a business.' And, she adds, 'it's an obligation for the municipality to give us water'.

The second misunderstanding came from the fact that the provision of water, as a basic service, is the legal responsibility of the municipality – which for many people meant it should be provided for free. In theory, each *Gobierno Autonomo Decentralizado* (GAD) [Autonomous Decentralised Government] receives money for that purpose from the central state – something that the inhabitants were often aware of. But as Franklin Cox, the mayor, clarifies, 'the construction is one thing and the service is another. It should always be charged for.' Indeed, as underlined by César, a Quichua man working for PAM, 'The water system needs a generator, which consumes a lot of fuel. And people are needed for the maintenance.' Katy similarly considered that 'We have to pay because it's a good service, because it's being maintained by people who know what they are doing. Here, in the community, we wouldn't know.' According to Inocencio, 'The people don't understand that when there is a service, it has to be charged. It costs the municipality to *manejar* [operate] the system.' And for Marcia, the explanation was that 'Here we are not used to pay for basic services. We never had any!'

Deception...

I finally understood, while talking to Juan Carlos, a councillor, *mestizo*, and *socio* of the Quichua community of Vicente Salazar, that the real issue was the initial investment made by the community, which should have been made by the municipality – as part of its responsibility to provide for the drinking water. 'They ask for basic services [as part of the social compensation]. It's fine, on the one hand, but on the other hand it's the responsibility of the municipality to provide for the water. And the mayor pushes them a bit to ask the company such things', he explains. 'PAM gave the money to the community, as

24 The picture was taken in 2016 by Patricia González Toro and was originally named 'Nueva era petrolera en Samona Yuturi, bloque 31' (González Toro, 2017, p. 136).

compensation, and the community gave the money to the municipality for them to do the work. They want this service for free. It's very logical', he adds. 'If we analyse the case of Samona well, he goes on, what happened is that they had to sacrifice this money from the compensation for a work which normally the municipality should pay with its own money, as an institution of the state. And they have to pay for the service, when they could have invested that money in other things, which would have provided a return, instead of a cost' – an argument with which Marcia concurred, as she exclaimed, 'The community could have done something else with the money from the compensation.'

'The issue is the deception', Juan Carlos concludes, 'PAM gave them money from the social compensation, they had to pay the municipality to build the plant, and now the municipality is charging them for the maintenance. They feel tricked.' As a prospective mayor of Aguarico (*Pachakutik*) and opponent to the mayor (*Alianza País*), he had his own idea of the way he would deal with the conflict in Samona, 'I would (…) discount the 500,000 they have put for the payment of the service. Then they pay.' 'It's normal that they pay', he adds. It's not that they had to put their own money for the construction.'

'We supported you!'

According to Juan Carlos, 'There's also a personal issue with the mayor. They voted for him, they supported him, and he's changed his behaviour. He doesn't *atiende* [look after] them anymore. The conflict is very political', he goes on. 'If it was my project, they would pay me. Because I do respect their freedom when they speak with me.'

Corruption and 'paternalism'

The inhabitants were effectively upset by the mayor, and the community's support for him was called into question by the conflict. A group of young men tell me, 'We've been supporting the mayor for 15 years. Because he was a good mayor. But it's no longer the case. Now we are going to support Juan Carlos. He helped us a lot, with advice and with money too.'

They also complained that in Chiro Isla and Centro Ocaya, two neighbouring communities, the inhabitants are not paying for the water. 'How can this be?', Saul asks. After some investigation, the reason appeared to be twofold. First, the community of Chiro Isla did not have drinking water but piped water, which does not involve the same operating costs. Saul confirmed that in Chiro, 'the water is not drinkable and isn't good'. Still, that did not justify the difference in treatment for him, 'But it can't be!', he adds. 'Either they don't charge anyone, or they charge all of us!' Second, while the communities are usually being charged by the *municipio* even for *agua entubada*,[25] it seemed that Chiro Isla had a 'political

25 US$1 per month for the standard consumption, which increased to US$2 after the 2015 reform of the ordinance, as explained in the first section.

agreement' with the municipality. Juan Carlos reframed it that way, 'In Chiro, they do not pay for the water because the people whom the mayor likes do not pay. There's a lot of corruption.' He adds, 'The municipality is like the oil firm. They cheat the people. (…) in our country, all which is from the State is corrupted'.

Lack of consultation

Moreover, the inhabitants complained that there had been no proper discussion between the municipality and the community, but a decision imposed from above.

While the mayor maintains that 'we socialised a lot in the community that the water was going to be charged for (…) – and they agreed', according to Saul, the people did not know they were going to pay, because 'it was not *socializado*'. For Roque Andy, 'The issue is that they socialised after the plant was built.' Other *socios* argue that the municipality had actually socialised the introduction of the payment, but that it was only when the first payment was due that they realised it was actually not fair to be charged so much. Ángel concludes, 'the people accepted without knowing. *No somos preparados* [we lack knowledge].'

Whether the people were actually informed is one thing. But the issue seemed to be one of negotiation, and discussion, rather than mere information. Inocencio explains the difference to me, 'There was no consensus, they did not consult us on the price. If they had, we could have reached an agreement.' Juan Carlos concurs, 'It was "*socializado*" rather than "consulted". *En el pueblo* you "socialise" that, but in the communities, due to the cultural difference, you have to "consult" them, meaning you have to ask them whether they are in favour or not.[26] This is in one of the laws of the municipality, but we don't respect it as a municipal council. (…) Here there wasn't any [fiscal education].' He adds, 'The municipality is like a dictator. It imposes things.'

'We are free people'

Free from taxes

One day, coming back from Samona, Juan Carlos tells me, 'I realised the issue is not political, it's custom. They are not used to paying services and taxes. They are free people. (...) People are used to drinking, spending money to share, etc., but *recaudacion* [taxes] no, they don't want this, they want to be free'. Two months later, returning from another meeting in Samona, he adds, 'Good that you didn't come. They were screaming at the mayor. That they would not pay anything. That they are free. That they want to remain nomads. The mayor was not willing to negotiate either. They say this: they want to be free. Like the other communities which are not paying the water.'

26 *Pueblo* usually refers to the village (Tiputini) or the city (Coca and Quito).

Influence of Juan Carlos?

For the municipality, opposition was triggered by Juan Carlos himself. 'The councillor, Juan Carlos, walks around telling them that they shouldn't pay. Because he wants to get elected in the next elections.' 'It's because of Juan Carlos, who *se ha metido en esto* [got himself into this].' He continues, while explaining the issue to Julio, a fellow worker of the municipality, during breakfast in Tiputini. He's putting into people's heads that [water] shouldn't be charged for'. The vice mayor also complained that 'the fat guy [Juan Carlos] always visits them and tells them not to pay. They are in a mechanism of opposition to the mayor.' And indeed, Juan Carlos was now defending publicly that ancestral communities should not pay for the water, '(…) They have that right, as native people. This is in the constitution, they must not pay taxes. (…) It will change the culture if they charge them.' He concludes, 'The mayor *desconoce* [ignores] the law, and he *desconoce* their culture too.'

For the mayor, this is not true. During the same breakfast in Tiputini, he adds, 'The constitution says that the legalisation of territories should not be charged for. But the basic services do. Juan Carlos is misinterpreting the constitution.' In the meantime, the argument of some opponents to the municipality was being fed by Juan Carlos indeed. During an interview, Roque Andy tells me, 'Now we are writing a letter to talk about an article in the constitution, stating that ancestral communities should not pay. Juan Carlos told us so.'

Katy, the operator, disagreed with such view. 'What's that?' she exclaims. 'We no longer live in a world where everything is free. It's no longer like that. *Hay que pagar para vivir* [You need to pay in order to live].' She goes on, 'They do the native discourse, but they all know they have to pay to get services. *En el pueblo*,it's normal to pay for the water. They say that we are natives and I don't know what. But I think we have to leave this discourse of natives etc. Most of us know *el pueblo* by now and we know that it's normal to pay for services.'

'We don't have the money to pay'

Lack of money – or money mismanagement?

The inhabitants finally complained about the lack of a monthly income. According to César, an oil worker, 'The issue is that many people do not have a fixed salary. They cannot pay. This is why there is a conflict.' Saul tells me, indeed, 'Nobody's got an income. Before, there were jobs with the company. But there aren't anymore. With the crisis, they cut all the staff. They need technicians, but unqualified people, better at home!' It seemed that after the period of abundance of short-term low-skilled jobs offered by the oil company (in a seismic study), the inhabitants no longer had jobs and argued they did not have the money to pay for the water – an argument which Katy dismissed. 'No, there isn't that', she exclaims. 'We all have an income, from what we sell from the *finca*.'[27]

In fact, it seemed that as they had engaged in wage labour, the inhabitants had abandoned the *finca*. Many of them thus no longer had an income from agriculture either. Inocencio summarises the situation, 'People do not have money to pay for that. From agriculture: no money. From oil extraction: they drank and ate everything.[28] Or they built small houses, or they bought beer and beer and even more beer.' And according to Marcia, '(…) Here it's passive. There is no trade. Production is long term; it's not monthly. So some people could pay and some others could not.'

Katy was still not convinced, however. 'Some people say that, she goes on, but you realise that here, there's a shop. We buy rice, US$2. We buy jugs of beer; it costs US$22. They have money for petrol [for the canoes].' Money mismanagement was also the preferred explanation of the municipality – as made clear on various occasions, in particular during the *asamblea*. For the mayor, 'It's because of their culture, *'Plata que se coge se gasta'* [money which you get has to be spent]. They don't want to invest, they drink, they go and *farrear* [they go out drinking] with friends in Coca and done. Everything's over.' It appeared, in fact, that due to the lack of income, the inhabitants bought most of their products from the shop on credit – and the different debt accumulated by the *socios* was a recurrent issue raised during the *asamblea*.

More expensive than in the city

In addition, the cost for standard consumption (15 cubic meters per month) – US$3.70, including US$1 for administration – was considered too high – when compared to the *pueblo*, Coca and Quito in particular, where some of the inhabitants have relatives or, more rarely, have lived. Saul tells me, 'In Quito for example, they pay US$1. And here, they charge us almost US$5 for the basic amount.[29] How come we are going to pay 5 if they pay 1 in Quito?' Providing water to indigenous communities is more expensive than for cities, because of the size of the territories and the distance between the houses. Indeed, the territories span thousands of hectares, with only one house every 200 metres. According to the *municipio*, this fact, coupled with the small number of inhabitants in the community, justified why people were being charged more than in the cities of Quito and Coca. Katy explains, 'People say that it's less

27 The *finca* includes the Quichua house and the *chakra* [farm], which includes both crops and animals. Every family normally has one and they usually grow yucca and plantain.

28 The inhabitants had also spent the *indemnización*, an amount of money which is paid by the oil company to the inhabitants to compensate for the use of territory and which is decided by the Dirección Nacional de Avalúos y Catastros (DINAC) (National Directorate of Valuation and Land Registry) according to the quality and quantity of land used. In Samona it amounted to some US$3,000 per *socio*.

29 This exaggeration of Saul is probably due to the fact that people often consume more than the basic amount, as I explain below.

expensive *en el pueblo*, it's true, because there are 2,000 inhabitants! Here we are 83 [people]. So of course it's more expensive for each person.'

Huge bills: measurement problem or overconsumption?

While the standard cost was already considered too high, the issue was further amplified by huge bills that the people did not understand – something I understood as Juan Carlos tells me, 'People want to pay US$1 or 2 (…). At the moment they are paying bills of 20, 5, etc.' According to Marcia, 'It's very expensive. I lived in the city before and I am surprised by the prices here. For four people, I've received bills of US$20, 23, 30.' The inhabitants sometimes thus accused Katy of not measuring it well. 'I am currently paying US$27 per month, Saul tells me, and I don't consume more than 5 cubic meters. It could be that the woman in charge does not measure it well, I don't know what it could be.' Katy, on the other hand, was convinced that people simply wasted the water. 'They wanted to have a meter in each corner of the house!' she says. 'They had huge bills. And they say it's the operator's fault, because she does not see well!'

What was sometimes considered a 'measurement problem' was simply due to overconsumption, for the municipality, '(…) People use too much water. They don't take care of it, they leave the taps open.' The argument, made extremely clear during the *asamblea*, was recurrent during subsequent interviews and conversations and was shared by some of the inhabitants. Inocencio, for instance, considered that 'the problem is that the people consume too much: they leave the taps open. The same happens with the lights. Sometimes they are on the whole day.' Marcia thought, for her part, that 'maybe for lack of knowledge, we didn't save the water enough at the beginning?' Overconsumption was, for Ángel, a good reason why the water should be paid for. 'We have to pay for the *operadora*', he tells me. 'If it's free, people consume too much.'

Accumulation over time

A related issue was the total amount of the bills, accumulated over months. Katy, while showing me the list of all the indebted people, exclaims, 'some people owe 15 months of water! Look. This *señor*, Roque Andy: he has two meters. In total he owes something like US$80. Of course, if you accumulate, it's a lot.' Ángel comments, 'I think US$3 is good, if you pay it monthly. Obviously, it becomes huge if we let the months go by and pay everything at once.' Marcia seemed to accumulate both issues. 'I have invoices of US$200 since the beginning [for 11 months],[30] she tells me. And I consume almost nothing. My family is small.' She concludes, 'The price is towering. And in Coca [where Marcia used to live], they pay US$20 a year!'

30 According to official documents from the municipality, in December 2016, Marcia has accumulated a debt of US$189 for 17 months.

Attempts of resolution

The community in charge?

At some point, Juan Carlos concludes, 'What they want is to be able to manage it themselves. That's what I understood yesterday. It's not so much an issue of paying, but of paying the municipality. They want to do it themselves.' The mayor had reached the same conclusion already. In an interview, he tells me, 'For me, the only way to solve the crisis is to put the community itself in charge of the maintenance of the plant. If they don't pay, I'm going to contact the *Senagua*[31] to see if they could give them some training, so that they can manage the project themselves.'

But none of the inhabitants I talked to saw this as a possible way out. They thought they did not have enough resources, knowledge, and organisational skills to do it, and that it would be the end of the drinking water. Rodrigo, an ex-president, explains, 'The mayor also told us that he would transfer the maintenance to the community. But it's not a good idea, as our operator [Katy] would disappear. At the moment, she's getting paid by the municipality. And there will be no more water.' According to Marcia, similarly, 'The community cannot be in charge, because it's not a public firm. The community does not have the training to manage that, nor the resources to pay for the operator.' For once, Katy shared the view of the rest of the community. She thought that 'people don't want to be in charge of the service either, as the mayor has been proposing. Because we don't know how it would be managed. I personally think that if we take over the service, it's going to be much more expensive. People don't want to pay US$3, where are they going to find the money for the operator, etc? It will be much more than US$3. (…) Even if *Senagua* is directly in charge, I think they are going to charge us. Maybe more than now. And they are not here so it's better to deal with the mayor [who is in Tiputini].' Ángel summarises, 'The mayor has to pay for the *operadora*. So, the mayor says, "OK, you can be in charge of the whole thing." But we don't want that either. The people want the municipality to pay Katy and to give us the water for free.'

As I ask Katy whether the mayor will end up cutting off the water from people who do not pay, she responds, 'But if they cut the water completely, we'll have to go back to the river. How awful! I can't even imagine that.'

A way out

By December, the stance of the community seemed to have changed following the November *asamblea*. They were now asking for i) a period of exoneration and ii) a water bill of US$1 per month. Marcia later tells me, 'Of course we would be happy to pay, but not this price (…) People want to pay US$1.

31 *Secretaria Nacional del Agua* (National Water Secretariat) is a state institution in charge of managing the water resources and access in Ecuador.

Because it's a right we all have, it's a basic service, it's something vital. We are all very surprised by the price.' One dollar, however, was still not an option for the mayor, 'There are only 80 families, and with US$80 we can't repay any of the costs. Ten years ago it was enough, but it's not anymore.'

Some alternative proposals were made, 'What we want is to pay only half of the price. Because the project is not only from the municipality, but from Petroamazonas too. More than half of the money. Therefore, Petroamazonas should pay for half of the service.' And, according to Marcia, 'US$1 or 3 we could agree. Even barter. We could exchange it with local products.'

On 5 December, I learnt from Juan Carlos that a resolution had been found. He tells me, 'The conflict is now solved. The mayor went there and proposed to decrease the cost [of the standard consumption] to US$2.70 instead of US$3.70. It seems that they agreed.' When I returned to Samona, two weeks later, I was told about the meeting which had been held on 4 December, 'We agreed on US$2.70. Now they agreed and they need to pay.' 'Some people are starting to reimburse.'

Katy explains to me, 'The people committed to pay. They are already starting to pay. The financial director came too, in the *asamblea*, to explain well that they are not charging us for the water (the water is not a business, it's free) but for the work [maintenance] they have to do. And the people understood. This helped a lot because, as you said before, the issue was that they said the water was theirs. Now they know that the cost is not for the water. The municipality also agreed to buy some food [yucca and plantain] from the community, so that people can use that money to pay.' 'But the money that people had to pay for a year now is not going to decrease', Ángel clarifies. 'And there is a 30 per cent fine for paying late.'

That day, however, Saul still disagreed: 'We want to pay US$2 instead of 2.70. And without the *moras* [fine]. Nobody is paying this.'

And official documents from the same municipality indicated that, in January 2017, the total debt had reached US$4,896, and 32 households had either never paid, or just paid one month, to the municipality in 17 months of provision.

'The same will happen everywhere': questioning Juan Carlos's prediction

One day, while returning from Samona, Juan Carlos tells me, 'The same will happen in Puerto Quinche and in Bello Horizonte', two other communities further down the Napo River. Indeed, as part of the social compensation from the ITT oil project, which entered the *ribera* in 2016, most of the communities have asked for some kind of 'basic services' – drinking water, electricity, and a sewage system in particular – often through similar *convenios* between the oil firm and the municipality.

In the communities on the lower part of the river, where I discussed the conflict in Samona with the inhabitants as a way to understand their views and perceptions on the idea of paying for the water, I often heard, indeed, that 'they must not charge us', 'there is no reason for us to pay the municipality' because 'the water is from the community', or that it comes from the company which 'is using our land' and 'affecting fauna and flora'. For Franklin, a Quichua man and *socio* of Vicente Salazar, 'as a "frontier", as a community, as a Quichua people from that community, they don't have any tax to pay to the state.' Instead, his view was that 'The institutions have to give this opportunity to the people who never had it.'

'They want to change our culture by charging us!', his sister Carmen exclaimed. 'The municipality, because it puts meters, wants to charge them, but the people are not used to paying', Franklin concluded.

Alongside the arguments against the payment, however, I also heard from the presidents and *socios* of different communities that 'it's going to be charged for' but 'at a minimum price', 'less than in Samona' or that 'the amount of the investment should be deduced [from what they charge]' – although Alicia considered that 'maybe if it's PAM, they will do it for free.' Vicente Salazar, with a relatively high number of *mestizos*,[32] of salaried workers, and of *socios* who have a second house in the village, Tiputini, where they are already used to paying for water (in this case for *agua entubada*), was particularly heterogeneous. 'We have to pay, Jaime Salazar told me. Here, the politicians *nos pusieron en la cabeza* [made us believe] that everything was free, but it's not like that. *Las cosas se pagan* [You have to pay for things].' When I asked whether the fact of paying could change the culture, his response was unequivocal, 'No, because the culture is not to be poor.'

The issue was even reframed as a technical one by Efren, another *mestizo, socio* of the community, who considered that 'Here, some people *se dedican al trabajo* [work]. If we all had a job, it would no longer be a problem, [because anyway], the maintenance is not free.'

While in this part of the river the inhabitants are given jobs (by the same oil company) before (or at the same time as) they are provided with different 'basic services', it does make sense to question Juan's prediction and imagine that there might be much less resistance to the idea of paying for those services.

Discussion

Drinking water, 'difference' and 'equality'

This chapter discusses a case where the oil company comes with a drinking water plant, as compensation for the pollution of the Napo River, which is already

32 *Mestizos* are people of combined European and indigenous descent. In the lower Napo River, it refers to anyone who is not indigenous or comes from another part of Ecuador.

polluted, largely due to past extraction projects further upstream, thereby furthering (while at the same time fixing), a long-standing issue which has not been addressed by the state. The provision of drinking water to the inhabitants, however, does not come without difficulties. The chapter shows how the need and desire for drinking water, which has motivated the inhabitants to ask for a drinking water plant as part of the social compensation from oil extraction, slowly leads to a conflict between the municipality, in charge of the service, and the inhabitants, most of whom refuse to pay for such a service. The conflict is multidimensional and reveals clashes of worldviews between the municipality and most of the inhabitants, on multiple levels which are at least legal, political, cultural, and economic. As Goodwin and Alderman put it in the Introduction, infrastructure is a 'contested space[s] where different meanings and practices collide and interact' (p. 3). In this particular case, the water plant holds ideas about money, what should be paid for, and who should pay for things. It also acts as an accelerator of change, and as in other chapters of the book, infrastructure has the potential to shape the recipients in particular ways. More specifically, this case sheds light on the mechanisms through which the inhabitants will slowly negotiate and compromise on what they consider to be fair, until they ultimately agree to a compromise (which involves a payment) that they are nonetheless apparently not willing to meet. Analysed from a 'difference' and 'equality' perspective, the only available alternative offered by the *municipio* (paying for the service) presents an inherent tension between two claims of the inhabitants: the right to have clean water (which is arguably and mostly about 'equality'), and the right to have water for free (which is arguably and mostly about 'difference'). While embracing change (paying for the water service) implies a change of paradigm on many levels, resisting change (by refusing to pay for the water), in the present case a source of conflict, could potentially lead to health issues if the water ended up being cut off from the inhabitants – an 'awful' prospect, according to Katy. All in all, the need for drinking water legitimises certain worldviews while rendering others impractical, and the inhabitants necessarily have to 'change' (and compromise on their worldview) to gain 'equal' access to basic services. In that vein, one can predict that even Saul – who reminds us, towards the end of the conflict, of the fact that the new agreement is not what the people initially wanted – will end up accepting, because his position is simply untenable in the present context. The chapter finally suggests that in the lower part of the river, where the inhabitants obtain jobs in the oil company at the same time as they are provided with the different basic services which come as part of the social compensation from oil extraction in the ITT block, the issue could be reduced to its more technical aspect (lack of income) and be solved with the provision of jobs. It would thus result in further change – the transformation of the inhabitants into wage labourers – and a potentially much less conflictive situation. The infrastructure here acts as a turning point in the oil extraction process. It has the potential to 'transform its users into modern citizens' (Introduction, p. 13).

'Difference-in-equality' in practice: who should pay for the water?

As pollution levels rise globally, instances where the forest may no longer constitute the infrastructure people need are multiplying, leaving many indigenous people around the world living in poverty, vulnerability and dependence. In that vein, Neale and Vincent question 'the extent to which the kinds of Indigenous or ontologically alter worlds that scholars seek out are extant, or are better understood as fundamentally enmeshed, in violently unequal ways, with "our" world' and 'argue for the importance of engaging with contemporary Indigenous realities' (2017, p. 418). The question of access to 'equality' for indigenous people with different worldviews has thus become a crucial one – in a context where, according to Escobar, development is often about providing 'equality' at the expense of 'difference',[33] thus denying people's right to what he calls 'difference-in-equality'[34] (2006).

At a second, more practical level, the chapter raises the question of how 'difference' – which, as Goodwin and Alderman highlight in the Introduction, has been largely ignored by states in the Latin American context in the case of indigenous people – can be taken into account in infrastructural projects and basic service provision. While rights to clean and free water claimed by the inhabitants of Samona are easily compatible in settings where clean water is available in abundance in the natural environment, it gets trickier in the present situation tainted by the pollution of the Napo River, which means someone has to pay for the drinking water. The matter is further complicated by the size of the land holdings (which means the service is more expensive than in the cities), the impecuniousness of the inhabitants (who are often part-time farmers without a regular income), and their apparent vulnerability and dependence on the Ecuadorian state: while the management of the water plant by the community itself could potentially reduce the operative costs of water provision, the inhabitants do not feel sufficiently knowledgeable or qualified to be able to organise their own provision, in contrast to arguably more empowered and better organised indigenous communities in highland Ecuador.[35]

The case raises equally difficult questions regarding legitimacy and fairness. Who should invest in the drinking water plant, given that it is a legal obligation of the *municipio* to provide the communities with drinking water, but that the river (which is public) has been partly polluted by oil firms, because of present and past oil exploration and extraction projects? On the other hand, why would

33 Different illustrations of this extremely common tension can be found in Dinerstein (2015), Sheild Johansson (2018), Carrasco (2016), and Alderman (2021) in the Latin American context.

34 For Escobar, development presents the opposite problem of colonialism, which recognised 'difference' but denied 'equality' – while both enterprises deny 'difference-in-equality' (Escobar, 2006).

35 See for instance Goodwin (2019).

indigenous communities benefit from free water when other Ecuadorian citizens have to pay for it? Is it a cultural right, or a mark of poverty, as Jaime Salazar sees it? More generally, how can considerations of 'difference' be reconciled with the need to pay for infrastructure provision, in those cases where the forests (and rivers) no longer constitute the infrastructure people need? And where can the answers to such questions be found? In law? In international law? In the Ecuadorian constitution, or in indigenous institutions and rules?

These difficult yet fascinating questions cannot be avoided in the search for concrete translations to the abstract concept of 'difference-in-equality' – a policy goal which is not mine here. They can only be raised through the investigation of cases where (changing) economic and ecological situations mean that 'difference' might be sacrificed in the search for 'equality' – or, in Neale and Vincent's words, 'where "they" are not as different as "we" might hope them to be' (2017, p. 417). Indeed, and in relation to water more particularly, sidelining such situations has arguably resulted in a 'dearth of knowledge regarding culturally adapted sanitation and hygiene promotion strategies and culturally acceptable solutions for indigenous communities' (Jiménez et al., 2014).

References

Aanestad, C. (2011) 'Ecuador charges indigenous activists with terrorism', DW News, 23 September, <www.dw.de/ecuador-charges-indigenous-activists-with-terrorism/a-15398230> (accessed 5 April 2022).

Acosta, A., E. Gudynas, E. Martínez, and J. Vogel (2007) *Leaving the Oil in the Ground: A Political, Economic, and Ecological Initiative in the Ecuadorian Amazon* (Americas Program Policy Report No. August 13). (Washington, DC: Center for International Policy).

Alianza País.(2006). *Plan de Gobierno de Alianza país, 2011*.

Alderman, J. (2021) 'The houses that Evo built: autonomy, vivir bien, and viviendas in Bolivia', *Latin American Perspectives*, 48(3): 100–18.

Banco Central del Ecuador (BCE) (2013) Cifras del sector petrolero ecuatoriano, 77, <https://contenido.bce.fin.ec/documentos/Estadisticas/Hidrocarburos/cspe201377.pdf> (accessed 5 April 2022).

Barrientos, A., J. Gideon, and M. Molyneux (2008) 'New developments in Latin America's social policy', *Development and Change*, 39(5): 759–74.

Bass, M.S., M. Finer, C.N. Jenkins, H. Kreft, D.F. Cisneros-Heredia, S.F. McCracken, and T.H. Kunz (2010) 'Global conservation significance of Ecuador's Yasuní National Park', *PloS one*, 5 (1): e8767.

Bebbington, A. (2009) 'The new extraction: rewriting the political ecology of the Andes?', *NACLA Report on the Americas*, 42 (5): 12–20.

Bebbington, A. (2012) *Social Conflict, Economic Development and Extractive Industry: Evidence from South America* (Abingdon: Routledge).

Becerra, S., E. Paichard, and L. Maurice (2013) 'Vivir con la contaminación petrolera en el Ecuador: percepciones sociales del riesgo sanitario y capacidad de respuesta', *Revista Lider*, 15 (23): 102–20.

Becker, M. (2011) 'Correa, indigenous movements, and the writing of a new constitution in Ecuador', *Latin American Perspectives*, 38 (1), 47–62.

Beristain, C.M., D. Páez Rovira, and I. Fernández (2009) *Las palabras de la selva: estudio psicosocial del impacto de las explotaciones petroleras de Texaco en las comunidades amazónicas de Ecuador* (Bilbao: Instituto de Estudios sobre Desarrollo y Cooperacion Internacional).

Bissardon, P., S. Becerra, and L. Maurice (2013) 'Le risque sanitaire lié aux activités pétrolières en Amazonie équatorienne: des alertes aux décisions', *Environnement Risques Santé*, 12 (4): 338–44.

Blaser, M. (2014) 'Ontology and indigeneity: on the political ontology of heterogeneous assemblages', *Cultural Geographies*, 21 (1): 49–58.

Boelens, R., J. Hoogesteger, and J.C. Rodríguez de Francisco (2014) 'Commoditizing water territories: the clash between Andean water rights cultures and payment for environmental services policies', *Capitalism Nature Socialism*, 25 (3): 84–102.

Bustamante, T. (2007) *Detrás de la cortina de humo: dinámicas sociales y petróleo en el Ecuador*, Quito: Flacso-Sede Ecuador.

Carrasco, A. (2016) 'A biography of water in Atacama, Chile: two indigenous community responses to the extractive encroachments of mining', *The Journal of Latin American and Caribbean Anthropology*, 21(1): 130–50.

Cepek, M.L. (2016) 'There might be blood: oil, humility, and the cosmopolitics of a Cofán petro-being', *American ethnologist*, 43 (4): 623–35.

Cevallos, G. (2014) 'La redistribution de la rente pétrolière en Amazonie équatorienne au profit du développement local: le cas de Sucumbíos et Orellana' (unpublished master's thesis, Toulouse: GET-IEP).

Dangl, B. (2010) *The Price of Fire: Resource Wars and Social Movements in Bolivia* (Edinburgh and Oakland, CA: AK Press).

de la Cadena, M. (2019) 'Uncommoning nature: stories from the anthropo-not-seen', in P. Harvey, C. Krohn-Hansen, and K.G. Nustad (eds.), *Anthropos and The Material* (Durham, NC: Duke University Press), pp. 35–58.

Dinerstein, A. (2015) *The Politics of Autonomy in Latin America: The Art of Organising Hope* (London: Palgrave Macmillan).

Escobar, A. (2006) 'An ecology of difference: equality and conflict in a glocalized world', *Focaal, 2006*, 47: 120–37.

Escobar, A. (2008) *Territories of Difference: Place, Movements, Life, Redes* (Durham, NC: Duke University Press).

Finer, M., C.N. Jenkins, S.L. Pimm, B. Keane, and C. Ross (2008) 'Oil and gas projects in the western Amazon: threats to wilderness, biodiversity, and indigenous peoples', *PloS one*, 3 (8): e2932.

Finer, M., R. Moncel, and C.N. Jenkins (2010) 'Leaving the oil under the Amazon: Ecuador's Yasuní-ITT Initiative', *Biotropica*, 42 (1): 63–6.

Finer, M., V. Vijay, F. Ponce, C.N. Jenkins, and T.R. Kahn (2009) 'Ecuador's Yasuní Biosphere Reserve: a brief modern history and conservation challenges', *Environmental Research Letters*, 4 (3): 034005.

Fontaine, G. (2004) 'Enfoques conceptuales y metodológicos para una sociología de los conflictos ambientales', In H.A. Fazio Vengoa, *Guerra, sociedad y medio ambiente*. Foro Nacional Ambiental, 503–33.

Fontaine, G. (2009) 'Los conflictos ambientales por petróleo y la crisis de gobernanza ambiental en el Ecuador', *Boletín ECOS*, 6: 1–7.

González Toro, P.A. (2017) Nueva Amazonía: reconfiguraciones socioterritoriales y ambientales a partir de la implementación de políticas de desarrollo, extractivas y de integración regional en las riberas del río Napo y norte amazónico del Ecuador (unpublished master's thesis, Facultad Latinoamericana de Ciencias Sociales Sede Ecuador – FLACSO).

Goodwin, G. (2019) 'The problem and promise of coproduction: politics, history, and autonomy', *World Development*, 122: 501–13.

Guzmán-Gallegos, M.A. (2012) The governing of extraction, oil enclaves, and indigenous responses in the Ecuadorian Amazon', in H. Haarstad (ed.), *New Political Spaces in Latin American Natural Resource Governance* (New York: Palgrave Macmillan), pp. 155–76.

Haley, S. (2004) 'Institutional assets for negotiating the terms of development: indigenous collective action and oil in Ecuador and Alaska', *Economic Development and Cultural Change*, 53 (1): 191–213.

Harvey, P. (2018) 'Infrastructures in and out of time: the promise of roads in contemporary Peru', in N. Anand, A. Gupta, and H. Appel (eds.), *The Promise of Infrastructure* (Durham, NC: Duke University Press), pp. 80–101.

Hetherington, K. (2014) 'Waiting for the surveyor: development promises and the temporality of infrastructure', *The Journal of Latin American and Caribbean Anthropology*, 19 (2): 195–211.

Hurtig, A.K. and M. San Sebastián (2002) 'Geographical differences in cancer incidence in the Amazon basin of Ecuador in relation to residence near oil fields', *International Journal of Epidemiology*, 31 (5): 1021–7.

Jameson, K.P. (2011) 'The indigenous movement in Ecuador: the struggle for a plurinational state', *Latin American Perspectives*, 38 (1): 63–73.

Jiménez, A., M. Cortobius, and M. Kjellén (2014) 'Water, sanitation and hygiene and indigenous peoples: a review of the literature', *Water International*, 39 (3): 277–93.

Jochnick, C., R. Normand, and S. Laidi (1994) *Violaciones de derechos en la Amazonía ecuatoriana: las consecuencias del desarrollo petrolero* (No. 323 J63v). Quito: Ed. Abya-Yala.

Juteau, G. (2012) 'L'Exploitation du pétrole en Équateur: à la recherche d'un nouveau modèle de développement, entre enjeux économiques et conflits socio-environnementaux' (unpublished master's thesis, IEP de Toulouse).

Juteau-Martineau, G., S. Becerra, and L. Maurice (2014) 'Ambiente, petróleo y vulnerabilidad política en el Oriente Ecuatoriano: ¿hacia nuevas formas de gobernanza energética?', *América Latina Hoy*, 67: 119–37.

Kimerling, J. (1990) 'Disregarding environmental law: petroleum development in protected natural areas and indigenous homelands in the Ecuadorian Amazon', *Hastings Int'l & Comp. L. Rev.*, 14: 849.

Lalander, R. and P.O. Peralta (2012) 'Movimiento indígena y revolución ciudadana en Ecuador', *Cuestiones Políticas*, 28 (48): 13–50.

Larrea, C. (2017) '¿Existen alternativas frente al petróleo en la Amazonia Centro-Sur?', in Larrea, C. and Arroyo, L. (ed.), *¿Está agotado el periodo petrolero en Ecuador?, alternativas hacia una sociedad más sustentable y equitativa: un estudio multicriterio* (Madrid: Ediciones La Tierra), pp. 49–108.

Martínez-Alier, J. (2002) *The Environmentalism of the Poor: A Study of Ecological Conflicts and Valuation* (Cheltenham: Edward Elgar Publishing)

Muratorio, B. (1991) *The Life and Times of Grandfather Alonso, Culture and History in the Upper Amazon* (New Brunswick, NJ: Rutgers University Press).

Neale, T. and E. Vincent (2017) 'Mining, indigeneity, alterity: or, mining Indigenous alterity?', *Cultural Studies*, 31(2–3): 417–39.

O'Connor, T.S. (1994) 'We are part of nature: indigenous peoples' rights as a basis for environmental protection in the Amazon basin', *Colo. J. Int'l Envtl. L. and Pol'y*, 5: 193.

Orta-Martínez, M. and M. Finer (2010) 'Oil frontiers and indigenous resistance in the Peruvian Amazon', *Ecological Economics*, 70 (2): 207–18.

Paichard, E. (2012) 'Vivre avec les activités pétrolières, capacités et vulnérabilités économiques, sociales et sanitaires', *Le Cas de la paroisse de Dayuma-Orellana* (unpublished master's thesis, Sciences Po Toulouse).

Perreault, T. (2001) 'Developing identities: indigenous mobilization, rural livelihoods, and resource access in Ecuadorian Amazonia', *Ecumene*, 8 (4): 381–413.

Perreault, T. (2003) '"A people with our own identity": toward a cultural politics of development in Ecuadorian Amazonia', *Environment and Planning D: Society and Space*, 21 (5): 583–606.

Reider, S. and R. Wasserstrom (2013) 'Undermining democratic capacity: myth-making and oil development in Amazonian Ecuador', *Ethics in Science and Environmental Politics*, 13 (1): 39–47.

Reygadas, L. and F. Filgueira (2010) 'Inequality and the incorporation crisis: the left's social policy toolkit', in M. Cameron, and E. Hershberg (eds.), *Latin America's Left Turns: Politics, Policies, and Trajectories of Change* (London: Lynn Rienner), pp. 171–91.

Rival, L. (1998) 'The right to life, or the right to a way of life?', *Resurgence*, 189: 10–12.

Rival, L. (2012) 'Planning development future in the Ecuadorian Amazon: the expanding oil frontier and the Yasuní-ITT initiative', in A. Bebbington (ed.), *Social Conflict, Economic Development and The Extractive Industry: Evidence from South America* (Abingdon: Routledge), pp. 153–71.

Rival, L. (2017) 'Quegoki Cönwi: Risiliencia waorani. Resiliencia y el futuro de la reserva del Yasuní', in C. Larrea and L. Arroyo (eds.), *¿Está agotado el periodo petrolero en Ecuador?, alternativas hacia una sociedad más sustentable y equitativa: un estudio multicriterio* (Madrid: Ediciones La Tierra), pp. 216–87.

Sabin, P. (1998) 'Searching for middle ground: native communities and oil extraction in the Northern and Central Ecuadorian Amazon, 1967–1993', *Environmental History*, 3 (2): 144–68.

San Sebastián, M. and A. Karin Hurtig (2004) 'Oil exploitation in the Amazon basin of Ecuador: a public health emergency', *Revista Panamericana de Salud Pública*, 15: 205–11.

Sawyer, S. (2004) *Crude Chronicles: Indigenous Politics, Multinational Oil, and Neoliberalism in Ecuador* (Durham, NC: Duke University Press).

Schlosberg, D. and D. Carruthers (2010) 'Indigenous struggles, environmental justice, and community capabilities', *Global Environmental Politics*, 10 (4): 12–35.

Sheild Johansson, M. (2018) 'Taxing the indigenous: a history of barriers to fiscal inclusion in the Bolivian highlands', *History and Anthropology*, 29 (1): 83–100.

Simbaña, F. (2012) 'Consulta previa y democracia en el Ecuador', *Chasqui. Revista Latinoamericana de Comunicación*, 120: 4–8.

Valdivia, G. (2005) 'On indigeneity, change, and representation in the northeastern Ecuadorian Amazon', *Environment and Planning A*, 37 (2): 285–303.

Vallejo, I. (2014) 'Petróleo, desarrollo y naturaleza: aproximaciones a un escenario de ampliación de las fronteras extractivas hacia la Amazonía suroriente en el Ecuador', *Anthropologica*, 32: 115–37.

Venkatesan, S., L. Bear, P. Harvey, S. Lazar, L. Rival, and A. Simone (2018) 'Attention to infrastructure offers a welcome reconfiguration of anthropological approaches to the political', *Critique of Anthropology*, 38 (1): 3–52.

Wilson, N.J. and J. Inkster (2018) 'Respecting water: Indigenous water governance, ontologies, and the politics of kinship on the ground', *Environment and Planning E: Nature and Space*, 1 (4): 516–38.

Ziegler-Otero, L. and L. Ziegler-Otero (2006) *Resistance in an Amazonian Community: Huaorani Organizing against The Global Economy* (New York: Berghahn Books).

3. Water storage reservoirs in Mataquita: clashing measurements and meanings

Ursula Balderson

Introduction

Water-infrastructure developments in Andean Peru have great symbolic and practical importance, particularly in 'territories of abandonment' where state presence is limited and water may be scarce (Rasmussen, 2016b, 2016c; Harvey and Knox, 2015). Like other types of infrastructure, water infrastructures can 'emerge out of and store within them forms of desire and fantasy and can take on fetish-like aspects that sometimes can be wholly autonomous from their technical function' (Larkin, 2013). Despite this, water infrastructures are generally presented as apolitical and technocratic, a characterisation which obscures the intense wrangling and negotiation processes that can accompany even small-scale localised interventions. In the case I discuss below, the desire for water infrastructures was intertwined with issues of citizenship, legitimacy, and respect and therefore inherently political.

The data for this chapter is drawn from observations of a 'working group'[1] formed to resolve a low-level mining conflict taking place between the mining

1 'Working group' has been translated from the Peruvian Spanish term *mesa de diálogo*. As part of the post-Fujimori transition back to democracy in the Democracy and State Rights section of the 2002 National Agreement, the state committed itself to promoting and consolidating a culture of dialogue and negotiation. This institutionalised the channels and mechanisms through which citizens could contribute to state processes (Willaqniki, 2013). *Mesas de diálogo* were introduced specifically to help reduce the proliferation of conflicts that developed around mining activities from the mid-2000s onwards (Defensoría del Pueblo, 2017). They are institutional spaces where stakeholders in a conflict can meet, in the presence of the state, to discuss their disagreements and hopefully reach an agreement about how to move forward. In practice this has meant that they are primarily spaces where communities and companies negotiate projects or activities which extend the cover of public services (Willaqniki, 2013). Mining affected communities are heavily encouraged to engage in these working groups instead of expressing their anger and frustration via more direct actions such as road blockages or protests.

U. Balderson, 'Water storage reservoirs in Mataquita: clashing measurements and meanings' in *The Social and Political Life of Latin American Infrastructures*, ed. J. Alderman and G. Goodwin (London, 2022), pp. 79–100.

company Barrick Gold[2] and the village of Mataquita in the Ancash region of Peru. The conflict revolved around the village's inadequate access to drinking water as a result of damage caused to water resources during mining activities. Although the mining company initially dismissed the complaint brought by the community as illegitimate, after substantial pressure a working group overseen by state representatives was formed. The outcomes of the process included a hydrological study outlining the extent of the water deficit in the village (the *Diagnóstico*), a document detailing engineering designs for a series small water storage reservoirs which were posited as a means of resolving the crisis (the *Expediente Técnico*) and the reservoirs themselves.

In my discussion, I seek to illustrate the complex relationship that communities can have with promised infrastructure developments and the ways in which they try to mould the form that these interventions take. I show how infrastructural developments are never politically neutral and how their affective nature allowed the community to challenge the abstract depoliticised rationalities that legitimate them.

Hybridity and hydrosocial territories

Infrastructures have been viewed as 'socio-technical assemblages through which it is possible to tease out the arrangements of people and things and ideas and materials that make up larger technological systems' (Harvey and Knox, 2015, p. 5). Infrastructures generate political effects and structure social relations. Work on assemblages shifts the focus from what things are to what they do (Deleuze, 1990, p. 218 in Fox, 2015, p. 305). The concept of 'hybridity' and the interrelation of natural/physical and social worlds which underpin concepts such as 'socio-technical assemblage' and 'hydrosocial territory' emerged from the influential work of Bruno Latour (Latour, 2004). The term 'hydrosocial territory' is used to indicate the hybrid relationship between nature, society, and technology which facilitates or constrains access to water resources (Zwarteveen and Boelens, 2014; Boelens et al., 2016). Hydrosocial territories have been conceptualised as 'the contested imaginary and socioenvironmental materialization of a spatially bound multi-scalar network in which humans, water flows, ecological relations, hydraulic infrastructure, financial means, legal and administrative arrangements and cultural institutions and practices are interactively defined, aligned and mobilized through epistemological belief systems, political hierarchies and naturalizing discourses' (Boelens et al., 2016, p. 2). Hydrosocial territories are therefore both plural and multidimensional. In the example I discuss below, they included physical infrastructures, legislation such as the Peruvian Water Resources Law, discursive understandings of adequate water access, epistemological assumptions about what constitutes valid

2 I refer to the mining company as Barrick Gold throughout although its actual name was Barrick Misquichillca as it is a wholly owned subsidiary of Barrick Gold.

knowledge of the hydrosphere, the technical documents which underpinned the design of the water-storage reservoirs, local and global conceptualisations of water rights and the institutions and actors who were engaged in the process of resolving water conflicts.[3]

Hydrosocial territories make visible the political decisions which underpin water-infrastructure construction. The disproportionate ability of powerful actors to influence the production of norms and knowledges which serve their own agendas means water infrastructure is not rolled out evenly across countries but tends to prioritise the needs of already affluent communities (Anand, 2011; Zwarteveen and Boelens, 2014; Loftus, 2009). Latour's approach to knowledge emphasises its political nature and the futility of trying to enforce the fact/value distinction. Although sometimes considered a social constructivist, Latour is uncomfortable with work that leaves the study of nature to the scientists and works only with our perceptions of it (Harding, 2008). Rather than denying the possibility of facts or truth, he indicates that the how, where, and why a 'fact' was created ought not to be regarded as irrelevant to the fact itself (Latour, 2004). Knowledge inevitably serves some agendas better than others and the ability to produce facts that bolster one's own agenda is a socially contingent process. Facts also rely on concepts such as 'sufficiency', 'normality', and 'legality' which inevitably have a political dimension. Throughout the conflict, values, ideologies and affective relations could be observed impinging on the 'facts' that supposedly underpinned the solution to the water crisis that was being performed. By excavating the power relations underpinning access to water the issue of water justice becomes pertinent. Demands for water justice combine demands for more just socio-economic distribution of water and far more or better cultural-political recognition such as the acknowledgement of local pre-existing norms and value systems (Zwarteveen and Boelens, 2014).

Background to the dispute

The Pierina mine is located in Ancash, a central northern region in Peru, and run by Barrick Gold, a Canadian multinational gold mining company, and the second largest gold mining company in the world. When Barrick Gold acquired the Pierina concession and the company which had been carrying out the exploration work in 1996 the hopes of the local populations living nearby were high.[4] As this area has a long history of mining activity and it has often complemented incomes from subsistence agriculture or small-scale farming (Assadourian et al., 1980; Deustua, 1994) there was little organised resistance to the arrival of the mine. State investment in agriculture had been declining since the 1980s (Gonzales de Olarte, 1996; Yashar, 2005, p. 236) and low levels of water availability meant that agricultural productivity in the

3 This is not an exhaustive list.

4 It acquired the company including its assets and liabilities.

Jangas region where the mine would be located was lower than in other nearby districts which had greater access to water resources. The settlements in the area around Mataquita, the village where I conducted most of my fieldwork, are a mixture of villages, hamlets, and small-scale campesino communities. Quechua is the first language spoken in most of the villages and although Spanish is also spoken men tend to be far more proficient in it than women. Local people generally describe themselves as campesinos and there has been limited resurgence in indigenous identification and organisation around issues affecting this group in this part of Peru (see de la Cadena, 2000; Oliart, 2008; Scarritt, 2011; Yashar, 2005 for more detailed discussion of these topics).

When Barrick Gold arrived, it was hoped that the company's Corporate Social Responsibility (CSR) programme would improve access to further education and training and that agricultural productivity would be improved via the installation of *reigo tecnificado* (sprinkler systems). Over 20 years later, although there has been some progress, most feel that Barrick Gold's promises have not been fulfilled. Although the initial reception to the mine was relatively positive, as soon as the local employment boosting construction phase ended, local relationships went quite quickly downhill. Between 2002 and 2005 the company was involved in a tax avoidance scandal which led to the loss of US$141 million in taxes from the Peruvian Treasury, although the tax authorities pursued Barrick Gold through the courts they eventually lost the case. Soon after that, low-level water conflicts began to develop around the mine. These conflicts periodically flare up into more serious episodes of violence. For example, in 2012 one protester was killed and four were injured during protests about water scarcities in Mareniyoc, a neighbouring village to Mataquita. Despite similar complaints, coalition building between affected actors has remained limited (Himley, 2013; de Echave et al., 2009; Gamu and Dauvergne, 2018; Balderson, forthcoming). Not only has the mine failed to fulfil expectations of development, many of the communities around the mine feel their situation is now even more precarious as water availability has reduced since the mine's arrival as a representative of the Junta Administradora de Servicios de Saneamiento (JASS) (Mataquita Water and Sanitation Committee) explained to me:

> In the Environmental Impact Assessment Barrick planned to bring water from the Cordillera to use in their operations but they never brought it. As an agreement or a commitment Barrick said they would bring water and share it with the communities. But what has happened is the opposite. When they began their operations they began extracting subterranean water. This is now affecting the surface water and many streams have dried up. (Representative of JASS)[5]

5 The president of the JASS committee represented community interests during working-group meetings.

The Cordillera Negra where the mine and village are located has always been short of water. After significant pressure from the local government, the mine funded a water transfer scheme from across the other side of the valley where glaciers provide relatively abundant water. However, when this was eventually built in 2015, it did not benefit the communities which have been most affected by the mine's activities as pumping water to their altitude was not considered economically feasible. Barrick Gold did not view this situation as problematic as their overall contribution to water availability in the region was positive: 'We have brought 150 litres and we have taken away 20 litres.[6] Mathematically it is this', a community relations representative told me during an interview.

Water supply in Mataquita was delivered by a series of 'water capturation points', built where springs emerged and constructed throughout the 1990s and early 2000s. Until the initiation of mining exploration activities in 1996, an important contributor was the Uliyacu stream whose water was shared between the villages of Mataquita and Mareniyoc, a village slightly higher up the catchment. Unfortunately, during mining exploration work, the flow rate of that stream dramatically diminished and there was no longer enough water for the villagers to share and so from 1996 onwards the Uliyacu stream was only used by Mareniyoc. Initially, there was sufficient water for both villages from other sources, however, as the population increased, other water sources decreased, and flushing toilets became more common, water regularly began to run out in Mataquita. In 2013, fed up with the intermittent drinking-water connection, the community wrote to the local water authority to lodge a formal complaint (*denuncia*) against the mining company. The aim of this *denuncia* was to convince the company to provide water to replace that which had been lost as a result of mining activities. In the next sections, I discuss events that emanated from and underpinned this *denuncia* in order to illustrate some of the social and political dimensions of the resulting infrastructure project.

Demands for water as demands for citizenship

When the community sent their letter to the local water authority demanding that Barrick Gold intervene to replace the water that had disappeared as a result of mining activities they framed their intervention in terms of their rights as Peruvian citizens:

> as human beings and citizens of PERU we have the right to water because it guarantees our life and as such will allow that our Nation has peace and tranquillity as long as citizens such as us will be able to continue our activities without the threat of an uncertain future.

The letter goes on to request that the state:

> enforce the Mining Company Barrick with the duty to provide us with

6 The figures refer to litres-per-minute flow rates. The community allege a greater reduction in flow in the stream around the mine as later discussion illustrates.

> drinking water and water for our agricultural activities because the Uliyacu stream has disappeared since exploration and exploitation of mining activities were initiated.[7]

In the letter, they drew on the Water Resources Law[8] to suggest the loss of water meant their human right to water was not being respected. In Mataquita, the enmeshing of concerns about water and citizenship reveals the extent to which water availability is used as an indicator of social wellbeing and is inseparable from people's expectations of development, recognition, and respect from the state. Since the early 2000s, water has become an extremely salient political topic in Peru, and it has been central to many of the nation's mining conflicts (Defensoría del Pueblo, 2015). Perhaps the most emblematic of all has been the conflict with the Yanacocha Mining Company, which has a history of intense conflicts running back as far as the early 2000s. In 2011, the conflict re-intensified when the company announced plans to extend mining activities and construct a large open-pit copper-gold mine (Li, 2015; Triscritti, 2013; Sosa and Zwarteveen, 2016). This new project would be located in the headwaters of three provinces reliant on agriculture and would involve draining three lagoons and their replacement by artificial reservoirs. Previous experience of high-level conflict relating to the Yanacocha mine means that activist networks are much stronger in this part of Peru than in the Ancash region (de Echave, 2009; Tanaka, 2005). In February 2012, around 1,000 campesinos and representatives of groups defending water rights marched from the threatened lagoons to Lima 800 km away. A manifesto produced by the organising committee stated, 'The Peruvian state's current legislation does not recognize that potable water and sanitation are a human right; a right that is essential for all other human rights, since without water there is no life.'[9] The Mataquitans registered their grievance against Barrick Gold shortly after the 2012 Water March and echoes of this strategy can be seen in their approach to the conflict. This tendency towards using the language of rights in water conflicts relates to neoliberal ideas about citizenship and what constitutes a recognisable and legitimate concern for campesino communities, constraining the type of grievances that can be aired as I discuss in more detail below (Hale, 2007).

The importance of citizenship in claims for water was particularly evident during a protest event I observed in Mataquita in September 2015. As the water had been disconnected for nearly a week, in an attempt to convince

7 A copy of this letter was printed in the Appendix of the hydrological study 'Diagnóstico de Agua para Uso Poblacional de Mataquita Distrito de Jangas, Huaraz, Ancash' produced as part of the working group.

8 The Water Resources Law was introduced in 2009. It replaced the General Water Law of 1969 (see del Castillo Pinto, 2011; Paerregaard et al., 2016 for a more detailed analysis of the implications of this change).

9 Although much of the subsequent activism relating to this conflict was less focused on the idea of water rights and instead tended to promote the people's connection to the local landscape (Chanduvi 2012; Peñafiel and Li 2019; Li 2015).

Barrick Gold to arrange water deliveries to the village by lorry the community partially blocked the road to the mine.[10] During this protest the villagers raised a Peruvian flag in the middle of the road (see Figure 3.1). Their desire for water and water infrastructure was intimately connected to their desire to feel valued Peruvian citizens rather than abandoned and neglected by their state. As Baviskar notes: '[a]ppreciating the inseparability of the material and symbolic dimensions of the conflict helps us understand that the political economy of a natural resource is meaningful only through the wider networks of cultural politics through which it is embedded' (Baviskar, 2003, p. 5051).

Anand (2011, 2017) has used the term hydraulic citizenship to refer to the way that belonging is enabled through articulations between politics and technology as residents of Mumbai attempt to access reliable water from the urban distribution system. Similarly, Paerregaard et al. (2016) propose water citizenship to describe how actors understand the right to use and access water and the distribution of responsibilities relating to governance. If citizenship is to be conceptualised as 'an imperfect, unstable set of processes and practices always in the making rather than a singular status being negotiated' (Paerregaard et al., 2016, p. 200) then the quote from the letter above implies a transactional relationship with the state in which the community's compliance to the norms expected of them rests upon the state, and by proxy, the ability of the mining company to deliver a sufficiency of this critical resource. The

10 They allowed collective taxis (*colectivos*) to villages higher up in the catchment area to pass but stopped all mine traffic.

Figure 3.1 The Peruvian flag was raised emphasising the link between issue of water access and citizenship. Photo by the author.

quote echoes Anand's discussion of the iterative, cyclical process of citizenship formation whereby social histories, political technologies, and material semiotic infrastructures all contribute to people's quest to secure reliable water access (Anand, 2017) as well as Lemanski's claim that 'citizenship is embodied in infrastructure for both citizens and the state' (Lemanski, 2020, p. 1).

However, the way citizens engage with infrastructures is uneven: in Mataquita they protested in favour of water infrastructure whilst in Cajamarca they protested against it. In both cases, their arguments were buttressed by rights-based framing tactics. After significant community pressure (explored in more detail below) the company agreed to build water-storage reservoirs to help address the drinking-water crisis in the village. These structures would capture water that fell as rain during the rainy season and distribute it during the dry season when supplies were often scarce. Although some concerns were expressed about the suitability of potentially stagnant water for drinking and cooking, the commensurability of the replacement water source was not extensively debated in meetings. This is unlike the Conga conflict discussed above in which the rejection of the reservoirs and thus the conflict itself hinged on the incommensurability of lagoon versus reservoir sourced water. In Mataquita, it was not that the water sources were regarded as equal, but rather their need for some form of water-infrastructure intervention and a weak bargaining position meant the rejection of what was being offered by the mine was not an option. Instead, unease around the equivalence of the intervention mainly focused on whether the water-storage reservoirs would deliver sufficient water for their needs to be adequately met.

As ethnographic research by Dayot in this volume makes clear, responsibility for infrastructure provision in contexts where extractive companies are active is complex and tends to shift between local actors depending on changes to the political economy of extraction. This uncertainty around responsibility is exploited by both the company, local state actors, and prospective politicians (Dayot, 2022). When the Mataquita conflict took place, although the Water Resources Law recognised the right to water, it was not considered to be a constitutional right. In October 2016 however, amendments were made to the constitution and universal access to drinking water has now been included and will be guaranteed by the prioritisation of human consumption over other uses.[11] The decision to construct water capture infrastructure in Mataquita is indicative of a moment when water access has crept up the political agenda such that demands that try to activate the human right to water, even before constitutional formalisation, were acted upon. Yet demands for more water are still narrowly interpreted as demands for drinking-water provision rather than fuller conceptualisations which recognise the role that water plays more broadly in allowing human flourishing to take place (Jepson et al., 2017).

11 Ley 30588 – 'Artículo 7º-A' of the constitution, see http://sinia.minam.gob.pe/normas/ley-reforma-constitucional-que-reconoce-derecho-acceso-agua-derecho (accessed 16 April 2022).

Below I explore this issue more fully through a consideration of the role that documentation played in determining the response to the water crisis.

Documents and the epistemological underpinnings of infrastructure design

When the community initiated their complaint to Barrick Gold, it was partly because two *actas*[12] had recently been rediscovered in the community archives in which the company appeared to admit responsibility for causing damage to the Uliyacu stream in 1996. The rediscovery of these *actas* was crucial because previous interactions[13] with the company had taught the community that without the proper documentation convincing them to accept responsibility for damages was impossible. On one occasion when complaints about the disappearance of streams used for agriculture were raised in a meeting, the community relations representative reminded them, 'It is necessary to demonstrate with legal documents [that water resources have been affected]. It is easy [just] to say they have been impacted.' This emphasis on the necessity of formal studies as a means of knowing scarcity disadvantages local communities who struggle to access this type of information (Shah et al., 2019; Li, 2015). The necessity of having legal documents in order to make a claim for water loss conscribed the community's ability to successfully claim for the loss of other streams which had been gradually disappearing since the initiation of mining activities.

As such, in their letter to the mining company the community focused on damages caused to the Uliyacu stream, rather than their perception that water availability was reducing more generally. At first, the company refused to recognise the legitimacy of their complaint.[14] The community's use of the Uliyacu stream had previously occurred under an informal sharing agreement with the neighbouring village of Mareniyoc, thus, as a formal permit had never been obtained for the water's use, Barrick Gold stated[15] that they had no right to claim for its subsequent reduction in flow. Such informal agreements are a common feature of water allocation configurations across the country (Gelles, 2000; Boelens, 2009). However, Peru's legal system does not recognise the plurality of ways that water is shared and used, despite the ubiquity of this type of arrangement in highland communities (Boelens, 2008). 'Local water rights, organisational norms and operational rules in the Andean region are not only dynamic, extremely diverse, puzzlingly intertwined and even

12 *Actas* are minutes of meetings or events; they record who was present, what was discussed and any decisions taken. They are considered to have legal validity.

13 For example, their earlier efforts to get the damage to irrigation streams recognised.

14 See Balderson (2018) for a more detailed history of conflict trajectory.

15 The mine's formal response to the initial letter sent by the community was also printed in the Appendix of the hydrological study.

mutually contradictory; often they also stand in clear contradiction to national legislation' (Boelens, 2009, p. 310; Cremers et al., 2005).

When Barrick Gold continued to refuse to recognise the legitimacy of their claim despite the existence of the *acta,* the Mataquitans pointed to the existence of physical infrastructures (pipes, a storage tank and hydraulic brake systems) buried in the ground, and which had previously been used to distribute the water from the Uliyacu stream. These orientations are typical of peasant frameworks for understanding water rights, which rarely rest on the acquisition of specific state permits. Instead, legitimate mechanisms for the right to make a claim include socio-territorial rights, historic rights (i.e. the use of water over a given historical period) and hydraulic property creation (Boelens, 2009; Boelens and Vos, 2014). In Mataquita, the historic use of the water and the materiality of the previously existing infrastructure was regarded as 'overwhelming proof'[16] of water rights.

As the Mataquitans only had an *acta* linking water disappearance to mining activities for one stream, the only part of their claim that might be considered legitimate related to drinking-water scarcity rather than the more generalised water crisis that was affecting the village. As a response to a much more generalised water crisis, the construction of the reservoirs made both the state and the mine complicit in the enactment of a political ideology which was willing to concede the necessity of drinking-water provision for highland communities but did not recognise the interconnected nature of natural and social systems, and the role that water plays in allowing a flourishing life to take place (Jepson et al., 2017). As such, the reservoirs are indicative of a political ideology that prioritises large-scale extractive projects to the detriment of smaller-scale productive activities which are more likely to contribute a sustainable income to households in the area. A point echoed by Guarneros-Meza and Torres-Wong in this volume whose case study illustrates how infrastructural decision-making in the presence of mining activity is often not always made in the best interests of local populations.

Despite the formation of a working group overseen by the state, the mining company continued to claim that the *denuncia* lodged by the community was a spurious complaint that aimed to secure undeserved compensation and that the community already had sufficient water to meet their daily living needs. In 2015, the working group addressed this difference in opinion via the production of a document called the *Diagnóstico de Agua para Uso Poblacional de Mataquita Distrito de Jangas, Huaraz, Ancash* (henceforth referred to as the *Diagnóstico*) which was a hydrological study that aimed to determine the water balance in the village. This report used hydrological and meteorological data to quantify expected stream flows and then combined this information with current and future population water-use needs to determine how much

16 This is how it was described to me: *prueba contundente.*

water was needed in comparison to how much water was available. The study indicated that although the water balance was positive across the year, there was a deficit between June and December especially during August, September, and October. This document served to 'scientifically verify' the scarcity which the community were reporting and its results placed Barrick Gold under increased pressure to respond to their complaint. As a result, they agreed to fund the production of an engineering document known as the *Expediente Técnico,* which arrived nearly a year later and outlined how the scarcity in the village could be addressed. The water deficit figures in the *Diagnóstico* directly informed the follow-up document, which proposed addressing the scarcity via the construction of water-storage reservoirs that would collect water during the rainy season for distribution later in the year. The study noted that there was a small but significant water deficit in the present but as the population increased this would increase in the future. It outlined volumetric designs for the reservoirs as well as recommending that existing water distribution infrastructures were renovated to reduce water losses.

Although it is common practice to treat documents such as the *Expediente Técnico* as purely technical endeavours, they are nevertheless constrained and moulded by specific regulatory guidance, normative expectations, and epistemological assumptions. The *Expediente Técnico* makes clear that any infrastructure development must consider the needs of not just the current population but the projected population over a period of 20 years.[17] Therefore, the designs presented in the *Expediente Técnico* were supposed to meet the needs of the projected population of Mataquita, which is expected to increase from 681 to 919 people by 2035. This apparently necessitated the construction of five water-storage reservoirs in total: three of 870 and two of 355 cubic metres capacity. This seemingly mundane government recommendation became 'a site of opportunity' (Pinker and Harvey, 2015, p. 16) as it allowed the community to potentially gain access to water in *excess* of their *current* supposed requirements.

As the *Expediente Técnico* itself stated 'Due to the location being found within the influence of the mine the project will be financed by the Civil Association NeoAndina'[18] (2M Group/Asociation Civil Neo Andina, 2016, p. 1) the community had expected that water infrastructures would be built according to the designs presented in the document. However, during subsequent working-group meetings the mining company representatives denied they had ever committed themselves to building water infrastructures for the village. Instead, representatives began to claim that only one of the five reservoirs included in the *Expediente Técnico* needed to be built. As the community had begun to feel that significant water-infrastructure development was within their grasp, there

17 This requirement was established via a government document titled 'Design Parameters for Water and Sanitation Infrastructures in Rural Villages' (Gobierno del Peru, 2004).

18 The subsidiary of Barrick Gold that organises infrastructure projects as part of their Corporate Social Responsibility programme

was great disappointment and moral outrage when they realised that again the company was backtracking on its commitments despite their apparent formal codification into documents. In the words of the president of the Water and Sanitation Committee:

> [A]ll this has been worked [out] in an engineering manner, it hasn't been done without thought [*así por así*], no? They have submitted to the laws and in agreement with the laws (...) it has been designed in agreement with the work of engineers, Mr [Ling[19]] cannot avoid this. Why did they commit themselves on principle to make an *Expediente* in agreement with the *Diagnóstico* that [Manual Martínez] did? Because why not just say, you know what, the mine has the intention of only making a reservoir of so much, so let's make this *Expediente* just for this?' (President of JASS)

In the quote above, the speaker tries to appeal to the indisputable materiality of the figures in the *Expediente Técnico* and the 'authority' of the law to challenge the refusal of the mine to acknowledge both the neediness of the community and the legitimacy of their expectations. Using a legal frame to address perceived miscarriages of justice has a strong historical precedent in highland regions (de la Cadena, 2015; Salomon and Nino Murcia, 2011; Wilson, 2013). The legitimacy of concepts such as law and science are derived from their association with objectivity and neutrality. Their apparent strength is that they are designed to be a non-political tool in conflict resolution (Sosa and Zwarteveen, 2016). The villagers expected, as citizens of Peru, that the legal framework which had insisted that their claim could not be considered fully valid due to the lack of a formal permit for water use in this instance would work in their favour. They expected that their willingness to negotiate with the mining company, their prioritisation of technical and scientific knowledge would make them 'rational' subjects and respected citizens (Li, 2015). In her analysis of the way that documents are operationalised by Turkish Cypriots, Navaro-Yashin writes about how their ability to produce particular effects means they can 'discharge affective energies' and 'be perceived or experienced as affectively charged phenomenon ... within specific webs of social relations' (2007, p. 81). In Mataquita, the hope that documents would allow them to hold the mining company to account is part of what electrified the conflict and working-group negotiations (Balderson, 2022). Further, in rural Peruvian communities documents are seen as very powerful: '[t]he written word [is] mightier than the spoken one; its leverage in legal disputes (local ones included) [is] undeniable, and it [can] only be countered with another written word' (de la Cadena, 2015, p. 15; see also Allen, 1988, p. 67).

As the mine continued to insist that the community already had sufficient water, community members brought forth emotional accounts of their lived experience of water scarcity.

> I am there daily, I live there (...) and your study doesn't convince us, and

19 All names used are pseudonyms.

> why? Because we live on this side, as I have said we have tried to collect water from the roofs, for what? In order to survive. (Unknown speaker at a working group meeting)

Or in the words of another:

> [H]ave you at least checked that there is sufficient water in the lower part? At least have you lived [there] for a couple of days? Of course, it is there at some moments, [but] there are moments when it disappears. (Unknown speaker at a working group meeting)

The speakers are challenging the figures in the documents by presenting their own epistemology of 'seeing is believing', which is a situated and embodied approach to understanding scarcity (Phillimore, 1998). Li has also highlighted the weight given to experiential knowledge by campesino communities (Li, 2015). In the quotes above knowledge is accessible, and knowledge of a situation can be acquired by the straightforward process of visiting the neighbourhood in question. As such, it became clear that the appeal to the legal force of the figures contained in the *Expediente Técnico* was not so much a genuine commitment to the authority of science but was instead related to their *faith in what documents do*. In Mataquita, codification of the community's needs in engineering documents according to the formal state-sponsored protocol created the expectation that the solution to the water crisis enacted would be the same as those laid out in writing. Again, we can see immaterial aspects of the hydrosocial territory shaping both processes of contestation and the response to the water crisis in the village via the embedded but conflicting norms about what constitutes valid knowledge of water availability.

Water infrastructures as the materialisation of social value

The Pierina project is an example of *nueva minería*, a type of mining that promises negligible environmental impact, local development, and fair treatment of local communities. However, as I indicated earlier, many feel that Barrick Gold has not lived up to its slogan of 'Responsible Mining'. One woman reported how she had gone from village to village in the 1990s, evangelising on the part of the mine, trying to make sure that the project went ahead. 'At the moment they enter [the zone] they offer everything, but up until now they have completed nothing', she told me angrily 20 years later. The frustration that the mine had not fulfilled expectations was palpable. It was a grievance they knew carried little political weight, but which was deeply felt, nonetheless. In this context, the promise of tangible water-infrastructure investments had meaning that went beyond their use value as structures able to ameliorate the impending water crisis. The water-storage reservoirs were viewed as a way of forcing the company to fulfil its moral obligations to the community who were resentful of the dismissive attitude shown during nearly 20 years of operations (Balderson, 2022). The community wanted as much water-storage as possible capacity to be built partly to alleviate the water crisis but also as the material presence of reservoirs in the village served as visible indicators of the community's social worth.

The logic of Barrick Gold was that building more than one reservoir would give the community water in excess of their requirements. In a meeting a community relations representative commented:

> It is unnecessary to construct for 20 years, the current deficit that Mataquita has could be satisfied with one infrastructure, with one part of the infrastructure investment which is proposed here (...) Why? Because to construct it all in one effort is unnecessary; it is going to deteriorate, you are not going to use it. It is unnecessary. (Community relations representative: Barrick Gold)

Velho and Ureta (2019) have explored the fragility of infrastructure and its innate propensity to decay. They note how in the neoliberal era rather than being the materialisation of state power as was previously the case, infrastructures often turn out to be manifestations of incapacity, corruption, and state failure. The ubiquity of infrastructural disrepair and decay is being exploited here by the Barrick Gold representative who uses this essential characteristic to undermine the case for infrastructural investment in the village. This is distinct from its implications in other contexts where the continuous experience of unreliability can result in a stabilised and embedded momentum in terms of the way that people interact with that system and find ways to adapt to and mitigate for its failures (Furlong, 2014).

In this context, rather than building five storage reservoirs according to the engineering solution proposed in the documents, instead the company offered one reservoir of 870 cubic metres for the upper part of the village and another daily regulation reservoir of 30 cubic metres for a neighbourhood situated at a lower location. The representative present claimed that as according to the figures in the documents as the population had not yet reached 919 inhabitants this would be sufficient to meet the community's needs in the present. This squabble over access to a few extra hundred litres of water also needs to be contextualised in relation to other less visible infrastructure interventions such as the deep-well pumps built on the mining company's property which allow the company to extract 120 litres a second of water from the water table below the mine as referenced in the quote at the start of this chapter. Again, the terrain of conflict as a hydrosocial territory is useful here; the idea of an excess of water reflects a particular social imaginary which was at odds with the way in which the community experienced daily life in the village in which there was always an insufficiency of water. For the community, the decision about what size to construct reservoirs was not an abstract concept related to the number of litres deemed a sufficient allocation per person per day, but rather it was linked to lay normativity and the understanding that they ought to have access to sufficient water for necessary daily living activities. The president of JASS commented:

> look we have lost time waiting for the 3,300 cubic meters, (...) it is something illogical gentlemen. (...) we have always been present, we can make [them] respect our rights.

Framing their disappointments in terms of the mining company's failure to respect their rights brings the relationship between infrastructure development and practices of citizenship back into focus again. Rasmussen has discussed how 'by claiming specific rights that highland protestors believe are granted by the constitution, they attempt to re-possess a citizenship that may be constitutionally secured but which all too frequently fails to be a lived reality in the high Andes of Peru' (Rasmussen, 2016a, p. 15). Their claim for 'rights' is a claim for visibility and recognition which they felt could be enacted by the construction of water-storage reservoirs in the village. However, the desire for tangible forms of social recognition is often viewed as an attempt to gain undeserved personal or community advancement by mining companies, the state, and in popular discourse.

In Peru since the 1980s, multiculturalism has been integrated into the neoliberal model of citizenship operating there. This has both progressive and regressive qualities in that it enables the cultural rights of indigenous populations to be given greater symbolic recognition whilst simultaneously denying the possibility of meaningful improvements, political representation, or economic opportunities (Hale, 2007; de la Cadena, 2015). Within this model of citizenship, certain types of indigenous activism are permitted in the political space whilst others are excluded, for example, demands for language rights are acceptable, but demands that interfere with global capital accumulation, such as full-scale opposition to *megaminería* projects, are far more problematic. Charles Hale and Rosamel Millaman have used the term *indio permitido* to describe the acceptable practices of multicultural citizenship that are admitted by the neoliberal state (Hale, 2007). This model of citizenship creates two types of indigenous subject:

> The 'Indio permitido' has passed the test of modernity, substituted 'protest' with 'proposal' and learned to be authentic and fully conversant with the dominant milieu. Its Other is unruly, vindictive and conflict prone. These latter traits trouble elites who have pledged allegiance to cultural equality, seeding fears about what empowerment of these Other Indians would portend. (Hale, 2007, p. 5)

As noted above, throughout the conflict it seemed that the Mataquitans were trying to position themselves as 'modern' actors. Their appeal to the power of law and science is an attempt to distance themselves from the disruptive protesters active at other conflict sites around the country. Despite this, their focus on implicitly economic issues such as access to water and sustainable livelihoods were considered 'unruly', and their demands and ways of doing business did not quite fit within the boundaries of what was considered acceptable by the mining company and the state. Their intentions of obtaining concessions that went beyond the symbolic realm contributed to the construction of their demands as issues of '[personal] interest', and therefore invalid claims on the resources of Barrick Gold. In the words of one mining company representative:

> They are trying to extract an economic advantage from a situation of scarcity in a village like Mataquita (...) Tell me this is not miserly? Or tell me this is not manipulative? It is manipulative, pure manipulation in order to extract material benefits. Obviously, it is manipulation.

The economic implications of said scarcity seem to be lost on the speaker. This tendency to question the moral worth of the community was consistent across various interactions I both initiated and observed. It is a delegitimation strategy that has been observed in numerous social conflicts in the region (Boelens, 2015).

Eventually, the working group managed to thrash out a deal on the size of the reservoirs and the compromise solution of one reservoir of 870 cubic metres and another of 100 (rather than the 30 originally offered by Barrick Gold) metres cubed was agreed. This small concession was extracted as a close examination of the technical documents by interested parties revealed that the figure of 30 metres cubed did not fit the calculated needs of the community even in the present. Thus, the potency of formally codified scientific figures remained largely intact, even if interpretation of their implications was more politically fraught than had initially appeared.

In 2017, these reservoirs were built and when I returned to the site in 2018 the community seemed relatively satisfied with the outcome of the conflict. During my period away, two villagers contacted me separately via Facebook to share pictures as the construction of the reservoirs progressed. The community was allowed to form a *microempresa* and a few people were then contracted to build the reservoirs under the supervision of a more technically qualified foreman. In these photos, they looked pleased and proud that the mining company had finally been convinced to offer tangible investment to the community. The water-storage reservoirs also improve their standing locally, something they felt was neglected, and from a practical point of view improves water access at the site (Balderson, 2022). By my 2018 visit, the paint was already looking flaky but for the previous two years there had been a much more reliable drinking-water connection. Water for agriculture remained in very short supply.

Discussion and conclusion

This case study reveals a number of insights pertinent to understanding the social and political life of water-infrastructure projects in this part of Peru. Analysis of the politics and ideological assumptions behind the wrangling process which led to the construction of the Mataquitan water-storage reservoirs has shown how important features of the hydrosocial territory around the community and the mine influenced the type of infrastructure intervention received at the site.

First, the value accorded documentation – both terms of water permits which formalise access to specific water sources and scientifically accredited studies that legitimise experiences of scarcity – reduced the ability of the community to contest water scarcities which go beyond inadequate access to drinking water. Complex layers of mutually contradictory understandings of water rights, imaginaries of community behaviours, and historic infrastructures form part of the hydrosocial territory which shaped the type of water access intervention – i.e. the type of infrastructure – the community would go on to receive.

My discussion has highlighted how water can operate as a socio-technical assemblage: the documents created by the engineers conjured water into being for the community, the hydrological study made their experience of scarcity 'real', and so made an intervention to improve access (and thus 'produce' water) also a reality (Zwarteveen and Boelens, 2014). As Harvey and Knox point out, 'infrastructures do not simply reference or represent political ideology but actively participate in often unexpected ways, in the processes by which political relations are articulated and enacted' (Harvey and Knox, 2012). Thus, the construction of reservoirs which do not facilitate an increase in local productive (agricultural) capacities is a means of ensuring that current political relations remain unchallenged. Limited access to irrigation water reduces the likelihood that the Mataquitan campesinos will have sufficient economic security to participate fully in the political life of the country and be able to challenge the marginalisation of rural indigenous groups across the country.

Long (2001) has used the term 'knowledge interface' to conceptualise the discontinuities between lifeworlds and ways of knowing. For him 'interface entails an acute awareness of the ways in which different possibly conflicting forms of knowledge intersect and interact'. It highlights how 'different social constructions of "reality" developed by various parties' have important social implications (Long, 2001, p. 191). In the case discussed above, during working-group meetings experiential knowledge crunched up uncomfortably against the apparently scientific figures in the *Diagnóstico* and *Expediente Técnico*. Whilst the community were not necessarily willing to recognise the legitimacy of scientific representations of reality what was recognised was the immutability of knowledge codified into formal documents and the power of modernist discourses such as law and science.

The imbrication between these frameworks and infrastructure projects both constrains and opens up possible resistance strategies in marginalised communities. On one hand, the totalising nature of these narratives squeezes the possibility that their lived experience of water scarcity will be taken seriously by powerful actors such as the mining company and the state. However, the tendency for citizenship 'to be mediated through infrastructure' (Goodwin, 2018, p. 13) creates space for communities to make redistributive claims in language that is acceptable to the state. Thus, as well as creating liberal subjects via the imposition of these logics as Alderman and Goodwin suggest in the introduction, contestations around infrastructures also offer previously 'unruly' citizens a means through which to perform their identities as modern rational citizens who understand the value (and power) which science and law have to shape their water reality. The construction of water infrastructure in Mataquita was riven with tensions. Although the infrastructure was longed for and viewed as a tangible indicator of the community's social worth, the specificities of the design were contested. The end result was somehow a physical expression of their hopes and disappointments. Anand (2011) has posited 'pressure' as a useful analytic for understanding how settlers claim water in Mumbai and certainly the Mataquitans had to apply significant pressure to secure water infrastructure for the village in the face of an obdurate attitude from the mining company. However, in doing this they worked creatively with the discursive flow in which law and science were sacrosanct and the state was increasingly sensitised to the link between suffering and access to water.

References

2M Group/Asociation Civil Neo Andina (2016) *Elaboración del expediente técnico: 'construcción de reservorios de almacenamiento de agua para uso poblacional de Mataquita, distrito de Jangas, Huaraz, Ancash'.* Mataquita: NeoAndina, 2M Group/Asociación Civil.

Allen, C. (1988) *The Hold Life Has: Coca and Cultural Identity in an Andean Community* (Washington, DC: Smithsonian Institution Press).

Anand, N. (2011) 'Pressure: the politechnics of water supply in Mumbai', *Cultural Anthropology,* 26 (4): 542–64.

Anand, N. (2017) *Hydraulic City: Water and the Infrastructures of Citizenship in Mumbai* (Durham, NC: Duke University Press).

Assadourian, C.S., H. Bonilla, A. Mitre, and T. Platt (1980) *Minería y espacio económico en los Andes siglos XVI–XX* (Lima: Instituto de Estudios Peruanos (IEP)).

Balderson, U. (2018) 'Wrangling Over Water: Emotion, agency and uncertainty in a mining conflict in Ancash, Peru', PhD Thesis (Newcastle: unpublished)

Balderson, U. (2022) 'Emotional subjectivities and the trajectory of a Peruvian mining conflict', *Environment and Planning E: Nature and Space.*

Baviskar, A. (2003) 'For a cultural politics of natural resources', *Economic and Political Weekly,* 29 November, pp. 5051–5.

Boelens, R. (2008) *Rules of the Game and the Game of the Rules: Normalisation and Resistance in Andean Water Control* (Wageningen: Wageningen University).

Boelens, R. (2009) 'The politics of disciplining water rights', *Development and Change,* 40 (2): 307–31.

Boelens, R. (2015) 'Water justice in Latin America: the politics of difference, equality, and indifference', Inaugral Lecture, University of Amsterdam 21 May 2015, s.l., s.n.

Boelens, R., J. Hoogesteger, E. Swyngedouw, and J. Vos (2016) 'Hydrosocial territories: a political ecology perspective', *Water International,* 41 (1): 1–14.

Boelens, R. and J. Vos (2014) 'Legal pluralism, hydraulic property creation and sustainability: the materialised nature of water rights in user managed systems', *Current Opinion in Environmental Sustainability,* 11: 55–62.

Chanduvi, E. (2012) 'National mobilisation in defense of water in Peru', *Latin America Data Base New and Educational Service,* 24 (2): 2012: 1–4.

Cremers, L., M. Ooijevaar, and R. Boelens (2005) 'Institutional reform in the Andean irrigation sector: enabling policies for strengthening local rights and water management', *Natural Resources Forum,* 29: 37–50.

Dayot, J. (2022) 'They want to change us by charging us: drinking water provision and water conflict in the Ecuadorian Amazon', in J. Alderman and G. Goodwin (eds.), *The Social and Political Life of Latin American Infrastructures* (London: University of London Press).

de Echave, J., A. Diez, L. Huber, B. Revesz, X. R. Lanata and M. Tanaka (2009) *Minería y conflicto social,* (Lima: IEP).

de la Cadena, M. (2000) *Indigenous Mestizos: The Politics of Race and Culture in Cuzco, Peru, 1919–1991* (Durham, NC: Duke University Press).

de la Cadena, M. (2015) *Earth Beings Ecologies of Practice Across Andean Worlds* (Durham, NC and London: Duke University Press).

Defensoría del Pueblo (2015) *Conflictos sociales y recursos hidricos – informe no. 001–2015-DP/APCSG* (Lima: Defensoría del Pueblo).

Defensoría del Pueblo (2017) *El valor del diálogo: ajuntia para la prevencion de conflictos sociales y la gobernabilidad* (Lima: Defensoría del Pueblo).

del Castillo Pinto, L. (2011) 'Ley de recursos hídricos: necesaria pero no suficiente', *Debate Agrario,* 45: 91–118.

Deleuze, G. (1990) *Expressionism in Philosophy.* New York: Zone Books.

Deustua, J. (1994) 'Mining markets, peasants, and power in nineteenth-century Peru', *Latin American Research Review,* 29 (1): 29–54.

Fox, N. (2015) 'Emotions, affects and the production of social life', *British Journal of Sociology,* 66 (2): 301–18.

Furlong, K. (2014) 'STS beyond the "modern infrastructure ideal": extending theory by engaging with infrastructure challenges in the South', *Technology in Society*, 38: 139–47.

Gamu, J.K. and P. Dauvergne, (2018) 'The slow violence of corporate social responsibility: the case', *Third World Quarterly*, 39 (5): 959–95.

Gelles, P. (2000) *Water and Power in Highland Peru: The Cultural Politics of Irrigation and Development* (New Brunswick, NJ: Rutgers University Press).

Gobierno del Perú (2004) *Parámetros de diseño de infraestructura de agua y saneamiento para centros poblados rurales* (Lima: Gobierno del Perú).

Gonzales de Olarte, E. (1996) *El ajuste estructural y los campesinos* (Lima: IEP; Ayuda en Accion-Peru; Action Aid-UK).

Goodwin, G. (2018) 'Water, infrastructure and power: contention and resistance in post-colonial cities of the south', *Development and Change*, 49 (6): 1616–30.

Hale, C. (2007) 'Rethinking indigenous politics in the era of the "indio permitido"'. *NALCA Report on the Americas*, 38 (2): 16–21.

Harding, S. (2008) *Sciences from Below: feminisms, Postcolonialities, and Modernities* (Durham, NC: Duke University Press).

Harvey, P. and H. Knox (2012) 'The enchantments of infrastructure', *Mobilities*, 7 (4): 521–36.

Harvey, P. and H. Knox (2015) *Roads: An Anthropology of Infrastructure and Expertise* (Ithaca, NY: Cornell University Press).

Himley, M. (2013) 'Regularizing extraction in Andean Peru: mining and social mobilisation in an age of corporate social responsibility', *Antipode*, 45 (2): 394–416.

Jepson, W., J. Budds, L. Eichelberger, L. Harris, E. Norman, K. O'Reilly, A. Pearson, S. Shah, J. Shinn, C. Staddon, J. Stoler, A. Wutich and S. Young (2017) 'Advancing human capabilities for water security: a relational approach', *Water Security*, 1: 46–52.

Larkin, B. (2013) 'The politics and poetics of infrastructure', *Annual Review of Anthropology*, 42: 327–43.

Latour, B. (2004) *The Politics of Nature: How to Bring the Sciences into Democracy* (Cambridge, MA: Harvard University Press).

Lemanski, C. (2020) 'Infrastructural Citizenship: (de)constructing state-society relations', *International Development Planning Review*, 42 (2): 115–125.

Li, F. (2015) *Unearthing Conflict: Corporate Mining Activism and Expertise in Peru* (Durham, NC: Duke University Press).

Loftus, A. (2009) 'Rethinking political ecologies of water', *Third World Quarterly,* 30 (5): 953–68.

Long, N. (2001) *Development Sociology: Actor Perspectives* (Abingdon: Routledge).

Navaro-Yashin, Y. (2007) 'Make believe papers, legal forms and the counterfeit', *Anthropological Theory,* 7 (1): 79–98.

Oliart, P. (2008) 'Indigenous women's organizations and the political discourses of indigenous rights and gender equity in Peru', *Latin American and Caribbean Ethnic Studies,* 3 (3): 291–308.

Paerregaard, K., A.B. Stensrud, and A.O. Anderson (2016) 'Water citizenship: negotiating water rights and contesting water culture in the Peruvian Andes', *Latin American Research Review,* 51 (1): 198–217.

Peñafiel, A.P.P. and F. Li (2019) 'Nourishing relations: controversy over the Conga Mining Project in northern Peru', *Ethnos,* 84 (2): 301–22.

Phillimore, P. (1998) 'Uncertainty, reassurance and pollution: the politics of epidemiology in Teesside', *Health & Place,* 4(3): 203–212

Pinker, A. and P. Harvey (2015) 'Negotiating uncertainty: neoliberal statecraft in contemporary Peru', *Social Analysis,* 59 (4): 15–31.

Rasmussen, M.B. (2016a) 'Reclaiming the lake: citizenship and environment-as-common-property in highland Peru', *Focaal Journal of Global and Historical Anthropology,* 74: 13–27.

Rasmussen, M.B. (2016b) 'Tactics of the governed: figures of abandonment in Andean Peru', *Journal of Latin American Studies,* 49, 327–53.

Rasmussen, M.B. (2016c) 'Water futures: contention in the construction of productive infrastructure in the Peruvian highlands', *Anthropologia,* 58: 211–26.

Salomon, F. and M. Nino Murcia (2011) *The Lettered Mountain: A Peruvian Village's Way with Writing* (Durham, NC: Duke University Press).

Scarritt, A. (2011) 'Broker fixed: the racialsied social structure and the subjugation of indigenous populations in the Andes', *Critical Sociology,* 37 (2): 153–77.

Shah, E., R. Boelens, and B. Bruins (2019) 'Reflections: contested epistemologies on large dams and mega-hydraulic development', *Water,* 11(3), 417: 1–6.

Sosa, M. and M. Zwarteveen (2016) 'Questioning the effectiveness of planned conflict resolution strategies in water disputes between rural communities and mining companies in Peru', *Water International,* 41 (3): 483–500.

Tanaka, M. (2005) La importancia del estado y de las instuciones', in R. Barrantes, P. Zarate, and A. Durand (eds.), *'Te quiero pero no': minería, desarrollo y poblaciones locales* (Lima: IEP), pp. 9–15.

Triscritti, F. (2013) 'Mining development and corporate-community conflicts in Peru', *Community Development Journal,* 48 (3): 437–50.

Unknown (2015) *Diagnóstico de agua para uso poblacional de Mataquita, Distrito de Jangas – Huaraz – Ancash.* Mataquita: n/a.

Velho, R. and S. Ureta (2019) 'Frail modernities: Latin American infrastructures between repair and ruination', *Tapuya: Latin American Science, Technology and Society,* 2 (1): 428–41.

Willaqniki (2013) *Mesas de dialogo, mesa de desarrollo y conflictos sociales en el Peru: no. 5* (Miraflores: Oficina Nacional de Diálogo y Sostenibilidad – ONDS/Presidencia del Consejo de Ministros de la República del Perú – PCM).

Wilson, F. (2013) *Citizenship and Political Violence in Peru: An Andean Town 1870s–1970s* (New York: Palgrave Macmillan).

Yashar, D. (2005) *Contesting Citizenship in Latin America: The Rise of Indigenous Movements and the Postliberal Challenge* (Cambridge: Cambridge University Press).

Zwarteveen, M. and R. Boelens (2014) 'Defining, researching and struggling for water justice: some conceptual building blocks for research and action', *Water International,* 39 (2): 143–58.

4. Planning a society: urban politics and public housing during the Cold War in Natal, Brazil

Yuri Gama[1]

Introduction

In Brazil, until the late 1930s, private industries were the main constructors of public housing. These companies let houses and rooms to their own workers. After 1940, the state played a progressively larger role in building more affordable housing intending to provide shelter for a new urban working class and give a sense of private ownership to people who used to rent or squat. This chapter focuses on revealing the reasons for the strong presence of public housing in Natal, the capital of the north-eastern state of Rio Grande do Norte. Much of the extensive literature on housing infrastructure in Brazil emphasises industrialisation and mass protests as drivers for housing policy mainly in large south-eastern cities such as São Paulo and Rio de Janeiro. A relatively small, poorly industrialised, and relatively quiescent city such as Natal fits poorly into these existing explanations. However, looking specifically between 1960 and 1980, public housing projects proliferated with a real drive from different government units to attend to popular needs and their own ideas. While the prevailing literature focuses on unveiling the impact of present government practices on changing popular consciousness, this chapter questions the origins and the reasons behind these governmental efforts. More specifically, this chapter analyses the role of state-led social housing in shaping the urban working class during the Cold War.

Throughout the modern history of Natal, affordable housing for people on low incomes or the middle classes was the purview of the state with the help of private initiatives. Beyond providing shelter for people, mass housing infrastructure and

1 The author would like to thank the History Department at the University of Massachusetts Amherst and the Potash Travel Award for the endless support of his research. Without them his research would not exist. He would also like to thank Geoff Goodwin and Jonathan Alderman; his adviser Joel Wolfe; Jason Higgins, Kevin Young, Mark Healey, Priyanka Srivastava, and all the reviewers for their very helpful comments and edits suggested for this chapter.

Y. Gama, 'Planning a society: urban politics and public housing during the Cold War in Natal, Brazil' in *The Social and Political Life of Latin American Infrastructures*, ed. J. Alderman and G. Goodwin (London, 2022), pp. 101–126.

urban planning served as a tool of sanitary education, political propaganda, Cold War strategy, and economic development between 1900 and 1986, when the federal government closed its main housing agency. In the first 40 years of the 20th century, local and regional authorities along with urban planners developed comprehensive neighbourhood plans that were never completely fulfilled, but influenced the city's growth and hygiene habits. Although these plans did not focus on affordable housing per se, they changed Natal's architecture and construction laws and measures through sanitary urbanism, such as the 1924 Plano Geral de Obras de Saneamento [Comprehensive Sanitary Works Plan] by engineer Henrique de Novais and Saturnino de Brito's 1935 Plano Geral de Obras [Comprehensive Works Plan]. Among several aspects of planning, these massive works destroyed buildings and alleys, and changed the sizes of pavements and houses while implementing rubbish disposal and sewer infrastructure that influenced the urban expansion of Natal and Rio Grande do Norte.

After 1930, with the creation of agencies such as Institutos de Aposentadoria e Pensões (IAP) [Pensions and Retirement Institutes] in 1933, the Fundação Casa Popular (FCP) [Casa Popular Foundation] in 1946, and the Banco Nacional de Habitação (BNH) [National Housing Bank] in 1964, the federal state, through different administrations prioritised the construction of *conjuntos habitacionais*[2] with the support of local states and private-construction companies. As the state planned and constructed affordable homes conforming to modernist architecture, an anti-communist discourse, and sanitation requirements, I argue that state-sponsored housing in Natal became an instrument to shape citizenship and to form a new society based on old ideas. Considering infrastructure's capacity to reveal insights into governance, culture, and ideology (Larkin, 2013), this chapter examines ideas and practices of politicians, bureaucrats, and planners behind public housing construction in the state of Rio Grande do Norte. I posit that by using housing to tame communist inroads and to control a new growing urban working class, transnational and national meetings of local and international urban planners, politicians, diplomats, and academics fostered an ideal of moderate citizenship and particular political subjects based on Cold War ideals.

Specifically analysing the most active years of housing construction, between the late 1950s and the late 1970s, I situate Natal's history in Adrián Gorelik's discussion about the social construction of the Latin American city in the 20th century (Gorelik, 2005).[3] Natal's public housing emerged directly

2 A Brazilian expression for public housing.

3 In 'The Latin American city' (2005), Adrián Gorelik argues that the Latin American city became a place of the 'encounter between the discourses and material practices of modernisation and development' during the Cold War. Scholars such as Leandro Benmergui also discuss the influence of clashing economic policies developed by modernisation theorists and CEPAL's economists in housing development in Buenos Aires and Rio de Janeiro. The influences in Natal are manifest in the different architectural choices for different public housing complexes built by different sections of the state in regional political disputes.

influenced by transnational Cold War politics in a local context. Different from industrial centres such as São Paulo, in which public housing construction mostly followed the emergence of new companies, in Natal, a poorly industrialised region, housing investment became a way for authorities and elites to implement cultural transformations connected to Cold War politics. Thus, Natal's public housing infrastructure between 1945 and 1980 developed as a cultural model that attempted to shape a new society. By associating new sanitary, economic, and political habits with the provision of social housing restricted to the working class alone, authorities and elites fostered a model citizenship visualising a new and modern urbanised Rio Grande do Norte.

After a coup d'état in 1930, the governor of the state of Rio Grande do Sul, Getúlio Vargas and his allies ousted all the existing governors and replaced them with their own choices creating a provisional government up to 1934. Vargas's coalition expanded and strengthened the federal government with new agencies that coordinated national policies in education, health, labour relations, commerce, and industrial policy (Williams, 2001). Suffering backlashes and fearing possible coups, in 1937 Vargas instituted the Estado Novo [New State] an authoritarian-nationalist regime. Among many programmes, in conjunction with the Rockefeller Foundation, the Vargas regime coordinated a campaign of national hygiene with sanitation workers and disseminated public information on tropical and venereal diseases (Williams, 2001). At the same time, the state policy promoted social harmony and class collaboration with massive support for industrialists and workers' rights. In this sense, with the creation of Institutos para Aposentados e Pensionistas (IAPs), during the Getúlio Vargas administration, and Banco Nacional de Habitação (BNHs), during Castelo Branco government, the federal government and its state interveners assumed the responsibility of providing housing for and regulating the labour conditions of the working class (Holston, 2008). The example of housing in Natal reflects James Holston's analysis of Getúlio Vargas's administrations in which the state considered the workers to be special citizens 'by bestowing social rights they had never had and celebrating a dignity of labour it had never recognised' (2008). However, in contrast to Holston's engagement with the residents' struggles in his book *Insurgent Citizenship* (2008), I investigate the politics behind state initiatives of building affordable housing complexes equipped with schools, open spaces, and community centres.

Initially created in 1933 to organise the social security of the emerging working class, the IAP was divided into several different sections according to each labour category and soon became the first country-wide federal housing agency.[4] Turning the IAP into a housing agency using a self-financing mechanism also helped the state to obtain data about industrial activity. The IAP's profit came from four different sources: a mandatory monthly contribution made by the

4 IAP was a collection of several federal institutes that organised labour affairs according to different categories: IAPC (merchants), IPASE (civil servants), IAPB (bank workers), IAPM (maritime workers), IAPI (industrial workers), IAPETEC (dockers and cargo transport workers).

workers, a mandatory annual contribution made by the industrial company, a symbolic percentage deducted from each project undertaken by the company, and donations (FGV/CPDOC, IAP). Created in 1964 by the new military regime, the National Housing Bank (BNH) fulfilled the IAP's promise of centralising housing construction in the hands of the federal government. Actively influencing regional states such as Rio Grande do Norte, the BNH became the most important agency of the military regime between 1964 and 1985. During these two decades, Natal's labour power also participated in a couple of self-built house construction schemes called *mutirão* and *autoconstrução* (Filho, 2011). However, in contrast to cities such as São Paulo, Brazil and Bogotá, Colombia, Natal's government did not focus its efforts on assisted self-built housing. Most of the self-built initiatives were autonomously organised by neighbourhood associations or the owners, which is not this chapter's focus. Constructed by the Catholic Church along with residents and the municipal government, Bairro Mãe Luíza and Rocas were the only assisted self-built experiments that stood out and still, they did not provide the expected number of homes (de Araújo, 2014). In conversation with Holston (2008), I understand here, that before 1960 with Vargas and after 1960, the state of Rio Grande do Norte used housing construction to reformulate the citizenship of workers in order to organise labor laws, foster the region's industrialisation and to stimulate a certain dependence on the government's structure.[5]

As part of the state structure, the IAP supported workers from different industries: banking staff, industrialists, public servants, maritime workers, and commercial workers benefited the most. These sections of the IAP established a degree of transparency in all of the construction phases through newspaper announcements. In Natal, local newspapers such as *Diário de Natal* and *Tribuna do Norte* published competition advertisements for companies to tender and win the right to build housing complexes for the state. The creation of the IAP along with the establishment of labour legislation such as the Consolidação das Leis do Trabalho (CLT) [Consolidation of Labour Laws],[6] and the construction and funding of private homes for the same social class meant an expansion of the state in registering the new working class. The state used CLT to gather data on unemployment and employment to build a social profile of its citizens as workers while improving its demographic census.

In contrast to Holston's discussion of citizenship formation with its focus on mass movements, my research examines the ideas and practices of architects, urbanists, governors, mayors, land surveyors, and sanitation experts who

5 In conversation with Holston's idea in *Insurgent Citizenship* (p. 186) that this manipulation of the workers' citizenship mainly happened before and during Vargas era, I posit that in Natal and Rio Grande do Norte authorities and elites attempted to culturally shape the working class throughout most of the 20th century at least until the mid-1970s, when housing lost its appeal.

6 Consolidação das Leis do Trabalho (CLT) [Consolidation of Labor Laws] was a document signed in 1943 by Getúlio Vargas that regulated the relationship between workers and managers prescribing rights and duties for both parties) https://cpdoc.fgv.br/producao/dossies/AEraVargas1/anos37-45/DireitosSociaisTrabalhistas/CLT (accessed 16 April 2022).

participated in the history of public housing construction in Natal. In order to present this analysis, the present chapter discusses the connection between urban planning and the construction of sanitation infrastructure up to 1940, the role of urban experts and housing agencies, the peak of public housing development in the 1960s, the electoral uses of residential complexes in the Cold War context, and the dismantling of housing investment after the mid-1970s.

Sanitation and public housing

Vargas's first government implemented reforms in the fields of public administration, education, and city planning that reinforced the urban renewal destructions and constructions of the early 1900s. As the federal state prioritised housing, Vargas provided enough support to his state intervener, Rafael Fernandes Gurjão, who governed Rio Grande do Norte from 1935 to 1943, to invest in a few comprehensive urban projects that intended to improve city hygiene, the water supply, and sewage systems (*A Ordem*, 13 May 1939). The urban project, Plano Geral de Obras, was partially implemented through a public-private partnership between the private engineering office Escritório Saturnino de Brito and Gurjão's state department of sanitation under the guidance of the sanitary engineer Saturnino de Brito (Dantas, 2003).

The Plano Geral de Obras (1935–43) did not focus on housing, but it had two main neighbourhood plans that influenced local engineers after the 1950s: the Bairro Residencial and the Vila Operária Saneamento. The projects followed a historical trend in Natal's urban history of creating planned communities such as Cidade Nova in 1904, Bairro Operário by Henrique de Novais in 1924, and Bairro Jardim by Giacomo Palumbo in 1929. However, more than following a local trend, Escritório Saturnino de Brito's plan for the Bairro Residencial followed the concept of neighbourhood units developed in the USA by Clarence Perry. The precepts of neighbourhood units emerged with the construction of cul-de-sacs, the separation of community leisure facilities from homes, and heavy car traffic, allied with the local tradition of sanitary interventions such as wide avenues and open public squares (Dantas, 2003). Defending the construction of infrastructure such as schools, public spaces, and avenues within workers' villages, Brito believed that 'educating people with the good principles of hygiene' was the role of the engineers, urban experts, and authorities (de Brito, 1943).

The Plano Geral de Obras, produced by Gurjão and de Brito in 1935, was inspired by the 1924 Plano Geral de Obras de Saneamento created by the engineer Henrique de Novais that implemented the elites' discourse of reforming and expanding Natal through a sanitarian urbanism (Governo do Rio Grande do Norte, 1924). The plan fomented by the governor and the architect referenced the 1904 Cidade Nova's spirit by emphasising sanitation. According to the plan's writers, a good sanitation system connected other public projects without neglecting the aesthetics and the technical aspects of urbanism (Dantas, 2003). The Plano Geral de Obras kept alive the idea that hygiene signified progress and the necessity of implementing a comprehensive set of interventions in the city (Dantas, 2003).

The fact that until 1940 state actions focused more on sanitation projects than housing provision proved to be an initiative to educate people for a well-defined concept of cleanliness connected to modernity and progress. Land surveyors, sanitation technocrats, engineers, and politicians, in a public and private partnership, set up a cultural and social mentality in which sanitary conditions became a state priority in Natal.

The housing crisis turned out to be a recurring subject in the news within state sectors and among Natal's residents throughout the 1940s. Reporting the inauguration of Vila dos Estivadores on 22 July 1940, the local newspaper *A Ordem* pressured authorities to extend the right to housing not only to dockers and to move towards maritime, railway, transport, commerce, banking, and industrial workers (*A Ordem*, 22 July 1941). In a section called *Reflexões*, the newspaper posited that the state had to prioritise housing provision for those on low incomes (*A Ordem*, 22 July 1941). In 1948, supporting President Jânio Quadros' call to action concerning the lack of housing, the largest newspaper of Rio Grande do Norte, *Diário de Natal* defended the 'construction of cheap and hygienic housing for the poor classes' (*Diário de Natal*, 13 January 1949). The population increase in Natal from 60,203 to 103,215 between 1940 and 1950 demonstrated the lack of infrastructure in the city and contributed to the increase in housing deficit (IBGE, 1940). The alliance of the USA and Brazil in World War II emerged as one of the main factors related to this growth. As the war began to influence South American countries, worried about the expansion of Nazism in France and Africa, the USA built the Parnamirim Field military base, in the city of Natal.

In order to build the base, the USA pushed for infrastructural transformations. In 1943, the city implemented a bus transportation system that rapidly replaced the trams, and the international military commando at the Parnamirim Field demanded that the Electricity and Power Company of Northeast Brazil install 500 telephones all over Natal (Souza, 2008). Even with these infrastructural changes, the city's capacity remained insufficient to support the US base. Lacking enough homes, sewage, and water infrastructures for the incoming residents, the city of Natal became overburdened by this military presence and influx of people. At the end of the 1940s, a series of claims denounced a continuous housing crisis: the financial instability of the IAP (*Diário de Natal*, 8 August 1949), a 22 per cent hike in the cost of housing (*Diário de Natal*, 17 September 1948), and a structural reform at the Fundação Casa Popular to remedy institutional deficiencies (*Diário de Natal*, 13 January 1949).

Although World War II and the Cold War enhanced the political use of affordable housing construction in Natal, communist expansion in north-eastern Brazil had already attracted the attention of the elites and the authorities in the 1930s. During the Coluna Prestes communist threat in 1935, Getúlio Vargas already feared agitation in Natal (Camara, 1935). With Vargas back in power in 1951, the federal government soon reintroduced heavy investment in residential units for workers through the Instituto de Aposentadorias e Pensões dos Industriários (Retirement and Pension Institute for Industrialists). Vargas understood that state-sponsored housing could be a way for the state to control workers' and socialist movements. The political use of housing was manifested when the minister of the Civil Office of the Presidency, President Vargas's assistant, Lourival Fontes, affirmed to the national president of the IAPI, Gabriel Pedro Moacyr, that 'constructing houses to sell for members of the institute gives immunity against communism as it gives the member a sense of homeownership'.[7] Almost four months later, the Rio newspaper *A Noite* reported that Moacyr had authorised thousands of industrial workers, residents in the north-eastern state of Maranhão, to acquire a state-sponsored housing unit (*A Noite*, 4 June 1952). Although not heavily emphasised, Vargas's administration regarded the construction of *conjuntos habitacionais* as a means of taming communism in Brazil. However, the political use of housing provision against communism only became clear during the peak of the Cold War in the 1960s.

Alliance for Progress and the case of Cidade da Esperança (1960)

The national housing crisis was once again a frequent topic in Rio Grande do Norte newspapers throughout the 1960s. Capturing electoral anxieties and the importance of housing in Brazil, Juscelino Kubitschek's party's presidential candidate, Marshal Henrique Teixeira Lott wrote an address to the nation, on the front page of *Diário de Natal* entitled 'O problema da habitação'. Lott dissected the 1950s context in which large Brazilian cities ended up having a housing shortage due to demographic growth (*Diário de Natal*, 23 September 1960). Using data from the demographic census and analysing the crisis, Lott advocated the building of at least 2.5 million homes to end this shortage (*Diário de Natal*, 23 September 1960). Lott advocated that the construction of affordable housing for poor people needed to be a task for private companies with state leadership allied to the stimulus of capitalists' interests. According to Lott, the key factor responsible for the emergence of *favelas*, *mocambos*, or occupations, was the 'mismatch between the high cost of construction in the main cities that generated expensive rents and the reduced income capacity of the workers that forces them to occupy empty properties and build informal settlements' (*Diário de Natal*, 23 September 1960). The marshal concluded his article advocating the collaboration of all governmental spheres, the use of worker collaboration to build their own homes, the fostering of construction credit and mortgages,

7 In Portuguese 'A construção de casas para venda aos associados é um privilégio contra o comunismo, pois dá ao associado o sentido de propriedade.' See Vargas (1952).

the development of low-cost building methods and standardised construction materials, and the prioritisation of federal funding to produce mass housing (*Diário de Natal*, 23 September 1960). In one way or another, Lott's piece explained the public housing construction zeitgeist and predicted the incoming changes in the relationship between the state and housing.

Capturing the 1950s solidification of urban studies research centres and public housing agencies all over Brazil and in Rio Grande do Norte, federal and local authorities along with US housing experts and diplomats signed the Alliance for Progress, an economic and technical document in August 1961. The alliance was designed at the height of the Cold War to tackle communist insurgency in Latin American countries demonstrating capitalism's ability to enable a welfare state. In April 1962, the USA and Brazil signed the North-east Agreement in which the United States Agency for International Development (USAID) promised US$131 million over two years to the Development Superintendency of the North-east (SUDENE) (United States Senate, 9 February 1968, 90th Congress). One year later, Rio Grande do Norte's governor Aluízio Alves and the chief of the US mission for technical and economic cooperation, John Dieffenderfer approved 12 billion cruzeiros of foreign aid support specifically to implement the plans of the Alliance for Progress in the state (*Diário de Natal*, 13 April 1963). For public housing, USAID contributed 1 billion and 200 million cruzeiros (*Diário de Natal*, 13 April 1963). As the alliance allocated funding for state-led housing in the north-eastern region and the state of Rio Grande do Norte, urban experts and authorities got together to plan and build the necessary infrastructure.

In September 1963, the government of Rio Grande do Norte sent four people to the Centro Interamericano de Vivendas y Planeamiento (CINVA) in Colombia, an international aided self-help housing workshop sponsored entirely by the Organisation of American States (OAS) (*A Tribuna do Norte*, 26 September 1963). As an international hub of urban experts, CINVA consisted of researchers from Rio de Janeiro, Recife, Natal, Bogotá, Buenos Aires, Lima, La Paz, and many other cities. Among those selected were Natal architect Ubirajara Galvão, the technocrat Domingos Gomes de Lima, the social worker Eunice Pereira de Araújo, and the military police construction worker Eneas Pereira dos Santos (*A Tribuna do Norte*, 26 September 1963). A month later with the support of USAID, SUDENE announced the investment of 400 million cruzeiros for the creation of the housing agency Fundação Casa Popular, an institutional reform demanded by the USA (*Diário de Natal*, 12 October 1963). Alliance for Progress bureaucrats, technocrats, and diplomats understood the importance of assisting Latin America's affordable housing projects for low-income families in not only providing shelter. Social housing for them signified establishing 'a base in well-being and in tangible standards of living that also contribute[d] to productivity' (United States Senate, 9 February 1968, 87th Congress, 1963).

Created in 1951, CINVA became a workshop in the early 1960s that prepared professionals to participate in the Alliance for Progress/USAID housing construction all over the Americas. It was a hub of different professionals based on the work of Jacob L. Crane, a veteran of US public housing administration who had participated in Puerto Rico's home construction projects in the 1940s and coined the term 'aided self-help housing' (Offner, 2019). In this case, 'aided self-help housing' construction meant that governments could consistently help families build their own homes. This was different from the idea of 'self-help housing' in which low-income families built their own dwellings themselves entirely without support.

The Alliance for Progress helped to jumpstart housing projects elaborated by Aluízio Alves and Carlos Lacerda, allies of the USA, the governors of Rio Grande do Norte and Rio de Janeiro, and political opponents of Brazil's left-leaning president, João Goulart. Born in Rio de Janeiro, Lacerda was a journalist and a liberal politician who made his career in national politics by opposing Vargas's and Goulart's administrations, becoming Rio's governor in 1960 – approximately at the same time that Aluízio Alves became governor of Rio Grande do Norte (FGV/CPDOC, Carlos Lacerda, Online). Aluízio and Lacerda were friends, partners, and key political actors in Latin America's Cold War that reached its peak in 1959 after Fidel Castro came into power in Cuba.

Nothing reveals the connection between Cold War politics and the housing of rural migrants in urban areas in north-eastern Brazil more clearly than the case of Natal's Conjunto Residencial Operário Cidade da Esperança. As part of this post-war developmentalist context fostered by SUDENE and the Alliance for Progress, Cidade da Esperança appeared to be one of the largest state-sponsored housing enterprises in Brazil during the early 1960s (de Almeida, 2007). In order to realise this project, the state governor Aluízio relied on USAID, and the recently created regional housing agency Fundação da Habitação Popular do Rio Grande do Norte (FUNDHAP) (de Almeida, 2007).

Along with the construction of Cidade da Esperança between 1964 and 1966, two other neighbourhoods also followed the spirit of the time and tried to emulate international urban planning in Natal. A little bit different from Cidade da Esperança, the neighbourhoods Mãe Luíza and Rocas emerged as state-led self-built housing experiments with much less support from the state. In Mãe Luíza's case, municipal authorities renovated the bus station, built a public space, and a school (*Diário de Natal*, 20 May 1964). Through a working group led by the Catholic Church, the community developed a process through which residents with little construction knowledge were in charge of building their own houses (*Diário de Natal,* 13 March 1966). By 2 March 1965, counting on the labour of 115 men and women, the group had built some new roads and four houses (*Diário de Natal,* 13 March 1966). Because of a lack of cement in the area, donations running out, and the Aluízio Alves government and the mainstream media focusing solely on Cidade da

Esperança, the Mãe Luíza neighbourhood self-built experiment ended, leaving many residents without new homes (de Araújo, 2014).

Contrasting with Mãe Luíza, Rocas's case benefited from greater state participation through FUNDHAP's support of residents' self-built housing promoting the assisted self-help housing advocated by US housing expert Jacob Crane. Alluding to Bogotá's self-built Ciudad Kennedy without mentioning it, the newspaper *A Tribuna do Norte* reported on 5 January 1965, the beginning of Rocas's reconstruction of low-cost houses through a 'mutual support' system, which was 'used in many countries of Latin America' (*A Tribuna do Norte*, 5 January 1965). Originally intended to be funded by USAID, Rocas's was entirely financed by the local government and implemented by the community's residents (*A Tribuna do Norte*, 11 June 1965). In contrast with most self-build projects of the Cold War era that developed new homes, the Rocas's plan only renovated houses (*A Tribuna do Norte*, 26 March 1965). Rocas's renovation was supervised by Domingos Gomes, a local technician who had recently arrived from the transnational housing workshop at CINVA (*A Tribuna do Norte*, 11 April 1965). The restoration processes counted on an estimated 12 groups formed by FUNDHAP's engineers, social workers, a couple of master masons, and residents (*A Tribuna do Norte*, 11 April 1965). FUNDHAP's characterisation of Rocas's reconstruction as 'the project that changed Brazilian housing policy', appeared to be an exaggeration in comparison to other self-build plans in Latin America, such as Ciudad Kennedy in Bogotá, and Cajueiro Seco in Recife since both involved more residents, built completely new houses instead of adapting them, and added more urban facilities than Rocas (*A Tribuna do Norte*, 9 June 1965). The Alves-family-owned newspaper *A Tribuna do Norte* was the main medium responsible for spreading the news that housing developments such as Rocas and Cidade da Esperança were projects elaborated by Aluízio Alves's group, Comando da Esperança (*A Tribuna do Norte*, 7 August 1965). In contrast to Cidade da Esperança that ended up with almost 3,000 houses after its last construction phase, Rocas only managed to rebuild around 200 houses (*A Tribuna do Norte*, 25 July 1965). Following the same path as the Mãe Luíza neighbourhood, the Rocas project stopped its development with the government focusing on finishing Cidade da Esperança.

The literature on Natal's housing construction paid attention to municipal, state, and federal relations with architects and institutes. However, these accounts often missed the transnational connections in which many of the urban experts and financial actors were involved.[8] Alliance for Progress funded planned communities in places all over Latin America, such as Buenos Aires, Bogotá, and Rio de Janeiro. Although different from each other, Natal's Cidade da Esperança

8 Scholars such as Angela Lucia Ferreira, Caliane de Almeida, Felipe Tavares de Araújo, and Sara Raquel de Medeiros, approached the north-east region's housing issues by analysing the government's role in providing these goods and examining the formation of Instituto de Aposentadoria e Pensões in Natal, RN.

and Rocas fitted into this pattern. In particular, the Cidade da Esperança project constructed residential units with facilities such as an elementary school, a chapel, a public market, a local commercial block, a mother's club, a community centre, police headquarters, a football pitch, among others (Galvão, 2007). Inspired by President Juscelino Kubitschek, Rio's governor Carlos Lacerda, the city of Brasília, and the CINVA workshop, Natal's urbanist Ubirajara Galvão created the initial plan of the neighbourhood (Galvão, 2007).

As a technical agency sponsored by the OAS, CINVA trained housing officials from all over the Americas. One of these experts, Galvão was trained to develop the housing sector of the Alliance for Progress in north-east Brazil, more specifically in his hometown Natal (Galvão, 2007). The workshop fostered the idea of sharing knowledge among technocrats and housing experts in the Americas and creating new ways of providing self-built homes for low-income families (Galvão, 2007). Under the Alliance, Galvão and FUNDHAP's Director, Agnelo Alves, also went to Maceió, in the north-eastern state of Alagoas to learn about the low-income housing condominium of 1,000 residential units under construction funded by the USAID (*A Tribuna do Norte*, 11 July 1964). After Galvão's experiences in Colombia and Maceió, he went back to Natal to design and build Cidade da Esperança.

As part of the process to build USAID-funded housing projects, the state government began the registration process for home ownership in Cidade da Esperança in 1964 (*A Tribuna do Norte*, 14 July 1964). The conditions for registration were as follows: not having previously owned any property of any kind, being married or having a family formed by your household, having a family income based on one minimum wage, being over 21 years of age, having been resident in Natal for at least two years, and being in a regularised military situation (*A Tribuna do Norte*, 11 July 1964). Besides these conditions, the applicant needed documentation of their personal life details such birth certificates, marriage certificates, proof of income, professional, residential, and electoral records (*A Tribuna do Norte*, 4 August 1964).

The construction of Cidade da Esperança in the mid-1960s perpetuated the authorities' concerns with sanitation developed in the late 1800s. Hired by the municipal government, the sanitary physician José Carlos Passos developed and implemented a sanitation programme with an informative magazine called *How to Inhabit Public Housing* and a schedule of activities for the Health Centre of Cidade da Esperança (*A Tribuna do Norte*, 21 July 1964). As part of the registration of new residents, the state conducted a survey that collected information on 3,000 applicants in order to reassure the 'sociological and meritocratic character' of their choice (*A Tribuna do Norte*, 19 August 1964). According to FUNDHAP, the socio-economic survey researched the real status of the urban population in Natal and the future residents of Cidade da Esperança (*A Tribuna do Norte*, 19 August 1964). The use of the surveys and the sanitation workshop in these 1960s housing projects demonstrated the interest of the state in learning about the workers of the city. Moreover, it showed a continuation of the practice of registering and learning about the Brazilian working class initiated in the 1890s by private companies and emphasised during Vargas's administrations between 1937 and 1954. Authorities used this information to decide who could live in Cidade da Esperança and encourage the community to promote a modern, healthy lifestyle among the residents.

Similar to Rio de Janeiro's housing development,[9] in Natal the USAID and the Alliance for Progress served specifically to jumpstart the construction of the first batch of residential units. On 30 January 1966, Aluízio Alves left his position as governor while inaugurating Cidade da Esperança with 540 units built out of the 1,000 planned in the first project.[10] Cidade da Esperança had two more construction stages after the first one in 1966; both were implemented by Governor Cortez Pereira without foreign aid and with the help of the federal state and the local agency FUNDHAP.

In 1966, the National Housing Bank (BNH), the largest state habitation development agency, took over the construction of Cidade da Esperança by incorporating FUNDHAP. However, even though the BNH funded most of the housing construction in Natal, the political character of FUNDHAP as a regional state agency lasted for several years. It endured mainly because all three state deputies and Natal's mayor Agnelo Alves were Aliança Renovadora Nacional (ARENA) members – making Rio Grande do Norte the most solid ARENA state in the union with a cohesive pro-US agenda aligned with conservative values.[11] Taking into account the fact that ARENA governed the state, the strong US relations with Natal through the military base in 1943, and President Roosevelt's visit in 1944, by 1967, the US State Department considered Natal, of all the north-eastern cities, 'the most pro America' (United States Department of State, 1967). This political agreement between the US and the Rio Grande do Norte governments strengthened pro-US allies in Brazil and made housing an insurance policy against communism during the Cold War era.

This solid alliance was vital to kickstart the building of Cidade da Esperança during a time of housing insufficiency and an electoral campaign. In fact, Aluízio Alves' plan of building the housing complex was his main campaign promise and helped him to become governor of Rio Grande do Norte in 1961 and elect his ally Walfredo Gurgel in 1966, just like Vila Kennedy and Vila

9 See Benmergui (2018).

10 See more at *A Tribuna do Norte*, 'Povo sai hoje na vigília da despedida com Aluízio Alves', 30 January 1966, *A Tribuna do Norte*, 'Aluízio Alves advertisement to sell homes in Cidade da Esperança', 15 December 1964. *A Tribuna do Norte*, 'Energia de Paulo Afonso para as Casas Populares', 9 July 1964.

11 The ARENA (National Renewal Alliance) Party was founded in 1966 in order to support the military regime that followed the civil-military coup d'état of 1964. Before the coup, the party used to be called the União Democrática Nacional (UDN).

Aliança helped Carlos Lacerda continue in power as Rio de Janeiro's governor in 1964, at least until he was ousted by the military dictatorship.

USAID, electoral politics, and Cidade da Esperança

Between 1961 and 1966 Aluízio Alves created a series of plans for infrastructural changes in the state of Rio Grande do Norte and more specifically its capital, Natal (Medeiros, 2015). However, among all of these projects, Aluízio chose the construction of the planned community Cidade da Esperança as his main campaign platform in 1961. Predicting support from the USA, Aluízio used his concept of housing to attract foreign capital. Soon after his election, he went to the newspapers to appeal for funding for the building of social housing in the west-side of Natal (*Jornal da Tribuna*, 30 August 1964). Contradictorily, during the Alliance for Progress meeting in Punta del Este in 1961, all the north-eastern states sent project representatives to receive funding from USAID through SUDENE, except Rio Grande do Norte. The state alleged a lack of infrastructure to implement any project and rejected the agreement (DeWitt, 2009).

One year after the approval of the alliance in Punta del Este, the US ambassador Lincoln Gordon told President John F. Kennedy that they needed to trust Rio Grande do Norte's governor Aluízio Alves. After Gordon's seal of approval, Alves travelled and convinced Kennedy in person that his state wanted to collaborate in a direct agreement. In 1962, a committee from USAID visited Rio Grande do Norte and declared that the USA wished to establish an agreement with the state without mentioning SUDENE or the Northeast Development Master Plan (DeWitt, 2009). Two years later, through an auction notice in a newspaper, Aluízio publicly announced his intentions of building Cidade da Esperança through a direct agreement between the state of Rio Grande do Norte and USAID, leaving aside the mediation of SUDENE and the Brazilian federal government (*Jornal da Tribuna*, 30 August 1964). While Getúlio Vargas managed to implement his housing policies in Natal in the early 1950s with the support of the state governor Sylvio Piza Pedroza (1951–6), João Goulart (1961–4) did not have the same luck when Aluízio Alves disobeyed the federal government's directions (Pedroza, 1953). Since the beginning of his electoral campaign, Aluízio focused on the modernisation of Rio Grande do Norte using foreign funding and his media companies. With Cidade da Esperança's population slowly growing, Aluízio managed to elect his brother Agnelo Alves mayor of Natal in 1966 and named him president of FUNDHAP (United States Department of States, 1967). The Alves family established a successful method of using housing for political purposes with the support of their own media.

Coalition of media and politics: spreading the modernisation discourse

Aluízio Alves's campaign was inspired by Lacerda's campaign (Trindade, 2003). Five years after Lacerda created the newspaper *A Tribuna de Imprensa* in Rio, Alves formed *A Tribuna do Norte* in Natal. Alves's newspaper followed similar editorial lines to Lacerda's with a regional focus. Both also had slots in local radio stations. In the radio station *Rádio Poty*, Alves had 15 minutes every day for his political speeches (Trindade, 2003).

The media played an important role in building the image of Aluízio with the masses. Combining radio and newspapers, Alves had the power and the means of communication. With headlines such as 'Aluízio: I know that the people are with me' and 'On foot, Aluízio followed the people in the first March of Hope',[12] *A Tribuna do Norte*, the Alves family's newspaper, followed the line established by Aluízio in the rallies, motivating the voter and captivating his allies. In contrast with *A Tribuna do Norte*, *Diário de Natal* offered space in their daily editions for political propaganda from other candidates for the state governorship such as Djalma Marinho (*Diário de Natal*, 23 September 1960). Local mainstream media established its role in society not as neutral, impartial, or in favour of people's common good, but politically engaged with one candidate or another.

A couple of years before Aluízio Alves, Lacerda became the governor of Rio as a stepping stone to his attempted presidential candidacy (Benmergui, 2018). He wanted an efficient modernising administration, focused on expertise and technical knowledge while caring about the poor and the masses by providing affordable housing and trying to renovate favelas. Using the same modus operandi as Alves, Lacerda understood that the transformation of favela residents into homeowners was a way to modernise and formalise the urban poor (Benmergui, 2009). In Rio de Janeiro, the governor created the Guanabara Housing Programme with the financial and technical assistance of the Alliance for Progress. The programme included four communities: Vila Aliança, Vila Kennedy, Vila Esperança, and the initial stage of Cidade de Deus (Benmergui, 2009). Redefining citizenship as purchasing power, governors Aluízio Alves in Rio Grande do Norte and Carlos Lacerda in Rio de Janeiro believed that homeownership would help people living in poverty to become a new middle class.

The Alliance for Progress defined a construction pattern for these housing projects, and the same concept in Rio de Janeiro also took place in Natal. According to Leandro Benmergui, in Rio's case 'the blueprints of individual dwellings already prescribed the layout for future additions as a way to control improvisation, a characteristic of spontaneous construction in the favelas' (Benmergui, 2009). Guanabara Housing Programme conceived Vila Kennedy as an ideal community open to reforms and changes according to different needs of different residents' lives,

12 See both headlines here: *A Tribuna do Norte*, 'Aluízio: Eu sei que o povo está comigo', 23 June 1960. *A Tribuna do Norte*, 'A pé, Aluízio seguiu o povo na primeira Marcha da Esperança', 1 July 1960.

in other words, a modernism different from the rigid vision of modernist Brasília (Benmergui, 2009). This flexible characteristic of the affordable housing complexes in Rio was the basis of Cidade da Esperança in Natal: the Fundação Casa Popular and the BNH built two-bedroom houses in a scheme that allowed the construction of another bedroom by the owner (*A Tribuna do Norte*, 15 July 1964). In this sense, affordable housing developed by Aluízio in Natal and by Carlos Lacerda in Rio emerged as a pillar in the structure of the Alliance for Progress. As a product of the Cold War context, the economic agreement landed in Latin America to promote a liberal citizenship through homeownership in opposition to communism.

Another influence of Aluízio's politics was Brazilian President Juscelino Kubitschek's way of combining politics and urban planning as a main electoral campaign promise in the late-1950s. Kubitschek's 1955 presidential campaign and his building of Brasília directly influenced Aluízio Alves to build Cidade da Esperança to win the Rio Grande do Norte state elections of 1961. Unlike Getúlio Vargas, who focused mainly on state and national private funding, Kubitschek promised an economic national development scheme in alliance with foreign private capital. His speeches during the campaign promised the acceleration of Brazilian development towards this imagined world of modernity with his Targets Plan. His politics incorporated two approaches that could be seen as conflicting: on the one hand, the capacity to deal with the traditional political system based on patronage, and on the other, bringing a new sense of hope for Brazil's development with an economic programme of modernisation that had to overcome state bureaucracy (Maram, 1990).

Kubitschek's programme signified the feeling of hope that represented the political zeitgeist used by institutional politicians to captivate hearts and minds (Benevides, 1991). Brasília's unofficial and official anthems, written by Capitão Furtado, claimed that the city was the capital of hope.[13] The spirit of Brasília as a *cidade da esperança* was shown in the documentary *Brasilia: City of Hope* by Robert W. Schofield and Leona Carney produced by Tangent Films and funded by the Standard Oil Company.[14] Analogous to Kubitschek, Alves emerged as the candidate of hope, the one who campaigned for the integration of the north-east in the national economy and to show the importance of the region, or at least of Rio Grande do Norte in Brazil.

The fact that in the 1960s politicians used their own media outlets and their presence in inaugurating housing complexes in their election campaigns set up a cultural and social mentality in which workers' home construction became a priority for authorities. Public housing in Natal thus emerged as a tool of electing and keeping in power politicians who managed to raise funds and promote their actions through mainstream media. The Alves family and Carlos Lacerda were perfect examples of that.

13 Unofficial anthem of the Federal District with words by Capitão Furtado.

14 See *Brasília: City of Hope* (1960), https://archive.org/details/18204journeytobrasiliavwr (accessed 16 April 2022).

Post-1970: mass housing and economic crisis

After the 1964 coup d'état that ousted left-leaning President João Goulart, Brazil faced a military dictatorship that suspended national elections and centralised all local agencies. In contrast to Getúlio Vargas's coup, the military regime attacked unions and froze wages. Similar to the Vargas governments, this new regime continued to invest in affordable housing and anti-communist projects. However, instead of developing the social aspects of housing, authorities used it more as economic leverage, following the same strategy used in the automobile industry.[15] In the early years of the dictatorship, the recently created federal housing agency, BNH, incorporated local housing agencies. The military control of national institutes meant the reduction of local state autonomy and people's participation (Diário Oficial Lei no. 6.008, 26 December 1973). This centralisation signified a top-down approach that emphasised mass housing construction with a lack of urban facilities.

After years of foreign aid being reallocated to build housing in Brazil,[16] the 1970s authoritarian regime started to use other economic development mechanisms such as the Sistema Financeiro de Habitação [Housing Finance System] (SFH), voluntary savings, and the Fundo de Garantia do Tempo de Serviço [Severance Indemnity Fund for workers] (FGTS) (*A Tribuna do Povo*, 21 January 1965). Between 1970 and 1991, the federal agency SFH together with the BNH built approximately 50,000 housing units in Natal (Bentes et al., 2005). Organised into large and medium-sized condos, these groups of units appeared scattered throughout various neighbourhoods on the periphery of the city, leading to the urban expansion of infrastructure networks throughout the municipal territory. The outcome of this mass investment could be seen in 1980 when Natal was considered completely urbanised.[17] As post-1964 Brazil faced an aggressive investment in infrastructure construction, industrialisation, and an operation against communist agitation, the military regime proved to be a more efficient choice to implement the US Cold War interests in Latin America than a highly polarised international economic cooperation such as Alliance for Progress.[18]

After the transfer of power from General Emílio Garrastazu Médici to General Ernesto Geisel in 1974, the federal housing agency BNH lost regulatory capacities

15 See Joel Wolfe discussing automobility after 1964 in Wolfe (2010). See Sara Medeiros on housing as economic leverage in Medeiros (2007).

16 The US Senate estimated an investment of 23 million cruzeiros spent on technical assistance during the active years of Alliance for Progress. See United States Senate, Committee on Government Operations, *USAID Operations in Latin America under the Alliance for Progress*, Testimony of the Housing Commission of USAID Mission in Brazil, February 1968, 90th Congress, Second Session (Washington, DC, 1969).

17 According to Bentes et al. (2005), Natal's population growth between 1980 and 1990 was of 45.27 per cent.

18 I borrow this idea from Leandro Benmergui when he writes about housing in Rio de Janeiro and Buenos Aires in Benmergui (2018).

in the mortgage and loan system to the private sector (de Mendonça, 1980). While in 1968 BNH dedicated 96 per cent of its loans to housing construction, by 1975 the National Housing Bank only used 60 per cent, and even less in the next year with only 47.1 per cent (de Mendonça, 1980). Moreover, the military regime progressively shifted from providing housing to low-income and destitute families to focusing on the middle and upper-middle classes with a regulatory power transfer to private funds and individuals instead of working-class associations such as the IAPs of the 1940s (Bolaffi, 1981). This change relied on the creation of massive bank loans for workers to purchase a home in a public housing complex. Similar to Argentina's public housing construction, the modernisation of the mortgage market in Natal considered the individual responsible for saving money instead of the collective notion in which groups such as unions (IAPs) were responsible for a general welfare. Post-1970 changes in the public housing market created new economic habits in which individuals searched more often for loans and mortgages, and accumulated debts.

Before housing losing its appeal, the BNH faced its peak of house construction by expanding its programme to the interior of Brazil. Although the BNH focused more on rural towns, the population of Natal still managed to grow. The number of affordable housing residents in Natal, in 1981, impressed regional authorities: only the neighbourhood of Candelária alone with 2,140 houses and 10,700 residents was larger than 125 towns in Rio Grande do Norte, a state with 150 towns by the end of that year (de Andrade et al., 1987). Similar to the Alves family in the 1960s, between 1975 and 1982, the Maia family controlled the state's and the capital's politics with constant investment in affordable housing for middle and low-income earners and used the constructions as promises in their electoral campaigns (Petit, 1990).

Natal's largest *conjuntos habitacionais* were built between 1975 and the 1984 as the table on p. 118 shows.[19] Among all of these housing complexes, Natal received three important *conjuntos habitacionais* that became large neighbourhoods and represented the infrastructural and economic decline that emerged in the 1980s and culminated with the demise of the National Housing Bank: Soledade with 2,485 homes, Ponta Negra with 1,837 homes, and Cidade Satélite with 3,545 homes. All of them were built in different regions of Natal and for different kinds of people. Together with Cidade da Esperança, these projects were connected by similar challenges. All of the neighbourhoods found themselves in a state of decay, with a lack of urban infrastructure and poor public provision by the mid-1980s. Residents of Cidade da Esperança complained about the lack of paving and water (*A Tribuna do Norte*, 25 June 1982). Soledade's residents mostly complained about lack of secondary schools and teachers (*A Tribuna do Norte* 16 April 1985). All of the residents complained about the precarious sewage system, rubbish disposal

19 List of neighbourhoods in Sara Medeiros (2007).

Affordable housing	Number of units	Affordable housing	Number of units
Candelária	2,140	Bairro Latino	564
Conjunto Universitário	192	Jardim Botânico	552
Lagoa Nova I	264	Parque das Pedras	300
Jiqui	623	Parque dos Rios	204
Panorama	260	Felipe Camarão	672
Potengi	379	Gramoré	1708
Lagoa Nova II	174	Nova Natal I	1,863
Igapó	113	Nova Natal II	1,000
Ponta Negra	1,837	Brasil Novo	324
Soledade	2,485	Santarém	2,764
Alagamar	158	Cidade Satélite	3,545
Panatis	123	Santa Catarina	1,722
Pirangi	2,100	Colina dos Flamoyants	504
Pitimbu	1,925	Pajuçara I	992

services, and lack of safety, with growing violence and burglaries (Medeiros, 2018). Throughout the 1980s, Natal's daily newspaper headlines announced that poverty and neglect provoked riots and demonstrations in Cidade da Esperança, Soledade, Ponta Negra, and Cidade Satélite (*A Tribuna do Norte*, 15 November 1984).

The process of abandonment and growing poverty in these four neighbourhoods provides a snapshot that was reflected all over Natal, a feature that denounced the sensation of the 'lost decade' in Latin America.[20] As Brazil faced a deep financial crisis; suffering from corruption claims, the BNH experienced a large disinvestment campaign that forced its closure by the new democratic transitional government of José Sarney in 1986.

Conclusion

The history of state-sponsored housing in Natal is the history of Brazilian politics. Irrespective of the regime in power, housing infrastructure manifested the political. However, when it comes to analysing the Cold War era, housing infrastructure received special attention from local, national, and international authorities and elites. In Natal, as the state prioritised the construction of affordable homes for workers, the authorities aimed to promote the importance

20 The 1980s in Latin America was popularly known as the 'lost decade' due to economic crises faced by most of the region's countries. Most of the issues were related to austerity programmes adhered to by nations that ended up with unpayable foreign debts, inflation, and fiscal deficit.

of homeownership. Legally owning a house engendered a new relationship between workers and their dwelling. As a result of constant migration of people from rural to urban areas in search of jobs and escaping from droughts and floods, authorities redefined homeownership as a way for the state to acknowledge and control a new urban working class while satisfying their demands. As state-led public housing led Rio Grande do Norte workers into a consumer society by establishing where they were going to live and work, planned communities became a way of shaping identity and citizenship. As anti-communist politicians used mass housing projects as promises in electoral campaigns and to remain in power, housing provides a glimpse into the intricacies of electoral politics. Given that foreign funding and expertise in the housing construction circulated throughout the Americas – moving mainly from the United States to Latin America – Natal's housing construction demonstrated the state's attempt to define what it means to be a worker, a voter, and a homeowner in modern Brazil. The state, with the help of private urban planning companies and foreign aid, responded to popular demand and attempted to reconceptualise citizenship.

James Holston's (2008) studies on citizenship and city formation in Brazil provide a helpful guide for interpreting Natal's public housing history. By limiting habitation provisions to regulated workers only, authorities used homeownership to foster a conditioned citizenship. At least until 1970, if residents of Natal wanted to have a house and access to public services, they needed to be a registered worker, thus leaving out of the equation a mass of informal workers and the unemployed. Afterwards, public housing access became even more restricted. Housing agencies tailored housing provision mostly to middle-class citizens. Rather than investigating the agency of citizens as Holston has, the main purpose of this chapter has been to unveil the ideas and practices of authorities directly or indirectly connected to the construction of affordable homes.

Natal's housing experience places the north-eastern city in the debate about the Latin American city as a cultural construct fuelled by battles between modernising reformism and revolutionary actions (Gorelik, 2005). Researching Natal's affordable home construction is vital to understand city formation in Latin America between 1950 and 1970. As Adrián Gorelik argued, the Latin American city became a place of the 'encounter between the discourses and material practices of modernisation and development' during the Cold War (Gorelik, 2005). Like Ciudad General Belgrano in Buenos Aires, Ciudad Kennedy in Bogotá, and Vila Aliança in Rio de Janeiro, the public housing complex Cidade da Esperança, in Natal, emerged as an outcome of the transnational engineering and architecture workshop, CINVA. A key insight here is Leandro Benmergui's discussion about the Argentinian housing complexes Ciudad General Belgrano and Villa Lugano and the Guanabara

Housing Agency's constructions in Rio de Janeiro as contact zones[21] for the encounter between local, national and international flows of power, capital, aesthetics, and expectations about the modernisation of the working masses of Latin America (Benmergui, 2012). Just like the examples of Rio and Buenos Aires, I posit that Cidade da Esperança in Natal, a smaller city than both of these, also emerged as a contact zone, an abstract site of transculturation that may represent, what Gilbert Joseph considered, a place in which the external was absorbed by the local and received new meanings through exchanges and borrowings of a diverse amalgam of behaviours and discourses (Joseph, 1998). Cidade da Esperança, thus, appeared in the middle of the Cold War built by local engineers influenced by foreign expertise. Similar to Amy Offner's analysis of Bogotá's housing construction, fostering public planned communities of private homes in Natal emerged in its own unique form, as a way of transforming 'an unruly population, endowing the poor with new social and political loyalties that would restore order to the country' (Offner, 2019).

In light of the discussion about modernisation efforts, considering the patterned infrastructure that came along with houses, state-led housing in Natal became a way for the authorities to try to attract development to the city and to the state of Rio Grande do Norte. Housing during the era of developmentalism was key in the search for modernisation – a hub that served as an excuse to disseminate a new way of living that left behind radical politics and congregated new hygiene habits with the expansion of the middle class. Shying away from James Scott's (1998) condemnation of high modernist projects as failures, this chapter shows that assessing failure or success would require an examination of many historical actors' evaluations about their places of living, an analysis I did not attempt here.

Although the United States maintained a self-interest by funding housing through the Alliance for Progress (1961–74) in Latin America because of the Cold War, Brazil's adoption of state-sponsored housing at the beginning of the 1960s appeared not as a one-sided demand coming from the USA, but one also proposed by Rio Grande do Norte anti-communist politicians such as Aluízio Alves, Agnelo Alves, and Walfredo Gurgel, who understood the effective political and ideological use of housing provision by the state. Hence, Rio Grande do Norte government's historical use of housing as a way of taming communism was a continuation of a strategy also used by the Getúlio Vargas administrations between 1930 and 1954, that also served to fulfil people's demands for cheap housing. In a closer reading of urbanisation practices and speeches, the political adoption of common signifiers such as *hope* tied to the construction of housing

21 The term 'contact zone' is also used by Leandro Benmergui while discussing housing and the Alliance for Progress in Rio de Janeiro and Buenos Aires in Benmergui (2018). The term was first elaborated by Mary Louise Pratt in Pratt (1992); I situate Natal's housing development in this discussion.

infrastructure and modernising ideals between 1950 and 1970 helped politicians elaborate a sophisticated manner of doing politics and winning elections.

Taking into account the Vargas regimes (1930–45 and 1951–4), the Juscelino Kubitschek administration (1956–61), the João Goulart government (1961–4), and the military regime (1964–86), the provision of housing infrastructure by the state emerged as a convenient insurance policy against communism in Brazil and in Natal, Rio Grande do Norte. Vargas's use of IAPs to register the working class, Kubitschek's creation of SUDENE, Aluízio's co-option of FUNDHAP, the USAID funding of the Alliance for Progress, and the largest investment in Brazil's history in housing through the military regime's BNH, all of these ventures considered, directly or indirectly, along with state provision of modern public housing fostered a sense of private homeownership and a new citizenship.

By planning and building public housing infrastructure while establishing ideals of sanitation, fighting communism with homeownership provision, registering a new urban working class, and using the construction industry for electoral purposes, local, regional, and foreign experts allied with politicians in private and public partnerships, understood that state-led public housing could shape the urban workers of Natal and Rio Grande do Norte into a consumer society based on Cold War moderate politics that could result in a new, modern society in an urbanised and integrated Latin America.

References

Secondary Sources

de M. Benevides, M.V. (2005) *O governo Kubitschek: desenvolvimento econômico e estabilidade política* (São Paulo: Editora Paz e Terra).

Benmergui, L. (2009) 'The Alliance for Progress and housing policy in Rio de Janeiro and Buenos Aires in the 1960s', *Urban History*, 36 (2): 303–26.

Benmergui, L. (2012) 'Housing development: housing policy, slums, and squatter settlements in Rio de Janeiro, Brazil and Buenos Aires, Argentina, 1948–1973' (unpublished doctoral thesis, University of Maryland).

Benmergui, L. (2018) 'Building the alliance for progress: local and transnational encounters in a low-income housing program in Rio de Janeiro, 1962–67,' in A.K. Sandoval-Strausz and N.H. Kwak (eds.), *Making Cities Global Again: The Transnational Turn in Urban History* (Philadelphia, PA: University of Pennsylvania Press), pp. 71–97.

Bentes, D., Ferreira, A., Tinoco M., and Pessoa, Z. (2005) 'Política habitacional de interesse social em Natal: revisando conceitos, formulando estratégias e apontando caminhos', *Scripta Nova: Revista Electrónica de Geografía y Ciencias Sociales* IX (194), <http://www.ub.edu/geocrit/sn/sn-194-27.htm> (accessed 6 April 2022).

Bolaffi, G. (1981) 'Para uma nova política habitacional e urbana: possibilidades econômicas, alternativas operacionais e limites políticos', in L. do Prado (ed.), *Valadares habitação em questão* (Rio de Janeiro: Zahar), pp. 167–96.

Dantas, A.C. de C.L. (2003) 'Sanitarismo e planejamento urbano: a trajetória das propostas urbanísticas para Natal entre 1935 e 1969' (unpublished master's thesis, Universidade Federal do Rio Grande do Norte).

de Almeida, C.C.O. (2007) 'Habitação social: origens e produção, Natal, 1889–1964' (unpublished master's thesis Universidade de São Paulo).

de Andrade I.A.L. et al. (1987) 'Mapeamento e análise dos conflitos urbanos em Natal – 1976–1978', *Relatório de Pesquisa, Natal.*

de Araújo, F.T. (2014) 'A argamassa da casa e do conflito: os usos políticos da construção da cidade da esperança feitos pelo grupo aluizista 1964–1966' (unpublished master's thesis, Universidade Federal do Rio Grande do Norte).

de Brito, F.S.R. (1943) 'Projetos e relatórios. O saneamento de Santos', in *Obras Completas de Saturnino de Brito,* vol. VII (Rio de Janeiro, Imprensa Nacional), n.p.

de Witt, J. (2009) 'The Alliance for Progress: economic warfare in Brazil (1962–1964)', *Journal of Third World Studies,* XXVI (1): 57–76.

de Mendonça, L. (1980) 'A política habitacional a partir de 1964', *Revista de Ciência Política,* 23 (3): 141–61.

FGV/CPDOC Carlos Lacerda, <https://cpdoc.fgv.br/producao/dossies/Jango/biografias/carlos_lacerda> (accessed 5 March 2020).

FGV/CPDOC, IAP, <https://cpdoc.fgv.br/producao/dossies/AEraVargas1/anos30-37/PoliticaSocial/IAP>(accessed 5 March 2020).

Filho, O.C. (2011) 'As políticas de habitação no Brasil (1964–2002) e a reprodução da carência e da escassez da moradia dos trabalhadores' (unpublished doctoral thesis, Universidade de Brasília).

Galvão, M.G. (2007) *Ubirajara Galvão: trajetória* (Natal, RN: Mariz Design e Editor Ltda).

Gorelik, A. (2005) 'The Latin American city', *Tempo Social, Revista de Sociologia da USP,* 17 (1), <www.scielo.br/scielo.php?script=sci_arttext&pid=S0103-20702005000100005> (accessed 6 April 2022).

Holston, J. (2008) *Insurgent Citizenship: Disjunctions of Democracy and Modernity in Brazil* (Princeton, NJ and Oxford: Princeton University Press).

Joseph, G.M. (1998) 'Close encounters: toward a new cultural history of U.S.–Latin American relations', in G.M. Joseph, C.C. Legrand, and

R.D. Salvatore (eds.), *Close Encounters of Empire: Writing the Cultural History of U.S.-Latin American Relations* (Durham, NC and London: Duke University Press), 3–46.

Larkin, B. (2013) 'The politics and poetics of infrastructure', *Annual Review of Anthropology*, 43: 327–43. https://doi.org/10.1146/annurev-anthro-092412-155522.

Maram, S. (1990) 'Juscelino Kubitschek and the politics of exuberance, 1956–1961', *Luso-Brazilian Review*, 27 (1): 31–45.

Medeiros, S.R.F.Q. (2007) 'A casa própria: sonho ou realidade? Um olhar Sobre os conjuntos habitacionais em Natal' (unpublished master's thesis, Universidade Federal do Rio Grande do Norte).

Medeiros, S.R.F.Q. (2015) 'Produção do espaço residencial em Natal: renda, segregação e gentrificação nos conjuntos habitacionais' (unpublished doctoral thesis, Universidade do Rio Grande do Norte).

Medeiros, S.R.F.Q. (2018) *Segregação e gentrificação: os conjuntos habitacionais em Natal* (Natal: Editora da Universidade Federal do Rio Grande do Norte).

Offner, A.C. (2019) *Sorting Out the Mixed Economy: The Rise and Fall of Welfare and Developmental States in the Americas* (Princeton, NJ: Princeton University Press).

Pedroza, S.P. (1953) 'Telegram to Getúlio Vargas communicating the Partido Social Trabalhista's decision in collaborate with his administration', Getúlio Vargas. Classificação: GV c 1953.05.18/3 Data: 18/05/1953, <http://docvirt.com/docreader.net/DocReader.aspx?bib=CorrespGV4&PagFis=10918> (accessed 1 March 2020).

Petit, A. M. C. de M. (1990) *A produção de moradias na cidade de Natal no período de 1977 a 1981* (Rio de Janeiro: Editora da UFRJ, Ippur).

Pratt, M.L. (1992) *Imperial Eyes: Travel Writing and Transculturation* (London: Routledge).

Scott, J.C. (1998) *Seeing Like a State: How Certain Schemes to Improve the Human Condition Have Failed* (New Haven, CT: Yale University Press).

Souza, Itamar de. (2008) *A nova história de Natal* (Natal: Departamento do Estado do Rio Grande do Norte).

Trindade, S.L.B. (2003) *Aluízio Alves: populismo e modernização no Rio Grande do Norte* (Natal: Sebo Vermelho Edições).

Williams, D. (2001) *Culture wars in Brazil: the first Vargas regime, 1930–1945* (Durham, NC and London: Duke University Press).

Wolfe, J. (2010) *Autos and Progress: The Brazilian Search for Modernity* (New York: Oxford University Press).

Primary Sources

Brasília: City of Hope documentary, <www.youtube.com/watch?v=By6qi_V4lGE> (accessed 1 March 2019).

Camara, Mário Leopoldo Pereira da, (1935) *Telegramas sobre preparação de movimento subversivo em Natal, envolvendo elementos do exército* (Natal, Rio de Janeiro). Getúlio Vargas Archive. Classification: GV c 1935.03.16 Date: 16/03/1935 (Vol. XVII/64a e 64b), <www.fgv.br/cpdoc/acervo/arquivo-pessoal/GV/textual/telegramas-sobre-preparacao-de-movimento-subversivo-em-natal-envolvendo-elementos-do-exercito-natal-rio-de-janeiro-vol-xvii-64a-e-64b> (accessed 1 March 2022).

Capitão Furtado, *Unofficial anthem of the Federal District of Brasília*, <https://pt.wikisource.org/wiki/Bras%C3%ADlia,_Capital_da_Esperan%C3%A7a> (accessed 6 April 2022).

Diário Oficial (1973) Lei no. 6.008: 'Dispõe sobre a execução, no Distrito Federal, do Plano Nacional de Habitação popular (PLANHAP) e dá outras providências 26 de dezembro de 1973', <https://www2.camara.leg.br/legin/fed/lei/1970-1979/lei-6008-26-dezembro-1973-357359-publicacaooriginal-1-pl.html> (accessed 6 April 2022).

Governo do Rio Grande do Norte (1924) *Mensagens do Governador do Rio Grande do Norte para Assembléia (RN) – 1890 a 1930,* edição 00001.

Instituto Brasileiro de Geografia e Estatística, IBGE (1940) *Estudos do Gabinete Técnico do Serviço Nacional de Recenseamento, Censo 1940*, <https://seculoxx.ibge.gov.br/images/seculoxx/arquivos_download/populacao/1941_45/populacao_m_1941_45aeb_003.pdf> (accessed 1 March 2020).

United States Department of State (1967) *Classified Airgram from Recife, Pernambuco, Brazil, 1967.*

United States Senate, Committee on Government Operations (1963) *United States Aid Operations in Latin America: Hearings before a Subcommittee on Government Operations.* 87th Congress, First Session (Washington, DC).

United States Senate, Committee on Government Operations (1969) *USAID Operations in Latin America under the Alliance for Progress*, statement of Stuart H. Van Dyke, Director USAID Mission to Brazil, (Friday 9 February 1968, 90th Congress, Second Session, Washington, DC).

Vargas, G. (1952) *Report on his meeting with Gabriel Pedro Moacyr to discuss IAPI's new phase of development*, Getúlio Vargas at FGV-CPDOC 1952.02.04/2. Date: 04/02/1952 URL: <http://docvirt.com/docreader.net/docreader.aspx?bib=CorrespGV4&pasta=GV%20c%201952.02.04/2> (accessed 6 April 2022).

Newspapers

A Noite, 'Milhares de trabalhadores vão ter agora casa própria', 4 June 1952, p. 2.

A Ordem, 'As brilhantes festas da inauguração do saneamento de Natal', 13 May 1939.

A Ordem, 'Reflexões', 22 July 1941.

A Tribuna do Norte, 'Aluízio: Eu sei que o povo está comigo', 23 June 1960.

A Tribuna do Norte, 'A pé, Aluízio seguiu o povo na primeira Marcha da Esperança', 1 July 1960.

A Tribuna do Norte, 'Potiguares têm Bolsas de Estudo: Casas Populares', 26 September 1963.

A Tribuna do Norte, 'Energia de Paulo Afonso para as Casas Populares', 9 July 1964.

A Tribuna do Norte, 11 July 1964, p. 1.

A Tribuna do Norte, 14 July 1964.

A Tribuna do Norte, 'José Carlos Passos fará plano de higiene das casas populares', 21 July 1964.

A Tribuna do Norte, 'Programa de Casas Populares está sendo intensificado na FUNDHAP', 4 August 1964.

A Tribuna do Norte, 5 August 1964.

A Tribuna do Norte, Seção JORNAL WM, 19 August 1964, p. 2.

A Tribuna do Norte, 'Aluízio Alves advertisement to sell homes in Cidade da Esperança', 15 December 1964.

A Tribuna do Norte, 5 January 1965.

A Tribuna do Norte, 'Além de construir FUNDHAP reconstrói', 26 March 1965.

A Tribuna do Norte, 'TRIBUNA política', 11 April 1965.

A Tribuna do Norte, 'FUNDHAP Vai comemorar 1º aniversário de realizações em Benefício do Povo', 9 June 1965.

A Tribuna do Norte, 'FUNDHAP vence "guerra da pobreza" no primeiro ano de lutas', 11 June 1965.

A Tribuna do Norte, 'TRIBUNA Política', 25 July 1965.

A Tribuna do Norte, 7 August 1965.

A Tribuna do Norte, 'Povo sai hoje na vigília da despedida com Aluízio Alves', 30 January 1966.

A Tribuna do Norte, 'Caos e abandono provocam revolta na Cidade da Esperança', 25 June 1982, p. 1.

A Tribuna do Norte, 'Moradores denunciam abandono do conjunto', 15 November 1984, p. 1.

A Tribuna do Norte, 'Soledade enfrenta um total abandono', 16 April 1985, p. 1.

A Tribuna do Povo, 'Gordon declara nos EUA que o Brasil não precisará de ajuda a partir do ano de 1971', 21 January 1965.

Diário de Natal, 'Casas populares e financiamentos', 17 September 1948.

Diário de Natal, 'Habitação', 13 January 1949.

Diário de Natal, 'Crise de habitações', 8 August 1949.

Diário de Natal, 'O problema da habitação', 23 September 1960, p. 1.

Diário de Natal, 'O problema da Habitação', 23 September 1960, p. 4.

Diário de Natal, 13 April 1963.

Diário de Natal, October 12, 1963.

Diário de Natal, 20 May 1964.

Diário de Natal, 'A frente de trabalho João XXIII', 13 March 1966.

Diário de Natal, 'Djalma Marinho empolga a cidade nos últimos dias de sua campanha', 23 September 1960, p. 3.

Jornal da Tribuna, 30 August 1964, p. 6.

5. Contested state-building? A four-part framework of infrastructure development during armed conflict

Clara Voyvodic

Introduction

From the significant economic investment of the Marshall Plan in post-war Europe to the construction efforts in Afghanistan and state-building in South Sudan, infrastructure has long been a tool aimed at stabilising and strengthening fragile states. According to mainstream narratives, infrastructure interventions are intended to provide energy, water, and connectivity crucial to local mobility and businesses as well as opening up peripheries to both national and international markets (Mardirosian, 2010; Collier et al., 2015; Ali et al., 2015). In areas of internal armed conflict, infrastructure interventions also become a strategy of contested state-building. The assumed efficacy of infrastructure in opening previously inaccessible territories to wider licit markets is meant to reduce the reliance of local populations on illicit markets and the monopoly of armed-group control. These assumptions posit that infrastructure projects not only represent state power and presence (and access for state troops as well as state institutions), but also undermine armed-group control over illicit markets and local populations. As such, significant concern in infrastructure interventions is structured around the potential targeting and attack of infrastructure by non-state armed groups. These state-building logics assume that armed groups consider infrastructure interventions a symbol of state power and a threat to territorial control that invite an aggressive response.

This chapter seeks to go beyond these narratives by providing a more nuanced analysis of infrastructure and conflict. I argue that non-state armed groups do not always respond to infrastructure construction with aggression and that the state does not always perceive armed groups as spoilers to development. Drawing from empirical data in Colombia, and supported with evidence from other conflict areas, this chapter proposes a four-part framework on how

C. Voyodic, 'Contested state-building? A four-part framework of infrastructure development during armed conflict' in *The Social and Political Life of Latin American Infrastructures*, ed. J. Alderman and G. Goodwin (London, 2022), pp. 127–150.

infrastructure interventions shape interactions between the state and armed groups. I argue that an over-emphasis on confrontation risks obscuring less visible interactions, including subcontracted, co-opted, and complementary. This framework offers new insights and points of departure for future research into the nature of state-building and development, hybridised governance, parastatism, and the effect on authority-society relations.

In order to critically expand the significance of infrastructure in conflict, this chapter explores four key variations in how armed groups and the state interact that go beyond narrow conceptualisations of armed groups as spoilers: confrontation, subcontraction, co-option, complementarity. While I recognise the value in the orthodox assessment of state and armed-group confrontation around infrastructure, I seek to deepen and problematise its assumptions by drawing from theories and diverse literature on non-state orders, organised crime and criminology, corporate-crime complicity, parastatism, and theories of mediated stateness and hybrid governance. In examining the Colombian case – and drawing supporting evidence from other conflict areas such as the Democratic Republic of the Congo, Myanmar, and Afghanistan – I argue that in the milieu and complexity of one conflict multiple interactions, relationships, and strategies can emerge between armed groups and the state that bely reductive assessments.

In the first section of this chapter, I identify the uncritical instrumentalisation of infrastructure in policymaking of fragile states and conflict-affected regions. I then discuss the relationship between infrastructure and state-building and the limited nature of research on infrastructure in state-building in conflict areas. This literature largely approaches the development of infrastructure as orthogonal to the aims of non-state armed groups and assumes a contentious relationship between existing armed groups and attempts by the state or international interveners in constructing infrastructure. Colombia serves as a useful case study to understand not only how infrastructure construction is a state-building mission but also how it is politicised and weaponised in the context of armed conflict. Colombia particularly exemplifies state-led infrastructure intervention which offers a unique case among the scope of infrastructure in conflict areas where the central state, rather than international actors, leads the development of infrastructure in its peripheries.

Infrastructure, state-building, and conflict

Through infrastructure, governments act not on people directly but through the control of their physical environment; infrastructure is both a good the state provides and an instrument for state power. Influential work by Mann (1984) and Scott (1998) has been fundamental in understanding the physical machinations that enabled the modern Western state to centralise power, capital, and decision-making through the building of roads and railways, communication networks, electrical systems, and organising social relations through the built environment. Mann (1984, p. 189) coined the term 'infrastructural power' to describe 'the capacity of the state to actually penetrate civil society and to implement logistically political decisions throughout its territory'. Through infrastructure, a state does not need to act upon people directly but can do so through the control of their daily physical environment that both makes populations legible to the state and makes the state visible to groups even in its most peripheral territories (where it has limited presence). Scott (1998) argues that the state's survival (control over population in a territory) entails a drive to make society 'legible' where states must 'permeate' their society by reaching the remotest region or social groups. Scott terms this infrastructural project 'high modernism', where authorities and engineers attempt to realise grand plans of social and physical engineering. However, he argues that these ultimately fail to take into account local conditions. While Mann (1999) has critiqued Scott's narrow concentration on the state and his overvaluation of state capacity, Scott's analysis of the physical manifestation of state-building remains an excellent roadmap for developing new insights into its impact.

The critique of top-down infrastructural state-building is not always reflected in literature nor in practice that finds correlations between the absence of infrastructure and stalled development. Weak and conflict-affected states are thought to be products of truncated territorial extension and presence. Therefore, in state-building and peace-building, basic hard infrastructure – such as telecommunications, transportation, energy, and water – are prioritised (Mardirosian, 2010). They are meant to play a strategic and political role in linking rural territories into regional and international networks that strengthen the state and reduce the probability of conflict (Blattman and Miguel, 2010; Collier et al., 2015). This capacity-building approach to infrastructure is apparent in the strategies and agendas of many international interveners. Public works and infrastructure rehabilitation was one of four of the United Nations Development Plan (UNDP) stabilisation programme's primary areas of engagement in fragile states (UNDP, 2016). The World Bank stressed that access to markets was necessary to restore economic growth and generate the preconditions for peace and reconstruction (Ali et al., 2015). This approach to state-building is not new however; as Yuri Gama describes in Chapter 4 on urban politics and public housing in Brazil, long-term interest in international infrastructural development is also apparent with projects such as the Alliance for Progress in the 1960s where the USA – with some assistance from the UK – sought to invest in Latin America's infrastructure in order to halt the spread of communism in the region (Fajardo, 2003).

The infrastructural reach of the state has been linked in determining the probability of armed conflict; Fearon and Laitin (2003) demonstrated how state capacity was critical for variation in onset of civil conflict. In areas of conflict, the absence of infrastructure represents the lack of reach by the central state to all territories within its domain and therefore its ability to adequately govern, including the effective deployment of military strength (Soifer, 2008). In Colombia, Boudon (1996, p. 288) linked the Colombian armed conflict to the central state's inability 'to establish its legal authority and legitimacy throughout the entire national territory.' As Soifer and Vom Hau (2008, p. 222) note, the FARC and Ejército de Liberación Nacional (ELN) (National Liberation Army) 'confront a state that has not built significant infrastructure in the rural regions of the country, but that remains quite effective in the major cities – and particularly in the capital of Bogotá'. Concern with the unstable periphery has led to peace-building and stabilisation missions to make efforts to introduce infrastructure earlier and earlier in interventions during armed conflict (Bachmann and Schouten, 2018).

However, these peripheries are not inherently unstable but rather inscribed with the risks of 'underdevelopment'; as Richard (1992) notes, the concept of centre in Latin America is built around a metropolitan, Westernised ideal of intense capital accumulation and modernism. The periphery was that which in the modernising trend was justified as territory to be penetrated by foreign capital investment against backwardness in order to develop (also see Grosfoguel, 2000).[1] Efforts to build infrastructure in order to stabilise the state reinforces this project; when these 'peripheries' are occupied by non-state armed groups then infrastructure interventions also become part of a militarised penetration that is meant to capture or recapture territories for the state. Infrastructure becomes part of an explicit counterinsurgent strategy. Van de Walle and Scott (2011) document how historically states not only use the provision of services for the purposes of penetration and establishing presence, but also in order to suppress alternative power sources. Infrastructure construction in Afghanistan and Pakistan is aimed at capturing 'Hearts and Minds', where both the provision of goods and the economic growth it produced was meant to undercut the Taliban's appeal and the dependence of communities on the illicit markets controlled by the Taliban (Unruh and Shalaby, 2012). Kilcullen notes that the construction of roads in Afghanistan was meant to 'send a message' to potential spoilers of stabilisation efforts (2011, p. 65). Infrastructure provision becomes explicitly a strategy of counterinsurgency and a reflection of state power in conflict-affected areas.

From this logic of penetration and capture, it is assumed that armed groups would seek to destroy infrastructure in order to retain their control. This counterstrategy has been observed in multiple studies. Balcells (2011, p. 403) notes that 'military-strategic factors normally play a crucial role in the decision to bomb a location … infrastructure locations are most likely to be targeted'. Bertelsen (2016, p. 32) argues that the destruction wrought by the Resistência Nacional Moçambicana (RENAMO) (Mozambican National Resistance) in

1 These strategies of high modernism are not always driven by external actors. In Colombia attempts to control the periphery was not managed by direct international intervention but rather a growing corpus of national elites and bureaucracies (González, 2004).

Mozambique was effectively a deterritorialisation of the state through the razing of its building and erasing of its infrastructure that lost the state its physical territorial presence. These attacks are valuable to the insurgents because they destabilise the state, reduce state capacity, force concessions, and avoid high levels of civilian casualties that could emerge as a reputational cost. In Colombia, infrastructure sabotage, such as attacks on oil pipelines or electrical towers, is considered a primary military strategy by armed groups aimed at producing economic losses and disruptions of service (Beittel, 2014). Wood (2003, p. 23) notes that the Frente Farabundo Martí para la Liberación Nacional (FMLN) (Farabundo Marti Front for National Liberation) in El Salvador shifted its strategy from conventional to unconventional warfare that depended on attacks on infrastructure in order to undermine the government's economic strength as the conflict progressed. Infrastructure's role in civil conflict is its antithesis in state-building; where its construction emphasises the power of the state, its destruction strengthens the position of armed groups. These studies and the visible examples of armed-group attacks on infrastructure have resulted the characterisation of armed groups in the 'so-called' peripheries as spoilers to infrastructure construction since they would naturally oppose any effort to reduce their isolation, autonomy, and increase economic opportunities for local communities that form their support group (de Boer and Bosetti, 2017; Jones and Howarth, 2012).

However, these studies on armed groups' responses to infrastructure projects demonstrate a tendency to examine visible instances of aggression. A focus on more bombastic violence obscures other dynamics and limits understanding of how infrastructure interventions restructure state and armed-group interactions. It also tends to examine pre-existing infrastructure, rather than consider the implications of building infrastructure projects during conflict. Instances of successful infrastructure constructions in territories under armed-group control are rarely examined. As Scott (1998) argues, understanding the local conditions in the 'periphery' is hugely important in determining infrastructure's failure or success. This is even more pressing when conditions at the periphery and centre are also characterised by violence, contested authority, and securitisation. The particular conditions of infrastructure and its impact on conflict areas receive only cursory attention in the literature on peace and conflict, reduced to an indication of state capacity or – in its destruction – armed-group strength. In this chapter I seek to address this gap in the literature and oversight in practice by producing a framework of different interactions between the state and armed groups during infrastructure construction, of which only one results in violent contestation between the two.

Colombia: armed groups, infrastructure, and state-building

In order to exemplify the ubiquity of this framework, I draw from empirical examples of the Colombian conflict and complement with cases from other armed conflicts. This allows me to demonstrate how different types of interaction can proliferate even in the same conflict. Colombia is a perfect case study to explore the variation in interaction. The internal armed conflict in Colombia dates back to the 1960s, formally initiated in 1966 with the foundation of the Revolutionary Armed Forces of Colombia (FARC). The longevity of the conflict has included multiple other armed groups, including the ELN, Autodefensas Unidas de Colombia (AUC) (United Self-Defence Groups of Colombia), and various splinter groups and organised criminal groups that have emerged since. While both the AUC and FARC were disbanded in the last two decades, multiple armed groups continue to operate in the country, including splinter factions of both the FARC and AUC.

Unlike many states with internal armed conflict, Colombia does not resemble the so-called 'fragility' of Sudan, the Democratic Republic of the Congo, or Afghanistan in its institutional framework, GDP, industrialisation, and rule of law. Its urbanisation, development, and institutionalisation in the centre make its absence in the peripheries all the more striking (Calderón and Servén, 2010). It also has a comparatively low level of international intervention in managing its state-building and peace-building processes. While the USA has invested millions of dollars in the last few decades in supporting Plan Colombia, and various other international organisations, including the UN, have assisted in Colombian development programmes, these interventions are much more limited in scope compared to other peace- and state-building projects across the world. Berdal and Zaum (2012) note that while the majority of the state-building literature focuses on the role and impact of international intervention, Colombia has largely managed these processes internally.

This internal process has seen a boom in infrastructural investment in Colombia over the last few decades (Yepes et al., 2013). Since the early 1990s, these interventions have aimed to 'produce the requisite conditions for economic development while conveying the permanence of the state commitment to the region' (World Bank, 2004). In a report for USAID, Hartzell et al. (2011, p. 20) reported that between 2007 and 2009, '50 percent of the 422 billion Colombian pesos in PCIM investments was targeted at infrastructure, including road rehabilitation and construction projects that are instrumental in connecting producers to markets and local populations to the rest of Colombia'. In 2011, the Ministry of Transportation alongside the National Infrastructure Agency also rolled out a list of proposed transportation infrastructure for the following decade that would include US$50 billion worth of investment. This was later incorporated into the 2014–18 Plan for National Development (DNP, 2014), where the infrastructure would provide marginalised communities new economic opportunities, particularly incentivising growth in licit industries, improve access to basic services and general quality of life. Infrastructure was also geared to broader economic growth in the regions including paving the way for mining and oil production industries (UPME, 2017).

This investment in infrastructure in the 'periphery' was not only about development and consolidating state presence, but also, as previously discussed, a counterinsurgency strategy. Zeiderman (2019, p. 8) notes that since the mid-20th century public works 'were conceived as antidotes to insurgency' while in most recent years, infrastructure such as highways 'became a popular index of national security'. The assumption that isolation and poverty (framed as a lack of connection to economic markets) allowed armed groups to flourish unchallenged motivates the construction of infrastructure to remedy this isolation and underdevelopment. The 2003 Democratic Security Programme report by the Colombian Ministry of Defence – under President Uribe's (2002–10) administration – explicitly outlines the protection of infrastructure as the defence of Colombian sovereignty and the consolidation of the rule of law (Ministry of National Defence, 2003, p. 37). The counterinsurgency and state-building elements of infrastructure are echoed in the words of the Major General Solarte, chief of military engineers, who noted that 'the worst enemy of the groups at the margins of the law is a paved road' (PARES, 2015).

Confrontation

The assumptions held by the Colombian government echo those in the international arena; infrastructure interventions strengthen state power and undermine or pressure non-state armed groups in areas of state absence. As a result, the expectation is that armed groups respond aggressively to state-led infrastructure projects. From 1988 to 2012 the National Centre for Historical Memory (2013) registered 1,739 attacks by armed groups against infrastructure in Colombia. Petrol infrastructure was particularly targeted: in the last 10 years, armed groups have attacked petrol pipelines over 1,010 times (Ochoa Suárez, 2019). In the southern department, Nariño, the state-owned Ecopetrol pipeline that ran from end to end of the department was often a military target, particularly by the ELN and occasionally the FARC, who would bomb the pipeline, drawing national attention and producing significant environmental damage.

Violence against infrastructure, however, does not fully capture the security dynamics at sites of infrastructure intervention. Ross (2004, p. 64) observes that government efforts to protect infrastructure by force might actually serve to aggravate and further intensify conflict as armed groups respond aggressively to the perceived threat of armed troops. One of the key offices of the Colombian military is the protection of strategic infrastructure around the country, including oil and gas pipelines, electrical installations, and road networks (Ministry of National Defence, 2011). Large-scale infrastructure is often preemptively accompanied by increased military presence to secure the project. This militarisation often provokes responses by armed groups. Operation Hercules, a 2,000-soldier strong military task force, was deployed into Nariño in order to seize back control of the region from armed groups and to secure the '116 km of oil pipelines, 640 power line pylons, and the Espriella–Río Mataje road project, which connects the ports of Tumaco and Esmeraldas' in the region (Dussán, 2018). For the Awa, a local indigenous group, this presence generated more fear than security. As the Colombian military entered the indigenous territory in their bid to secure the land and existing infrastructure, the community became more vulnerable to aggressive clashes. One Awa leader explained that 'the anxiety is great, the people do not trust that there is military … there is more fear because the people do not know now which [armed] group might come now' (Interview with Awa leader reported in La Liga, 2019). The indigenous community feared that the close presence of the military to schools and community centres not only undermined indigenous autonomous control of their territories but might also provoke attacks by armed groups.

This escalation through militarisation is not only evident in Nariño. Human rights groups across Colombia have critiqued the government's heavy-handed involvement in large-scale infrastructure projects for affecting the security situation as the increasing levels of militarisation lead to escalations of conflict with armed groups (CITPAX, 2012). The construction of the Hidroituango dam in northern Antioquia provides a clear example. The dam's construction – initiated in 2009 – by the Public Enterprises of Medellín sought to generate the largest quantity of hydroelectricity in the country as well as invest in the local communities in the form of better infrastructure and royalties. The infrastructure project was accompanied by high levels of militarisation, particularly in the small urban centres. Troops came in and not only occupied battalions around the mountains and valley of the construction, but also took over buildings in the centre of the village of Ituango. Civil leaders flagged the presence of the military and their proximity to these schools and civilians' homes and petitioned for their removal (Wåhlin, 2015). In Briceño, a town further down the valley near the dam's construction, a confrontation between the guerrilla and the military led to the FARC placing new anti-personnel mines near the school the military had occupied (CCEEU, 2013). While the attack was targeted at the infrastructure, it was a response to the presence of state troops rather than the infrastructure itself.

As Weintraub (2016) notes, the incursion by the state into land governed by non-state armed actors is perceived as a threat, and non-state armed actors will respond through increased violence. This leads to a chicken-and-egg dilemma: where infrastructure is militarised as a supposed target for armed-group attack then it reinforces its importance as an object of war. Increased stationing of state military in order to protect the infrastructure provokes more attacks by armed groups concerned about the presence of hostile armed forces. The effects of securitised infrastructure are not only apparent in Colombia. Lacher and Kumetat (2011) explain that in Algeria attacks were more often targeted against security forces or private guards tasked with protecting pipelines rather than the infrastructure itself. In Myanmar, the government accompanied oil companies to help secure construction from the non-state armed groups; Larsen (1998) reports that, as a result, many of the attacks supposedly against the infrastructure were instead a response to escalating confrontation between Karen ethnic nationalists and the military.

These empirical examples only serve to problematise the causal processes behind the assumption of armed-group response to infrastructure, not to ignore the phenomenon of infrastructure destruction by armed groups. Armed groups have motive to attack infrastructure outside the presence of the military. As noted in Colombia, attacks were still levied directly at infrastructure rather than just military personnel. However, it is worth considering the exacerbating role that militarisation due to perception of aggression, can play in escalating tensions and particularly in making life difficult for local communities now caught between the armed group and the military. The framing of armed groups as potential spoilers and the peripheries as dangerous sites means that states are more likely to send (and private companies more likely to demand) military support to protect these projects. The presence of military personnel in a conflict region poses a threat to armed groups and provokes a stronger response, instead of assuming, *sine qua non*, that armed groups would inherently oppose and attack infrastructural projects in territories they occupy. In doing so, the state-building project becomes concerned with the protection of infrastructure over the safety of local communities. There is little analysis on how attacks are not always responses to infrastructure but rather a response to its securitisation and militarisation. The following sections also serve to illustrate the overgeneralisation of the assumption that infrastructure is intrinsically a target and site of contestation between the state and armed groups.

Subcontraction

States do not always interpret the presence of armed groups as a source of instability and threat for the roll-out of infrastructure. The existence of autonomous militias or armed groups are not necessarily indicators of state failure (Mazzei, 2009; Raleigh, 2014). In many cases these actors will often cooperate or collude with state forces, either out of financial interest, local territorial power, or shared ideology. This collusion does not undercut state capacity but instead can serve its state-building aims. In her exploration of civilian targeting by militias, Stanton (2015) argues that militias do not represent a loss of government control in a territory but rather a strategic extension of its power through both military and paramilitary means. The ability of states to operationalise violence is often a strategy of deniability that can increase their success in repressing counterinsurgency (Rudbeck et al., 2016). Armed groups' knowledge of the local territory and extra-legal violence offer capabilities that the state does not possess (Sanford, 2003). As insurgent groups challenge the state's control, the state can use non-state partners as a source of intelligence, deterring insurgent support in civilian populations through threat, supplying the state with auxiliary forces in operations, and providing plausible deniability (Eck, 2015; Ahram, 2016). This form of patronage allows the non-state armed groups to contract out their capacities to exert violence without accountability in exchange for some level of judicial protection or economic compensation (Eaton, 2006).

While this violence is often used for counterinsurgency purposes, armed groups can also be subcontracted for state-led infrastructural intervention. Armed groups act in order to secure land and prevent civilian opposition to projects. The deployment of subcontracted violence is better presented in the literature on corporate complicity in human rights abuses and conflict. Non-state armed groups, including private security, paramilitaries, and criminal groups, are utilised not for military purposes but in service of corporate profit-seeking (Stephens, 2017). For Reno (2004, p. 623), the collaboration between foreign firms and local strongmen re-emerged in contemporary times as '[t]he cheapest and most efficacious option for indirect management of disorder'. Civil conflict shapes the availability of these extra-legal mechanisms; Bartilow (2019) argues that the expansion of the drug war across Latin America resulted in the privatisation of terror at the hands of corporations, colluding with non-state armed paramilitary or criminal groups. Privatisation allows for more opaque interactions with armed groups, subject to fewer calls for transparency and accountability than governments.

Unlike private companies and foreign corporations, infrastructure is an explicit state-led strategy of state consolidation, economic development, and service provision. While it may have private stakeholders and contractors, it is public funds and political institutions that tender these projects. Grajales (2011, p. 774) argues that the logic of paramilitary violence in Colombia should not be understood as totally separate and independent of state authority, but rather as 'constitutive of logics of competition, accumulation and economic development' that are the elements of state formation. Infrastructure is a more explicit interpretation of these elements; it is a combination of state power and presence as well as private gain. Ballvé (2012, p. 605) explains that in Colombia:

> the paramilitary structures more broadly helped to socialise and materialise the state's territorialisation through repression, infrastructure construction, bureaucratic procedures, agribusiness plantations, NGO activities, political participation, and public services – backed in all instances by ultraviolent force.

Paramilitarism therefore became an integral part of the state's development into the peripheries of Colombia. Subcontracting armed groups to support infrastructure projects does not solely benefit the private sector at the expense of state capacity; it actively contributes to an infrastructural definition of state-building.

These dynamics are apparent in strategies of land clearance and civilian intimidation. Ituango, the site of the Hidroituango dam, was a hotspot of paramilitarism in the late 1990s and early 2000s as state forces and paramilitary groups clashed with the FARC. However, the presence of paramilitarism and massacres carried out in that territory have been linked to territorial cleansing for the large-scale dam project that would begin a few years later. In the 12 municipalities in the area of Hidroituango's influence, there had been 62 massacres recorded in the 10 years before the dam's construction began (Agencia Prensa Rural, 2019). The Rios Vivos group, an environmental and human rights activist organisation, denounced how – under the guise of counterinsurgency and the violence of armed conflict – paramilitary actions were aimed at removing communities from the territories to then build the large-scale dam (Tejada Sánchez, 2018). During the construction of the dam, there has been a clear threat against the human rights activists who have opposed the construction of the project by persisting neoparamilitary, state, and criminal organisations in the territories (Wåhlin, 2015).

In Buenaventura, the largest port city on the west coast of Colombia, violence by paramilitaries is also pervasive and at times linked to the construction of the port. One local leader explains to a journalist: 'what's at the bottom of this violence is not just drug trafficking, but territorial control over the city. It's a tactic of terror to get the people to move from the paramilitary-controlled waterfront areas and flee to the rural zones so that the megaprojects can have free rein. The mafiosos, allied with businessmen, want to force people out through fear' (Molano Jimeno, 2013). This port, however much it enjoys private investment, is a public project: The National Infrastructure Agency granted the Port Society of Buenaventura its public concession so that private companies could invest in the port for public use for Colombia (ANI, 2020). Large-scale projects to expand the port and increase trade and connectivity between Colombia and the world have been accompanied by violence leading to an 'exodus of residents fleeing the threat of death or dismemberment' that 'feeds back to encourage capital investment in the development of port infrastructure' (Zeiderman, 2016, p. 17).

Subcontraction in the Colombian case is often linked to armed groups whose ideology predisposes them to support large-scale development and landowners' interests. However, in the aftermath of the paramilitary groups demobilisation in 2005 and the FARC's demobilisation in 2016, an increasingly fragmented landscape of armed actors presents opportunities for collusion with the state even by actors traditionally ideologically opposed (HRW, 2021). Other conflict contexts around the world demonstrate how non-state armed groups can support large-scale infrastructure projects. In the Niger Delta, the Movement for the Emancipation of the Niger Delta opposed large-scale oil development in the region. However, despite emancipatory rhetoric or secessionist interests, observers noted that aggressive stances towards foreign oil companies was more likely a product of rival national companies recruiting 'some of the Delta militants to harass Chinese oil interests in Nigeria' (Page, 2018, p. 11). Lund (2018) details how palm oil production in Aceh in Indonesia was complicit with both military, para-state militia, and even insurgency leadership in land grabs and dispossession of territory, as well as the brutal suppression of dissent and mobilisation. These do not always involve autonomous armed groups, but rather take advantage of civil conflict for illicit abuse of military power; in Myanmar, military forces were implicated in forced displacement and forced labour of the civilian population in the implementation of infrastructure projects (O'Connor, 2011).

By subcontracting armed groups and extra-legal violence, the state takes advantage of existing civil conflict and disorder to secure infrastructure interventions. Through less licit uses of violence that can evade public scrutiny, the state secures the land through displacement and threat, and removes civilian opposition for the infrastructure project. The issue of legitimacy at the national and international levels therefore means that states and companies are careful to put these forms of human rights abuses out of sight. Armed conflict and disorder – often cited as deterrents or obstacles to the roll-out of infrastructure – can instead be weaponised for the sake of the project at the expense of local communities.

Co-option

In some cases, armed groups may also find they would prefer to make use of state resources that the state finds inconvenient to withdraw (Kasfir, Frerks, and Terpstra, 2017, p. 259). Gledhill (2018, p. 706) argues that 'when authorities are not willing or able to suppress armed groups, structures of opportunity favour insurgency'. While he refers more broadly to civil war onset, such a distinction can be made at the micro level. When states are not willing or able to suppress armed groups in the territories where they seek to build infrastructure, the armed group can take advantage of the infrastructure instead. In his work on the effect of natural resources and war, Ross (2004) contends that lootable resources (such as drugs, precious metals, or any high-value product that can easily be extracted and transported) produces a core set of financing for armed groups that allows them to effectively carry out the necessary actions of controlling a territory and a population. Infrastructure provides its own set of easily lootable resources: either rents, materials, or better logistical capabilities. When their survival is not at risk, armed groups can extract and benefit from the material resources that accompany infrastructure interventions.

In territories of contested statehood, private contractors for public projects are not always able to rely on the state to protect them while they work. Instead, contractors often pay the armed group's 'taxes' in order to gain access to the territory and construct the infrastructure project without violent repercussions. Rent seeking and taking advantage of new infrastructure does not require the armed group to invest into any industry of their own and instead they can take advantage of a new influx of resources while retaining authority in the region.

This relatively easy form of extraction only requires the armed group to be able to leverage sufficient coercive power to assert authority. In Colombia, the Brazilian construction firm Odebrecht was revealed to have paid between US$50,000 to US$100,000 monthly to the FARC in order to have 'authorisation' to construct infrastructure in the areas controlled by the groups. Two executives of the company confessed to these accounts and stated that these extortions appeared in Odebrecht's accounts as 'operating costs' or 'territorial tribute' (Semana, 2017). This arrangement emerges from an agreement between the company and the guerrilla in the 1990s that was mediated by an American group that had gone in to negotiate the freedom of two Odebrecht executives kidnapped by the FARC. Among others, these projects would include the *Ruta del Sol* [Route of the Sun] motorway that connects the centre of Colombia with the Caribbean coast. This insight into co-option raises serious questions about armed group attacks against infrastructure. If the failure to pay 'tax' also leads to violence against infrastructure, workers, and machinery, this complicates measurements of armed-group aggression as a product of isolationist tendencies and anti-state ideologies.

Armed groups can even take advantage of infrastructure they also deliberately target for attack. As noted in the previous section, the ELN and FARC would bomb oil pipelines, gaining swift public condemnation and government response. However, less visible was the daily perforation of the same pipeline by the same groups to use the fuel in cocaine production. Perforations are often referred to as 'artisanal perforations', denoting an unsystematic and ad hoc approach by local civilians (El País, 2014). The overwhelming coverage of how armed groups approach this pipeline is in the irregular bombing and attacks levied against it by the insurgents in the territory. However, armed groups account for a significant proportion of this crude oil theft, which was used for refining cocaine production (Verdad Abierta, 2016). These operations can sometimes involve machinery that the armed groups themselves contribute, attaching valves and spigots to the main pipeline (Portafolio, 2019). Local farmers and indigenous populations would also be employed in this effort; as indigenous leader Francisco Cortes explained, 'with the lack of alternatives, natives do what can be done here. The earth is no longer fertile to plant, and one needs to work, whether scraping coca leaves or stealing oil' (interview recorded in Bonet, 2016). Oil theft becomes part of the local economy under armed-group control. Attacks still occur against the infrastructure, but the armed group is equally content to take advantage and co-opt the pipeline. When the armed group requires a performative demonstration of strength (or is threatened by the possible installation of state military around sections of the project) then it uses force. However, in daily life, the armed group's frequent interaction with infrastructure as a resource and an opportunity stand in stark contrast to more infrequent destructive incidents.

Infrastructure is also strategic for armed groups' control over territory and illicit economies. Across Colombia, armed groups would utilise roads to levy taxes, set up roadblocks, and control territory (Alsema, 2018). In northern Antioquia, the main arterial highways through the town of Amalfi in the north-west were considered vital points of access and control over wider illicit economic markets for the armed group in those territories (Defensoría del Pueblo, 2016). This is not only limited to road infrastructure, Rubio notes a correlation between levels of telecommunication infrastructure in a region in Colombia and the presence of armed groups, in particular those who engage in drug-trafficking activities. He concludes that for drug-trafficking activities to work (a main source of financial income for armed group) 'a minimum physical infrastructure is required' (Rubio, 2005, p. 122). Rather than indicate how lack of state presence (via infrastructure) created the best conditions for armed groups, this finding goes against the 'current discourse in the country' (Rubio, 2005, p. 15).

These dynamics of co-option are not exclusive to Colombia. In the Democratic Republic of the Congo, the M23 rebel military group operating in the North Kivu province became very proficient at extracting money at road blocks, even establishing a de facto customs duty (Schouten, 2019). The Mexican cartels would also take advantage of existing or new infrastructure projects to improve their illicit operations and secure their ability to monitor and control populations (Sullivan, 2014). In Myanmar, leaders of the KIO ethnic armed group began to get involved in mining infrastructural projects, enabling the expansion of services and the construction of infrastructure by enriching themselves. This new group of rebels turned profiteers were perceived as having become 'unfaithful to the KIO' (Brenner, 2015, p. 348). When armed groups exploit easily lootable resources from an external source, this often leads to weakened relationships with local communities. Not only is there little systematic assessment of how armed groups respond positively to infrastructure projects – ostensibly meant for state-building – but also how it affects their relationship with civilian populations.

Complementarity

While co-option and subcontraction are dynamics that involve one side directly benefiting from the other's presence in the territory, other interactions involve more tacit coexistence. Often less visible than acts of aggression or histrionic violence, complementarity emerges when the armed group and the state find a way, despite opposing ideologies or aims, to occupy the same space with the construction of infrastructure projects without taking advantage of the other. This type of interaction is drawn from a rich literature on hybrid or mediated governance. Menkhaus' (2007) analysis of mediated states identifies more pragmatic engagements of the state that allow it to govern alongside non-state actors, just as Boege et al. (2009) argue that the state is merely one actor among many offering services and that hybrid political orders can emerge between the state and informal authorities. There does not have to be a monopoly of authority by one group over all the functions of governance for some form of governance to exist; as long as they enact non-contradictory rules on different functions of governance, multiple agents of authority can exist (Zanker et al., 2014; Gledhill, 2018). When there is an absence of direct threat and neither governance actors are able or willing to extract direct benefit from the other, both the state and the non-state are left with few additional resources in their arsenal.

In constructing infrastructure, the state is able to provide to local communities something the armed group cannot. Armed groups that exert rebel governance often place a premium on being perceived as effective and responsive by local communities to pursue legitimation strategies (Menkhaus, 2007; Arjona et al., 2015, p. 3). However, the desire to be perceived as a legitimate authority by the local community is undermined when the armed groups cannot provide desired infrastructure projects that require significant resources and expertise. In areas governed by armed groups, infrastructure represents a delivery of services that communities are rarely privy to. Therefore, armed groups seeking legitimacy with local communities would be more receptive to allow infrastructure construction that they themselves cannot provide.

In order to avoid confrontation and escalating violence, the state also refrains from militarisation and instead actively seeks to communicate and respond to communities. Staniland's (2012, p. 256) wartime order of tacit coexistence offers useful theorising for this type of interaction. Where both actors operate in the same region and do not wish to confront each other, they allow intermediaries to negotiate terms for both. Unlike confrontational or co-optive interactions, the state can turn to civilian intermediaries to restrict over-taxation or aggressive response by armed groups. They are in turn more responsive to community needs as it is local communities who negotiate their access to the territory. Both the armed group and the state must find ways to coexist or even complement each other's authority; the functions of governance, of protection, of taxation, of service provision, of regulation, and their accountability, can emerge piecemeal and fragmented rather than in competition.

The FARC and ELN have had histories of building simple roads in areas under their control, both for their own mobility and the communities, and as a form of social punishment for transgressions (Pearce, 1990, p. 186; Molano, 2000). However, anything more complex or expensive than a simple path runs into issues of resources and logistics. The state and private contracted companies, on the other hand, have the resources and experience to construct these projects, but do not have knowledge of the territory or a monopoly of force to guarantee safe access to the territories. A significant percentage of Colombia's tertiary roads, which are currently targeted for improvement and maintenance, were in fact constructed clandestinely, and in many cases, by the FARC (Acosta Ariza and Alarcón Romero, 2017, p. 123). Rather than an infrastructure project being solely the proviso of the state, this hybridity is built on the local governance and resources of the FARC with later implementation of state capacity. This interaction is not cooperative or collusive; neither of these authorities is acting in concert, nor a desire to be in concert, with the other. However, the resulting tertiary road and its maintenance is an exercise of complementary governance. In some cases, this complementarity is more direct. In Arjona's (2016, p. 189) influential work on rebel governance in Colombia, she observes that:

> armed actors in Colombia do not directly engage in the creation of health or education systems as insurgents have done in other countries. Instead, they usually influence how local government officials provide those services, and sometimes fund certain projects. Armed groups frequently gave orders to mayors and council members directing expenditures of public funds for infrastructure, education, or health projects.

The state is willing to accept (if grudgingly) the presence of armed groups in order to carry out service provision through the needs of local communities. Armed groups seeking to respond to local needs also direct their own resources and authority at the provision of services by taking advantage of state resources and expertise – not for their own profit – in order to build needed infrastructure in the area.

Similar complementary dynamics in the provision of public goods can be found elsewhere. In Sri Lanka the LTTE did not always reject state institutions in rebel-held territory but instead took over functions of security and justice while permitting the continuation of health and education services by state institutions as they did not have the skills or resources to build these from scratch (Mampilly, 2012, pp. 112–13). In Myanmar, this complementarity also emerges in some townships. In an interview with Kim Jolliffe (2015, p. 53), a community organiser describes how 'the government built all the infrastructure, but the DKBA [ethnic rebel groups] is still in control' as 'they are the ones that people will go to if they need to solve a dispute or get permission for something'. The separate provision of infrastructure and dispute resolution by the state and armed groups produced complementary public goods that created a hybrid form of local governance.

Colombia, like many regions affected by armed conflict, is not always a parcellation of smaller competing sovereignties; as the previous sections noted, states and non-state armed groups can and often do overlap in their territorial presence and their interests. Governance by armed groups can exist concurrently, in reaction to, or involved with the state as it extends its infrastructural presence into areas occupied by armed groups. Kasfir et al. (2017, p. 275) argue that 'armed groups may be in conflict with the national government in one sector, while allowing that government's service provision to continue on rebel-held territory in other sectors'. The provision of infrastructure is not inherently at odds with armed group authority, but it does symbolise a public good that the armed group is often unable to provide. Equally, the state's ability to build the infrastructure does not inherently assure their territorial authority. Instead, both the state and armed group can negotiate the provision of infrastructure as a way to complement both of their authorities. Complementarity offers not only a new way to understand armed groups and state dynamics but also a new lens into how infrastructure and the provision of public goods is not a zero-sum gain in authority.

Conclusion

The state extends, builds, and consolidates its presence through physical infrastructure. While a wealth of literature exists on the nuanced significance of infrastructural roll-out in the context of statehood, economic growth, and legitimacy, it rarely engages with these notions in contexts of conflict. Instead, infrastructure is either an indicator of conflict onset or state failure. Where infrastructure interventions occur during conflict, the preoccupation is with armed groups as spoilers, inherently opposed to processes that strengthen the state and reduce the isolation that allows them to control territory unchallenged. Colombia provides a unique case of this dynamic: a state that is centralised and wealthy enough to invest (along with private stakeholders) its infrastructural power in peripheries that for decades has been occupied by multiple types of armed groups. Infrastructure is not solely for economic development, but also part of a state-building process. By the admission of the Colombian state and in line with existing literature, this connectivity, economic development, and service provision is meant to undercut the power and territorial control of armed groups.

This chapter proposed instead that infrastructure produces four types of interactions between armed groups and states, drawing from the literature on corporate complicity and parastatism, crime-conflict nexus, and mediated stateness and empirical evidence from Colombia as well as other conflict-affected states. While these four types are not necessarily discrete, they do demonstrate crucial distinct characteristics which I detail in the table on p. 144. Variation in these interactions (confrontation, subcontraction, co-option, complementarity) depend on the armed group and the state's perception of threat, capacity to extract resources, and relationship with the local communities. I examined each of these interactions by drawing empirical examples from Colombia, a case study that embodies the overlapping realms of infrastructural state-building from the centre and the (in)secure peripheries occupied by non-state armed groups. However, while this chapter examines each of these interactions statically, they rarely (particularly in Colombia) emerge completely independent of each other. The interactive effects of temporality (a co-optive interaction following confrontation if the state backs down) and concurrence (a confrontational interaction between the state and one armed group at the same time as a subcontracted interaction with another) are worth further examination in future research.

These typologies of interaction are neither meant to discard existing research nor present an exhaustive explanation for the interaction between armed groups and infrastructure implementation. Instead, they offer a framework to explore the affective impact of infrastructure on state-building and violence during armed conflict. The implementation of infrastructure allows local communities to experience the state in new ways, as Diego Valdivieso (Chapter 1) argues in the

Confrontation	**Subcontraction**
1. Escalating security dilemma 2. Securitisation of infrastructure and increased militarisation by the state 3. High threat perception leads to clashes between armed groups and state forces 4. Victimisation of local communities	1. Collusion between state and armed group 2. The state takes advantage of the armed group's capacity for extra-legal violence 3. Forced displacement or threats against civilians opposing infrastructure projects 4. Extra-legal violence supports infrastructure project without implicating the state
Co-option	**Complementarity**
1. Armed group take direct advantage of infrastructure for their own ends 2. State must accept or face retaliation against infrastructure 3. Taxation of contractors 4. Use of infrastructure by armed groups to profit from illicit markets	1. Armed group and state have tacit coexistence 2. Armed group allows infrastructure in order to gain community support 3. The state uses civilian intermediaries 4. Division of public goods provision by armed group and the state (security and dispute resolution vs infrastructure construction)

in the arrival of the state to the islanders of Quehuli in Chile or Sam Rume's analysis of tram development in Ecuador (Chapter 8). During armed conflict, infrastructure becomes a physical representation of the state and armed group's varied interactions that communities must experience. By identifying these different interactions, I seek to address existing gaps in the literature, building a potential framework for how infrastructure reshapes dynamics between states and armed groups and the implications for the civilians caught between the two.

References

Acosta Ariza, M.A., and P.A. Alarcón Romero (2017) 'Análisis de la cantidad y el estado de las vías terciarias en Colombia y la oportunidad de la ingeniería civil para su construcción y mantenimiento'.

Agencia Prensa Rural (2019) '62 masacres en los 12 municipios donde se desarrolla proyecto hidroituango', *La Nueva Prensa*, <https://lanuevaprensa.com.co/component/k2/62-masacres-en-los-12-municipios-donde-se-desarrolla-proyecto-hidroituango> (accessed 6 April 2022).

Ahram, A.I. (2016) 'Pro-government militias and the repertoires of illicit state violence', *Studies in Conflict & Terrorism* 39 (3): 207–26. https://doi.org/10.1080/1057610X.2015.1104025.

Ali, R., A.F. Barra, C.N. Berg, R. Damania, J.D. Nash, and J. Russ (2015) *Infrastructure in Conflict-Prone and Fragile Environments: Evidence from the Democratic Republic of Congo* (Washington, DC: The World Bank).

Alsema, A. (2018) 'Colombia's 10 top corporations, or mafia organizations?', *Colombia Reports*, 29 October, <https://colombiareports.com/colombias-10-top-corporations-or-biggest-mafia-organizations/> (accessed 6 April 2022).

ANI (2020) 'Sociedad Portuario Regional de Buenaventura', Agencia Nacional de Infraestructura, <www.ani.gov.co/proyecto/puertos/sociedad-portuaria-regional-de-buenaventura-sa-21406> (accessed 6 April 2022).

Arjona, A., N. Kasfir, and Z. Mampilly (2015) *Rebel Governance in Civil War* (Cambridge: Cambridge University Press).

Bachmann, J. and P. Schouten (2018) 'Concrete approaches to peace: infrastructure as peacebuilding', *International Affairs,* 94 (2): 381–98. https://doi.org/10.1093/ia/iix237.

Balcells, L. (2011) 'Continuation of politics by two means: direct and indirect violence in civil war', *Journal of Conflict Resolution,* 55 (3): 397–422.

Ballvé, T. (2012) 'Everyday state formation: territory, decentralization, and the narco landgrab in Colombia', *Environment and Planning D: Society and Space,* 30 (4): 603–22.

Bartilow, H. (2019) 'Corporate power, US drug enforcement and the repression of indigenous peoples in Latin America', *Third World Quarterly,* 40 (2): 355–72. https://doi.org/10.1080/01436597.2018.1552075.

Beittel, J.S. (2014) *Peace Talks in Colombia* (Washington, DC: Congressional Research Service).

Berdal, M. and D. Zaum (2012) 'Introduction: power after peace'. in M. Berdal and D. Zaum (eds.), *Political Economy of Statebuilding: Power after Peace* (Abingdon: Routledge), 1–14.

Bertelsen, B.E. (2016) *Violent Becomings: State Formation, Sociality, and Power in Mozambique*, vol. 4 (New York: Berghahn Books).

Blattman, C. and E. Miguel (2010) 'Civil War'. *Journal of Economic Literature* 48 (1): 3–57. https://doi.org/10.1257/jel.48.1.3.

Boege, V., M.A. Brown, and K.P. Clements (2009) 'Hybrid political orders, not fragile states', *Peace Review,* 21 (1): 13–21.

Bonet, E. (2016) 'Siguiendo el rastro de la guerra sucia del petróleo trasandino', *El Confidencial*, 2016, <www.elconfidencial.com/

mundo/2016-08-23/petroleo-colombia-oleoducto-trasandino_1249791/> (accessed 6 April 2022).

Boudon, L. (1996) 'Guerrillas and the state: the role of the state in the Colombian peace process', *Journal of Latin American Studies,* 28 (2): 279–97.

Brenner, D. (2015) 'Ashes of co-optation: from armed group fragmentation to the rebuilding of popular insurgency in Myanmar', *Conflict, Security & Development,* 15 (4): 337–58. https://doi.org/10.1080/14678802.2015.1071974.

Calderón, C. and L. Servén (2010) 'Infrastructure in Latin America', World Bank Policy Research Working Paper (5317).

CCEEU (2013) 'Entre el sueño de la paz y la continuidad de la guerra', <http:/ / debatehidroituango.blogspot.se/2013/06/retiro-de-basemilitar-de-ituango-ya.html> (accessed 6 April 2022).

CITPAX (2012) 'Actores armados ilegales y sector extractivo en Colombia', Observatorio Internacional sobre DDR y la Ley de Justicia y Paz, <www.citpaxobservatorio.org/sitio/images/stories/Resumen_ejecutivo_DDR_Definitivo. pdf> (accessed 6 April 2022) <www.interpares.ca/en/publications/ pdf/Land_and_Conflict.pdf> (accessed 6 April 2022).

Collier, P., M. Kirchberger, and M. Söderbom (2015) *The Cost of Road Infrastructure in Low and Middle Income Countries* (Washington, DC: The World Bank).

de Boer, J. and L. Bosetti (2017) 'The crime-conflict "nexus": state of the evidence.' United Nations University Centre for Policy Research (New York: United Nations Organization).

Defensoría del Pueblo (2016) 'Sistema alerta temprana de inminencia remedios: informe de riesgo no. 029–16', Republic of Colombia.

DNP (2014) 'Plan nacional de desarrollo 2014–2018 "todos por un nuevo país"', Departamento Nacional de Planeacion.

Dussán, Y. (2018) 'Colombia and Ecuador heighten security on shared border', *Dialogo Americas,* <https://dialogo-americas.com/articles/colombia-and-ecuador-heighten-security-on-shared-border/>(accessed 6 April 2022).

Eaton, K. (2006) 'The downside of decentralization: Armed clientelism in Colombia', *Security Studies,* 15 (4): 533–62.

Eck, K. (2015) 'Repression by proxy: how military purges and insurgency impact the delegation of coercion', *Journal of Conflict Resolution,* 59 (5): 924–46. https://doi.org/10.1177/0022002715576746.

El País (2014) 'Defensoría denuncia contaminación en Tumaco por extracción ilegal de petróleo', *El Pais Colombia Prensa,* <www.elpais.com.co/judicial/defensoria-denuncia-contaminacion-en-tumaco-por-extraccion-ilegal-de-petroleo.html> (accessed 6 April 2022).

Fajardo, L.E. (2003) 'From the alliance for progress to the Plan Colombia: a retrospective look at US aid to Colombia', Crisis States Programme working paper no. 28. https://www.lse.ac.uk/international-development/Assets/Documents/PDFs/csrc-working-papers-phase-one/wp28-from-the-alliance-for-progress-to-the-plan-colombia.pdf.

Fearon, J.D. and D.D. Laitin (2003) 'Ethnicity, insurgency, and civil war', *American Political Science Review,* 97 (1): 75–90.

Gledhill, J. (2018) 'Disaggregating opportunities: opportunity structures and organisational resources in the study of armed conflict'. *Civil Wars,* 20 (4): 500–28. https://doi.org/10.1080/13698249.2018.1525676.

Grajales, J. (2011) 'The rifle and the title: paramilitary violence, land grab and land control in Colombia', *The Journal of Peasant Studies,* 38 (4): 771–92. https://doi.org/10.1080/03066150.2011.607701.

Grosfoguel, R. (2000) 'Developmentalism, modernity, and dependency theory in Latin America', *Nepantla: Views from South,* 1 (2): 347–74.

Hartzell, C., R.D. Lamb, P. McLean, and J. Mendelson Forman (2011) 'USAID/OTI's initial governance response program in Colombia', *USAID Transition Initiatives Evaluation,* April.

HRW (2021) 'Left undefended: killings of rights defenders in Colombia's remote communities', *Human Rights Watch,* <www.hrw.org/report/2021/02/10/left-undefended/killings-rights-defenders-colombias-remote-communities> (accessed 6 April 2022).

Jones, S. and S. Howarth (2012) 'Supporting infrastructure development in fragile and conflict-affected states: learning from experience', *Oxford Policy Management,* 3 (6): 13.

Kalyvas, S.N. (2006) *The Logic of Violence in Civil War,* Cambridge Studies in Comparative Politics (Cambridge: Cambridge University Press).

Kasfir, N., G. Frerks, and N. Terpstra (2017) 'Introduction: armed groups and multi-layered governance', *Civil Wars,* 19 (3): 257–78. https://doi.org/10.1080/13698249.2017.1419611.

Kilcullen, D. (2011) *The Accidental Guerrilla: Fighting Small Wars in the Midst of a Big One* (Oxford: Oxford University Press).

La Liga (2019) 'Comunidades de Llorente, silenciadas bajo presión', *La Liga Contra El Silencio,* <https://ligacontraelsilencio.com/2019/11/20/comunidades-de-llorente-silenciadas-bajo-presion/>(accessed 6 April 2022).

Lacher, W. and D. Kumetat (2011) 'The security of energy infrastructure and supply in North Africa: hydrocarbons and renewable energies in comparative perspective', *Energy Policy,* 39 (8): 4466–78.

Larsen, J. (1998) 'Crude investment: the case of the Yadana pipeline in Burma', *Bulletin of Concerned Asian Scholars,* 30 (3): 3–13.

Lund, C. (2018) 'Predatory peace. Dispossession at Aceh's oil palm frontier', *The Journal of Peasant Studies,* 45 (2): 431–52. https://doi.org/10.1080/03066150.2017.1351434.

Mampilly, Z.C. (2011) *Rebel Rulers: Insurgent Governance and Civilian Life during War* (Ithaca, NY: Cornell University Press).

Mann, M. (1984) 'The autonomous power of the state: its origins, mechanisms and results', *European Journal of Sociology/Archives Européennes de Sociologie,* 25 (2): 185–213.

Mardirosian, R.C. (2010) 'Infrastructure development in the shadow of conflict: aligning incentives and attracting investment', Working Paper.

Mazzei, J. (2009) *Death Squads or Self-Defense Forces?: How Paramilitary Groups Emerge and Challenge Democracy in Latin America* (Chapel Hill: University of North Carolina Press).

Menkhaus, K. (2007) 'Governance without government in Somalia: spoilers, state building, and the politics of coping', *International Security,* 31 (3): 74–106. https://doi.org/10.1162/isec.2007.31.3.74.

Molano, A. (2000) 'The evolution of the FARC: a guerrilla group's long history', *NACLA Report on the Americas,* 34 (2): 23–31.

Molano Jimeno, A. (2013) 'Buenaventura, entre la pobreza y la violencia', *El Espectador*.

National Centre for Historical Memory (2013). 'Daño a bienes civiles 1988–2012', Republic of Colombia, <www.centrodememoriahistorica.gov.co/micrositios/informeGeneral/basesDatos.html> (accessed 6 April 2022).

Ochoa Suárez, M. (2019) 'Voladuras: una cruda arma de guerra'. *Semana,* <http://especiales.sostenibilidad.semana.com/voladuras-de-oleoductos-en-colombia/index.html> (accessed 6 April 2022).

O'Connor, J. (2011) 'State building, infrastructure development and Chinese energy projects in Myanmar', *Irasec's Discussion Papers,* 10: 1–22.

Page, M.T. (2018) *The Intersection of China's Commercial Interests and Nigeria's Conflict Landscape* (Washington, DC: United States Institute of Peace).

PARES (2015) 'Vias para los olvidados', *Fundacion Paz y Reconciliacion,* <https://pares.com.co/2015/12/07/vias-para-los-olvidados/> (accessed 6 April 2022).

Pearce, J. (1990) *Colombia: Inside the Labyrinth,* London: Latin America Bureau.

Portafolio (2019) 'Cada mes, la red de oleoductos del país recibe seis atentados', *Portafolio*, 22 September, <www.portafolio.co/economia/cada-mes-la-red-de-oleoductos-del-pais-recibe-seis-atentados-533815> (accessed 6 April 2022).

Raleigh, C. (2014) 'Pragmatic and promiscuous: explaining the rise of competitive political militias across Africa', *Journal of Conflict Resolution,* 60 (2): 283–310. https://doi.org/10.1177/0022002714540472.

Reno, W. (2004) 'Order and commerce in turbulent areas: 19th century lessons, 21st century Practice', *Third World Quarterly,* 25 (4): 607–25.

Ross, M.L. (2004) 'How do natural resources influence civil war? Evidence from thirteen cases', *International Organization.* 58 (1): 35–67. https://doi.org/10.1017/S002081830458102X.

Rubio, M. (2005) 'Illegal armed groups and local politics in Colombia', *Journal of Drug Issues,* 35 (1): 107–30. https://doi.org/10.1177/002204260503500105.

Rudbeck, J., E. Mukherjee, and K. Nelson (2016) 'When autocratic regimes are cheap and play dirty: the transaction costs of repression in South Africa, Kenya, and Egypt', *Comparative Politics,* 48 (2): 147–66.

Sanford, V. (2003) 'Learning to kill by proxy: Colombian paramilitaries and the legacy of Central American death squads, contras, and civil patrols', *Social Justice,* 30 (3 (93)): 63–81.

Schouten, P. (2019) 'Roadblock politics in Central Africa', *Environment and Planning D: Society and Space,* 37 (5): 924–41. https://doi.org/10.1177/0263775819830400.

Scott, J.C. (1998) *Seeing like a State: How Certain Schemes to Improve the Human Condition Have Failed* (New Haven, CT: Yale University Press).

Semana (2017) 'Odebrecht admitió haber pagado "vacunas" a las Farc', 3 April, <www.semana.com/nacion/articulo/odebrecht-admitio-haber-pagado-a-las-farc/517434> (accessed 6 April 2022).

Soifer, H. (2008) 'State infrastructural power: approaches to conceptualization and measurement', *Studies in Comparative International Development,* 43 (3–4): 231.

Soifer, H. and M. Vom Hau (2008) 'Unpacking the strength of the state: the utility of state infrastructural power', *Studies in Comparative International Development,* 43 (3–4): 219.

Staniland, P. (2012) 'States, insurgents, and wartime political orders', *Perspectives on Politics,* 10 (2): 243–64. https://doi.org/10.1017/S1537592712000655.

Stanton, J.A. (2015) 'Regulating militias: governments, militias, and civilian targeting in civil war', *Journal of Conflict Resolution,* 59 (5): 899–923. https://doi.org/10.1177/0022002715576751.

Stephens, B. (2017) 'The amorality of profit: transnational corporations and human rights', in *Human Rights and Corporations* (Abingdon: Routledge), pp. 21–66.

Sullivan, J.P. (2014) 'Narco-cities: Mexico and beyond', https://smallwarsjournal.com/jrnl/art/narco-cities-mexico-and-beyond.

Tejada Sanchez, C. (2018) 'Las aguas turbias de hidroituango', *Semanario Voz.* https://semanariovoz.com/las-aguas-turbias-hidroituango/.

UNDP (2016) 'Funding facility for stabilisation', United Nations Development Programme.

Unidad de Planeación Minero-energética (UPME) (2017) 'Plan nacional de desarrollo minero con horizonte a 2025'.

Unruh, J. and M. Shalaby (2012) 'A volatile interaction between peacebuilding priorities: road infrastructure (re)construction and land rights in Afghanistan', *Progress in Development Studies,* 12 (1): 47–61. https://doi.org/10.1177/146499341101200103.

van de Walle, S. and Z. Scott (2011) 'The political role of service delivery in state-building: exploring the relevance of European history for developing countries', *Development Policy Review,* 29 (1): 5–21. https://doi.org/10.1111/j.1467-7679.2011.00511.x.

Verdad A. (2016) 'El "oro negro" del Catatumbo, atractivo de los grupos ilegales', *Open Society,* <https://verdadabierta.com/el-oro-negro-del-catatumbo-atractivo-de-los-grupos-ilegales/>(accessed 6 April 2022).

Wåhlin, M. (2015) 'Derechos ahogados, responsabilidades diluidas', Swedwatch.

Weintraub, M. (2016) 'Do all good things go together? Development assistance and insurgent violence in civil war', *The Journal of Politics,* 78 (4): 989–1002. https://doi.org/10.1086/686026.

Wood, E.J. (2003) *Insurgent Collective Action and Civil War in El Salvador* (Cambridge: Cambridge University Press).

World Bank (2004) 'Colombia: recent economic developments in infrastructure (REDI)', *Balancing,* <http://Documents.Worldbank.Org/Curated/En/315721468770067432/Pdf/303790CO.Pdf> (accessed 6 April 2022).

Yepes, J., M. Ramírez, L. Villar, and J. Aguilar (2013) 'Infraestructura de transporte en Colombia', *Fedesarrollo,* Cuadernos de Fedesarrollo, 011563.

Zanker, F., C. Simons, and A. Mehler (2014) 'Power, peace, and space in Africa: revisiting territorial power sharing', *African Affairs,* 114 (454): 72–91.

Zeiderman, A. (2016) 'Submergence: precarious politics in Colombia's future port-city', *Antipode,* 48 (3): 809–31.

Zeiderman, A. (2019) 'Concrete peace: building security through infrastructure in Colombia', *Anthropological Quarterly,* 93 (3): 497–528.

6. Competing infrastructures in local mining governance in Mexico

Valeria Guarneros-Meza and Marcela Torres-Wong[1]

This chapter explores how infrastructures relate directly and indirectly to and against mining as a means for defining governance and policy of place by focusing on two Mexican case studies: southern, indigenous communities in Oaxaca and northern, non-indigenous communities in Sonora. By unpicking the mechanisms underpinning the operation of power and governance, we argue that mining infrastructures bring into question the role of government authorities (local, state, and federal), especially their organisation, procedures, and policymaking practices.

Larkin (2013, p. 330) argues that 'the act of defining an infrastructure is a categorizing moment' comprising 'a cultural analytic that highlights the epistemological and political commitments involved in selecting what one sees as infrastructural … and what one leaves out'. In this sense, this chapter understands infrastructures as more than the physical dimensions that a bridge, road, or a thermoelectric dam represent; rather they are a group of relations (often networked) between actors (social and institutional) and mediators (policies, mechanisms, conducts, resources, and discourses) (The Critical Infrastructure Collective, 2022). These relationships underline the importance of state, business and social actors, all of which, through daily living, contribute to the design, development, and maintenance of the infrastructure in place.

Although infrastructures rely on specific technologies, they become systemic when different dimensions beyond the technological, such as administrative and financial, begin to be amalgamated into the technical layer which gave origin to an infrastructure (Larkin, 2013). These new dimensions are developed through the social relations that emanate from what is defined as

1 The authors are grateful to Lourdes Gallardo, Gisela Zaremberg, and Adrián Jiménez for collecting data for the Sonoran and Oaxacan case studies. All data collected was part of the project Conversing with Goliath, funded by the British Academy (Ref. AF160129). Thanks also to the fruitful discussions held with the Critical Infrastructure Collective in May 2017 – sponsored by the Centre for Urban Research on Austerity, De Montfort University – and to the book editors, all of whom contributed to developing this chapter.

V. Guarneros-Meza and M. Torres-Wong, 'Competing infrastructures in local mining governance in Mexico' in *The Social and Political Life of Latin American Infrastructures*, ed. J. Alderman and G. Goodwin (London, 2022), pp. 151–174.

infrastructure and through the affect and sensory apprehension generated in the use-value given to that infrastructure (Harvey, 2012; Shove, 2016). Among the different uses given to their value, Shove (2016, p. 255, f. 3) argues that infrastructures can be carriers of moral and political ideas that 'have various organising and "disciplining" effects on those who interact with them'. In other words, a biopolitical approach can be developed in the study of infrastructures (McFarlane and Rutherford, 2008; Larkin, 2013; Lemke, 2015). Building on these authors' work, the chapter argues that infrastructures can be a mode of governmentality, which is used as a governing technology not only to discipline but also to create capacity of the targeted populations (von Schnitzler, 2008). It is enacted in the everyday through the reproduction of patterns and practices of exclusion/inclusion of citizens' voices and needs into infrastructural decisions affecting their lives and environments. We argue that many of these practices resort to arrangements of governance that not only underpin the operation of power concentrated by political and economic elites, but also by empowered, subaltern groups that challenge dominant views of what infrastructures mean.

In critical literature on infrastructures (Arce, 2014; Kirkpatrick and Smith, 2011; Stirling, 2008) it is common to find the extent to which knowledge differential between experts and non-experts and social movements' protests expose the predatory logics of infrastructures by pointing out the lack of accountability and openness that contribute to community displacement, contamination of their environment and living conditions, and/or fragmentation of social cohesion existing before the infrastructure was built. In other words, these studies underline the exclusionary/inclusionary effects of infrastructures. Because grassroots groups find a voice to express discontent with the dispossession effects that specific types of infrastructures have on their territories (Arce, 2014), we argue that they are able to develop innovative political technologies to challenge appropriation and distribution of resources through, for example, competing understandings of infrastructures that entail the advocacy of collective goods. By engaging in conflict against companies and the state, opposition groups help to reveal the downside of normative assumptions that underpin the operation of power in governance of place (The Critical Infrastructure Collective, 2022:125). Conflict has inspired our understanding of infrastructure; it underlines that infrastructure cannot be divorced from assessments of space; hence it is key to understanding governance arrangements and policy. In this sense, the chapter aims to unpack our understanding of infrastructure through the everyday relationships that different governing technologies unfold. Through the Sonoran and Oaxacan cases, the chapter underlines how everyday life is unavoidably shaped by (mining) infrastructure. In particular, it focuses on local governance institutions to understand how planning is implemented and moulded not only by state actors, but also by businesses and social actors who use infrastructure as a vehicle to either build empowerment or maintain the status quo.

Articulating infrastructure and mining

This chapter addresses in a threefold manner the infrastructures associated to mining: i) those physical materialities (tailings dams, energy generators) that are directly required to either explore or exploit the extraction of a mineral; ii) the physical materialities that are indirectly required to help develop the value chain of minerals, such as roads and other means of communication, storage, transportation, and urban infrastructure that provides services to the immediate community, workers and suppliers in the mining industry; iii) and alternative (social) infrastructures that challenge the mining paradigm as an engine of development, with a particular focus on eco-tourism.

The scale of accumulation that modern mining and other extractive industries generate requires a continuous investment of capital in creating an imposing built environment for its production (Smith in Arboleda, 2016, p. 101). Therefore, it is unsurprising to find debates on mining infrastructure in Latin America alongside debates on development, extractivism and its impact on natural resources (Arboleda, 2016; Bebbington et al., 2008; Svampa and Antonelli, 2010). We find Svampa's (2018) threefold classification of 'development discourses' (orthodox neoliberal; neo-structuralist; radical) helpful for identifying the different meanings given to mining infrastructure.

Orthodox neoliberal and *neo-structuralist* discourses consider the mining sector a contributor to the provision of services that require 'network infrastructures', such as roads, electricity, and telecommunication systems (Graham and Marvin, 2001). These two discourses align to the modernisation ideology which assumes that, through mining, development is achieved not only because communities will have access to services to cover their basic needs (for a critique on this point see Chapter 7 on broadband Internet), but also because employment, their purchasing power, and the scholarly level of the population will increase over time. Because industrialised mining has been blamed for the environmental degradation it generates, through 'sustainable mining' values the neo-structuralist discourse differentiates from its orthodox neoliberal counterpart. Mining corporations – through reports published by different international organisations such as the International Institute for Environment and Development (Bastida, 2002) or resolutions reached by the UN General Assembly (UN, 2012) – are encouraged to minimise the negative impact to the environment through innovative management systems and geo-technologies that not only require information and communication systems, but also models of social responsibility. However, as Vogel (2010) argues, the socio-environmentally-friendly approaches of these types of corporations respond more to risk management decisions required to obtain investment than to genuine commitments of environment and social care as they tend to curtail profit. Hence, the neo-structuralist discourse illustrates the amalgamation of beliefs encompassing mining infrastructure, sustainable technologies, and the global financialisation of the sector.

In Latin America social conflicts are on the increase as anti-mining communities reveal the incompatibility between mining operations and the sustainability of natural resources that local populations depend on to survive (Martínez Alier, 2002; Arce, 2014). While some communities can prevent the implementation of mining infrastructures through different means including social mobilisation, intercommunity alliances, and the development of competing governance models (i.e. self-governance and autonomy) on their lands, most are incapable of counteracting the effects of national mining policies targeting their territories. Anti-mining movements lead us to Svampa's (2018) third and *radical* discourse. It underlines the inadequacies of modernisation and development, especially when social non-state actors reveal in their everyday practice that state-service provision is limited as businesses and government authorities are uninterested in, or incapable of assuming, social responsibility. Refusal to assume social responsibility results from lax/non-existent regulation to mitigate and sanction environmental or human damage or from authorities not having capacity for enforcing the management of scarce resources, such as (potable) water.

The deeply rooted narrative of modernisation in Latin America, which is supposed to be achieved through infrastructure networks, is also associated with peace and political stability. However, the social conflicts generated by mining[2] and the infrastructure that accompanies mining generate instead social instability which is generally targeted with repression. These downsides of mining (or other) infrastructures not only explain anti-mining mobilisations, but also highlight the 'fetishism of infrastructures' (Larkin, 2013). Despite their failures, infrastructures are operated by state and non-state actors on a level of fantasy to symbolise what these actors desire. In this sense infrastructures can become part of a political address to help build identity through the symbolic meaning of traditions and memories given throughout the practice of ceremonies, rituals, or other type of congregation.

Throughout this chapter we will refer to the neo-structuralist and radical discourses as vehicles for potential change. Although Mexican mining policy is framed under the orthodox neoliberal discourse, the resistance and opposition against this orthodoxy merits attention. First, a brief update on the relevance that mining infrastructure has in the country's national policy is provided. A description of the Sonoran and Oaxacan cases is presented before discussing how the former case uses, what we coin, a disciplinarian approach in mining infrastructure. In contrast, the Oaxacan case underlines a potential alternative to mining infrastructure as a means of empowering its community, while also resorting to repressive disciplinarian tactics through the importance of indigenous traditions. Finally, conclusions are presented focusing on the value of the comparison in order to articulate infrastructure, space, and governance.

2 Many of these social conflicts interweave with violent techniques of criminal organisations, such as kidnapping and extortion to ensure that the political context for mega-projects to develop prevails (Gledhill, 2015, p. 25). See also Chapter 5 on infrastructure and armed conflict.

Mining infrastructure in 21st-century Mexico

In 1992, following the spirit of neoliberal reforms implemented since the 1980s, the Mexican government approved a new mining law which allowed foreign companies to develop mining operations in the country. Mexico, like other Latin American countries, benefited from the commodities boom, for example, between 2010 and 2016 the amounts of gold extracted doubled those extracted between 1521 and 1830 (Sariego, 2016, p. 24). In 2013, a series of reforms intensified Mexico's natural resource extraction and although these reforms pertain mostly to the energy sector, such as oil, hydrocarbons, and non-renewable energies, during the same period, minor reforms to mining regulation were also carried out to streamline the issuing of concessions. These reforms spurred the number of contracts with transnational corporations for up to 50 years. By 2019, 10.6 per cent of the national territory was allocated to mining operations (Excelsior, 2019) many of which have been accompanied by increased social conflict (OCMAL, n.d.).

In 2014, a new mining tax was introduced, the Fund for the Regional Sustainable Development of Mining States and Municipalities, commonly known as Fondo Minero (FM) (Mining Fund). Up to 2019, the FM aimed to reinvest the tax paid by mining companies into the states and municipalities from where minerals were extracted. The aim of this tax was to improve the quality of life for residents in extractive communities; 80 per cent of the collection was directed to earmarked social infrastructures chosen and managed by states (37 per cent) and municipalities (63 per cent). These ranged from basic (urban) to more sophisticated infrastructures to improve water and air quality and build renewable energy sites.

In 2016, the Ley de Zonas Económicas Especiales (ZEE) (Special Economic Zones Law) and its subsequent decrees were introduced. It was foreseen that four free-trade zones, including extractive industries, were to be developed in the south-eastern states that were overlooked by the industrial development that occurred after the North American Free Trade Agreement was introduced in 1994. The ZEEs exempted corporations from levies and taxes, while providing them with labour and training subsidies. These free-trade zones require mega-infrastructure projects to which mining and hydrocarbon industries contribute through the demand for services that the different stages of their value chains require: roads and transport, water and energy, and local services (food, housing, administration).

The López Obrador administration (2018–) has not followed the ZEE strategy set by its predecessor. Moreover, the president publicly declared that during his government no more mining concessions were to be allocated (Excelsior, 2019). Yet, rhetorically, infrastructure is still present in the development plans for the country. Examples include the construction and location of a new international airport to relieve Mexico City's current airport from its overcapacity, the Tren

Maya which aims to have an extension of 1,500 km uniting key tourist sites and cities throughout the Yucatán Peninsula, and the oil refinery 'Dos Bocas' in Tabasco State which aims to revive this national subsector after decades of importing gasoline. It is interesting to note that in July 2019 the Tabasco State Legislature approved changes to its penal code intensifying the sanction (high fees and imprisonment) to social protesters blocking the transit of people, vehicles, and machinery. These changes have been referred to as Ley Garrote (Cudgel Law) and they have been criticised because they can potentially work as a precautionary mechanism to repress and control any social protest against the construction of Dos Bocas and Tren Maya.

Case study description

Focusing on the cases of the Sierra of Sonora and the Sierra Norte in Oaxaca State (see Figure 6.1), we will show the extent to which infrastructure has been used by state and non-state actors as a technology to discipline local populations, and also as a means to contest the unequal distribution of resources that define the relationships between local communities and mining corporations. These technologies take different shapes that range from administrative procedures and practices enacted in the everyday by government officials and mining corporations to indigenous autonomic procedures developed within traditional communitarian assemblies, and everyday local management of natural resources. As they are enacted, the reproduction of patterns and practices of exclusion/inclusion are identified in both extremes of the spectrum.

Figure 6.1 Map of Mexico, including two case studies. Wikimedia Commons, designed by Alexis Rojas. Areas indicated on the map added by the authors. CC BY-SA 3.0

The Sierra of Sonora encompasses eight municipalities and the region is known as the Sonora River Region. One of these municipalities, Cananea, has had a strong history of mining. The mine, Buenavista del Cobre (BdC), is owned by Grupo México Corporation. Its productivity focuses on three branches: mineral extraction, construction, and railways. BdC is considered to be the biggest mine in the country and the world's fourth biggest in copper extraction (Milano, 2018). Grupo México bought the mine in 1989 during the privatisation of many state-owned enterprises in the first wave of structural adjustment policies. The presence of BdC has generated labour, environmental and territorial conflicts that have been latent to date (more below). The communities living in the river region are mostly peasant and non-indigenous. Municipal authorities, formed by their respective mayors and councillors, are democratically elected. Historically, municipalities in the region have been characterised by their institutional weakness: limited resources to respond to citizens' needs and demands. In Cananea this void has been plugged to a great extent by the mining company, whose ownership over time has been held by public and private, national and international stakeholders. Although Cananea is no longer considered a 'colonial' mining enclave, it is still a modern enclave insofar as mining hinders diversification of the regional economy and relies heavily on export markets and foreign direct investment.

The renowned 2007 strike, led by Branch 65 of the Sindicato Nacional de Trabajadores Mineros, Metalúrgicos, Siderúrgicos y Similares de la República Mexicana, resulted from changes in labour contracts and working conditions that undermined many of the benefits that the union enjoyed when the mine was state-owned. Concomitantly, the death of 65 miners in another mine owned by Grupo México in Coahuila State prompted Branch 65 to strike as workers were experiencing similar health and safety risks. In 2018, nearly 650 workers and their families were still affected by the strike as they could not be redeployed in the regional mining sector (SoyCobre, 2018). Apart from mining unions, the region has had a history of low-social mobilisation until August 2014 when 40 million litres of acidulant copper were leaked from the pipeline connected to the mine's tailings dam into the Sonora River. Communities along the river began to mobilise demanding not only compensation for the damage caused by the disaster, but also that their communities be consulted by Grupo México and to have a voice in future decisions of infrastructure development that mining production requires.

Oaxaca is a state formed by 570 municipalities, most of which ascribe to an indigenous ethnicity. In 1995, the system of *usos y costumbres* was legally approved enabling indigenous municipalities to elect their political authorities according to customary laws that underline the prospect of autonomy, self-determination, and recognition of difference and diversity. The legal recognition of this system is depicted by some scholars and activists as a political conquest for indigenous peoples in Oaxaca as it represents the legitimation of indigenous political systems vis-à-vis the state (Vásquez, 2008). Capulalpam de Méndez (hereafter Capulalpam), like other Oaxacan indigenous municipalities, is co-governed by three types of authorities that hybridise in practice. First, state municipal authorities (i.e. the mayor and councillors) work very closely with other state institutions, the agrarian authorities. The agrarian authorities date from the Mexican Revolution, which redistributed land to peasants and indigenous peoples to be collectively owned, worked, and maintained by the agrarian assemblies. And third, there are indigenous authorities in the form of the (Consejo de Caracterizados) [Council of the Elderly]. In line with the *usos y costumbres* system, all of these authorities are elected through communitarian assemblies. Capulalpam is not only famous for its use of communitarian assemblies, but also for making decisions about significant political affairs involving territorial organisation.

In this vein, the conflict between the indigenous municipality of Capulalpam and the Canadian firm Continuum Resources has been framed by the local community as an attack against the political rule of indigenous peoples over their jurisdiction. In 2006 Continuum Resources began exploration activity. It had plans to begin an open-cast mine which is considered the worst type in terms of the environmental degradation and contamination of water aquifers given the immensity of the infrastructure that mining extraction requires. Capulalpam, through a long-standing advocacy network formed by academics and environmental and human rights NGOs, has been able to challenge and hinder the renaissance of gold mining in the area. This mobilisation has, on the one hand, been supported by the development of social infrastructure that enabled alternative economies competing with mining such as forestry, handcrafts, and eco-friendly tourism. On the other hand, the mobilisation against mining has generated intimidation and conflict not only against the mining company, but also against the neighbouring municipality of Natividad.

Capulalpam and Natividad have had a long history of gold mining. The mine, Natividad, which still undertakes minor operations in the Natividad municipality, is currently owned by a small Mexican firm, Minera Natividad y Anexas. The production of the mine declined substantially by the mid-1960s, hence the economic wealth that benefited communities began to decline as well, including urban infrastructure and roads required by mining companies. Unlike Capulalpam, Natividad does not ascribe to an indigenous ethnicity. It lacks an alternative economic model and depends on the mine to survive. In 2006, when Canadian investors attempted to reactivate mining operations, Natividad members welcomed the company in the hopes of recuperating the golden years when mining infrastructure was a sign of development and progress. In supporting mining operations, Natividad residents have suffered different types of reprisals by Capulalpam authorities. Intercommunity conflict in building the governance of place is common in many indigenous communities in Mexico (Dehouve, 2000) and in Oaxaca the mining industry has recently accentuated divisions among neighbouring communities (Hernández, 2014).

Fieldwork was carried out in the municipalities of Capulalpam, Natividad, and Oaxaca City in 2017 and 2018. Data collection included informal conversations, newspaper reviews, and 31 semi-structured interviews with local leaders, state officials, mining employees, and academics between July of 2017 and August of 2018. Fieldwork in Sonora was carried out in Hermosillo, Cananea and three other municipalities along the river: Arizpe, Banámichi, and Ures in August 2018. Thirty-nine in-depth interviews were conducted with state-level and municipal officials, mining employees, trade unions, local journalists, and community members.

Coercive consensus: infrastructure as a disciplinarian mechanism

We observed that the way infrastructure becomes a governing technology in the case of the Sonora River Region was through consensual mechanisms that were accompanied by coercion in everyday governance. First, the consensual mechanisms are discussed; these are reflected in government programmes that promote citizen participation and economic development, alongside Grupo México's policy of corporate social responsibility (CSR) which underpins its open participation with different tiers of government and citizens. Through these programmes, we reveal the productive side of infrastructural governmentality by unpacking the level of citizen inclusion.

Participatory budgeting in Cananea

The substantial revenue that Cananea has received from the FM became an unprecedented opportunity for state-government and municipal authorities to begin strategising tax distribution and expenditure. In Cananea the first municipal administration that benefited from this resource was the 2015–18 administration. In the first two years of the administration, the FM was invested in road infrastructure. By 2017, and advised by the World Bank, 40 per cent of Cananea's FM budget was allocated to participatory budgeting, entitled 'Cananea tú decides' (CTD) [Cananea you decide]. Participatory budgeting was originally a mechanism of innovative indirect democracy that originated in Porto Alegre, Brazil. Afterwards, it became the World Bank's flagship of participation under a managerial rubric of transparency and accountability that helped local governments to reduce patronage and corruption (Goldfrank, 2012).

Unsurprisingly, CTD was coupled with ideas of citizen inclusion and associated with the broader discourse on transparency pursued by both municipal and federal governments. The 13 projects voted by citizens prioritised basic infrastructure, such as paved roads, piped water, and sewerage connections or street electrification. Works were built by private firms which tendered for the work commissioned by the municipality and financed by the FM, while citizen groups monitored the works to see if they were built on time and as planned. The number of urban infrastructure projects was noticeable; it more than doubled the investment that the previous two administrations undertook together. Interviews with residents and municipal authorities underlined how this exercise created a space to begin trusting the municipal administration after citizen consultations materialised in the construction of required public works.

For residents it was also the first time they experienced having a voice in the policymaking of their municipality. Their participation was intense for almost 12 consecutive months in which they were asked to propose freely the public works that their neighbourhoods needed, discuss other options suggested by peers, vote for the option which they considered the most important, and oversee that public works were built as planned by municipal authorities. Citizens had to attend meetings after work and at weekends and were exposed to regular municipal government advertisements on social media, radio, and public loudspeakers. It was in the quotidian that citizens were continuously immersed in the importance of urban infrastructure.

Although Grupo México did not have a direct role in the design, management, and allocation of resources of participatory budgeting, during the first three years of the FM's implementation Grupo México staff were the representative of the mining sector in the state-level regional committee overseeing effective expenditure by the fund. The corporation's role in this regional committee can be interpreted as a tactical step to understand how far its taxation can influence not only the design and monitoring of fiscal monies, but also municipal government decisions in infrastructure that indirectly benefit mining.

Sonora River Special Economic Zone (SRSEZ)

Following the same logic as the federal ZEE, the state government of Sonora published the SRSEZ law, which aims to promote the economic development of the region by reactivating agriculture and livestock productivity affected by the 2014 river spill. The law also emphasises the promotion of tourism as one of the first pillars in consuming the goods produced in the region, while also being a new source of income after plans for many of the towns in the region to obtain the category of *pueblo mágico* [magic town – a national recognition of towns that stand out for their attractiveness and customs]. Agriculture, gastronomy, and tourism are accompanied by the importance of road infrastructure which is necessary for transportation of goods and services that the SRSEZ will generate. Curiously mining is neither mentioned in the law nor implementation programme document. However, the regulation (which translates law clauses into implementation) does emphasise that the SRSEZ also promotes mining. Local newspaper articles and interviews with government officials and NGOs also emphasised that the SRSEZ was about developing mining infrastructure. The development of mining infrastructure threatens the communities which have been affected by the 2014 mining spill as more infrastructure involves territorial expansion of mining. It is in the law, regulation, and implementation of policy that infrastructure becomes the pillar of development as underlined by Svampa's (2018) orthodox neoliberal and neo-structuralist discourses.

Grupo México's corporate social responsibility policy (CSR)

CSR introduces concepts of rights, democracy, and sustainability into profit-making understandings of business corporations. Grupo México's CSR began in 2009 in Cananea after three years of labour conflict with the main mining union and which until today has not been completely resolved. The main ethos of the CSR, according to staff, is to be a 'good neighbour' and to ensure that the activities of the BdC benefit the immediate communities. The CSR policy encompasses a community development programme that promotes education and skills training for the community as well as providing seed-corn funding for civil society groups to implement social and cultural projects. Before the FM was implemented, the CSR policy included urban infrastructure projects, but since the introduction of the tax, infrastructural needs are no longer covered by the CSR programmes. However, urban infrastructure and equipment are still an area in which Grupo México invests in other municipalities along the Sonora River that do not receive income from the FM. Particularly, the sponsorship by Grupo México to seven of the municipalities in the region to pay consultancy services to prepare their municipal development plans (2018–21) illustrates how the influence of Grupo México reaches planning projects that involve infrastructure at municipal and regional levels. This illustrates how mining infrastructure, planning of space, and everyday policy are intertwined.

In the subsequent paragraphs, we discuss the coercive side of the disciplinary mechanism that Grupo México uses, alongside other actors, to consolidate mining infrastructure. We observe coercion in the continuous threat caused by the negligent maintenance and expansion of mining infrastructure and in the meaning given by Grupo México and communities to the use of space by infrastructure in everyday practice.

Infrastructure as threat

The 2014 toxic spill from BdC was the result of bad maintenance in one of the pipelines and valves controlling pressure in the tailings dams. Regulations stipulated that there had to be an emergency dam to capture any potential leaks filtrating out of the main dam. However, on the day of the accident, this emergency dam was still under construction (Lamberti, 2018). The origins of the disaster point to the negligence of maintaining mining infrastructure according to environmental regulation, but also the lack of capacity of environmental federal authorities in monitoring that regulation is followed (civil servant). These types of shortfalls from federal authorities and Grupo

México's health and safety procedures were widely disseminated by media, and it was the mining union and human rights activists who alerted communities to the scale of the threat that mining toxic waste generated. Although Cananea's residents have normalised the pollution generated by mining over a century of existence (Madrigal, 2019), the magnitude of the 2014 spill instilled fear into residents of other municipalities along the river. In 2016, a group of residents, organised into Comités de Cuenca Río Sonora (CCRS) [Sonora River Basin Committees], found out that Grupo México was building a second tailings dam 138 times bigger than the community of Bacanuchi, which is closest to the dam construction (Infobae, 2019). The threat of dam construction has consolidated the legal struggle that CCRS have raised through a series of lawsuits presented at the National Supreme Court of Justice, demanding the participation of communities during the decision-making of infrastructural expansion.

Infrastructure as spatial exclusion

Although road signs indicate that Grupo México has funded the construction of some highways connecting Cananea with other municipalities in the river region, the corporation has also closed old roads as it bought land to expand mining infrastructure. As local residents explained, the new Cananea-Bacanuchi road built by Grupo México takes longer because it circumvents its private land. The new road contributes to the sense of isolation that Bacanuchi residents feel as the two town centres (Cananea and Arizpe) which provide them goods and services are each a two hour-drive away. As Grupo México mining activities increase, other privatisation of public space continues to ensure that the infrastructure of the value chain of mining is well safeguarded. For example, Cananea streets that led to the rail tracks have been fenced off, to ensure that no street protest by mining workers stop the trains transporting copper to the foundry and seaport depots. Similarly, all water wells owned by Grupo México, but also owned by peasants who lease them to the corporation, are fenced off to prevent any damage to the pumps directing water to the mining site. Finally, through our observations we found that the leisure centre in Cananea, Plaza Tamosura, the only example of urban infrastructure built by Grupo México, which includes a cinema, an ecological park, restaurants, a gym, and a hotel, provides services that are mostly used by high-ranking employees of BdC, their families, and suppliers who visit Cananea on a temporary basis. However, this excludes a significant portion of Cananea's population who cannot afford the private fees and find the centre hard to access.

Infrastructure as intimidation

As a result of the 2007 strike, which was accompanied by street protests and police repression, Grupo México followed a series of measures to protect the mining site premises in Cananea. These measures increased the security of the mine's entrances, relocated its entrances away from the city centre of Cananea, and as mentioned above increased security of wells. Also, the new road to Bacanuchi has been guarded by armed security as residents need to cross a section that is the corporation's private property. The increased presence of private security safeguarding the mining site and the infrastructure it requires generates an environment of not only exclusion, but also indirect intimidation of neighbouring communities. More direct forms of intimidation were also mentioned by a resident who lived in a rural district and was threatened by the local mafia after the agrarian assembly that he led complained to BdC about its breach of the water contract signed with them.

In summary, the disciplinarian approach has worked as mechanism used by the corporation and state actors to legitimise and impose consensually mining infrastructure, while discouraging communities, through coercion, from becoming a threat to mining. The combination of tactics of exclusion and violence in government and corporation policies also shows that infrastructure is key to understanding governance of place.

Eco-tourism: antidote to mining infrastructure and empowerment of local governance

The way infrastructure becomes a governing technology in the case of Oaxaca is through the opposition shown by the indigenous community of Capulalpam – and the hybrid composition of its local authorities (municipal, agrarian, and indigenous) – to an expansive open-cast gold mining project. In this municipality, opposition to mining is conjunctural to the emergence of a social type of infrastructure which is produced by collaborative effort between local leaders and ecologically progressive state actors. In Capulalpam, social infrastructure works in favour of local, indigenous authorities to maintain its autonomy and contributes to empower local governance institutions against the state-level and federal government narratives of modernisation and development. In this case, social infrastructure in the form of eco-friendly materialities, such as organic-food markets and restaurants, hospitals offering traditional medicine, ecological roads and accommodation, boosted alternative economies. These materialities have undermined the value of mining and have competed against the infrastructure accompanying it (Torres-Wong, 2019).

It has been more than a decade since eco-tourism and the sustainable management of the surrounding forest came to define the social and economic life of community members in Capulalpam. Community companies and collective businesses associated with tourism and the production of sustainable food and furniture provide employment for nearly 80 community members (Arango et al., 2018). In 2007, after a long and continuous municipal administration, the municipality became a *pueblo mágico*. Since then several state agencies are launching innovative marketing plans to expand tourism in

Capulalpam (Secretariat of Tourism, 2020). In our interviews with indigenous leaders, municipal and agrarian authorities emphasise that young men and women are now able to find jobs as tourist guides, food providers, traditional healers, among others. However, the downside of the eco-friendly option is the repressive acts that the Capulalpam authorities use to discipline some of their own community members and neighbouring Natividad. Mining is perceived as a major threat to the existence of Capulalpam; in this regard, actions perceived as capable of undermining anti-mining stances are severely punished.

Opposition and mine production

Opposition to mining has been led by the Capulalpam authorities in their three modalities: the agrarian, the indigenous and the municipal. They received wide support from community members when Continuum Resources began an exploration phase. Strong mobilisations against the corporation's plans began to develop through the broad networks that Capulalpam authorities created with Red de Afectados por la Minería [Network of Those Affected by Mining] and other indigenous forums that questioned and challenged the orthodox neoliberal discourse of economic development. Different street protests, road blockages, and acts of disobedience (vandalising the mine's premises and equipment) took place. As a result, Continuum Resources left, but Minera Natividad has continued to extract gold, albeit in very limited amounts, while plans for expansion still exist.

Opposition reached its climax when the Capulalpam authorities decided to begin a lawsuit in 2015 against Minera Natividad underlining that the land, in which the mine was located, was theirs and not Natividad municipality's, as was commonly believed. This claim accentuated the land conflict that the two municipalities have experienced over the last decade because the Natividad authorities are pro-mining and the entrance to the mine is located within Natividad's administrative boundaries. Before the conflict, Natividad was only a municipal type of authority. Unlike Capulalpam, Natividad does not ascribe to an indigenous ethnicity and does not own agricultural land, therefore indigenous and agrarian authorities were non-existent. Yet, after the legal battle against Capulalpam unfolded, Natividad strategically elected agrarian authorities to make their territorial control claims more legitimate and counterbalance the power of Capulalpam, but without much success.

The reasons Capulalpam opposes mining are threefold. The first, is local awareness of the negative impacts that mining has on environmental resources and people's health. When asked about why they opposed mining, it was common for people to remember previous experiences when the Natividad Mine was at its zenith back in the 1960s (Méndez, 2017). Miners and agrarian authorities of Natividad recall that although levels of employment were high, they also remember poor labour conditions for workers, their poor health, and water scarcity. The second reason is linked to the Capulalpam authorities' battle in the 1980s against the paper company, Papelera Tuxtepec, which was indiscriminately logging their forests. As a result, an environmental consciousness and awareness began to develop that later on became useful in emphasising the pollution of the rivers and aquifers caused by the toxic waste generated by open-cast mining.

The third reason is related to the arrival of the Canadian Minera Cuzcatlán in the Oaxacan Valley Region in 2006, which has generated violent conflict among community members (pro- and anti-mining groups) and several have been killed due to increased intracommunity tension. These experiences have helped Capulalpam authorities to resolutely reject gold mining in their territory despite the promises of development for the local population that generally accompany CSR mining programmes. One of Capulalpam's local leaders recalls the time when an employee from Continuum Resources came to Capulalpam to explain to the authorities how open-cast mining would create jobs and development for the youth. However, the authorities remained firm in their decision to reject the mining project.

Despite the strong opposition, Minera Natividad is still extracting some gold, but our data pinpoint that the extraction has been in a clandestine manner. One of the tactics of the Capulalpam authorities to discourage gold mining has been a series of environmental lawsuits against the company, underlining their lack of compliance with environmental regulation, especially with regard to toxic waste management. As a result, the Federal Attorney for Environment Protection (PROFEPA) closed down the mine while the lawsuit is being resolved. This recent lawsuit began in 2017, but while we were visiting, we observed that the mine was still in operation. Some workers told us that this was just maintenance work, but other residents mentioned rumours that small amounts of gold were still being extracted because of fully loaded lorries travelling during the night. PROFEPA officials denied that this was happening, while one official of the State Secretariat of Economy mentioned to us that low levels of extraction were happening in order to ensure maintenance. Although technically this may be a genuine reason to extract minerals, it is not administratively speaking, as the corporation is avoiding the FM which should be redirected to the Natividad municipality.

Although Natividad obtains few benefits from the operation of the mine (60 jobs for miners and sporadic economic donations to the mayor's office), this municipality continues to support mining. Natividad claims that mining does not represent an environmental threat; on the contrary, the authorities fetishise it through their belief that it will revive the economy and bring development for the population. As is frequently observed in localities where mining companies attempt to carry out operations, deep divisions were created between Capulalpam and Natividad over which of these municipalities has the right to decide whether mining should take place.

One of the lawyers of Minera Natividad argues that the conflict between Capulalpam and Natividad is in reality a territorial dispute and mining is window dressing that indigenous leaders use. In contrast, Natividad residents say that it is the other way around. The conflict is about whether mining should move forward and the territorial dispute is only about how this conflict is presented legally (more below). The fact remains that according to our respondents in both Natividad and Capulalpam, these two towns never experienced a territorial dispute before. Instead we observed that different stances over the implementation of the mining project by Continuum Resources was the main trigger of the conflict.

Infrastructure and identity formation

Before the outbreak of the conflicts, Capulalpam and Natividad were good neighbours, cooperative, and friendly. Capulalpam owns the land where Natividad is located through the agrarian land system. In 1995, a presidential decree confirmed that the owner of the land was Capulalpam. However, Capulalpam shared land and water with their neighbours. When Natividad aligned itself to the interests of the mining company in the 2000s, the relationship between these two communities deteriorated. Capulalpam claimed that Natividad, even when it had a population and the administrative power to govern its community, 'had no territory in which this rule can be proclaimed' (Member of agrarian committee, Natividad). This interpretation is the rationale that the Capulalpam authorities use to prohibit gold mining. As a result, a long legal battle at the Agrarian Tribunal was filed. In 2020, the Third District Court recognised Capulalpam as the legitimate owner of the land, yet it is unlikely that this decision will end the legal battle and contribute to restoring relationships between these neighbouring municipalities.

Opposing views regarding mining operations relate to the different experiences that both municipalities had regarding the mining industry. While Capulalpam is a pre-Hispanic community, Natividad did not exist until a mine was discovered in 1776, becoming a municipality in 1939. People from all parts of the country came to Natividad to work for the mining company and settled in Natividad. The whole town was designed and built to facilitate mining. As of today, visitors can observe that the town is full of one-room constructions that miners used to rent to sleep for a few hours after the end of their shifts in the mine. During the mining peak, Natividad was famous for its cantinas, good restaurants, hotels, and a cinema. Local residents recall with pride that these types of infrastructures did not exist in any other town in the state of Oaxaca. Residents of Natividad looked back with nostalgia to the golden years when the mining company employed nearly 1,000 workers. Several interviewees emphasise that because Natividad was born out of the mining industry it has a cosmopolitan identity made up of different cultures not only from Mexico but also from other countries. Romantic memories of this idealised past help to explain why people in Natividad received with joy the news of the arrival of Continuum Resources and the built environment that accompanies mining. It is in this sense that infrastructure is closely intertwined with space and identity.

Residents of Capulalpam also worked in the mine and several of the leaders who now oppose mining do not hesitate to say publicly that they are the sons of former indigenous miners who were able to improve the quality of life of their families because of the salaries they received for their work in the mine. Yet, while the identity of the people in Natividad was shaped by the extraction of gold and silver, Capulalpam kept its indigenous government which has favoured community decision-making. Because of the geographical closeness to Natividad and that most male residents of Capulalpam worked for the mining company (only 10 minutes away), it would have been expected that Capulalpam would become a mining town like Natividad. However, indigenous leaders never allowed the opening of foreign-owned restaurants or cantinas within the jurisdiction of Capulalpam. According to a Natividad resident, the people from Capulalpam were always very protective of their traditions.

Their tendency towards a more radical anti-mining stance has been shaped by indigenous collective systems of decision-making partly empowered by the collective resistance against Papelera Tuxtepec, which required cooperative mechanisms of self-organisation and management. In 2000, the local authorities took advantage of an opportunity to develop eco-tourism made available by the State Secretariat of Tourism. Tourism officials identified that developing an eco-tourism project was viable because most people in Capulalpam were professionals and at the same time maintained a strong political organisation based on customary laws. The Commission for the Development of Indigenous Peoples provided the funding for the eco-tourism project and Capulalpam provided labour to build the required infrastructure. State funding was aimed at restoring old indigenous architecture and improving the quality of services to make the community attractive. Decades ago, under a government initiative, traditional, indigenous roof tiles were replaced by more functional tin roofs. Hence, the restoration of the older indigenous roofs began alongside the painting of houses according to a specific colour scheme provided by the Secretariat of Tourism.

As mentioned above, local authorities contributed to the project with materials and labour, one leader explains, 'We put out the wood, the gravel, the sand, the stones, and the *tequio* (unpaid but recognised work by indigenous members).' As a result of joint efforts, eco-tourism is now a source of employment for Capulalpam residents. Local authorities received economic resources from the state but retained the power to develop a vision of tourist activities organised by community companies; they began to administer income without state interference. In contrast to Natividad, the development of eco-tourism as a new economic model contributed to the reinforcement of anti-mining attitudes in Capulalpam as part of their collective identity.

Empowerment and repression

The most important weapon that Capulalpam used to prohibit mining for good was its system of collective decision-making anchored in customary law, hybridised with state institutions. Indigenous Mexican communities are governed by values encompassed by what anthropological studies call the Mesoamerican civilising matrix (Bonfil in Sierra and López, 2013). The state through administrative and agrarian laws defines the legal framework to which indigenous communities have to align, but the community organisation also responds to its customary law. This underlines the 'collective', bringing local authorities into account while promoting commitment, respect, reciprocity, cooperation and collective work (Sierra and López, 2013, p. 33). These values are reflected in the community's overall organisation, where in principle, the municipal authorities (mayor and councillors) as well as the agrarian commission (president, secretary, and treasurer), and the indigenous council (Consejo de Caraterizados), are subject to the Communitarian Assembly, the highest authoritative body. This type of organisation was immediately recognised in our interviews with Capulalpam authorities.

Communitarian Assemblies served to reinforce anti-mining stances. Through collective scrutiny of positions to ban mining activities, local authorities were able to ensure that all community members complied with their decision to prohibit the entry of the Canadian company. We found that in practice the power of the agrarian commission was key to making decisions with regard to mining. Although the Communitarian Assembly met regularly and governing plans were presented and discussed, we were told that the proposals presented were led by the agrarian commission's president and agreed by the rest of the Communitarian Assembly. But as Natividad's local leader commented, not all people attended the assemblies and if they disagreed with the general decision fines or other informal sanctions, such as house evictions, took place.

These types of practices by the Capulalpam authorities have ensured that the threat of gold mining and the infrastructure accompanying it have not taken place, but instead repression against its own community was regularly used. Several residents and authorities mentioned that repressive acts were also perpetrated against Natividad through sanctioning tactics that resulted from land conflict; the most mentioned one was an infrastructural intervention – the cutting off of the water supply to Natividad in 2003 after the Capulalpam authorities broke the water pipes. Because the water source is within Capulalpam 'territory', they had the capacity to interrupt provision to Natividad. A resident of Capulalpam and the former municipal authority recalls that he did not agree with the decision to cut off water to Natividad, 'they were our brothers and sisters, there were children there, but the authorities made their decision and there was nothing we could do'.

Repression alone would not have been as effective without the political decisions that the Capulalpam authorities had made in the past and which have helped to provide economic wellbeing to the community. As a result of the mobilisation against logging in the 1980s, opportunities to develop forestry activities emerged. In turn, they became a gateway to other economic activities such as wood carving and eco-tourism. Over time they have developed and provided the community with income. Capulalpam's nomination as a *pueblo mágico* has been particularly helpful in developing local businesses dedicated to tourism, such as small hotels and restaurants selling local produce. In order to thrive, these economic activities, especially forestry and eco-tourism, work as opposition to open-cast, gold mining activities.

Capulalpam has thereby become a community with a more diversified economy that can dispense with gold mining. It has a governing institutional assemblage that empowers its local authorities, led by the agrarian commission, which have shown their resourcefulness: to accuse the mining corporation of violating environmental regulation, to challenge Natividad's local-government status by claiming that its lack of territory is supported by archival evidence and to build a network of alliances with state-level politicians, national and international academics and NGOs, and indigenous umbrella organisations that have fought not only against mining, but also against the orthodox neoliberal discourse of development. It is this conjuncture of factors that render Capulalpam as a potential example of radical discourse insofar as local customary laws fill-in the void left by the state's inability to respond consistently to social and environmental responsibilities. However, the potential that the Capulalpam case embodies is curtailed by the exclusion and violence inflicted on Natividad and some of its community members. Violence and exclusion break the reciprocity, interconnectedness, and respect for life that broader values of alternative transformative projects within the radical discourse pursue. Equally, the benefits obtained from the *pueblo mágico* programme can raise questions on the extent to which Capulalpam is really overcoming the neo-structuralist discourse of development.

Conclusions

Through the Sonoran and Oaxacan cases we have shown how infrastructures work both as a governing technology to discipline populations and to produce capacity or empower. In Sonora the governing technology has shown that discipline is achieved through a more conventional approach that combines consensual and coercive mechanisms to maintain the power of the traditional elites, in particular, local-government authorities and Grupo México and the broader mining industry. The consensual mechanisms have been identified through the creation of government programmes, state-led citizen participation initiatives, and the CSR. The CSR has adopted values on sustainable mining where participatory mechanisms are important to offer a more caring approach toward the environment and wellbeing of the population. However, these values are encompassed by the neo-structuralist discourse, which subject them to a growth-led-by-exports rationale. The coercive side is implemented through threatening and intimidating mechanisms that are materialised in the fragmentation of living space to ensure the protection of mining production while accentuating the exclusion of sections in the community. However, it is fear and extreme material precarity (displacement), a result of these coercive tactics, that mobilised communities (CCRS) to expose the downsides of the sustainable assumptions behind neo-structuralist development. How successful this mobilisation will be is still unknown, but it may be that their network of support will keep motivating their fight.

In contrast, the Oaxacan case through enforcement of indigenous political systems and customary laws shows how Capulalpam has been able to challenge the neoliberal discourse of development backed by mining infrastructure. Local leaders showed that their governance model based on indigenous-community values and collective memories can be more effective than mining in delivering development for local populations without damaging their health or environment. In this case territory, mediated by infrastructure acquires significance as social struggle is linked to the prospect of autonomy, self-determination, and recognition of difference and diversity, while building a relative distance from the market and the state. The experience of Capulalpam shows that community empowerment is created through the hybridisation of opportunities offered by state institutions (i.e. Secretariat of Tourism, the Commission for the Development of Indigenous Peoples) and by customary and agrarian laws. Nevertheless, the empowerment attained over the last 40 years is not exempt from disciplinarian mechanisms. The Capulalpam authorities use these to maintain the power acquired against neighbouring communities (Natividad) and if need be against their own population when the local leaders' interests are challenged. By building an alternative to gold mining, leaders have addressed eco-tourism, alongside the infrastructural materiality it involves (restaurants, hotels), to build their identity. However, this new identity would not have been acquired without the mining identity that previous generations held.

Overall, these two cases show the plurality and tensions of local governance that Mexican mining involves and which would not have been possible to discern without the focus on the system of dimensions (beyond technology) that give meaning to infrastructure (Larkin, 2013). Both cases show the importance of local governance institutions and related everyday arrangements to understand how policy is implemented and shaped not only by local state actors, but also by business and social actors who have used infrastructure as a vehicle to either build empowerment or maintain the status quo. In contrasting the two cases, we have shown that the orthodox neoliberal discourse (Svampa, 2018) is resisted and challenged. The labour and environmental conflicts in the Sonoran case have shifted the discourse, albeit very gradually, towards the neo-structuralist pole of the continuum. Therefore, the discipline and order in local governance follow a conventional approach to power, in which coercion is whenever possible masked by consensus. Oaxaca's more radical discourse responds to the presence of customary laws alongside indigenous identity. This conjuncture underpins a struggle against a double colonialism (resource extraction and the state ruling indigenous territories) that renders discipline and order more empowering and unconventional than the Sonoran case.

References

Arbolada, M. (2016) 'Spaces of extraction, metropolitan explosions: planetary urbanization and the commodity boom in Latin America', *International Journal of Urban and Regional Research*, 40 (1): 96–112.

Arce, M. (2014). *Resources extraction and protest in Peru*, Pittsburgh: University of Pittsburgh Press.

Arango, P., B. Cruz, and A. Toledo (2018) 'Iniciativas socioeconómicas y desarrollo sustentable de Capulalpam de Méndez, Oaxaca', <http://ru.iiec.unam.mx/3850/1/056-Arango-Toledo-Ru%C3%ADz.pdf> (accessed 9 April 2022).

Bastida, E. (2002) 'Integrating sustainability into legal frameworks for mining in some selected Latin American countries', January, International Institute for Environment and Development/World Business Council for Sustainable Development, <https://pubs.iied.org/sites/default/files/pdfs/migrate/G00577.pdf> (accessed 2 August 2021).

Bebbington, A., D. Humphrys Bebbington, J. Bury, J. Lingan, J.P. Muñoz, and M. Scurrah (2008) 'Mining and social movements: struggles of livelihood and territorial development in the Andes', *World Development*, 36 (12): 2888–905.

Critical Infrastructure Collective, The (2022) 'Infrastructures, processes of insertion and the everyday: towards a new dialogue in critical policy studies', *Critical Policy Studies,* 16(1): 121–130..

Dehouve, D. (2001) *Ensayo de geopolítica indígena: los municipios tlapanecos* (Mexico City: CIESAS-Porrúa).

Excelsior (2019) 'Concesionado a mineras, 10% del país: López Obrador', <www.excelsior.com.mx/nacional/concesionado-a-mineras-10-del-pais-lopez-obrador/1354852> (accessed 30 June 2020).

Graham, S. and S. Marvin (2001) *Splintering Urbanism* (London: Routledge).

Gledhill, J. (2015) *The New War on the Poor: The Production of Insecurity in Latin America* (London: Zed Books).

Goldfrank, B. (2012) 'The World Bank and the globalization of participatory budgeting', *Journal of Public Deliberation*, 8 (2): Art. 7.

Harvey, P. (2012) 'The topological quality of infrastructural relationship: an ethnographic approach', *Theory, Culture & Society*, 29(4/5): 76–92.

Hernández, U. (2014) 'Vivir la mina: el conflicto minero en San José del Progreso y sus efectos cotidianos en la vida individual y la existencia colectiva; rupturas, contrastes, reconstrucciones y resistencias', Master's dissertation, CIESAS: Oaxaca, Mexico.

Infobae (2019) 'A cinco anos de la tragedia, Grupo México prepara un proyecto que podría acabar con todo un poblado', <www.infobae.com/america/mexico/2019/12/30/a-cinco-anos-de-la-tragedia-grupo-mexico-prepara-un-nuevo-proyecto-que-podria-acabar-con-todo-un-poblado/> (accessed 3 May 2022).

Kirkpatrick, L.O. and M.P. Smith (2011) 'The infrastructural limits to growth: rethinking the urban growth machine in times of fiscal crisis', *International Journal of Urban and Regional Research*, 35 (3): 477–503.

Lamberti, J. (2018) *Análisis del Fideicomiso Río Sonora. Simulando la remediación privada en un estado capturado* (Mexico City: Project on Organizing, Development, Education and Research (PODER)), July.

Larkin, B. (2013) The politics and poetics of infrastructure, *Annual Review of Anthropology*, 42: 327–43.

Lemke, T. (2015) 'New materialisms: Foucault and the "Government of things"', *Theory, Culture and Society*, 32 (4): 3–25.

Madrigal, D. (2019) 'De la práctica antropológica en contextos de negación de conflicto: aproximaciones etnográficas a los derrames mineros en México', in J.L. Plata, A. Vázquez and D. Madrigal (eds.), *Experiencias de exploración y práctica antropológica: Querétaro, San Luis Potosí y otras latitudes* (San Luis Potosí: Colegio de San Luis), pp. 235–60.

Martínez Alier, J. (2002) *The Environmentalism of the Poor. A Study of Ecological Conflict and Valuation* (Cheltenham: Edward Elgar Publishing).

McFarlane, C. and J. Rutherford (2008) 'Political infrastructures: governing and experiencing the fabric of the city', *International Journal of Urban and Regional Research*, 32(2): 363–74.

Méndez, E. (2017). De relámpagos y recuerdos... minería y tradición de lucha serrana por lo común (Guadalajara, México: Cátedra Interinstitucional: Universidad de Guadalajara-CIESAS-Jorge Alonso, Grafisma editores).

Milano, F. (2018) *Extractive Sector and Civil Society, When the Work of Communities, Governments and Industries Leads to Development* (Washington, DC: Interamerican Development Bank – Canadian Extractive Sector Facility).

OCMAL (n.d.) Conflictos mineros en América Latina, <www.ocmal.org/> (accessed 29 June 2020).

Sariego, J.L. (2016) 'Extractivismo y sustentabilidad: la conflictividad actual en la minería mexicana', in A. Rodríguez López (ed.), *Sociedades mineras en América Latina: homenaje a Juan Luis Sariego Rodríguez*, part 1 (Mexico City: Instituto Nacional de Antropología e Historia), 21–67.

Secretariat of Tourism (2020) Plan de marketing turísitico, pueblos mágicos, Capulalpam de Méndez, <www.oaxaca.gob.mx/sectur/wp-content/uploads/sites/65/2020/12/Plan-de-Marketing-Capulalpam-de-Mendez.pdf> (accessed 9 April 2022).

Shove, E. (2016) Infrastructures and practices: networks beyond the city, in O. Coutard and J. Rutherford (eds.), *Beyond the Networked City: Infrastructure Reconfigurations and Urban Change in the North and South* (London: Routledge), pp. 242–57.

Sierra, M.T. and E.L. López (2013) *El dictamen pericial antropológico y los sistemas normativos indígenas en el municipio de San Luis Actlán, Guerrero* (Mexico City: CIESAS).

SoyCobre (2018) 'Mineros de la Secc. 65 seguirán su lucha ante JFCA y ante la CIDH', <www.soycobre.com/2018/01/mineros-de-la-secc-65-seguiran-su-lucha-ante-jfca-y-ante-la-cidh/> (accessed 14 June 2019).

Svampa, M. (2018) 'Latin American development: perspectives and debates', in T. Falleti and E.A. Parrado (eds.), *Latin American since the Left Turn* (Philadelphia: Penn Press), pp. 13–32.

Svampa, M. and M.A. Antonelli (eds.) (2010) *Minería transnacional, narrativas del desarrollo y resistencias sociales* (Buenos Aires: Biblos).

Stirling, A. (2008) '"Opening up" and "closing down". Pluralism in the social appraisal of technology', *Science, Technology & Human Values*, 33 (2): 262–94.

Torres-Wong, M. (2019) *Natural Resources, Extraction and Indigenous Rights in Latin America: Exploring the Boundaries of State-Corporate Crime in Bolivia, Peru and Mexico* (London: Routledge).

UN (2012) 'The future we want', resolution adopted by General Assembly, United Nations, 27 July 2012, available at <www.un.org/en/development/desa/population/migration/generalassembly/docs/globalcompact/A_RES_66_288.pdf> (accessed 2 August 2021).

Vásquez, G. (2008) 'Una conquista indígena. Reconocimiento de municipios por "usos y costumbres" en Oaxaca (México)', in A. Cimadamore (ed.), *La economía política de la pobreza* (Buenos Aires: CLACSO).

Vogel, D. (2010) 'The private regulation of global corporate conduct: achievements and limitation', *Business and Society*, 49 (1): 68–87.

von Schnitzler (2008) 'Citizenship prepaid: water, calculability, and techno-politics in South Africa', *Journal of Southern African Studies*, 34 (4): 899–917.

7. 'Somos zona roja': top-down informality and institutionalised exclusion from broadband internet services in Santiago de Chile

Nicolás Valenzuela-Levi

Introduction

The telecommunications sector plays a major role in the imaginaries that today link infrastructure and notions of progress and development (Harvey et al., 2016). Yet, situations such as the COVID-19 pandemic have exposed how inequalities are dramatically reproduced or even amplified by digital infrastructures. The promise of infrastructure (Anand et al., 2018), in the case of internet, could have led some to believe that tele-working and tele-schooling were a real alternative for the majority of the population, which, obviously, has proved not to be true.

More broadly, social studies of infrastructure have long stated that inequalities and exclusion of part of the population are inherent to the neoliberal governance of infrastructure networks (Graham and Marvin, 2001). Since the 1990s, 'cherry picking and social dumping' became a common mechanism to exclude communities and territories from service provision, based on profitability under finance-oriented business models (Graham and Marvin, 1994). 'Redlining', or 'redzoning', is a way of excluding specific areas, and the communities who live in them, from a certain service. This practice entails the abdication from the responsibility (Appel, 2012a) of providing a commodity that is expected to be universal, or at least to lack any form of discrimination beyond individual ability to pay. Redlining involves exclusion that is not just individual, but collective and spatially specific. Surprisingly, however, corporate-led exclusion via redlining is scarcely discussed by studies that focus specifically on internet access (for two of the few mentions of the issue, see Fernández et al., 2019, and also my own work).

In this chapter, I examine the case of the *zonas rojas* [red zones] of fixed broadband Internet in Santiago, Chile. Using qualitative semi-structured

N. Valenzuela-Levi, '"Somos zona roja": top-down informality and institutionalised exclusion from broadband internet services in Santiago de Chile' in *The Social and Political Life of Latin American Infrastructures*, ed. J. Alderman and G. Goodwin (London, 2022), pp. 175–197.

interviews that involved managers from telecommunication companies, public officials, and community leaders, this work aims to explore the *zonas rojas* as an institutionalised form of network disadvantage. Two neighbourhoods are the focus of attention: La Pincoya and El Castillo, in the northern and southern outskirts of Santiago, respectively (see Figure 7.1).

Apart from the empirical contribution within the realm of internet studies, this chapter pays attention to the need to extend the notion of informality, usually approached as a bottom-up phenomenon, into top-down processes by which powerful actors enforce unwritten rules. Far from just working within homogeneous universal institutional environments – shaped by neoliberal globalisation – internet provision markets operate on the basis of business models that significantly depend on informality exercised by the rich, and not just by the poor. These informal mechanisms are developed and enforced locally, and spark a range of economic and social dynamics at the neighbourhood level. The bottom-up notion of informality in infrastructure networks, usually associated with the influential concept of 'people as infrastructure' (Simone, 2004), does not seem to be enough to describe the dynamics in play in the *zonas rojas*. As discussed by Harvey et al. (2016), linkages between infrastructure and social dynamics tend to be more complicated than the usual narratives.

In the following paragraphs, I attempt to explain this particular story of infrastructural complications. The first section offers a background that reviews and discusses the literature of internet studies and social studies of infrastructure. The second section describes the case studies and the methodology. The third section provides a thorough view of how broadband access operates in the case studies, based on the results from the interviews. The final section concludes.

Background

The rules of the telecommunications sector: one size fits all?

The structural readjustment period during the 1980s and 1990s, summarised by the Washington Consensus, included a pledge to privatise state-owned enterprises and deregulate the sectors in which they operated (Williamson, 1990). This agenda had an enormous impact on network industries, to the point that some scholars talk about current debates as 'post-liberalisation technology policy' (Jamasb and Pollitt, 2008). The structural readjustment policies of the 1980s and 1990s have been paired, in the 2000s, with a 'good governance' agenda that keeps pushing for governments to 'adopt a one-size-fits-all approach to get things done' (Andrews, 2010, p. 7). Issues such as competition, corruption, and market failures are debated within a political economy environment that is left untouched in its fundamentals. In other words, especially in the telecommunications sector, 'there is no alternative' (Swyngedouw and Wilson, 2014).

However, recently, the expansion of broadband internet connections has not followed previous rapid adoption curves within the telecom sector, as was the case with fixed telephone lines and mobile phones (World Bank, 2016). Inequalities in access to quality internet services have become a problem, acknowledged not only by critics, but also by the same institutions that promoted the implementation of the neoliberal agenda in the first place. The best example is the World Bank, in its 2016 World Development Report:

> First-generation ICT [information, communication and technology] policies involving market competition, private participation, and light-touch regulation have led to near-universal access and affordability of mobile telephony, but have so far been less successful in spreading internet services. Much of the explanation lies in continued policy failures such as regulatory capture, troubled privatizations, inefficient spectrum management, excessive taxation of the sector, and monopoly control of international gateways. (World Bank, 2016, pp. 25)

Yet, ICT policies based on the neoliberal one-size-fits-all approach have not just been assumed as a given by policymakers, but often also by scholars. This supposedly universal and homogeneous rule-system of the internet sector is assumed by most researchers to be a framework to approach their analyses on internet access. By ignoring questions about the rules of internet access – in other words, the political economy of the internet – the environment in which internet adoption occurs is assumed to be one of a global market dominated by big transnational companies, under virtually invariant local frameworks of deregulation, privatisation, and financialisation. For instance, the most influential studies on the digital divide (van Deursen and Helsper, 2015; van Deursen and van Dijk, 2015; Helsper and Reisdorf, 2017), while contributing enormously to the understanding of individual access, appropriation and capacities, do not ask any relevant question about the political economy of internet service provision, and especially neglect the role of local and informal institutions. In other words, as I have attempted to summarise elsewhere (Valenzuela-Levi, 2020a), most studies of internet access tend to provide insightful analyses about the demand-side but to forget the supply-side.

If such a universal and homogeneous institutional framework is assumed, it seems natural to lack any attention to the unwritten rules of internet exclusion, which are enforced by specific actors, through specific mechanisms, at different territorial levels. Common institutional approaches to internet provision can be divided into two sectors. On the one hand, a series of studies focuses on small formal variations within the universal policy package: public investment, enforcement of regulation, prices policy applied to copper and fibre, tariff diversity, and the existence of national plans or strategies (Beltrán, 2014; Neokosmidis et al., 2015; Haucap et al., 2016; Ghosh, 2017). On the other hand, a number of studies have focused on shallow definitions of democratic 'cultures' or 'regimes' and how they link to internet adoption

(Milner, 2006; Gulati and Yates, 2012; Stier, 2017). The notion of institutional factors is reduced to abstract ideas about democracy that are usually measured by opinion polls, or to small variances within the good governance agenda (Andrews, 2010). Informal institutions that operate at the local level, through specific mechanisms, and enforced by specific actors, are out of the discussion.

Informality in social studies of infrastructure

As already mentioned, a specific aspect of rule-systems (Pamuk, 2000) – or the institutional political economy (Chang, 2002) – that is missing from internet studies is the role of informal institutions, or non-written rules, in the telecommunications sector (Valenzuela-Levi, 2020a). These informal institutions can be placed in three categories: tacit rules, traditions or customs, and unwritten rules that are 'enforceable', that is to say, they require action or inaction by somebody that holds enough power (Khan, 2010). When it comes to social studies of infrastructure, informality is mostly associated with people breaking the written rules of certain markets: land, transport, waste management, electricity, water, and sewage. They operate as providers within, or are served by, informal sectors. Illegal, semi-legal, or black markets, are usually allowed by authorities given the lack of force to control them, and/or the importance of these sectors in the livelihoods of the poor.

Informal settlements, or slums, as areas within a city, or pieces of land that are occupied by squatters, are the usual object of discussion about urban informality, especially after the publication of *Planet of Slums* (Davis, 2006). Nonetheless, some scholars have gone further from referring to specific administrative boundaries or spaces as informal, and thereby have assigned the category 'informal' to a specific population, usually the urban poor (McFarlane, 2008). Hasan (2006), for instance, shares the definition of informal as associated with the 'informal settlement', plus classifying infrastructure as informal (i.e. 'informal sewerage'). Dekel et al. (2019) differentiate between formal and informal spaces: however, the informal are the spaces instead of the people inhabiting them. Vollmer and Grêt-Regamey (2013) expand the informal category to cover urbanisation processes that forge informal settlements, discussing 'informal land conversion' activity. Similarly, Hill et al. (2014) use the informal to refer to a consequence of the formation of informal settlements, talking about informal urban growth. From transport geography, authors such as Evans et al. (2018) exemplify a growing attention to informal transport. Here, just as in 'informal recyclers', informal as a characteristic is assigned to a service sector.

Interestingly, a different kind of distinction comes from medical sciences and studies of chronic illness. For example, Van Houtven et al. (2010) discuss 'care infrastructure', and discriminate between formal and informal as paid and non-paid. 'Remaining at home often requires support, which may be provided by formal programs (e.g. home health agencies) or informal caregivers (e.g.

spouses or adult children who provide unpaid assistance). Informal caregivers of elderly adults often experience stress, economic hardship, and burnout, which increase the elderly adult's risk of nursing home admission' (Van Houtven et al., 2010, p. 57). Instead of the usual 'informality of the poor' that is present in discussions on 'informal labour', 'informal recyclers' or 'informal transport', the informal here is closer to the attention paid by feminist economics to unpaid care work (Braunstein et al., 2010).

Thus, informal are certain peoples or their activities: the poor, the trespassers, the precarious workers, the unpaid carers. What they have in common is a notion of a bottom-up informality. Informal are the activities and means for those excluded, marginalised, uncounted, and unpaid. These visions resonate with the already mentioned notion of 'people as infrastructure' (Simone, 2004). However, it is much harder to find accounts of informal means that come 'from above', which would be much closer to the 'black box' and the 'how of capitalism' discussed by Appel (2012b). There are increasing debates about the impacts of top-down decisions on local communities, as vividly explained by Anand et al. (2018) when describing the chain of decisions that led to a dramatic impact on access to drinkable water by communities of colour in Flint, Michigan. However, the problem of institutional political economy (Chang, 2002) of networked infrastructure, that is to say, of understanding both the written and unwritten rules of network disadvantage (Valenzuela-Levi, 2020a, 2020b), urges the incorporation of the perspective of informality as a top-down phenomenon too.

One of the works from the field of social studies of infrastructure that remarkably integrates a perspective that goes beyond bottom-up informality is the work by Pamuk (2000) on informal institutional arrangements in credit, land markets and infrastructure delivery in Trinidad. This author integrates informality as part of a broader conception of institutions. Pamuk formulates a fundamental critique, 'by focusing exclusively on informal housing settlements when discussing informality, previous studies of land and housing policy in developing countries have ignored informal institutions that permeate both formal and informal settlements' (Pamuk, 2000, p. 380). This author is able to escape the trap of the 'informality of the poor', by integrating informality and infrastructure into a broader institutional analysis. Nonetheless, what could be criticised from Pamuk's work is that, although informal customs and traditions are observed across groups in society, and linked to both the formal and informal markets – providing a much more comprehensive perspective on informality than the rest of the literature – the analysis lacks the dimensions of conflict, controversy, and illegality that are crucial in the political economy of infrastructure (Appel, 2012a, 2012b): for instance, corruption is absent from the analysis.

Some more recent attempts in institutional economics and urban issues, as exemplified by the use of the political settlements approach, include illegal institutions as part of informal rules, and understand them as sustained by a balance of power that enables a specific distribution of benefits (Goodfellow, 2018; Valenzuela-Levi 2020a, 2020b). According to the political settlements approach (Khan, 2010), conflict and illegality, and particularly corruption, emerge as informal rules that can be explained based on the specific distributional role that they play. By focusing on customs and informal rules that are part of specific 'cultures', analyses such as that in Pamuk (2000) pay less attention to informal rules that need to be enforced by intra or extra state actors (Khan, 2010). By omitting attention to corruption, the informality of the rich is most likely to be overlooked. In order to better approach the political economy of networked infrastructure, however, both top-down and bottom-up informality should be observed in detail, understanding the unwritten rules that define how each sector operates. In what follows, I use the case of the *zonas rojas* of broadband provision in Santiago, in order to illustrate the relevance of this much required conceptual expansion.

Case study and methodology

Two neighbourhoods in Santiago

This research focuses on Santiago, the capital of Chile. According to the 2017 census, the Santiago Metropolitan Region (SMR) had a population of 7 million, comprising 40 per cent of the total of 17.5 million living in the country (Instituto Nacional de Estadísticas, 2017). Santiago is the second southernmost national capital of the Americas, after Buenos Aires. As such, it was the epicentre of Spanish colonial rule in Chile, and of the Republic of Chile since 1810 (Rodríguez Weber, 2017). Santiago is characterised by extreme socio-economic residential segregation, structured by a unitary affluent sector in the north-east (see Figure 7.1), and a periphery that is almost entirely poor and residential – with no other major land uses that could, for instance, produce jobs outside the affluent areas of the city (Sabatini et al., 2009; Garretón, 2017). Furthermore, in the Chilean capital, the 'informal' is not directly linked today to what is expected of informal settlements in most of the Global South (Hasan, 2006; McFarlane, 2008). Although there are a number of small-scale slums in Santiago, the majority of the poor live in formal social housing financed by the state.

In their current form, the peripheral and peri-central areas where the poor live were defined mainly by three origins. The former informal settlements (Garcés, 2002) that grew during rapid urbanisation due to the expansion of urban economic activity and the collapse of both the nitrate mines in the north and agricultural production in the south during the mid-20th century were the first (Rodríguez Weber, 2017). The second is comprised of the destination areas populated by those forcibly evicted from slums in affluent areas during the dictatorship led by Augusto Pinochet (1973–90) (Morales et al., 1990). The third is an unprecedented investment in subsidising a private market for social housing (Gilbert, 2002), which produced millions of units built on cheap land. This third origin is the most common for the majority of neighbourhoods where the poor have lived in Santiago during the last three decades.

The Chilean subsidised housing policy has been considered an example of successful reduction of the housing deficit among the so-called developing countries (as thoroughly reviewed by Gilbert, 2002, 2004). The enabling approach (Chiodelli, 2016) in Chile had its origin during the military dictatorship led by Augusto Pinochet between 1973 and 1990 (Gilbert, 2002), while the same policies were continued later by democratic governments (Ducci, 1997; Özler, 2012). Mainstream literature has usually referred to this policy shift as the reason for the reduction of the number of residents in Chile

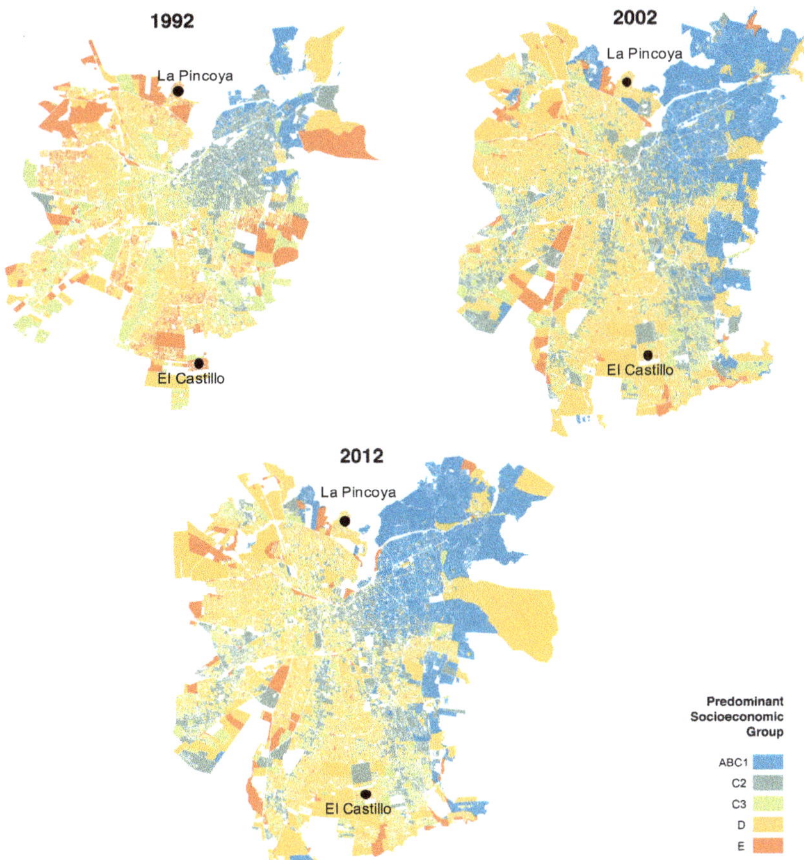

Figure 7.1 Location of La Pincoya and El Castillo in Santiago, including spatial distribution of socio-economic groups in 1992, 2002, and 2012, according to census data. Source: Cociña (2017)

living in informal settlements to less than 1 per cent of the total population (Valenzuela-Levi, 2017).

As recently described by Cociña (2018), the characteristics of the Chilean social-housing model can be summarised in four main features. First, the private for-profit sector develops the biggest portion of units. Second, the Ministry of Housing and Urbanism manages a centralised funding system based on vouchers. Third, the system promotes house ownership, and only recently has there been initial experiences of public rental. Fourth, those who have access to a subsidy require savings, and the loan had to be paid off before the mid-2000s, when – after years of protests by poor and indebted households – the social-housing system stopped generating debt among its beneficiaries.

As soon as the 1990s, scholars started to notice conflicts and social problems that started to be concentrated in the newly built subsidised housing. Ducci (1997) proposed the idea of quantitative success in terms of built units, paired with qualitative emerging problems. Discussion of the adverse effects of social-housing policies became mainstream among the Chilean housing and urbanism scholars after Rodríguez and Sugranyes (2004) called for attention to be paid to those 'with a roof' – in social-housing projects – instead of decades of mainly caring about those 'without a roof' – in the slums. The idea of a 'new urban poverty' (Tironi, 2009) then became widely accepted: since the mid-2000s, most of the urban poor live in formal housing and only a minority inhabit slums. Consequently, problems of distant locations of housing developments, concentration of the poor, increase of socio-economic segregation as an effect of state action, and clustering of social exclusion within new 'ghettos' became the usual topics of the debate concerning Chilean housing policies (Ruiz-Tagle and López, 2014).

The description of this particular landscape of urban poverty in Chile, and Santiago in particular, is relevant for the analysis of the case studies detailed in the next sections, because service provision is supposed to operate 'universally' in this strongly segregated city. For the selection of cases, neighbourhoods with two kinds of origins were selected, located in the northern and southern peripheries of the city, respectively (Figure 7.1). On the one hand, El Castillo is an example of forced eviction during the dictatorship and a later concentration of subsidised housing (Álvarez and Cavieres, 2016). On the other hand, La Pincoya was started by squatters at the end of the 1960s and later formalised (Salcedo and Torres, 2004; Barbera, 2009). Both are today part of formal neighbourhoods. However, they are also parts of working-class neighbourhoods which have stayed mostly poor, and where the effects of multiple forms of inequality are concentrated. They also experience permanent violence both from state repression and territorial disputes by drug gangs (Han, 2012). La Pincoya and El Castillo account for the imaginary of peripheral excluded places for any Santiaguinean.

In these neighbourhoods, access to network infrastructure services has become increasingly hard, not because of lack of physical infrastructure, but because of the cost of privatised services. Water bills, for instance, have had to be subsidised by the state: by 2015, more than 800,000 households received a water subsidy in Chile (Contreras et al., 2018). As is evident in the interviews, the Internet is increasingly being seen as a basic service, similar to water, sanitation, electricity, and waste collection. The story of the *zonas rojas* is partly a story of this transition of the Internet into an essential need.

Methodology

The data for this study was collected through fieldwork in Santiago de Chile, during the first semester of 2018. As part of the wider cycle of protests discussed in the introduction to this book, Chile has experienced what is now called the 'social outbreak' since October 2019. This research was conducted 18 months before that date. However, the forms of inequality and exclusion that are described here resonate with the demands raised by massive protests, and also with a body of work from social scientists who have thoroughly diagnosed the mounting tension that led to 'social outbreak' in 2019 (for a reliable account of this sentiment among people in Santiago, see Araújo, 2020).

The fieldwork consisted of 22 semi-structured interviews that included actors who have a role in the supply of internet services in the city. As already mentioned, two areas of the periphery of the city were selected as case studies, La Pincoya (municipality of Huechuraba) in the north, and El Castillo (municipality of La Pintana) in the south. Interviewees included managers and workers from telecommunication companies, small and medium enterprises (SMEs) from the same sector, national and local government officials, and community leaders. Whereas the views of managers, workers, and some SMEs are not anchored in a specific territory, local government officials and community leaders were specifically associated with the selected neighbourhoods. An interview schedule was utilised to organise semi-structured interviews. Depending on each interviewee, some topics were developed more deeply and extensively. Interviews were conducted in Spanish, recorded, and transcribed for analysis. Quotations are translated into English by the author. A set of preliminary codes was established based on pilot interviews. These codes were confirmed after transcription and used for content analysis. In what follows, excerpts from some interviews are mixed with secondary literature and a number of discussions that took place in the media during the period when this research was undertaken.

Broadband Internet in La Pincoya and El Castillo

Household broadband access in the SMR is provided by eight private companies. The Chilean telecommunications sector is an example of the tight links between global and national capital, as has been widely debated by social studies of infrastructure (Harvey et al., 2016; Anand et al., 2018). Among these companies, four are the main competitors: VTR, owned by the American holding Liberty Global, Carlos Slim's Claro from Mexico, the

Spanish company Telefónica, and the Chilean company Entel, owned by the Matte Group which belongs to one of the most traditional oligarchic families in Chile (Salazar, 2009).

Chile represents well what the World Bank (2016) identified as the widely accepted market-oriented policies of previous generations of telecommunication services that achieved high expansion, but have been less successful as regards broadband. For instance, by 2017, Chile was one of the leading countries in Latin America in terms of percentage of people using the Internet (World Bank, 2020). However, by the same year, Chile had only 16.6 fixed broadband subscriptions per 100 people, below the 17.9 reached by Argentina, and 27.7 by Uruguay, the nearest countries in terms of Gross Domestic Product (GDP) per capita within Latin America and the Caribbean. In the SMR, the percentage of people with internet access was 89.9 by 2017. According to a recent study by the Chilean government, by 2019 the percentage of households with fixed broadband subscriptions were near 100 in affluent areas, but only 28.2 in a municipality such as La Pintana (EMOL, 2019).

The contrast in fixed broadband access has sparked a public debate over the existence of *zonas rojas* [red zones], which are zones where users ask for the service but telecommunication companies say that they do not have infrastructural coverage there. This is how one of the interviewees describes the experience of being part of one of the *zonas*:

> If you call to sign up to the service, they will tell you that your area doesn't have technical viability. That is because it is a red zone, and red zones are all those sectors that big companies stay away from. They are defined by the fact that that at some point the copper cables were stolen, or that the residents have liquidity problems that exclude them from the big telecoms' business model. They call these neighbourhoods red zones and use a technical excuse to discriminate.

A remarkable debate occurred in 2017 between the then head of the Sub-secretariat[1] of Telecommunications (SUBTEL) and his immediate predecessor. A sub-secretary wrote an article questioning the public debate over the *zonas rojas*, arguing that these zones do not exist. He wrote that 'the law establishes the obligation of guaranteeing coverage, continuity of service, regularity, compliance of the regulations and quality standards. That makes the idea of the existence of *zonas rojas* in telecommunications unsustainable' (translated from Ramírez, 2017). In other words, according to the official, the illegal nature of the *zonas* is enough to deny their existence. The same official explains, in the article, the legal framework in which this debate is situated:

1 In Chile, ministries that consist of a number of sectors have vice ministers called Sub-secretaries. In the case of the Ministry of Transport and Telecommunications, the corresponding vice ministry is the Subsecretaría de Telecommunicaciones [Sub-secretariat of Telecommunications].

> The public service concession is an administrative contract in which the concessionaire assumes the commitment to provide a service of collective and social interest, and the supervision is there for that to be fulfilled. The satisfaction of a public need is mandatory for all and without distinction. There is no such thing as saying that poor commercial appeal can be disguised as a crime, a ghetto dispute, or recurrent vandalism. Neither are there zones of any colour. (Ramírez, 2017, p. 1)

This official discourse was extended among high-ranked officials. I was able to interview a former minister, who told me:

> If there is a neighbourhood taken over by drug dealers, that will affect everything. I would say that these are major public order problems. But something systematic, such as zones that do not have coverage … I never heard of, at least not in urban areas. A different thing is complaints about quality or continuity of the service.

The official discourse seems to deny the *zonas rojas* as a structural problem for the telecommunications sector. However, this discourse is not entirely monolithic. For instance, the above-cited article by the sub-secretary motivated a response from his predecessor, in which the existence of *zonas rojas* was acknowledged, and a pledge was made about the need to recognise the problem in order to solve it (Huichalaf, 2017).

Interviewing managers from the dominant telecommunication companies provided a contradictory narrative. On the one hand, they insisted that crime and vandalism was the justification for not providing services in some zones:

> In the case of the older technology, which uses copper, and particularly in poor zones, cables are stolen. Since having copper in the streets is the same as hanging out 1-dollar bills (laughs), if you have on 1-dollar bills hanging over the streets, evidently impecunious people will collect those dollars.

As we will see later, the 'older technology' of copper cables is not the only option for provision of internet connections, and is somewhat obsolete. There are other technologies being used now that would be more difficult to steal. On the other hand, when asked about possible policies to solve the problem of the *zonas rojas*, the response was closer to the issues of 'commercial appeal' named by the sub-secretary (Ramírez, 2017). This is how the same manager talking about 'dollar bills' puts it:

> Our position as a company is that the solution is subsidising demand (…) in Chile, that was the way we solved access to electricity and sanitation. This is similar. You have parts of the population that wouldn't have access to drinkable water without subsidies for utility bills. Well, that would be unacceptable, so the government offers the money. We believe it's the same with the Internet. If the government subsidises those in need within neighbourhoods that aren't currently economically viable, someone will say that here we will get the same benefit as a middle-class neighbourhood. This means that half of the users will hire us if we put a cable there. Therefore, we will invest and install the cable. Problem solved.

Thus, the official discourse among high-ranking managers and public officials is that *zonas rojas* do not exist as part of the rules-system of the telecommunications sector. If something like these zones exists, it is an issue of public order, an exception, and a *force majeure* that has nothing to do with decisions by providers. However, going lower in the hierarchies within big transnational companies brought in a different view. For instance, when I was able to interview technicians from one of the main telecommunication companies, they confirmed the existence of the *zonas*. They believe that their origin might have been crime and vandalism, but they think that it is currently about a commercial decision:

> If there are too many illegal connections, the network fails. You will have too many technical service requirements. It is not convenient for the company to send a technician 20 times to the same place during one week or one month. It is not efficient. So, what the company does is that it drops the services where it will have too many problems. (...) That is what happens, and that is why these areas are called red zones.

Talking to municipal officials, I was granted access to a formal communication sent by one of the poorest municipalities in the SMR, Renca, to the SUBTEL. In this communication, the municipality generated a map based on the claims of their neighbours about being excluded by telecommunication companies (see Figure 7.2). The municipality asked the SUBTEL to take action in regard to possible infractions by telecommunication providers. This communication occurred during the same year in which the sub-secretary in office denied the existence of the *zonas*.

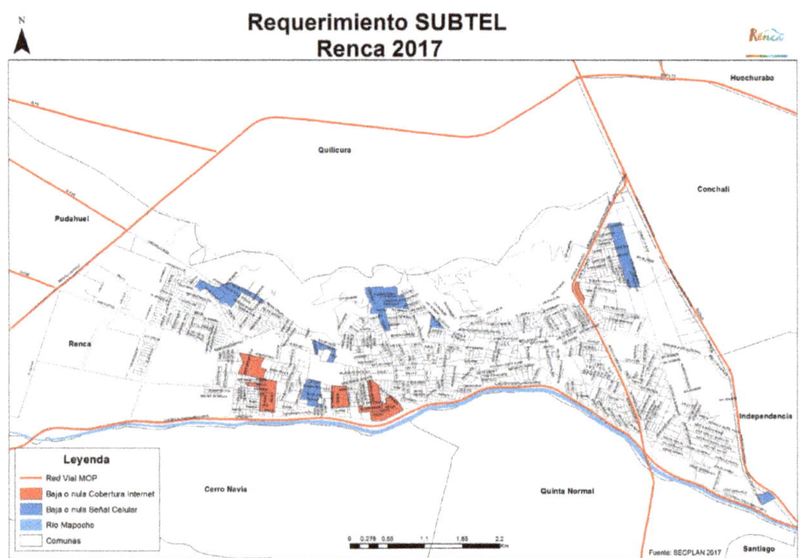

Figure 7.2 'Red zones'. Map elaborated by the Municipality of Renca (Santiago) from users' testimonies. Source: author

Interestingly, although high-ranking managers deny the existence of redlining, they acknowledge at the same time the limitations of government agencies to supervise compliance among internet providers. A manager from a transnational company gave me the following information about the government office responsible for supervising internet providers: 'Did you know that the SUBTEL is the smallest sub-secretariat in the whole of Chilean government? They have the smallest number of staff.' The claims – from users, workers, and local governments – about redlining and illegal exclusion being made possible by unilateral decisions by big telecommunication companies, emerges in tandem with a well-known low capacity for supervision of the market.

Just as in the case of the big telecoms, the discourse changed within the state when I talked to lower-ranking officials. For instance, a public servant in charge of ICT promotion programmes at the regional level used his origins in Rodelillo, a *población* in the city of Valparaíso, to explain that people have long used collaborative strategies to access telecommunications:

> The Internet is increasingly transforming into a basic service. Therefore, families make efforts to have some sort of internet connection (…). For instance, I am from Rodelillo in Valparaíso. What did we do in Rodelillo? One person hired internet access and shared it with the neighbours, splitting the bill. We used to do the same with Cable TV. Then it is about strategies, one could say, that are community based.

This public official also claims that these contemporary community-based strategies were already present in older telecommunication technologies, such as fixed telephone lines:

> When there were no fixed telephone lines, then there was always one neighbour that had a line and then they charged you for going to their house to make a call. Or, if somebody called you, the owner of the line went and knocked on your door. Then maybe we forget about that, of this collaborative logic that has long been there.

Lower-ranking state and big-telecom employees seem to have a much more nuanced knowledge of the rules of telecommunication service provision, as they operate on the ground. However, even this collaborative logic to pay the bill is not possible when an entire zone is excluded from hiring the service.

Nonetheless, this exclusion is so systematic that it has allowed the emergence of a new market. A key seems to be the 'economically viable' issue, mentioned by the same manager who talked about dollar bills hanging over the streets. This economically inviable nature of some areas as far as the big corporations are concerned, contrasts with the emergence of small local enterprises which are for-profit too but seem to be economically viable.

Community leaders both in La Pincoya and El Castillo, gave me practically the same information, 'Somos Zona Roja', and confirmed that the only access they have to broadband is not thanks to the big telecommunication companies, but to local providers. Surprisingly, both in La Pincoya and El Castillo, there were local small enterprises, each connecting between 300 to 500 users. As they explained to me in La Pincoya,

> Here we have our own internet company ... you know? Its name is Alcom. They are my friends. I worked with them. They have like a monopoly of Internet here in the hood. I have Alcom. It is a company from our neighbourhood.

A similar story was told in El Castillo:

> ... no internet provider that uses cables reaches us. Why? Because this is a *Zona Roja*, because here copper cables used to be stolen... so they decided to call us a *Zona Roja*, and now no one arrives with the Internet ... no one! ... here the only option is to use mobile Internet, but there is no good signal either. We only have one cell phone antenna in the area. (...) The Internet that I have now is provided by a guy from the neighbourhood.

Both examples of local providers share some elements. First, these are small, formal enterprises. Although conditions of hiring their services are less strict than those of big telecoms, people still have to sign formal contracts. As one interviewee from El Castillo told me:

> Big companies ask you to sign an 18-month contract. This guy just asks you to buy the router. There is a contract that you sign, which is for about six months. He promises to come and sort out any problem for 6 months, with no charge. For instance, if a bird breaks the antenna, which is his property. (...) Part of what you pay is for renting the antenna from him.

Figure 7.3 Houses with installed antennas that are used to get broadband connections from local providers in El Castillo, district of La Pintana. Photo by the author

Second, they were started by young entrepreneurs who come from the same neighbourhoods or areas of the city. The local provider in La Pincoya began as a social enterprise by a group of university students who grew up in a more affluent neighbourhood, within the same municipality of Huechuraba. In the case of El Castillo, it was a resident of the neighbourhood. I was able to talk to a provider from another municipality from the south of Santiago, Puente Alto (next to La Pintana, where El Castillo is located) who decided to start an internet provision business when he was in high school, motivated by the lack of access in his home. He also provides services in El Castillo.

This latter entrepreneur, a 27-year-old man whose name is of Mapuche origin, vividly explains how his personal experience led him to become an internet provider:

> My case is very particular, because it was born out of necessity. I lived in a zone where there was no Internet, and this was at the time of the Internet boom. So, sadly, I was not able to hire any company. I mean, I experienced it myself. I called all the companies, and there was no access. I was at high school, and there we designed an antenna … like … very handmade, made of aluminium … some of those antennas are still circulating over there … one of those antennas gave me access to the Internet. Partnering with a neighbour, we split the bill in two. So, this is how we realised that the need was not something affecting just me, but also the other neighbours, and it was the same all over the neighbourhood. In my case, it is about my own necessity, how to solve the problem, to face it… and now it is also about how to earn money.

Third, they use a similar technology: they install an antenna – like the one described above – in a place reached by optic fibre, and then they use smaller antennas or cables to transmit the signal (see Figure 7.3). One of the first experiences of this company from Puente Alto was actually in El Castillo, in the municipality of La Pintana. Interestingly, they recognise that it seemed risky to implement services there. This prototype was based on the same copper cables that the manager of the transnational company referred as '1-dollar bills'. But they mention the relevant role of the neighbours in generating a totally different relationship between the community and 'their' infrastructure:

> This was one of the first prototypes, using cables. We installed them in the municipality of La Pintana… the are still in service… in El Castillo. People told us 'how dare you to do it there, if they are going to steal you all the cables'. The first prototype was implemented five years ago, one year after our company started operating … and until now all the cables are there, all the customers pay their bills (…) we are talking about an alley (…) now we have more cable connections, from an antenna, connecting around 100 families. But the prototype was implemented in a place that is tremendously conflictive (…) it was like 'don't do it, they will steal everything', but until today the neighbours have been taking care of what is theirs. They know that in reality we are a help to them, and it is worth taking care of what is theirs.

A fourth element in common is that local providers in La Pincoya and El Castillo use local shops to buy groceries as a way of finding clients. For instance, the provider in La Pincoya made a deal with small corner shops in the neighbourhood to advertise the service, and also to install some of their main antennas in the shops, using cables to connect the houses close by. As my interviewee from La Pincoya explained, the way to hire the service is to 'go to the shop that is associated with them, and sign a waiting list'. Later, it is in that same shop where you 'go and pay the bill'.

One of the providers in El Castillo, in turn, used the local street markets to literally voice their services. As a local community leader told me, about his internet provider:

> I met him in the street market. (…) As I told you, here big internet companies don't come, although we need the Internet for studying, or watching YouTube videos during our free time … it's also very useful for finding a job. So … this guy was offering his Internet … I didn't hire him immediately … I didn't want to hire a company that I never heard of, doesn't have a TV commercial … you know? But my friend next door bought it, and it worked … so I called the guy and he installed the Internet that I have now.

The same interviewee described the organic spread of this supply, always using the need for the Internet and ingenious ways of advertising:

> There are other neighbourhood providers. For instance, here just in front of my house (…) I realised because their wi-fi network appeared in my devices. They used the name of the network to advertise themselves. Here my neighbour has another one … he is the provider now … I know because they installed a huge antenna (…) he has a different kind. My antenna is just a metal stick with a white ball on top. He has a frame. … yep … here the majority have the Internet from the neighbourhood, *internet de barrio*.

The usual narrative about informality and infrastructure needs to be challenged in the case of the Internet. What the *zonas rojas* show is a telecommunications sector in which informality is not how the poor operate outside formal rules to access or produce services. Actually, in a new and inverted narrative of informality, it is the rich – shareholders and managers from big telecommunication companies – who operate informally and illegally to sustain a business model that excludes the poor. These findings can be linked to a recent analysis of African cities (Meagher, 2018), in relation to 'frugal innovations' which enhance involvement by local informal actors among the urban poor, but always benefit corporate interests from 'above'. However, I insist, the 'formal versus informal' distinction must be detached from the 'top-down versus bottom-up'. In the work of other researchers, these two distinctions converge, but here they diverge. Or, one could say, they converge in the opposite direction: bottom-up is the formal and top-down the informal.

Yet, beyond the discussion on informality, the link between frugal innovation and the distribution of benefits is similar to that found by Meagher (2018). Another manager, different from the 'dollar bill' story, provided another view, that might explain why big companies are not bothered by the existence of the SMEs that create a local provision market that would otherwise be theirs to serve. About the *zonas rojas* and local providers, he says:

> I have seen it, and not just in Santiago, but also in other regions (…). Two or three providers that make you ask yourself 'Where are these guys getting their Internet from.' Now, from a certain point of view, these guys are still buying services (…). They are re-selling. And it is reaching a market that perhaps is not possible for you to serve. Much more atomised and cheaper than what you could do with your cheapest alternative. Then, in this way, you are still getting profits. Somebody is hiring you. Now, if this guy was connected illegally, that would be a different thing. But if they hire fibre or a dedicated link to our company (…) and re-sell it… well… what is wrong with that? (…) It would be great to have a product for those clients, but sometimes so, so cheap, can be hard.

Far from an exceptional case of *force majeure*, the *zonas rojas* seem to be a consolidated part of a well-functioning and profitable system of written and unwritten rules in the Chilean internet market. It appears that part of the mechanisms that are needed for sustaining a system of informal rules is a deliberately small supervisory government branch, and an official denial of redlining. Living what seems to be the effects of the informality of the rich and transnational capital, a top-down exercise of informality, the poor access services via formal entrepreneurial activities that emerge in places like La Pincoya and El Castillo, while conforming a new socio-productive local fabric in the periphery of Santiago.

Conclusions

Using broadband Internet in Santiago de Chile as a case study, this chapter illustrates ways in which the systems of rules in the telecommunications sector include informal institutions that need to be enforced to sustain the dominant business model for service provision. Illegal redlining seems to be a mechanism that is inherent in the functioning of the telecommunications sector, based on unilateral decisions by big telecommunication companies, which are possible thanks to the denial of the phenomena by national authorities that are in charge of supervising the sector. These informal mechanisms are far from being exceptional: they are a fundamental part of the systems of rules that shape the telecommunications market. For these unwritten rules to exist and operate, they require an active role by transnational capital, high-ranking managers, and public officials. They illustrate the informality of the rich, a top-down enforcement of unwritten rules, and sustain rules that distribute benefits towards corporate capital.

Thus, in this work I criticise the limits of the views that social studies of infrastructure tend to have on informality. A dominant attention to bottom-up experiences outside formal rules is linked to a well-established association between informality and the lives of the poor. In the context of rising debates about the role of the rich and informal institutions, the chapter provides some elements to overcome the dominance of the 'informality of the poor', and proposes to look at the 'informality of the rich'. This top-down informality should be incorporated into the analytical toolkit within social studies of infrastructure.

As I hope is evident in this chapter, my analysis aims to expand the analytical notions of informality. However, it is far from my intention to celebrate informality as has been done by scholars and policymakers in order to promote liberalisation reforms and pro-market policies in the contexts of weak states in Latin America (Gilbert, 2012; Meagher, 2014). Furthermore, this research pays attention to the distribution of benefits that both formal and informal rules allow, as it can be found in other technology-related works such as the those mentioned above by Meagher (2018). She eloquently talks about corporate interests 'cannibalizing the informal economy'. More locally, in Chile, a similar understanding of a top-down imposition of rules to both discipline the poor and extract value has been thoroughly developed by social historians who see local informal markets as 'residual spaces of sovereignty' (Salazar, 2003). Informality, expressed at the neighbourhood level by street markets, is seen as a stubborn resistance by the people paired with an extractivist existence by the elites, all which can be traced back to colonial origins (Salazar, 2009). Nonetheless, sharing most of these views on power balances, I insist on breaking the formal-rich and informal-poor associations that are so important in these influential narratives.

If looking 'above' for subjects of informality is a novelty in comparison to the usual narrative in social studies of infrastructure, another new element is the characterisation of service provision initiatives that emerge from poor areas of Santiago. The local enterprises that provide broadband are formal, not informal. They both interact and somehow compete with the dominant service provision model, which is sustained by rules that benefit the rich and transnational capital, and are in conflict with the local socio-productive fabric in peripheral places like El Castillo and La Pincoya. Without overcoming the usual association between informality and the poor, citizens, decision-makers, and scholars will have less analytical resources to confront the challenge of providing and developing key services such as broadband Internet. A question that remains is: what fundamental non-written rules could we be missing when only focusing on the poor to analyse informality and other infrastructure sectors?

References

Álvarez, A.M. and H. Cavieres (2016) 'El Castillo: territorio, sociedad y subjetividades de la espera', *EURE (Santiago)*, 42 (125): 155–74.

Anand, N., A. Gupta and H. Appel (eds.) (2018) *The Promise of Infrastructure* (Durham, NC: Duke University Press).

Andrews, M. (2010) 'Good government means different things in different countries', *Governance*, 23 (1): 7–35.

Appel, H.C. (2012a) 'Walls and white elephants: oil extraction, responsibility, and infrastructural violence in Equatorial Guinea', *Ethnography*, 13 (4): 439–65.

Appel, H.C. (2012b) 'Offshore work: oil, modularity, and the how of capitalism in Equatorial Guinea', *American Ethnologist*, 39 (4): 692–709.

Araújo, K. (ed.) (2020) *Las calles: un estudio sobre Santiago de Chile* (Santiago: LOM).

Barbera, R. (2009) 'Community remembering: fear and memory in a Chilean shantytown', *Latin American Perspectives*, 36 (5): 72–88.

Beltrán, F. (2014) 'Fibre-to-the-home, high-speed and national broadband plans: tales from down under', *Telecommunications Policy*, 38 (8–9): 715–29.

Braunstein, E., L. Van Staveren, I., and D. Tavani (2011) 'Embedding care and unpaid work in macroeconomic modeling: a structuralist approach', *Feminist Economics*, 17 (4): 5–31.

Chang, H.J. (2002) 'Breaking the mould: an institutionalist political economy alternative to the neo-liberal theory of the market and the state', *Cambridge Journal of Economics*, 26 (5): 539–59.

Chiodelli, F. (2016) 'International housing policy for the urban poor and the informal city in the Global South: a non-diachronic review', *Journal of International Development*, 28 (5): 788–807.

Cociña, C. (2017) 'Housing as urbanism: the role of housing policies in reducing urban inequalities. A study of post 2006 Housing Programmes in Puente Alto, Chile (unpublished doctoral dissertation, University College London), <https://discovery.ucl.ac.uk/id/eprint/1571836/. CC BY-NC 4.0> (accessed 9 April 2022).

Cociña, C. (2018) 'Housing as urbanism: the role of housing policies in reducing inequalities. Lessons from Puente Alto, Chile', *Housing Studies*, 7(3): 1–23.

Contreras, D., A. Gómez-Lobo, and I. Palma (2018) 'Revisiting the distributional impacts of water subsidy policy in Chile: a historical analysis from 1998–2015', *Water Policy*, 20 (6): 1208–26.

Davis, M. (2006) *Planet of Slums* (New York: Verso).

Dekel, T., A. Meir, A., and N. Alfasi (2019) 'Formalizing infrastructures, civic networks and production of space: Bedouin informal settlements in Be'er-Sheva metropolis', *Land Use Policy*, 81: 91–9.

Ducci, M.E. (1997) 'Chile: el lado obscuro de una política de vivienda exitosa', *EURE (Santiago)*, 69: (23): 99–115.

EMOL (2019) 'El mapa de la conectividad en la región metropolitana: qué comunas tienen mayor acceso a internet', <www.emol.com/noticias/Tecnologia/2020/03/25/980915/Mapa-Conectividad-Internet-Penetracion-Red.html> (accessed 9 April 2021).

Evans, J., J. O'Brien, and B. Ch Ng (2018) 'Towards a geography of informal transport: Mobility, infrastructure and urban sustainability from the back of a motorbike', *Transactions of the Institute of British Geographers*, 43 (4): 674–88.

Fernández, L., B.C. Reisdorf, and W.H. Dutton (2020) 'Urban internet myths and realities: a Detroit case study', *Information, Communication & Society*, 23 (13): 1925–46.

Garcés, M. (2002) *Tomando su sitio: el movimiento de pobladores de Santiago, 1957–1970*, Santiago: LOM ediciones.

Garreton, M. (2017) 'City profile: actually existing neoliberalism in Greater Santiago', *Cities*, 65: 32–50.

Ghosh, S. (2017) 'Broadband penetration and economic growth: do policies matter?', *Telematics and Informatics*, 34 (5): 676–93.

Gilbert, A. (2002) 'Power, ideology and the Washington consensus: the development and spread of Chilean housing policy', *Housing Studies*, 17 (2): 305–24.

Gilbert, A. (2004) 'Helping the poor through housing subsidies: lessons from Chile, Colombia and South Africa', *Habitat International*, 28 (1): 13–40.

Gilbert, A. (2012) 'De Soto's the mystery of capital: reflections on the book's public impact', *International development planning review*, 34 (3): V.

Goodfellow, T. (2018) 'Seeing political settlements through the city: a framework for comparative analysis of urban transformation', *Development and Change*, 49 (1): 199–222.

Graham, S. and S. Marvin (1994) 'Cherry picking and social dumping: utilities in the 1990s', *Utilities Policy*, 4 (2): 113–19.

Graham, S. and S. Marvin (2001) *Splintering Urbanism: Networked Infrastructures, Technological Mobilities and the Urban Condition* (London: Routledge).

Gulati, G.J. and D.J. Yates (2012) 'Different paths to universal access: the impact of policy and regulation on broadband diffusion in the developed and developing worlds', *Telecommunications Policy*, 36 (9): 749–61.

Han, C. (2012) *Life in Debt: Times of Care and Violence in Neoliberal Chile* (Berkeley: University of California Press).

Harvey, P., C.B. Jensen, and A. Morita (2016) 'Introduction: infrastructural complications', in P. Harvey, C.B. Jensen, and A. Morita (eds.), *Infrastructures and Social Complexity* (London: Routledge), pp. 19–40.

Hasan, A. (2006) 'Orangi Pilot Project: the expansion of work beyond Orangi and the mapping of informal settlements and infrastructure', *Environment and Urbanization*, 18 (2): 451–80.

Haucap, J., U. Heimeshoff, and M.R. Lange (2016) 'The impact of tariff diversity on broadband penetration – an empirical analysis', *Telecommunications Policy*, 40 (8): 743–54.

Helsper, E.J. and B.C. Reisdorf (2017) 'The emergence of a "digital underclass" in Great Britain and Sweden: changing reasons for digital exclusion', *New Media and Society*, 19 (8): 1253–70.

Hill, A., T. Hühner, V. Kreibich, and C. Lindner (2014). 'Dar es Salaam, megacity of tomorrow: Informal urban expansion and the provision of technical infrastructure', in *Megacities* (Dordrecht: Springer), pp. 165–177.

Huichalaf, P. (2017) ¿No existen las zonas rojas en telecomunicaciones?, <https://m.elmostrador.cl/noticias/opinion/2017/08/26/no-existen-las-zonas-rojas-en-telecomunicaciones/> (accessed 9 April 2022).

Instituto Nacional de Estadísticas (2017) 'Resultados CENSO 2017', <http://resultados.censo2017.cl/Region?R=R13> (accessed 9 April 2022).

Jamasb, T. and M. Pollitt (2008) 'Liberalisation and R&D in network industries: the case of the electricity industry', *Research Policy*, 37(6–7): 995–1008.

Khan, M. (2010) *Political Settlements and the Governance of Growth-Enhancing Institutions* (London: SOAS).

McFarlane, C. (2008) 'Sanitation in Mumbai's informal settlements: state, "slum", and infrastructure', *Environment and Planning A*, 40 (1): 88–107.

Meagher, K. (2014) 'Smuggling ideologies: from criminalization to hybrid governance in African clandestine economies', *African Affairs*, 113 (453): 497–517.

Meagher, K. (2018) 'Cannibalizing the informal economy: frugal innovation and economic inclusion in Africa', *The European Journal of Development Research*, 30 (1): 17–33.

Milner, H.V. (2006) 'The digital divide: the role of political institutions in technology diffusion', *Comparative Political Studies*, 39 (2): 176–99.

Morales, E., S. Levy, A. Aldunate, and S. Rojas (1990) 'Erradicados en el régimen militar: una evaluación de los beneficiarios' [Eradicated during the military regime: an assessment of the beneficiaries], Working Paper 1–199 (Ñuñoa: FACSO-Chile).

Neokosmidis, I., N. Avaritsiotis, Z. Ventoura, and D. Varoutas (2015) 'Assessment of the gap and (non)-Internet users evolution based on population biology dynamics', *Telecommunications Policy*, 39 (1): 14–37.

Özler, Ş.İ. (2012) 'The concertación and homelessness in Chile: market-based housing policies and limited popular participation', *Latin American Perspectives*, 39 (4): 53–70.

Pamuk, A. (2000) 'Informal institutional arrangements in credit, land markets and infrastructure delivery in Trinidad', *International Journal of Urban and Regional Research*, 24 (2): 379–496.

Ramírez, R. (2017) '¿Qué es eso de "zonas rojas"?', <https://m.elmostrador.cl/noticias/opinion/2017/08/22/que-es-eso-de-zonas-rojas/> (accessed 9 April 2022).

Rodríguez, A. and A. Sugranyes (2004) 'El problema de vivienda de los "con techo"', *EURE (Santiago)*, 30 (91): 53–65.

Rodríguez Weber, J. (2017) *Desarrollo y desigualdad en Chile (1850–2009): historia de su economía política* (Santiago: LOM Ediciones).

Ruiz-Tagle, J. and M.E. López (2014) 'El estudio de la segregación residencial en Santiago de Chile: revisión crítica de algunos problemas metodológicos y conceptuales', *EURE (Santiago)*, 40 (119): 25–48.

Sabatini, F., G. Wormald, C. Sierralta, and P.A. Peters (2009) 'Residential segregation in Santiago: scale-related effects and trends, 1992–2002', in B.R. Roberts and R.H. Wilson (eds.), *Urban Segregation and Governance in the Americas* (New York: Palgrave Macmillan), pp. 121–43.

Salazar, G. (2003) *Ferias libres: espacio residual de soberanía ciudadana* (Santiago: Ediciones Sur).

Salazar, G. (2009) *Mercaderes, empresarios y capitalistas: Chile, siglo XIX* (Santiago: Editorial Sudamericana).

Salcedo, R. and A. Torres (2004) 'Gated communities in Santiago: wall or frontier?', *International Journal of Urban and Regional Research*, 28 (1): 27–44.

Simone, A. (2004) 'People as infrastructure: intersecting fragments in Johannesburg', *Public culture*, 16 (3): 407–29.

Stier, S. (2017) 'Internet diffusion and regime type: temporal patterns in technology adoption', *Telecommunications Policy*, 41 (1): 25–34.

Swyngedouw, E. and J. Wilson, (2014) 'There is no alternative', *The Post-Political and Its Discontents: Spaces of Depoliticisation,* in J. Wilson and E. Swyngedouw (eds.), *The Post-Political and its Discontents: Spaces of Depoliticization, Specters of Radical Politics* (Edinburgh: Edinburgh University Press), pp. 299–312.

Tironi, M. (2003) *Nueva pobreza urbana* (Santiago: RIL Editores).

Valenzuela-Levi, N. (2017) 'Public housing investment to defeat poverty: looking into production and effectiveness through quantitative and qualitative results', in USAID (eds.), *Urban Perspectives Climate Change, Migration, Planning and Financing* (Washington, DC), pp. 147–67.

Valenzuela-Levi, N. (2020) 'Waste political settlements in Colombia and Chile: power, inequality and informality in recycling', *Development and Change*, 51 (4): 1098–1122.

Valenzuela-Levi, N. (2021) 'The written and unwritten rules of internet exclusion: inequality, institutions and network disadvantage in cities of the Global South', *Information, Communication & Society*, 24 (11): 1568–85.

van Deursen, A.J.A.M. and E.J. Helsper (2015a) 'The third-level digital divide: who benefits most from being online?', in *Communication and Information Technologies Annual* (Bingley: Emerald Group Publishing Limited), pp. 29–52.

van Deursen, A.J.A.M. and J.A.G.M. van Dijk, (2015b) 'Toward a multifaceted model of internet access for understanding digital divides: an empirical investigation', *The Information Society*, 31 (5): 379–91.

van Houtven, C.H., E.Z. Oddone, and M. Weinberger (2010) 'Informal and formal care infrastructure and perceived need for caregiver training for frail US veterans referred to home and community-based services', *Chronic Illness*, 6 (1): 57–66.

Vollmer, D. and A. Grêt-Regamey (2013) 'Rivers as municipal infrastructure: Demand for environmental services in informal settlements along an Indonesian river', *Global Environmental Change*, 23 (6): 1542–55.

Williamson, J. (1990) 'What Washington means by policy reform', *Latin American Adjustment: How much Has Happened,* 1 (Washington, DC: Institute for International Economics), pp. 90–120.

World Bank, The (2016) World Development Report 2016 (Washington, DC: The World Bank).

World Bank, The (2020) 'World development indicators', <http://datatopics.worldbank.org/world-development-indicators/> (accessed 9 April 2022).

8. The contradictions of sustainability: discourse, planning and the tramway in Cuenca, Ecuador

Sam Rumé

Introduction

Anthropologists have long taken on the challenge of analysing big urban paradigms in Latin America, such as modernist city building (Holston, 1989; Peattie, 1968), security urbanism (Zeiderman, 2016; Caldeira, 2000), and neoliberal urban renewal (Gandolfo, 2009; Low, 2000). These works have helped to shed light on the discourses of these paradigms, on the heterogeneous actors involved in their formulation, and the conflictual nature of their materialisations. An urbanist tendency still in need of a more elaborated anthropological look, I argue, is 'sustainable urbanism' in Latin America. Though not a new concept anymore, the notion of sustainability is becoming ever more central in the policy formulations of many Latin American cities (UN-Habitat, 2012). Several reasons account for this lack of detailed investigation of this emerging trend. In the first place, scholarship on sustainable urbanism has focused more on cities of the Global North, identified as hubs of sustainable development up until now (Jensen et al., 2019; Blok, 2012). Latin American cities are usually characterised instead by their 'unsustainable' aspects, being described as chaotic, segregated, dangerous, and contaminated places (see, for example, Duhau and Giglia, 2008, on the typical discourse on Mexico City). Second, as the edited volume *Anthropology of Sustainability* (Brightman and Lewis, 2017a) shows, anthropological studies on sustainability tend to focus on rural areas, where the interaction with 'nature' is more apparent.[1] Rival's (2017) chapter is the only one in the book based on the city, but it is also explicitly focused on people's relationship to 'nature' in the city. This point raises a third

1 See Isenhour et al. (2015) and Knox (2020) for interesting exceptions.

and central issue, namely what sustainability actually means: is it necessarily linked to 'nature' and environmentalism?

Many scholars have emphasised the vagueness of the notion of sustainability, which would make it a mere buzzword used in uncritical, often contradictory ways (Jensen et al., 2019; Isenhour et al., 2015). International conceptualisations of sustainability, such as the UN's Sustainable Development Goals (SDGs), include three realms, environmental, economic, and social sustainability, but the defined goals of these three realms are often difficult, if not impossible to reconcile (Homewood, 2017). In the vein of Brightman and Lewis's (2017b) critique of the distortions of sustainable ideas by powerful actors, many sustainable urbanism projects might simply be rejected as unworthy of this label. The inflationary use of the notion in policy discourses also suggests that one cannot consider 'sustainable urbanism' a consistent paradigm to be studied as such. Therefore, other scholars instead argue for an analysis of the *uses* of the term in order to see what it is made to mean in specific contexts, and how it thereby acts in these contexts (Jensen et al., 2019; Tahvilzadeh et al., 2017; Blok, 2013). In what follows, I will address the concrete case of sustainable urbanism in Cuenca, Ecuador, exploring the different meanings and uses of 'sustainability', as well as the tensions between policy, planning, and infrastructure in this process of urban change. My aim, thus, is not only to contribute to the scholarship on sustainable urbanism, but also to explore the interstices between the anthropology of infrastructures and the anthropology of policy and planning.

Cuenca, with its roughly half a million inhabitants, is Ecuador's third largest city, situated in the southern Andean region of the country. It is defined as a heritage city, due to the UNESCO-protected old city centre which combines colonial architecture with pre-colonial remnants and post-colonial, republican buildings. The heritage, along with the natural surroundings, crossed by four emblematic rivers, gives Cuenca a certain charm and makes it a much-appreciated city among Ecuadorians and foreign visitors alike. Cuenca is also a leading city in sustainable policies nationwide, for example in what refers to the protection of its water reserves and wastewater management (Latorre and Malo-Larrea, 2019). Also in terms of sustainable mobility, local authorities express their desire to be seen as frontrunners in Ecuador and the wider region. One of the most significant planning documents in terms of its sustainable vision statement and its supposed impact on the lives of Cuenca's inhabitants is the 2015 Plan de Movilidad y Espacios Públicos (PMEP) [Plan for Mobility and Public Spaces], (GAD Cuenca, 2015).

This document conceives a radical change in the organisation of the city. From the city streets congested by the steadily increasing motorised traffic, considered highly polluting and invading public space, the PMEP plans to shift to a more sustainable, comfortable, and socially just city by promoting walking and cycling and redeveloping public transport. The plan advocates a compact city model, which would be less resource-intensive, in which people would no longer depend on the car but be able to enjoy public space and sociality again. The biggest of the transport projects is the construction of a tramway, which is presented as the heart of the future public-transport system and will constitute a central axis through the city.[2] Initiated in 2013, the tramway project became the flagship of the city's transformation plans, embodying in the most visible form the values and expectations of the sustainability policies. However, the project was also heavily criticised from the beginning, because of the high cost of the project, the possible damage to the historic city centre and the political intentions behind the project. Later, complications in the construction paralysed parts of the city for several years, interrupting commerce and mobility in the surrounding areas and leaving the outcome of the project uncertain. As recently as May 2020, in the midst of the coronavirus pandemic, the tram was finally put into operation and presented as an emergency measure meant to transport people safely through a city threatened by the virus. This happened at a new moment for sustainable urbanism, in which its proponents saw the sustainable projects as even more justified and urgent in the fight against the pandemic.

I undertook fieldwork in Cuenca from 2017 to 2018,[3] observing the dynamics along the tram route under construction, and interviewing disparate social actors, from residents and shopkeepers to academics and municipal authorities. In this period of time, the construction process was constantly haunted by conflicts between these actors and by the seemingly endless ruinations (Gupta, 2018) of the building sites. These conflicts point toward a set of contradictions in Cuenca's sustainability policies and the ambiguous relationship between infrastructure construction and policy discourse. This ambiguity is also temporal, challenging the linearity of project time. Thus, the next section is dedicated to the changes the tram project has known over time, painting a picture which is much more uncertain than the usual 'practitioners' perspective' on policy (Shore and Wright, 2011, p. 4) and the temporal order of policy mobilities (McCann and Ward, 2011). Subsequently, I will analyse the official plans for sustainable mobility in the light of shifting political interests, questioning the divide between planning authorities and unruly society. The last section asks what it takes for the tram to become a sustainable infrastructure, focusing on the politics of urban assemblages.

2 Despite local discourses on Cuenca as a pioneer in the field of sustainable mobility, there are interesting parallels with developments across Latin America. Bus Rapid Transit (BRT) systems originated from Curitiba, Brazil, and are being reproduced with similar urban imaginaries of sustainability and modernisation in numerous cities of the Americas and beyond (see Munoz and Paget-Seekins, 2016). Bogotá's TransMilenio is one of the most famous BRT systems and has drawn much attention to the city and ex-mayor Peñalosa from international scholars and sustainability advocates. In Santiago de Chile, the Transantiago project created an intermodal public transport system, integrating metro, BRT, and other buses. For an assemblage analysis of these two emblematic mobility projects, see Valderrama (2010) and Ureta (2015) respectively.

3 At the time of writing, in 2020, I am undertaking fieldwork in Cuenca again.

What came first, the desire for sustainability or the tram?

In December 2013, towards the end of his mandate as mayor of Cuenca, Paúl Granda fulfilled his biggest electoral promise initiating the construction of a single tram line across the city. In the run-up to the construction, the tram was hyped as a radical innovation for the city, making Cuenca the first Andean city and the third city in Latin America with a modern tram. In television interviews, the mayor suggested that Cuenca could become a model for mobility on the continent. The tram's modern technology and aesthetics were displayed on billboards, in promotional films, and even in the form of a prototype carriage, which was presented ceremoniously in a public space. Although depicted as unprecedented in the regional context, its proponents however made sure to always link the tram project to the many European cities in which trams are operating. One promotional film[4] gives a lengthy list of such cities, praising the tram as 'the future of mobility', efficient and sustainable, which would introduce a 'new culture of mobility' in Cuenca. Sustainability here is understood as 'respectful of both the environment [as the tram is electrically driven] and the passengers [because of its levelled surfaces, its spacious interior, and its smooth locomotion]'. This would make it inclusive for people of all ages and physical conditions, in contrast to the old buses of the city which, apart from being extremely polluting, are considered uncomfortable, even dangerously shaky and inaccesible for some groups.

Various authors (Moraglio, 2014; Siemiatycki, 2006) have pointed out a global trend to reintroduce rail infrastructures in cities, after trams had been abandoned in most places towards the middle of the 20th century. This development can be understood in the context of growing concerns about climate change and pollution, and increasingly congested and fragmented cities. The new generation of tramways, heralded as non-polluting and inclusive technologies, are thus proposed by many city administrations as the best way to fight such problems and make the city more sustainable. The fact that very similar developments of sustainable planning involving tramway systems can be observed in different cities around the world can be fruitfully addressed through the policy mobilities literature (McCann and Ward, 2011). This scholarship shows how ideas, plans, and technologies travel around, supported and negotiated by consultants, construction companies, and politicians. This illustrates how connected cities are, and how complex processes of negotiation and power influence their development.

In much of the literature on this global spread of sustainable planning (Rapoport and Hult, 2017; Carr, 2014; Blok, 2012), it is taken for granted that first there is the desire to implement sustainable projects and then the election

4 See the promotional film uploaded to YouTube on 3 September 2012 by the publicity agency Barter Rubio, www.youtube.com/watch?v=_gu1zIIH2SU (accessed 18 April 2022). The cities mentioned in the film are Bilbao, Ghent, Vienna, Amsterdam, Angers, Vitoria, and Barcelona.

and concretisation of some of the possible projects. The case of the Cuenca tram, however, might tell a different story. Here, the idea for a tram was expressed for the first time in 2009 as part of Paúl Granda's electoral campaign for mayor. In a televised interview from that year,[5] Granda presented his embryonic vision of the tram. The computer-designed picture he held towards the camera showed a tram that looked very different from the one which was to be built four years later. It was a single angular carriage in a rustic reddish-brown tone that resembled less the contemporary trams and more the trams that had been built a century ago. So Granda was actually inspired by the older generation of tramways, and in this interview both Granda and the interviewer became quite excited about the idea. The interviewer found it 'formidable', comparing it to the San Francisco cable car, and Granda replied by calling it 'spectacular' and in turn invoking the Lisbon tram – both examples of preserved heritage trams. At this point, Granda might have found this aesthetically more suitable for the historic city centre of Cuenca, with its colonial architecture. His motivations for building a tram were, as he told the interviewer, that 'this is going to boost the economy enormously, it's going to create a lot of jobs and, above all, it's going to resolve the problem of the chaos that the city of Cuenca is living'. By chaos, he referred to the increasing traffic in the city, which he had mentioned earlier in the interview. When asked if the tram was going to be electrically driven, he denied it, saying that he preferred it to have an internal combustion engine.

So, as this interview shows, the Cuenca tramway started off with quite a different discourse from the sustainable one. Obviously, as a means of public transport, it was already conceived of as a measure against car traffic, but not fully in the vein of sustainable urbanism, as Granda dismissed the option of electrical locomotion. He might have been more concerned with the aesthetics than with the technical details – especially considering that he imagined a newly built 'retro' tram, which in fact only operates in cities in which it has a long history. Only in the course of the following years was the idea of the tram shaped into its 'modern', 'sustainable' form, through various exchanges Granda's administration had with European consultants. A group of local officials travelled overseas to inspect operating tram systems, and Spanish and French agents came to Cuenca to undertake feasibility studies. Backed by a loan from the French government, French and Spanish companies were then appointed for the construction of the tramway in 2013 (Cardoso, 2017). The earlier model had completely disappeared from view, eclipsed by a new-generation electric tram which was 'formidable' and 'spectacular' in a different way. Instead of the rustic vintage aesthetic, this new model stood out through its shiny red colour and its rounded-off, elegant design. In this form, the tram was more likely to correspond to Larkin's (2013) description of infrastructures' affective modernity. For many *cuencanos*, the tram came to represent something excitingly

5 See an excerpt of the interview, which aired on Ecuavisa, on journalist Carlos Vera's show *Contacto Directo*, www.youtube.com/watch?v=uhj8vP1dcco (accessed 18 April 2022).

Figure 8.1 The Cuenca tramway in 2020. Photo taken by the author

outlandish and futuristic, something which would undoubtedly make the city more modern. The fact, often voiced in public discourse, that it would be the first of its kind in the whole Andean region, resonated with the inhabitants' high opinion of their city.

Not everyone was equally excited about the project, however. As I was sitting with Diego in his workshop in the city centre, having a coffee and chatting about the changes in Cuenca, buses periodically drove by, emitting their black exhaust fumes through the open shopfront and cutting our conversation with their noise. Diego, a young artisan and passionate walker, hates these old contaminating buses and describes a ride on them as a rollercoaster, due to the bus drivers' aggressive driving style. But he does not consider the tram to be a viable alternative. According to him, the tram is useless for most inhabitants, as it only represents one route. It would rather constitute a means to transport tourists from the airport and the coach station through the city centre. Apart from the tram's considerable financial cost, Diego emphasises the material and symbolic threat to the city which he feels the tram poses. The Cuenca he loves and admires on his walks is characterised by the details of the heritage architecture and the natural surroundings. The essence of Cuenca, to him, is its tradition, and the tram is likely to damage the fragile heritage buildings, especially those made of adobe. Its modernist look would also clash with the city's traditional aesthetic. But Diego describes Cuenca as a 'city of many appearances', aspiring to appear in certain ways. He says people here are mestizos, cholos, indios, 'but people sometimes don't want to recognise this. They focus on this image on the television, on what they sell you. That might be why this futuristic tram is coming about now.'

This comment illustrates two opposed visions of the city, a traditionalising and a modernising one. Many people I have met in Cuenca feel as attached to the city's heritage as Diego does. Heritage conservation policies are reinforcing this sense of belonging, while promoting the city as a tourist destination. The first draft of the Cuenca tramway embodied a heritage aesthetic, although Cuenca has never had a tramway in the past. Instead, the new-generation tram which came to be built was presented as a revolutionising innovation, a technology which would lead the city into the future.[6] This future was presented as already a reality in European cities, thus feeding a sense that Cuenca was lagging behind a temporally advanced 'developed world'. Diego feels that the resolutely modern aesthetic of the tram clashes with the identity of the city and its inhabitants. However, he does not frame this clash in temporal terms, but rather in cultural, even racial ones. The racial implications of this conflict between the traditional and the modern in Cuenca is also described by Weismantel (2003). In her analysis, the modernisation discourse would represent indigenous people as the traditional, anti-modern past, and aspire towards the whitening of the population (see also the introduction to this volume). The explicit inspiration from urban Europe and the praising of its technology, expertise and supposedly orderly city life, might not go as far as implying racial superiority, but it does imply a cultural advance. Can the imagined 'new culture of mobility', proposed by the tramway project, thus be seen as a case of persistent 'colonial cultures of planning' (Horn, 2019, p. 39)?

The policy mobilities perspective helps us to understand how powerful global actors maintain their influence in the international arena of urban development, in this case asserting a Eurocentric view of the 'best practices' (McCann, 2017; Blok, 2012) to be reproduced. This Eurocentric view also explains why the discourse of sustainability accompanying the Cuenca tramway and the city's mobility planning in general almost completely blank out notions of *buen vivir*. The concept of *buen vivir* has been developed in national policy, including the new constitution of 2008, as an alternative to

6 In contrast to my argument, the theorisations of heritage usually do not see heritage-making as opposed to modernity, but rather as inherently modern. A modern elite would assert itself through heritage making, creating a contrast with modernity which would serve as a romanticised past and a consumable object (see Gandolfo, 2009; Hodges, 2009; Kingman and Goetschel, 2005). In part, this is certainly true of heritage-making in Cuenca as well. A newly built 'retro' tram would have exacerbated the sense that heritage is more about the aesthetic simulation of a past that has never been, rather than the mere conservation of history. However, as Weismantel (2003) suggests, much of what is considered heritage in Cuenca, such as the symbolic Chola Cuencana, is very much alive and resisting the objectification and stereotypification of heritage. This scholarship on heritage might also neglect how heritage can reinforce people's sense of belonging and identity, as is reflected in Diego's account.

the Western idea of 'sustainable development'. While sustainable development maintains modernist logics of progress, economic development, and control over nature, understood as resources, *buen vivir* is inspired by indigenous worldviews, uniting the social and the natural in a non-dualist, relational ontology (see Latorre and Malo-Larrea, 2019; Bretón, 2017; Merino, 2016). The supposed sustainability of the Cuenca tramway project is intrinsically linked to its modernity, its electric technology, and 'inclusive' design. Rather than the more holistic approach of *buen vivir*, it thus constitutes a technological fix understood to create sustainability. This trust in the power of technology to produce sustainable futures reveals the techno-modernist logic of the tram project, which, according to Latorre and Malo-Larrea (2019) would correspond to the general worldview of policymakers in Cuenca, despite the national policy discourse of *buen vivir*.[7] What these authors do not discuss, however, is the influence powerful international actors can have on the shape and discourse of local sustainability projects.[8]

The early development of the Cuenca tram project shows how an infrastructure project can change its forms, workings, and meanings over time (see Latour, 1996), and how the same project can involve different, even contradictory interests and visions of the city. The Cuenca tramway came into being as the electoral promise of a mayoral candidate seemingly inspired by heritage trams. His motivations, apart from being elected, appeared to be primarily to solve traffic problems and boost the local economy, while beautifying the city. These goals were maintained as the project materialised several years later, but they were integrated into a new discourse of sustainability and modernisation. At this point, international actors had participated in redirecting the tram into the global field of sustainable urbanism, thereby completely changing its shape and aesthetics. This modern aesthetic excited many residents, and clashed with others' sense of belonging. Also, national efforts to produce an alternative to Western conceptions of sustainability were overlooked. The tram had become a project in line with a global urban trend towards sustainable development and mobility, presented at the same time as a pioneer project in the region.

Thus, a tram can mean very different things: an old-fashioned means of transport that is turned into a picturesque heritage object and a cutting-edge technology that promises sustainable development. The Cuenca tram, rather than being *the result* of explicit sustainability policies, was only integrated into these in the course of its development. The tram project therefore challenges

7 The *buen vivir* policy discourse was particularly strong at the beginning of Rafael Correa's presidency, but weakened towards the end of his presidency. Under his successor, Moreno, *buen vivir* has been largely sidestepped, if not abandoned in national policymaking (Carranza, 2019).

8 For a historical account of both modernist urban planning in Latin America and the influence of international actors and ideologies on local projects, see Chapter 4 of this volume.

the 'practitioners' perspective' on policies (Shore and Wright, 2011, p. 4), which considers policymaking as a rational, temporally linear process with clear stages. This process would begin with a general vision statement offering a frame for concrete actions to be taken subsequently. This is also the common representation of urban planning (Abram, 2011). In the next section, I will address the relationship between the tram project and the broader sustainable planning efforts in Cuenca.

Who is planning?

Despite Cuenca usually being described as more peaceful than Ecuador's two largest cities, Quito and Guayaquil, the discourse of local authorities, as well as many residents, shifts when it comes to characterising traffic in the city. Streets are perceived as contaminated and overcrowded; bus, taxi, and private car drivers as irresponsible and aggressive. To make matters worse, street vendors are said to invade public space and crime to be on the rise. The picture drawn of urban space here corresponds to typical accounts of chaotic Latin American city streets (see Gandolfo, 2009; Duhau and Giglia, 2008). Municipal plans, such as the PMEP (GAD Cuenca, 2015) claim to profoundly change this cityscape. They imagine a mobility system which would prioritise and significantly increase pedestrian and bicycle mobility through (semi-)pedestrianisation, the implementation of bicycle lanes, and a public bicycle rental system.[9] These would be connected to non-polluting and inclusive public transport, constituted by a renovated bus fleet and the tramway as the central axis and 'articulator' (GAD Cuenca, 2015, p. 12) of the system. The different mobilities would work conjointly in an overarching intermodal system, which would not only be more efficient than current transport, but also it would also create a more sustainable and liveable city. It would have to emerge together with a more compact city, in which dense, mixed-use neighbourhoods would allow for shorter journeys and lively public spaces. The PMEP's broad vision of sustainability thus includes the reduction of pollution, as well as the physical and mental health, safety, and social inclusion of city dwellers. With its almost thousand pages, the plan leaves no doubt that these aspects have been thoroughly analysed and it shows how to improve them. But the PMEP, like the tramway project, might not correspond to the policy and planning ideal of a linear process, starting with the analysis of a problem, followed by an informed choice of response and its implementation (Shore and Wright, 2011).

One day in February 2018, I met up with Juan for lunch on campus. As one of the scholars in Cuenca focused on mobilities, he was participating in public debates and projects to improve mobilities in the city. An engaged advocate of

9 Some of these projects have already been realised at the time of writing, such as the public bicycle system. Others are constantly postponed and cancelled, such as pedestrianisation projects.

sustainability, he had also contributed to the elaboration of the PMEP, which came into being as a participatory project between the municipality, local universities, and certain civic groups. Juan considered the plan to go in the right direction, although it would still lack broader participation. Regarding the tram, he had mixed feelings, as the tramway project was not really a consequence of the plan: 'Everything was done the other way round, because first they thought of building the tram, and then, when they had already started building the tram, they thought of making the mobility plan. So completely in reverse. Also, the mobility plan kind of had to adjust to this heavy condition which was the tram.' According to Juan, thus, the tram constituted a certain constraint for the PMEP, to which other measures had to be adapted, rather than emerging from the plan as a logical and coordinated measure. Antonio, an engineer and transport expert who had only recently been hired by the municipality to work on the tram project, echoed this view during our interview. 'The tramway project did not exactly respond to planning', he said, 'it was an improvisation' which would have completely thrown previous mobility plans off track. So just as the tram project had emerged before its conceptualisation in terms of sustainability, it was also developed out of sync with the city's more general public-transport planning.

When the PMEP was published in 2015, two years after the beginning of the tram project, circumstances had changed in Cuenca. Paúl Granda, the left-wing originator of the tram project, lost the municipal elections in 2014 against the centrist Marcelo Cabrera, who had shown himself to be critical of the tramway in his campaign. Construction of the tram had already begun, when Cabrera reevaluated the details of the project. However, the previously concluded deals and the pressure from the national government apparently forced him to continue the construction. In fact, Granda's project had been supported from the beginning by the then President Rafael Correa, whose left-wing party Alianza País Granda was a member of. The tram project fitted into the government's large-scale modernisation project, which produced an unprecedented amount of infrastructure projects throughout the country. It also corresponded to national efforts to decrease dependence on fossil fuel and develop electrification. In this sense, although locally the tram caused confusion and disrupted planning, it was in line with the national agenda.[10]

The tram project was perceived by many locals as a primarily *political* project, the spectacularity of which had fulfilled its function of electing Granda as mayor in the previous elections. The view that infrastructure projects fulfil political interests rather than 'public' ones (see Harvey, 2017) is quite common in Ecuador, especially among opponents of Correa's government. Many big projects of Correa's administration have been criticised as entailing

10 The new-generation tram model corresponded to the modernisation and electrification agenda, but also the initial 'retro' tram draft would have had certain parallels with national developments, given that the government restored the country's historic trains as a tourist attraction.

false promises and white elephants (Wilson and Bayón, 2017), and as tools for political campaigns and corruption. The Cuenca tram played into this criticism, especially when problems arising in the construction hinted at flawed planning (Cardoso, 2017). In fact, many details given by the early promoters of the tram project turned out to be wrong in the course of the construction. The tram ended up costing much more than expected by feasibility studies, and the construction was considerably lengthier and more intrusive than Granda had claimed. Instead of going into operation in 2016, it only started to run in May 2020. In 2013, the municipality argued that the tram would transport 120,000 people a day. Today, the tram directorate has lowered its expectations considerably, as only a third of this number of passengers might be achieved. What may have seemed like a viable project, based on international expertise, at the outset, was revealed to be hugely problematic five years later, when it was commonly accepted to be irreversible.

Therefore, interlocutors like Juan, the scholar, and Antonio, the engineer, saw planning efforts like the PMEP as a necessity to restore order and make the tramway a success. However, Juan was sceptical about the actual outcomes of the PMEP. Although he and many other contributors had worked on this plan on behalf of the municipality, Juan had heard that Mayor Cabrera himself was actually not that keen on following the plan rigorously. 'There are contradictory positions [of the municipality] all the time, which shows again – irrespective of what is ultimately going to be done – the absolute lack of vision about how the city centre should work. [...] Many things have been done and will continue to be done on the go, searching for makeshift solutions rather than a more global vision and plan.'

So although Cabrera wanted to dissociate himself and his administration from previous errors, he quickly suffered from criticism himself about the handling of the tramway project. While his administration argued they had inherited a flawed project from his political opponent Granda (who in 2017 would become Minister of Transport), critics thought Cabrera and his team had made it even worse. The construction slowed down and eventually came to a halt, with inhabitants left amid fenced-off and broken streets, workers unpaid, and the municipality fighting with the Spanish construction company over prices.[11] For more than a year, the construction sites remained abandoned. Not only did this chaotic development of the project give people the impression of incompetence on the part of the municipality, Juan's quote above also suggests a lack of will. What his comment referred to in particular was the municipality's unclear position concerning pedestrianisation. The tram construction would have been a good opportunity to pedestrianise the

11 It still remains unclear who was at fault in this fight, a municipality which was not able to pay the contractors because of the country's increasing economic difficulties, linked to the significant drop in international petrol prices, or a contractor which turned out to be without funds and asked for unjustified surcharges. An arbitration tribunal in Chile will determine this.

areas along the rails – even a necessity for Juan, considering the narrowness of some of the streets hosting the tram. This measure would have been in line with the vision of the PMEP, but apparently it was too controversial for the mayor to realise it, risking his approval among car supporters. So Juan's mention of 'makeshift solutions' implies short-term political strategies, which may sometimes bring forth infrastructure projects – as had happened in the electoral campaign of the previous mayor – but which are inherently contrary to the long-term commitment of infrastructure projects and planning. There is thus a contradiction between the temporality of political interests and the temporality of planning which contributes to the intrinsic instability of infrastructure projects (see Harvey, 2017; Abram, 2011).

Two theoretical lines can be helpful to follow from here. On the one hand, the literature on infrastructures (Anand et al., 2018; Harvey et al., 2017b; Harvey and Knox, 2015) shows how, apart from the volatility of political actors, innumerable other forces participate in the course of infrastructure projects, 'enchanting' (Harvey and Knox, 2012) and simultaneously unsettling them – among these, the economic actors and market tendencies, the unruly actions of local residents, and the unpredictable behaviour of materials and climate. Infrastructure projects claim to hold these elements in place, promising different benefits for all of their publics. Unsurprisingly, they often fail to do so. In this sense, the official narratives of orderly development, as well as the critiques of incompetent authorities, stem from an overestimation of the decision-makers' ability to anticipate infrastructural futures (Harvey et al., 2017a).

On the other hand, the literature on the state (Krupa and Nugent, 2015; Sharma and Gupta, 2006; Scott 1998) shows how such projects are also meant to *conjure up* the state through those very narratives of planning and the emerging materials. This applies, on the national level, to Ecuador's 'postneoliberal' return of the state under Correa (Grugel and Riggirozzi, 2012), as well as, on the local level, to the municipality's projects to impose order in an uncontrolled landscape of mobilities. This performative state effect would counter the unruly heterogeneity, not only of the society to be governed, but also of the state itself. The state, or the municipality in this case, is seen through the same processual lens as its infrastructure projects. The uncertainty of the outcomes of infrastructure projects thus goes in hand with the uncertainty of the state effect, a failing infrastructure being likely to expose the flaws of the responsible entities and thereby damage their relationship with those to be governed. This was the case with the Cuenca tramway, especially during the construction phase.

What about the municipality's failure to comply with the PMEP? As Juan suggested, plans can be developed from the start with the knowledge that they are not going to be followed: '[The mayor] was interested in making the plan, not to improve mobility, I think, but in order to say "we have a mobility plan."' The state effect of a plan, although unrealised, might be enough to stimulate certain economic gains. At a time when sustainable development is

Figure 8.2 Shops along the paralysed tram construction in 2017. Photo taken by the author

advocated by international organisations such as UN-Habitat and generating a flourishing market, cities' sustainable policy initiatives give them an attractive and trustworthy image for investment (Rapoport and Hult, 2017). The municipality of Cuenca does indeed work a lot towards international cooperation, reaching out to organisations such as the UN, the Inter-American Development Bank, and the Development Bank of Latin America. The sustainable image might also attract businesses and tourists, as it makes the city appear well-organised, innovative, and secure. In this sense, sustainable urbanism is often criticised for maintaining the neoliberal logics of the entrepreneurial city. Sustainability would only be used as a superficial aesthetic, or a means in the inter-city competition for 'best practices' (McCann, 2017).

By all appearances, thus, the tramway project was hastily launched without the necessary planning, while the PMEP was carefully elaborated, but not to be realised. Based on the representation of a chaotic cityscape, the discourse of both the tram and the PMEP suggests the ordering of the city and its mobilities in more sustainable ways, implying a certain disciplining process through which a new form of citizenship, a 'new culture of mobility'[12] is supposed to emerge.[13] However, in the face of the apparent problems and contradictions within the municipality, it was increasingly residents who accused the municipality of being disorganised and creating chaos in the city. As the tram construction irrupted in the everyday spaces of city dwellers, obstructing their mobility and paralysing commerce over the course of several years, inhabitants started organising in order to improve their situation.

12 This is quoted again from the promotional film of the tram discussed in the previous section.

13 As noted in the introductory chapter, the ordering and disciplining efforts of infrastructure projects are a recurring theme throughout this volume, for example, between Chapters 2, 4, and 6.

A couple of shopkeepers and other engaged people formed a *veeduría*, in accordance with a legal mechanism in Ecuador which makes it possible for citizens to monitor and assess public works. Over several months, I attended the weekly *veeduría* meetings which were held in the ballroom of a hotel in the city centre. The half a dozen to a dozen participants would gather in the empty ballroom to discuss their monitoring work, their personal situations, and political opinions. These meetings offered a space for the participants to share their sorrow, as most of them were directly affected by the obstructive construction sites. Like many other shops along the unfinished tram route, their businesses were on the brink of collapse. In their meetings, they also programmed protest marches, prepared press conferences, and came up with actions in solidarity with other affected residents. In their efforts to monitor the progress of the tram construction, they struggled with an uncooperative, untransparent municipality. However, they got hold of a leaked timeline of the tramway project and publicly put pressure on the municipality to abide to it. This perspective further challenges the idea of planning as involving organised institutions, on the one hand, and unruly social forces, on the other[14] – akin to de Certeau's (1988) dichotomic view of urbanism. Municipal actors can just as well be indecisive and inclined to improvisation, while inhabitants prove able to plan themselves and pressure authorities to respect official plans.

A sustainable infrastructure?

At one of the *veeduría* meetings, Eugenia, the president of the group, informed the participants about a project presentation by one of the city's universities she had attended the week before. Given that new calculations gave the tram far fewer passengers than initially expected, the university had been commissioned by the municipality to develop a plan to solve this problem. Basically, they needed to make the tram useful, as Eugenia explained. The university had come up with a plan to densify certain areas along the tram route, outside the heritage perimeter, which were somewhat commercial and not particularly residential at present. It was the *veedores*' understanding that this meant high-rise residential buildings should be developed there in order to produce passengers. The *veeduría* participants were very sceptical of this idea. It seemed even more extravagant and unrealistic than the tram itself. It made Eugenia think of Brasília, Brazil's capital which had been designed from scratch. But Cuenca was an existing, historic city, which could not simply be replaced by a new design, she said, especially not from one day to the next.

This university project was aimed at developing a Master Plan for the Area of Influence of the Tramway, abbreviated as PMAIT.[15] The PMAIT project thus

14 Similar critiques are raised in Chapters 1 and 7 of this volume.

15 From the original title Plan Maestro para el Área de Influencia del Tranvía de los Cuatro Ríos de Cuenca en los Tramos de la Avenida España y Avenida Américas.

started from a recognition that the city was still in need of thorough planning with regard to the tram: 'the lack of planning for the integration of the tramway profoundly limits the potential for linkage and urban regeneration that a means of transport of these characteristics can achieve, becoming, on the one hand, an element of fracture in the urban fabric and, on the other hand, the origin of its possible unsustainability in the long term' (UDA, 2016, p. 118). How is (un)sustainability understood here? The inherent characteristics of the tram, such as its electrical drive and its inclusive design, are revealed not to be a sufficient condition anymore for it to be sustainable. Although this perspective leads the authors of this document to reject the technological determinism implied in the tram discourse (the idea that the city would become sustainable *through* the tramway), they still consider the tram as a potential catalyst for broader urban change. 'How to build a better city using the tramway as a tool?', they ask (UDA, 2016, p. 14). A more reciprocal understanding thus arises, with the tram depending on a range of other elements and actors, while the city's sustainable future is made to depend on the tram. What is suggested is a thorough re-assemblage of the city, which the *veedores*, as well as Diego the artisan, see as a threat to the historical city. Thus, the tension between the conservationist vision of the city and the sustainable projects emerges again, the tram being understood less as a means to sustain the present city as it is involved in the imagining of a more sustainable future. In this future-oriented logic, the recurrent critique that the tram does not respond to Cuenca's needs is not as relevant anymore. Instead of responding to present needs, it would create future possibilities. But these future possibilities actually create new needs in the present, the tram requiring a range of adjustments of the city in order to fulfil its promises. I will briefly discuss some of these adjustments, ranging from densification to the restructuring of buses and, more broadly, of social life along the tram route.

As mentioned, the main claim of the PMAIT project is for densification. This idea can be seen, as Eugenia put it, as a necessity to make the tram useful by producing passengers. If a sufficient number of paying passengers is not achieved, the tram becomes unsustainable: *financially*. On the other hand, the tram can be understood to make densification possible, as it is more appropriate for transporting large numbers of people than buses or private cars. In this sense, it indeed becomes a tool, namely in the quest for a compact city, counteracting urban sprawl (see also Hermida et al., 2015). The tramway's very need of financial sustainability becomes an incentive to pursue compact city policies more seriously. Apart from densification, this might include restrictions on car traffic, pedestrianisation, and the revision of land uses in order to create mixed-use neighbourhoods (mixing residence, work, commerce, and leisure). Environmental sustainability and financial sustainability turn out to be overlapping concerns in this case, the tram's promises coalescing with its needs.

Likewise, the tram makes this ideal of an overarching, intermodal mobility system both possible and necessary. It makes this system possible as it can work as its central axis and connect future pedestrian spaces with bus routes and public bicycle docks. In turn, this interconnection with other means of transport is necessary for the tram, again in order to attract people to it and increase tram passengers. In particular, the city's buses ought to become essential suppliers of passengers, through the adaptation of their routes to the tram line. The buses would thereby become more peripheral in this intermodal system, connecting the city centre – covered by the tram – to its surroundings. The image of harmonious and effective cooperation between these different means of transport, however, conceals the diverging interests of the actors involved. The buses in Cuenca are owned by private companies who see their spaces, passengers, and autonomy captured by the municipality and its tramway project. The relationship between the municipality and the bus companies was already tense before, but the negotiations around the creation of the intermodal mobility system is currently exacerbating this tension. As a result, for instance, the tram started operation without a unified fare payment system, although the municipality had established this as a requirement for the tram to start operating.

But perhaps most importantly, the emergence of the sustainable and orderly 'new culture of mobility'[16] (UDA, 2016, p. 113) relies on the shaping of social life in the city streets. The PMAIT recognises the spaces along the tram route as essential to the city's sociality and commerce. Several of those spaces, such as the Feria Libre (the city's biggest market) and the coach station, would attract large masses of people, especially from lower social classes, producing unwieldy settings of mobility, encounter, formal and informal commerce, alcohol consumption, and theft. The PMAIT argues that these spaces need to change together with the tram project. The inclusive design of the tram, along with municipal ordinances, educational campaigns, and police control should participate in making these public spaces safe, comfortable, and orderly. A sense of *social* sustainability (see Polèse and Stren, 2000) emerges from this vision, the tram, combined with other measures, being able to create more harmonious social ties. However, the ideal of the socially sustainable city, where everybody has equal rights and access, can easily be contradicted by the discriminatory implications of many 'urban regeneration' policies (UDA, 2016, p. 118; see Gandolfo 2009; Swanson, 2007). The implicitly middle-class aesthetic of sustainability and its particular vision of order might in fact exclude practices of informality from the spaces in question, profoundly changing the character of these spaces.

What is more, formal commerce along the tram route has also been undergoing important changes, as hundreds of shops have had to close down

16 The PMAIT document echoes the expression from the 2012 promotional film of the tram, quoted above.

since the construction of the tram began. The longer the construction dragged on, complicating access to surrounding streets, the more businesses nearby suffered. Several *veedores* expressed suspicions about the intentions of the municipality. Was the construction being retarded on purpose so as to force traditional small businesses to abandon their spaces and sell their properties for a reduced price, only for the municipality and allied investors to benefit from the revaluation of the area which was expected to occur with the tram in operation? Such speculations about possible intentions remain unproven. What is certain, however, is that the construction process has destabilised and devalued commerce and ownership in affected areas, and revaluation is likely to ensue from a working tram and connected urban regeneration efforts. Thus, as Siemiatycki (2006) showed in the case of the tram construction in Bilbao, the Cuenca tram is likely to reinforce gentrification in the city centre.[17]

Cuenca's sustainable planning documents emphasise their social conscience, mentioning ideas of 'social cohesion' and 'right to the city' (GAD Cuenca, 2015, p. 177), but their overly harmonious vision easily omits more conflictual realities. However idealised, their conceptualisation of sustainability might sound familiar to the anthropologist of infrastructures. The understanding of sustainability as relying on the tram becoming an inclusive system, seamlessly integrated into the 'urban fabric' (UDA, 2016, p. 118), ordering mobility and stabilising social relations, in fact comes close to the scholarly ideal type of infrastructure (Star, 1999). The PMAIT's vision of sustainability involves reciprocal relations between the tram and the urban environment, including its material and social organisation. This reciprocity between humans and materials can be understood through conceptualisations of infrastructures as socio-technical assemblages (see Harvey et al., 2017a).

One could therefore argue that the efforts to make the tram sustainable are synonymous with infrastructuring it. According to Star's (1999) by now classic definition of infrastructures, effectively intertwined and adapted infrastructures are seen to produce the systemic background of social life, defining the possibilities of action without being taken into account. Key to this background condition is the seamlessness of their interconnected working (Vertesi, 2014). The introduction of the tram would thus require the re-entanglement of infrastructures and infrastructured practices which were destabilised by the tram construction. This involves the physical reconnections of transport routes, as well as certain legal adjustments, the orientation of population growth, and changes to social life in public spaces.[18] The sustainability of the planned intermodality is linked to its seamlessness. The tram, buses, public bicycles, bicycle lanes, and pedestrian zones are supposed to form a coherent

17 Various authors have already observed gentrification processes in Cuenca before, linked to tourism and lifestyle migration (Cabrera-Jara, 2019; Hayes, 2015).

18 Chapter 6 in this volume offers a detailed description of how different layers and types of infrastructure, from material to social, interact.

whole, in which one could comfortably skip from one means of transport to another (e.g. by allowing bikes on the tram, by reducing waiting times, or by not paying twice when switching between tram and bus). The supposed sustainability of the tram itself, as a technology, also stems largely from its promise of seamlessness. People will not have to put up with exhaust fumes, loud motor noises, and uncomfortable, even dangerous rides – in contrast to the experience of the urban bus, which was elucidated at my visit to Diego's workshop. The tram offers smooth, silent movement and levelled surfaces, constituting a technology which includes the elderly, the disabled, and people with young children.

However, the ideals of sustainability and inclusiveness are contradicted by possible and actual instances of discrimination, coercion, and exclusion. This ambivalent reorganising effort of the city illustrates the politics of urban assemblages (Ureta, 2015; Blok, 2013; Farías, 2011). The building of a 'sustainable future', in accordance with the current planning imagination, requires its proponents to build alliances, making humans and non-humans behave according to plan by convincing people of the values of sustainability, successfully negotiating with companies and other interest groups, and making infrastructures work together. However, this alliance-building is not necessarily a peaceful process, unlike what might be represented in planning documents. These documents omit the diversity of agencies and interests which can resist official plans within a heterogeneous society. A heterogeneous society might include residents with contrary feelings of belonging, higher-class inhabitants who continue to prefer their suburb-car assemblage, lower-class inhabitants who continue to make 'informal' use of public space, bus companies and shopkeepers who defend their businesses, and even the very proponents of sustainability projects, who value their personal careers over their official plans. What becomes clear is that the sustainable assemblage is never a finished infrastructure, but rather a political terrain (von Schnitzler, 2013), with possibly as many alternatives, sometimes openly resisting worlds as there are stable alliances. This uncertainty makes the official definition of sustainability an ever-partial reality.

Conclusion

The Cuenca tramway project involves critical elements with which to think about sustainable urbanism and infrastructures. It shows how infrastructure projects are malleable and multiple, able to change their forms and meanings over time (Latour, 1996), as well as to enfold heterogeneous, conflicting forces in unstable assemblages (Harvey, 2018). As the tram emerged in the form of an electoral promise before being imbued with a globalised sustainable development discourse, it alludes to the uncertain politics of infrastructure. But by the time of its concretisation, not only had the discourse changed from a merely logistic and economic focus to imply a more radical transformation of the city, but the tram itself was also hardly recognisable anymore. The project had exchanged its technology under the same name – 'tram' – as transnational actors had engaged their expertise and money.

Represented henceforth as the embodiment of sustainable development and modernity in its advertising, the tram project however disrupted contemporaneous mobility planning and increased experiences of chaos in the everyday lives of city dwellers. It thereby illustrates the ambiguous relationship between infrastructure projects and planning, the former not necessarily ensuing from the latter but instead disturbing and constraining it. Despite the tram being non-polluting, its planning failures made it 'unsustainable' in various ways: The lack of organisation caused the construction site to durably affect infrastructured practices of dwelling, mobility, and commerce in the city. It thereby also compromised the state effect of the municipality and the relationships between inhabitants and their affective spaces. Inasmuch as sustainability includes considerations of human wellbeing and consolidated social ties, the tram became acknowledged as socially unsustainable in its impromptu form (see UDA, 2016). But the expected deficiency of 'integration', and thus of passengers, also contradicts the very goal of environmental benefit (by not decreasing motorised traffic) and threatens the financial sustainability of the tram.

The tramway appears as neither sustainable by itself, nor able to produce sustainability on its own – a diagnosis which challenges technological essentialism and determinism respectively. Instead, for it to be sustainable, it would need to be infrastructured by reassembling socio-material relations. Sustainability, in this sense, can be understood to correspond to the very ideal of infrastructure as a seamless technical support for social life, facilitating and ordering collective action. This reassembling effort equates to a large-scale transformation of the city, including changes in the legal frameworks, the built environment, the organisation of social life, and the practices and values of inhabitants. By acknowledging this, planning documents such as the PMAIT advance towards a deeper understanding of the implications of infrastructure production, hinting at the hugely complex challenge of such projects. If, as Star (1999) argued, an infrastructure is never an infrastructure for everybody, neither is sustainability. A considerable range of conflicts has already been sparked by the tramway construction, and the operational tram and the quest for an intermodal mobility system are likely to entail new ones. The anthropological analysis of infrastructures is well placed to describe the heterogeneous actors involved in this process. The inherent uncertainty of infrastructure projects leaves questions open about how the city will reassemble with the tram, and who is to win and who is to lose in this process.

References

Abram, S. (2011) *Culture and Planning* (Farnham: Ashgate).

Anand, N., A. Gupta, and H. Appel (eds.) (2018) *The Promise of Infrastructure* (Durham, NC and London: Duke University Press).

Blok, A. (2012) 'Greening cosmopolitan urbanism? On the transnational mobility of low-carbon formats in Northern European and East Asian cities', *Environment and Planning A,* 44: 2327–43.

Blok, A. (2013) 'Urban green assemblages: an ANT view on sustainable city building projects', *Science & Technology Studies,* 26 (1): 5–24.

Bretón, V. (2017) 'Three divergent understandings of *Buen Vivir* in the Ecuador of the Citizens' Revolution', *Latin American and Caribbean Ethnic Studies,* 12 (2): 188–98.

Brightman, M. and J. Lewis (eds.) (2017a) *The Anthropology of Sustainability. Beyond Development and Progress* (New York: Palgrave Macmillan).

Brightman, M. and J. Lewis (2017b) 'Introduction: the anthropology of sustainability: beyond development and progress', in M. Brightman and J. Lewis (eds.), *The Anthropology of Sustainability. Beyond Development and Progress* (New York: Palgrave Macmillan), pp. 1–33.

Cabrera-Jara, N. (2019) 'Gentrificación en áreas patrimoniales latinoamericanas: cuestionamiento ético desde el caso de Cuenca, Ecuador', *Urbe. Revista Brasileira de Gestão Urbana,* 11: 1–15.

Caldeira, T. (2000) *City of Walls. Crime, Segregation, and Citizenship in São Paulo* (Berkeley and Los Angeles: University of California Press).

Cardoso, E. (2017) *Ilusiones. Una ciudad para el tranvía* (Cuenca: Diego Demetrio Orellana).

Carr, C. (2014) 'Discourse yes, implementation maybe: an immobility and paralysis of sustainable development policy', *European Planning Studies,* 22 (9): 1824–40.

Carranza, C. (2019) *Emergencias epistémicas de modelos alternativos al desarrollo. El Sumak Kawsay y el buen vivir en Ecuador.* Hegoa Working Papers No. 80 (Bilbao: Universidad del País Vasco).

de Certeau, M. (1988) *The Practice of Everyday Life* (Berkeley and Los Angeles: University of California Press).

Duhau, E. and A. Giglia (2008) *Las reglas del desorden. Habitar la metrópoli* (México D.F.: Siglo XXI).

Farías, I. (2011) 'The politics of urban assemblages', *City,* 15 (3–4): 365–74.

GAD Cuenca (2015) 'Plan de movilidad y espacios públicos',

<www.cuenca.gob.ec/?q=content/plan-de-movilidad> (accessed 13 April 2022).

Gandolfo, D. (2009) *The City at its Limits. Taboo, Transgression, and Urban Renewal in Lima* (Chicago: University of Chicago Press).

Grugel, J. and P. Riggirozzi (2012) 'Post-neoliberalism in Latin America: rebuilding and reclaiming the state after crisis', *Development and Change,* 43 (1): 1–21.

Gupta, A. (2018) 'The future in ruins: thoughts on the temporality of infrastructure', in N. Anand, A. Gupta and H. Appel (eds.), *The Promise of Infrastructure* (Durham, NC and London: Duke University Press), pp. 62–79.

Harvey, P. (2017) 'Containment and disruption. The illicit economies of infrastructural investment', in P. Harvey, C.B. Jensen and A. Morita (eds.), *Infrastructures and Social Complexity. A Companion* (Abingdon and New York: Routledge), pp. 51–63.

Harvey, P. (2018) 'Infrastructures in and out of time: the promise of roads in contemporary peru', in N. Anand, A. Gupta, and H. Appel (eds.), *The Promise of Infrastructure* (Durham, NC and London: Duke University Press), pp. 80–101.

Harvey, P., C.B. Jensen, and A. Morita (2017a) 'Introduction: infrastructural complications', in P. Harvey, C.B. Jensen, and A. Morita (eds.), *Infrastructures and Social Complexity. A Companion* (Abingdon and New York: Routledge), pp. 1–22.

Harvey, P., C.B. Jensen, and A. Morita (eds.) (2017b) *Infrastructures and Social Complexity. A Companion* (Abingdon and New York: Routledge).

Harvey, P. and H. Knox (2012) 'The enchantments of infrastructure', *Mobilities,* 7 (4): 521–36.

Harvey, P. and H. Knox (2015) *Roads: An Anthropology of Infrastructure and Expertise* (New York: Cornell University Press).

Hayes, M. (2015) 'Moving south: the economic motives and structural context of North America's emigrants in Cuenca, Ecuador', *Mobilities,* 10 (2): 267–84.

Hermida, M.A., C. Hermida, N. Cabrera, and C. Calle (2015) 'La densidad urbana como variable de análisis de la ciudad. El caso de Cuenca, Ecuador', *EURE,* 41 (124): 25–44.

Hodges, M. (2009) 'Disciplining memory: heritage tourism and the temporalisation of the built environment in rural France', *International Journal of Heritage Studies,* 15 (1): 76–99.

Holston, J. (1989) *The Modernist City. An Anthropological Critique of Brasília* (Chicago: University of Chicago Press).

Homewood, K. (2017) '"They call It Shangri-la": sustainable conservation, or African enclosures?', in M. Brightman and J. Lewis (eds.), *The Anthropology of Sustainability. Beyond Development and Progress* (New York: Palgrave Macmillan), pp. 91–110.

Horn, P. (2019) *Indigenous Rights to the City. Ethnicity and Urban Planning in Bolivia and Ecuador* (Abindgon: Routledge).

Isenhour, C., G. McDonogh, and M. Checker (eds.) (2015) *Sustainability in the Global City. Myth and Practice* (New York: Cambridge University Press).

Jensen, J. S., M. Cashmore, and P. Späth (eds.) (2019) *The Politics of Urban Sustainability Transitions. Knowledge, Power and Governance* (London and New York: Routledge).

Kingman, E. and A. Goetschel (2005) 'El patrimonio como dispositivo disciplinario y la banalización de la memoria: una lectura desde los Andes', in F. Carrión and L. Hanley (eds.), *Regeneración y revitalización urbana en las Américas: hacia un Estado estable* (Quito: FLACSO), pp. 97–109.

Knox, H. (2020) *Thinking Like a Climate. Governing a City in Times of Environmental Change* (Durham, NC and London: Duke University Press).

Krupa, C. and D. Nugent (2015) 'Off-centered states: rethinking state theory through an Andean lens', in C. Krupa and D. Nugent (eds.), *State Theory and Andean Politics: New Approaches to the Study of Rule* (Philadelphia: University of Pennsylvania Press), pp. 1–32.

Larkin, B. (2013) 'The politics and poetics of infrastructure', *Annual Review of Anthropology*, 42: 327–43.

Latorre, S. and A. Malo-Larrea (2019) 'Policy-making related actors' understandings about nature-society relationship: beyond modern ontologies? The case of Cuenca, Ecuador', *Ecological Economics*, 156: 387–96.

Latour, B. (1996) *Aramis or The Love of Technology* (Cambridge, MA and London: Harvard University Press).

Low, S. (2000) *On the Plaza. The Politics of Public Space and Culture* (Austin: University of Texas Press).

McCann, E. (2017) 'Mobilities, politics, and the future: critical geographies of green urbanism', *Environment and Planning A*, 49 (8): 1816–23.

McCann, E. and K. Ward (eds.) (2011) *Mobile Urbanism. Cities and Policymaking in the Gobal Age* (Minneapolis: University of Minnesota Press).

Merino, R. (2016) 'An alternative to "alternative development"?: *Buen vivir* and human development in Andean countries', *Oxford Development Studies,* 44 (3): 271–86.

Moraglio, M. (2014) 'Shifting transport regimes. The strange case of light rail revival', in M. Moraglio and C. Kopper (eds.), *The Organization of Transport: A History of Users, Industry, and Public Policy* (New York and London: Routledge), pp. 155–72.

Munoz, J.C. and L. Paget-Seekins (eds.) (2016) *Restructuring Public Transport Through Bus Rapid Transit: An International and Interdisciplinary Perspective* (Bristol: Policy Press).

Peattie, L. (1968) *The View from the Barrio* (Ann Arbor: University of Michigan Press).

Polèse, M. and R. Stren (eds.) (2000) *The Social Sustainability of Cities. Diversity and the Management of Change* (Toronto: University of Toronto Press).

Rapoport, E. and A. Hult (2017) 'The travelling business of sustainable urbanism: international consultants as norm-setters', *Environment and Planning A,* 49 (8): 1779–96.

Rival, L. (2017) 'Anthropology and the nature-society-development nexus', in M. Brightman and J. Lewis (eds.), *The Anthropology of Sustainability. Beyond Development and Progress* (New York: Palgrave Macmillan), pp. 183–206.

Scott, J. (1998) *Seeing Like a State: How Certain Schemes to Improve the Human Condition Have Failed* (New Haven, CT and London: Yale University Press).

Sharma, A. and A. Gupta (eds.) (2006) *The Anthropology of the State. A Reader* (Malden, MA: Blackwell).

Shore, C. and S. Wright (2011) 'Conceptualising policy: technologies of governance and the politics of visibility', in C. Shore, S. Wright, and D. Però (eds.), *Policy Worlds. Anthropology and the Analysis of Contemporary Power* (New York: Berghahn Books), pp. 1–25.

Siemiatycki, M. (2006) 'Return to the rails: the motivations for building a modern tramway in Bilbao, Spain', Research Paper 60 (Universities of Glasgow and Oxford).

Star, S. (1999) 'The ethnography of infrastructure', *American Behavioral Scientist,* 34 (3): 377–91.

Swanson, K. (2007) 'Revanchist urbanism heads south: the regulation of indigenous beggars and street vendors in Ecuador', *Antipode,* 39 (4): 708–28.

Tahvilzadeh, N., S. Montin, and M. Cullberg (2017) 'Functions of sustainability: exploring what urban sustainability policy discourse "does" in the Gothenburg Metropolitan Area', *Local Environment,* 22 (1): 66–85.

Universidad del Azuay (UDA) (2016) 'Plan maestro para el área de influencia del tranvía de los cuatro ríos de Cuenca en los tramos de la avenida España y avenida Américas', <https://issuu.com/lau-uda/docs/pmait_diagnostico> (accessed April 2022).

UN-Habitat (2012) *State of Latin American and Caribbean Cities 2012. Towards a New Urban Transition* (Nairobi: UN-Habitat).

Ureta, S. (2015) *Assembling Policy. Transantiago, Human Devices, and the Dream of a World-Class Society* (Cambridge, MA and London: MIT Press).

Valderrama, A. (2010) 'How do we co-produce urban transport systems and the city? The case of TransMilenio and Bogotá', in I. Farías and T. Bender (eds.), *Urban Assemblages: How Actor-Network Theory Changes Urban Studies* (London: Routledge), pp. 123–38.

Vertesi, J. (2014) 'Seamful spaces: heterogeneous infrastructures in interaction', *Science, Technology, and Human Values*, 39 (2): 264–84.

von Schnitzler, A. (2013) 'Traveling technologies. Infrastructure, ethical regimes, and the materiality of politics in South Africa', *Cultural Anthropology,* 28 (4): 670–93.

Weismantel, M. (2003) 'Mothers of the patria: la chola cuencana and la mamá negra', in N. Whitten (ed.), *Millennial Ecuador. Critical Essays on Cultural Transformations and Social Dynamics* (Iowa City: University of Iowa Press), pp. 325–54.

Wilson, J. and M. Bayón (2017) *La selva de los elefantes blancos. Megaproyectos y extractivismos en la Amazonia Ecuatoriana* (Quito: Abya Yala).

Zeiderman, A. (2016) *Endangered City. The Politics of Security and Risk in Bogotá* (Durham, NC: Duke University Press).

9. The record keepers: maintaining irrigation canals, traditions, and Inca codes of law in 1920s Huarochirí, Peru

Sarah Bennison

Can infrastructures facilitate communication with sacred ancestors? What role do record-keeping practices have in supporting infrastructures ideologically? This chapter seeks to explore these questions through focusing on Andean canal-maintenance customs.[1] These customs require social and political coherence, achieved through adherence to codified precepts associated with the Inca era. The historical and anthropological study of irrigative infrastructure in the Andes has focused heavily on social organisation and ritual (Gelles, 1984; Mitchell and Guillet, 1994; Sherbondy, 1998; Valderrama and Escalante, 1988). The reason for this is quite simply because life in Andean communities makes it impossible not to acknowledge ritual's centrality in infrastructure maintenance.

Appel (2018) points out that visible infrastructure requires recursive substrates conducive to its construction and maintenance, such as legal climates. In canal-cleaning rituals which accompany the technical aspect of maintaining the canals prior to the dry season, community regulations simultaneously give order and structure to social organisation and cooperation (de la Cadena, 1989, p. 83). Community regulations for water rituals cover the fine detail; most Andean villages have strict rules on what ritual items are needed and who should contribute what (Rösing, 1995, p. 74). In this respect, channelling water through the canals is as much a socio-legal matter as it is an economic or religious one: how to make sure all contribute what they are obliged to?

From the pre-Hispanic era to the 20th century, irrigation system maintenance was documented by material infrastructure in the form of knotted string records

1 I am grateful to the authorities and members of the Comunidad Campesina de San Pedro de Casta for supporting this research with their time, insights, and trust. I also wish to thank Sabine Hyland, Jonathan Alderman, and Geoff Goodwin and the anonymous reviewers for their helpful suggestions and Silvia Soriano and Cesar Urrutia for their support. This chapter is an output from the project 'Hidden Texts of the Andes: Deciphering the "Khipus" (Cord Writing) of Peru', led by Professor Sabine Hyland and funded by the Leverhulme Trust. The University of St Andrews funded my fieldwork in Casta.

S. Bennison, 'The record keepers: maintaining irrigation canals, traditions, and Inca codes of law in 1920s Huarochirí, Peru' in *The Social and Political Life of Latin American Infrastructures*, ed. J. Alderman and G. Goodwin (London, 2022), pp. 223–251.

known as *khipus* (Salomon, 1998) and hybrid *khipu*-writing devices (Tello and Miranda, 1923; Hyland, 2016; Hyland, Bennison, and Hyland, 2021). Salomon (2004) demonstrated that *khipus* were fundamental in the structuring of water management and for expressing and legitimising authority in Tupicocha, Huarochirí. In the following discussion, I acknowledge *khipus* and associated records as instruments of governance.[2] In this respect, they resemble other forms of infrastructure in that they constitute political power and rely on being sustained through material politics and silent relationships holding them together (Harvey and Knox, 2015, p. 6, citing Lampland and Star, 2009). Despite the acknowledgement of the disciplining and controlling functions of infrastructure (Gupta, 2018; Harvey and Knox, 2015, p. 14), the role of codified regulations in promoting the level of social coherence required to maintain big material infrastructure has received little attention in the infrastructure literature.

As Salomon explains: 'It would be no exaggeration to call coding of information on textile fibre a core infrastructure of Andean social organization' (Salomon, 2013, p. 32). I build on this proposal by demonstrating the ways in which *khipu* infrastructure and *khipu*-inspired canal-maintenance regulations encouraged subjects to work effectively as an economic and social unit, drawing on community skills, knowledge, labour, and resources. *Khipus* functioned to regulate the social and political environment, promoting the cooperation required for mobilising the hard work of cleaning and maintaining long canal tracts and reservoirs. Furthermore, *khipus* facilitated communication with the ancestors whom Andeans understood to own (and have created and have dictated maintenance instructions for) the canals.[3] As Verónica Belén from San Damián, Huarochirí explained, 'the ancestors teach us how to behave'. Rigoberto Jiménez from San Damián explained that the ancestors are the *owner-governors* of the canals and the ritual specialists pay homage to them and to the laws they mandated for canal maintenance: 'Really, we're here obeying the sacred orders, right?' (Bennison, 2016, p. 226). As channels of communication and power, canals and *khipus* are temporally dynamic in a manner characteristic of infrastructure, which 'lies at the intersection of different temporalities: human and nonhuman, social and technical, and material and ideological' (Gupta, 2018, p. 76).

Although Andean ritual customary laws are thought to have been transmitted orally (de Pedro et al., 2018, p. 2), my findings suggest that Andeans historically codified customary laws [*la costumbre*] in *khipus* obliging participation and good conduct during canal-maintenance events (Bennison, forthcoming). Recent research on colonial and republican *khipus* shows that these devices were important for minimising conflict and for negotiation, and that post-Inca *khipus* were often integrated into written Spanish accounting systems (Curatola

2 On infrastructure as an instrument of governance, also see Chapter 6.

3 See, for example, Chapter 31 of The Huarochirí Manuscript (Salomon and Urioste, 1991, p. 141).

Petrocchi and de la Puente Luna, 2013; de la Puente Luna, 2019; Hyland and Lee, 2021; Hyland, 2021).[4] Furthermore, *khipus* were apparently used to propose and decline agreements relating to the organisation of community events (Pimentel, 2014, p. 193). *Khipus* were therefore instrumental for minimising conflict and maximising cooperation.[5] Even in post-*khipu* contexts in the late 20th century, cooperation in Andean communities had become institutionalised (de la Cadena, 1989).

The functions of *khipus* and canals I explore correspond with Gupta's perception of infrastructure as 'a channel that enables communication, travel, and the transportation of goods; a biopolitical project to maximise the health and welfare of the population at the same time as subjecting it to control and discipline; and its role as the symbol of a future being brought into fruition' (Gupta, 2018, p. 65). For Harvey and Knox (2015), infrastructural systems only function when they produce smooth flows and obscure the complex relational mechanisms on which such flows rely (p. 5). To explore the ways in which *khipu* and canal infrastructures overlapped to make Andean irrigation systems work, I explore the social dynamics of the period *khipus* stopped being used for canal maintenance in the Huarochirí province in the highlands of Lima. The chapter describes changes in social relationships – between people as well as between people and place – in the early to mid-20th century. I argue that a blend of political, legal, economic, and social factors contributed to the decline of *khipus* (in favour of paper regulations) as authoritative infrastructure. Drawing on archival material, I trace the ways in which changing attitudes towards ancestral infrastructure in the last century destabilised the relationships necessary for maintaining the cohesion of Andean institutions and their infrastructural manifestations.

First, I illuminate ideological continuities between the *wachu* (Quechua for *rank-file* or *furrow*) hierarchical model of social organisation and governance, which transcends the legal, political, and religious spheres, and the tangible infrastructure of canals and *khipus*, wherein the *wachu* system is legitimised and reproduced. Second, I introduce the reader to *The Entablo*, a *khipu*-inspired manuscript from Huarochirí containing Inca era-derived regulations for canal maintenance. I explain how *The Entablo* forces us to consider the role of record-keeping for organising irrigation, promoting a meritocratic hierarchy where cooperation and the avoidance of dissonance are essential for maintaining the irrigation systems. Finally, I look outwards in time and space to explore the impact of global political events at the turn of the 20th century on Andean community organisation throughout Peru. Based on the premise that canal-cleaning ritual accountancy *khipus* were inextricably tied to the *wachu* prestige hierarchy system, I hypothesise that the demise of tangible *khipu* infrastructure

4 I am grateful to Sabine Hyland for recommending these supporting sources.

5 It is important to note that *khipus* were also used to organise colonial native uprisings (Stevenson, 1825, pp. 50–1; Spalding, 2012, p. 88; Hyland, 2017).

was caused by the erosion of the intangible infrastructure expressed in codified form through *khipus*.

Sacred infrastructure: giving order to society and landscape in Huarochirí

In the highland Huarochirí province of the Lima region (Peru), irrigation rituals are key domains of reference in the (re)production of moral, ethnic, and cultural identity (Bennison, 2016). The Huarochirí Manuscript of 1608, an early colonial Quechua text of native authorship, describes the water customs and origin myths of many of the kin groups or *ayllus* in the province, many of which focus on the groups' respective water sources (inter alia Salomon and Urioste, 1991; Taylor, 2008). The Quechua word *ayllu* can be translated literally into English as *family*; however, *ayllus* as a functional entity are linked through shared resources and lands. As Spalding (1974) explains, in pre-Hispanic Andean society, *ayllus* had primordial access to lands, irrigation rights and other group resources, which were distributed among its members (p. 66). These shared resources were accessed through collective labour efforts, including ritual work. This work involved invoking the water-owning sacred ancestors through elaborate rituals carried out in and beside the irrigative infrastructure. As Paerregaard's work in the Peruvian village of Tapay elucidates, Andean people believe that '… the flow of water is controlled by spiritual beings that inhabit each of their water sources. Maintaining good relations with these spirits through periodic ritual offerings is crucial to securing adequate water flow and, therefore, agricultural success' (Paerregaard, 1994, p. 189).

Each *ayllu* group carried out rituals in honour of their tutelary *huaca* – sacred beings of varied material forms who represented, or were, a group's primordial ancestor (Salomon 1991, p. 21; Paerregaard, 1994, p. 199). Because members of *ayllus* were linked through shared tutelary ancestor *huacas*, this unit of social organisation 'figured as the basic unit of ritual action' (Salomon, 1991, p. 21). Allen's (2002) definition of *ayllu* is especially relevant here; she glosses the term: 'Indigenous community or other social group whose members share a common focus' (p. 272). Irrigation systems are domains where members commit to the group's common focus of securing water and maximising production. The commitment of all individuals in canal-cleaning rituals was closely monitored by the community authorities; in the moment of communicating with the sacred ancestors, the community needed to be able to materially demonstrate its collective commitment to upholding the laws instructing on the specific rules of reciprocity expected for each canal.

According to Rodolfo Cerrón Palomino, the toponym *Huarochirí* is of Aymara etymology, and its elements (huatru-cha-ri) can be translated as 'he who makes furrows for irrigation' or alternatively, 'he who makes terraces' (personal communication). The toponym therefore may attest to the extent to which groups in the province were known for their irrigative infrastructure in the pre-Hispanic era (Bennison, forthcoming b). The advanced pre-Hispanic irrigative infrastructure in Huarochirí functioned in a context of *verticality* or *vertical archipelagos* (Murra, 1975). It is in this context where Andean people attempted to lay claim to and control as great a variety of resource areas as possible to maximise production and minimise crop failure and famine (Spalding, 1984, p. 16). In pre-Hispanic Huarochirí, this strategy appears to have proven fruitful; early colonial chronicles describe the relative wealth of the province (Spalding 1984, p. 20).

This highly developed infrastructural system relied on a socio-legal system geared at promoting cooperation, minimising internal conflict, and maintaining the organisation of labour. Today, the Huarochirí village of San Pedro de Casta treasures its set of regulations for the annual canal-cleaning ritual, codified in a 1921 *khipu*-inspired manuscript called *The Entablo* [*El Entablo*].[6] This text describes the responsibilities of the traditional authorities known as *functionaries* including specifying the material obligations required by each authority and instructions for ensuring that the canal work is completed swiftly, with devotion and without complaint. In Casta, like other Andean villages, these authorities are also known as Autoridades de Vara (staff-holding authorities; Llanos and Osterling, 1982, p. 119).[7] Like the traditional staff-holding authorities in other Andean communities, they are responsible for policing compliance with ancestral community laws (Mayer, 2002, pp. 125–6; Salomon, 2004, pp. 78).

Analysis of *The Entablo* manuscript is helpful for exploring the changing legal environment in Huarochirí communities between the 1920s and the 1950s, since its production and content convey the impact of the 1920 national constitution and associated legislation – including roadbuilding conscription law – on social organisation. As Harvey and Knox explain, the Leguía presidency saw men in Peru's provinces gain additional labour obligations through national law:

> The first major road to the interior of the country, the Carretera Central, was initiated in 1918 and soon stretched 231 kilometres from Lima to Tarma. President Augusto Leguía, in office from 1908 to 1912 and from 1919 to 1930, was a modernizer, committed to enhancing national integration through the systematic implementation of a road construction program. He was not averse to deploying authoritarian means to bring about the changes he was looking for. In 1920 he famously passed a law of conscription that obliged men between the ages of eighteen and sixty to work on the construction and repair of roads in the province in which they lived for six to twelve days a year. (Harvey and Knox, 2015, p. 28)

6 I am indebted to the community authorities of the Comunidad Campesina de San Pedro de Casta, who granted me permission to borrow, photograph and publish about *The Entablo*. For a full transcription of *The Entablo* and a translation into English, see Bennison (forthcoming, *c*).

7 For detailed descriptions of the canal-cleaning ritual in Casta, see Tello and Miranda (1923) and Llanos and Osterling (1982).

The traditional authority system in Andean communities is based on a hierarchical model wherein members ascend a ladder of prestige on the successful completion of increasingly highly-graded *cargo* duties (Isbell, 1978; Fernández Osco, 2000; Valderrama and Escalante, 1988, 55–9; Seligmann, 1997). Within this framework, community members who have successfully fulfilled their obligations throughout their lifetime are deemed to be moral authorities and icons of good work ethic and as such are conferred a special social status (Fernández Osco, 2000; Soler, 1958, pp. 180–1). These individuals are referred to as *notables* and *mayores*, and were (and in Casta, still are today) central figures in the application of the traditional justice system. They were consulted on matters relating to community organisation and the negotiation of community agreements (Soler 1958, p.181). Ethnographies from Huarochirí describe the severe punishments within the traditional authority system supervised by the *notables* (Soler, 1958; Flora Tristán and CENDOC-Mujer, 2002) and elderly locals in Casta emphasised the strict nature of former ritual punishments to me. As I shall explore further, the hierarchical authority system meant that young community members were categorically low status. Younger generations across Peru encountered urban ideologies in the early 20th century and began to question and resist the existing power structures in their home villages (Bennison, forthcoming). Ritual punishments came to be seen by younger generations as an abuse of power and many became resentful of the traditional system and the power that the elders wielded over them. *Khipu* devices, as institutional infrastructure, emblemised this hierarchical system and may have come to symbolise tyranny among the young. In the following discussion, I explore how the *khipu* infrastructure and more recent *khipu*-inspired paper accounts aided the maintenance of canals. The *wachu* system, otherwise known as the community justice *ayllu law* system (Fernández Osco, 2000), was historically administered through *khipus,* and administered through written accounts from the early 20th century onwards in some communities. Prior to the 20th century, ritual *khipu* accounts recording individuals' performance played a central role in minimising conflict and maximising production, since all people in a given account category were bound by the pre-agreed terms for their rank. Expectations were clear.

It is worth noting that the Aymara noun *huatru* [*wachu*] in the toponym Huarochirí means *furrow*, *groove*, or *rank file*. *Wachu* therefore denotes a vertical, hierarchical ordering system as well as a furrow or irrigation canal; the material infrastructure is ideologically inseparable from the notion of social order (Pérez Galán, 2008). The noun *wachu* has related connotations in Quechua; the early colonial dictionary of González Holguín glosses huachu huachu as 'camellones, o renglera'[8] (González Holguín, 1952 [1608], p. 169). Synthesising the Aymara and Quechua definitions allows us to identify a semantic association

8 The Spanish *camellón* means 'ridge' or 'strip', while *renglera* means 'string', 'file', 'rank', or 'row'.

between canals, *khipu* cords, and ranked hierarchies. Broadly speaking, the noun *wachu* refers to a (sacred) linear structure or ordering system through which a substance or entity can travel.

Although *The Entablo* makes no mention of the word *wachu* in relation to its authority structure, at the time of its writing in the 1920s, a functionary known as the Wachiq communicated with the ancestors on behalf of the community (Tello and Miranda, 1923, p. 526; Bennison, 2019).[9] The first page describes the importance of all community members submitting to the 'legal-political regime' honouring water as a sacred lifeblood (f. 3). Within this conceptualisation of water, the canal system represents the ancestors' veins, which must be ritually penetrated for the sacred lifeblood to reach their children (Arguedas, 2002, p. 165, Bennison, 2019; also see Valderrama and Escalante, 1988, p. 102). As such, the *sacred vein* logic of the *wachu* system defines the regulations for canal maintenance and associated social organisation prescribed in *The Entablo*.

In Quechua-speaking parts of Peru and Bolivia, the hierarchical organising system through which the staff-holding authorities advance is known as *wachu* (Pérez Galán 2004, pp. 13–15; Rösing, 2003). In Pisac, *wachu* refers to a specific series of obligations within the rank-file system, and as such *pasar un wachu* is equivalent to the phrase *cumplir un cargo* [fulfil an obligation to completion] in Spanish (Pérez Galán, 2004, pp. 15). Hyland's research on a *khipu* from the Huarochirí village of Anchucaya suggests that the word *wachu* was used in Huarochirí communities until the early 20th century in the classification of work categories. Testimonial material from the ritual specialist Mariano Pumajulka in the Tello archive describes multiple functionary roles suffixed with the (hispanised) word *huacho*[10] (Hyland, 2016, p. 495). Multiple *huacho* obligations were encoded in *khipus* and, according to Tello, Inca *khipus* were organised in the same structure (Hyland, 2016, p. 495; citing Tello, 1935).

According to Pérez Galán, *wachu* – the Andean traditional system of authorities – manifests as the symbolic representation of a mode of social, political, and religious organisation transmitted through territory (Pérez Galán, 2004, p. 15). Given that canal maintenance requires the channelling of values rooted in the ancestral past, the *wachu* ancestral system of governance likewise requires the mobilisation of lines of memory in the mind. Abercrombie (1998) has described the intersecting pathways of memory through which Andean people navigate the landscape, their relationships with the sacred ancestors and social structures (p. 113).

9 Arguedas' description of the canal-cleaning ritual in Puquio describes sacred heroes known as the *wachok* who were said to have pierced the ancestors and channelled water from them (Arguedas, 2002, p. 164).

10 For example, the *Runa Huacho* obligations involved carrying messages from Anchucaya to Matucana or Lima (Hyland, 2016, p. 495).

Ritual record-keeping through *khipus* was central for canal maintenance in that these devices generated memories of the authoritative past. In the Inca era, *khipus* held people accountable to the moral codes of the past through the concept of *capac unancha*, 'the ancestral past as the present' (Fernández Osco, 2009, p. 62). As I shall explain later, the Inca state used *khipu*-like reminders describing the punishments to be issued if the ancestral legal codes were not upheld. Irrigation rituals were a context where regulation was especially important, since the legal system was geared towards ensuring the maintenance of the irrigation canals and maximising production through cooperation with ancestral precepts and with one's *ayllu* members. In precolonial Huarochirí, native priests known as *yancas* were in charge of monitoring the irrigative infrastructure. One aspect of this work involved ensuring there were no conflicts between *ayllu* members that might threaten the community's stability and hamper communication with the water-owning ancestors (Spalding, 1984, p. 66). The need to regulate conflict and ensure cooperation as part of the broader work of maintaining irrigative infrastructure persists today: in Tapay, matters undermining communication with water spirits 'sometimes leads to conflict' (Paerregaard, 1994, p. 189).

War and disorder: global politics and changes to the traditional order

To understand the demise of *khipu* infrastructural functionality in the Andean community justice system, we must look beyond national-level change-inducing processes such as roadbuilding. The economic aftermath of the First World War (ending in 1918) negatively affected the Peruvian economy, resulting in the emergence of new technologies and new ideologies (Soler, 1958, p. 180). In 1920s Peru, nation-building infrastructure and a growing international interest in the role of infrastructure for development led to social transformation: 'The 1920s was … an important period of social change in Peru in which road building played a key part. The hold of the aristocracy was diminishing, and the post-war era in Europe and the new technological dominance of the United States was opening up many areas of social and cultural life' (Harvey and Knox, 2015, p. 29).

Casta's use of hybrid *khipu*-script devices known as *khipu* boards[11] during the canal-cleaning ritual – known as the *champería* – in Casta was documented in a 1923 ethnographic paper (Tello and Miranda, 1923, p. 534). Recent research based on an analysis of *The Entablo* suggests that *khipu* boards were used for canal maintenance in Casta until the mid-20th century (Hyland et al., 2021). As such, social changes during this time are relevant for understanding their demise.

11 In their analysis of the Mangas khipu board, Hyland, Ware, and Clark (2014) provide information on the history and uses of these devices.

Figure 9.1 Tello and Miranda's 1923 article on the Casta champería featured a drawing of a khipu board they observed being used (Tello and Miranda, 1923, p. 534). Redrawn by Eleanor Hyland. Copyright Sabine Hyland[12]

Numerous mid- to late-20th century ethnographies attest to social transformations and resultant intergenerational conflict in Peruvian Andean communities (Arguedas, 2002 [1956]; Soler, 1958; Hyland, 2016, 497–8 citing Tello, 1935; Flora Tristán and CENDOC-Mujer, 2002; Gow and Condori, 1976; Huber, 2002). The importance of the generational transmission of values over time for the smooth functioning of the *wachu* authority system is evidenced in the conferral of social responsibility on the parents of youths, who were punished if their children did not show the elders or the authorities respect (Flora Tristán and CENDOC Mujer, 2002, p. 28).

Soler's mid-20th-century research describing intergenerational conflict in the Huarochirí community of San Pedro de Huancaire helps us understand why the elders in Casta insisted on producing a list of responsibilities that all community members would accept as a legal agreement. Soler (1958) states that tensions escalated to a crisis point in the 1940s, when the liberalised youth collectively challenged the authority of the elders, who would humiliate and punish young objectors in public during rituals for attempting to challenge them individually (p. 181). This resulted in a youth rebellion in 1940, which

12 I am grateful to Sabine Hyland for allowing me to use this image.

revolutionised community life, resulting in a more equitable distribution of lands and more power conferred to the youths. Liberal youth groups began cultural and sporting initiatives, which brought men and women into closer social contact; prior to this, the elders strictly controlled social relations (Soler, 1958, pp. 180–9). Crucially, the changes the youths in San Pedro de Huancaire effected were made possible through their gaining control of the community records; their rebellion was complete when they seized the community books during a meeting (Soler, 1958, p. 182).

Soler's ethnography links the emergence of the new social group, the *youths* (*jóvenes*), with the impact of World War I on Peruvian society and its economy (Soler 1958, p. 180). Various Andeanist ethnographies document the changes in community relationships brought on by the emergence of the youths as a coherent social group (Arguedas, 2002 [1956]; Mayer, 1989; Gow and Condori, 1976; Huber, 2002, p. 76). During my 2021 doctoral fieldwork in San Damián, Don Eugenio Anchelía Llata, a former *curandero* (ritual specialist and healer) born in 1920, lamented the erosion of ancestral traditions during his lifetime. He explained that canal-cleaning traditions and other traditions, such as behaving respectfully towards elders, began to erode 'when the youth began'.

In the 1970s, Isbell described the decline of the traditional prestige hierarchy *hatun* system in Chuschi, Ayacucho, exploring the impact of the Spanish-language bureaucracy of the government legal system and of urban ideology on the closed corporate village (Isbell, 1978, pp. 84–97). The *hatun* system persisted until 1970, when the *comuneros* in Chuschi voted to abolish it, claiming that 'the prestige and respect previously accorded the *hatun* authorities had all but disappeared' (Isbell, 1978, p. 94).

The spread of revolutionary thinking throughout the central Andean highlands in 20th-century Peru had profound impacts on village life and the distribution of resources decades prior to the Civil War in the 1980s. While increased articulation with cities brought educational and entrepreneurial opportunities in rural villages, individual accumulation of wealth was antithetical to the community hierarchy system founded on cooperation and reciprocity, and to the ideology of progressive youth groups committed to overseeing an equitable redistribution of community resources.

In Chuschi, migrants acted as extra-legal cultural brokers who 'sought solutions to village problems outside of the sanction of the law' (Isbell, 1978, p. 191). Members of a progressive society charged the local head teacher with prioritising his private business affairs over public office commitments, denouncing him an 'enemy of the revolution' (Isbell, 1978, p. 192).

Various communities in the province of Canta (Lima region) saw intergenerational conflicts lead to organised youth resistance movements during the early to mid-20th century (Alberti, 1972).[13] In 1930, youths in Lampián

13 I am grateful to Patricia Oliart, who helpfully recommended Alberti's chapter.

were discontented with their low rank within the community hierarchy system. They were denied access to the same resources (chiefly lands) afforded to members who had fulfilled all their community obligations (Alberti, 1972, p. 99). Since 1927, the new head teacher at the local school had encouraged his pupils to implement new agricultural techniques using the community's irrigated lands. He also disseminated new urban political ideas among pupils, advocating youth participation in political life (Alberti, 1972, p. 99). During community assemblies where decisions were agreed, the youths began to object to their lack of access to land. The authorities acted immediately:

> In a general assembly, they decreed the expulsion of the youths, accusing them of rebelling against the community's *costumbres* and traditions, and as such impeding their access to any resources that the community could offer. That is to say, they were banned from participating in any aspect of community life and at the same time, they were denied the right to receive lands, even in the event that lands should be redistributed in the future. Furthermore, the authorities reported the youths to the Ministerio de Fomento, Dirección de Asuntos Indígenas, accusing them of provoking disorder.[14] (Alberti, 1972, p. 99)

According to Alberti, the emergence of the youths as a distinct solidary group was a key factor in the conflict. As the Lampián case shows, the effects of urbanisation on the traditional community system manifested as in-situ exposure to new ideologies as well as direct engagement with these ideas in urban environments.

This case parallels that of San Pedro de Huancaire in Huarochirí, where in the 1930s, community authorities reported youths accused of communist ideology to the district authorities (Soler, 1958, p. 181). The expulsion of the Lampián youths meant they were forced to emigrate, resulting in an exodus of 30 youths in 1938 (Alberti, 1972, pp. 101–2). The resultant loss of labour had detrimental effects that highlight the importance of community cohesion and cooperation: the failure to collectively maintain the irrigation systems (due to a lack of assistance at community *faenas*) resulted in a lack of water for pastures and agriculture production (Alberti, 1972, p. 104). The impact of changing social relationships on the functionality of the irrigative infrastructure demonstrates that the continuous work of [social] maintenance is what 'keeps infrastructure functioning' (Gupta, 2018, p. 76).

14 My translation from the Spanish: 'En una asamblea general se decretó la expulsión de los jóvenes, acusándolos de rebeldes a las costumbres y tradiciones de la comunidad, impidiéndoseles por lo tanto el acceso a cualquier recurso que la comunidad podía ofrecer. Es decir, se les impedía participar en cualquier aspecto de la vida comunal y al mismo tiempo, se les negaba el derecho de recibir tierras, aún en el caso de nuevos repartos. Además, fueron denunciados por las autoridades ante el Ministerio de Fomento, Dirección de Asuntos Indígenas, como provocadores de desórdenes' (Alberti, 1972, p. 99).

Reflecting on the 20th-century shift from functional to patrimonial *khipu* use in Tupicocha, Huarochirí, Salomon has hypothesised that social change following the War of the Pacific (1879–83) contributed to a decrease in active *khipu* use to the point of virtual abandonment of cord record-keeping in the 1930s (Salomon, 2008, pp. 299–300).[15] As he explains, in 1898, *khipus* were described in a Tupicocha *ayllu's* books as artefacts *de anterior* [of former [times]]; by the 1920s – when the *comuneros* who were born around the year 1880 would have risen to power within the community – the *khipus* were no longer functional (Salomon, 2008, p. 299). Mayer has made a similar point about the period 1900–50, when the 'Libre Pensadores' [Freethinkers] were in power in the highland Lima community of Laraos (Mayer, 1989, p. 40). This period saw increased autonomy for individuals and less regulation in terms of land and water use until a group of *comunero* youths gained control, reinstating the community controls in three of the five production zones (Mayer, 1989, p. 40).

As Rösing has pointed out, the biggest danger to the persistence of Andean rituals is the undermining of ethics of reciprocity; she writes: 'introducing the value of individual profit maximisation with so-called modernisation, is infinitely more deleterious to the survival of Andean religion and ritual than all direct attempts by extirpation or other missionary efforts' (Rösing, 1995, p. 85). It is no wonder then that in 1921, when the elders in Casta observed individualist values among younger generations seeping into the *champería*, they acted quickly. In the intergenerational conflicts that emerged in Pinchimuro, Cusco, the more the youth clung to ideas about modernity, the more the elders adhered to the past (Gow and Condori, 1976, p. 23). *The Entablo* manuscript of Casta suggests that the elders in Casta responded similarly to the modern ideals of the youth.

The Entablo: a *khipu*-inspired text and Casta's constitution for cooperation in canal maintenence

The Spanish-language *Entablo* manuscript was written in Casta between 1921 and 1952 as a collective endeavour by community authorities in office at the respective times of writing, drawing on the knowledge of village elders.[16] The text sets out the agreed regulations for proper ritual discourse during the annual canal-cleaning ceremony (*champería*) carried out during the first week of every October. Written for an internal readership of ritual officials,

15 I wish to thank Sabine Hyland for recommending this source.

16 While the main corpus of the text was penned in 1921, the *Entablo* constitution appears to have taken three years to be approved as an official record or *constancia* in Spanish (Bennison, forthcoming). An entry in 1926 reaffirms the regulations on permitted kinds of alcohol in the 1921 entry. Subsequent entries in 1939 and 1947 are constitutional reforms; both provide further details of the functionaries' duties throughout the year. The final entry in 1952 provides regulations for the January traditions and an inventory of ritual items used for rain divination during the January rituals.

the content illustrates tensions regarding issues relating to autonomy and outside intrusions. Nevertheless, this internal constitution is by no means itself autonomous in an institutional sense; representatives of state institutions feature as legitimising forces in this document containing 'many laws of the archaic era'[17] (*The Entablo*, f. 19). Casteños align their water customs with the Inca era; in 2018, a collaborator in Casta explained that cigarettes brought to the ritual must be Inca branded and a 1939 entry in *The Entablo* regulations for the New Year customs dictate that an 'Inca meal' be served (*The Entablo*, f. 25r). Likewise, in San Damián, elderly collaborators recalled the 'Inca dances' of the Concha group's *champerías* in the early 20th century. The alignment of 20th- and 21st-century landscape customs with Inca traditions is not unique to Huarochirí. In the 1990s, people in Huanoquite repeatedly appealed to ancient modes of social organisation and Inca-era social relations in land litigation processes (Seligmann, 1997, p. 115). Likewise, *wachu* authorities in Pisac, Cusco take their authority system to resemble that of the Incas; a collaborator of Pérez Galán stated 'somos como Incas' (Pérez Galán, 2004). Similarly, community members in Hauynacotas, Arequipa claim their irrigation management methods are Inca (Trawick, 2002, p. 39). As I explain elsewhere (Bennison, 2019), in describing their cherished regulations as deriving from the 'archaic era', the makers of *The Entablo* echo the endeavours of Guaman Poma de Ayala, whose early colonial chronicle addressed to the Spanish king emphasised the admirable moral foundations of the *good justice* of the Inca empire (Guaman Poma, 1615/1616). Like *The Entablo*, Guaman Poma's Inca codes of law explicate and pinpoint the duties of the officials enforcing the laws (Harrison, 2015, p. 144).[18]

The word *entablo* refers to a text produced through a process of collectively agreeing on a memory as an official narrative or fact. It refers to a set of codified ordinances deemed conducive to achieving a moral or social goal – in other words, precepts. Casta elder Eufronio Obispo Rojas, defined *entablo* as 'a code of conduct or a law'. An elder named Porfirio explained that an *entablo* is: 'lo que queda en escrito' ('That which gets set down in written form', or 'a definitive version of events that ends up in the books'). In this respect, an entablo is a definitive agreement and, as such, represents the basis of the *justicia de acuerdos* system, where *khipu* records reflected collectively agreed-upon and approved sets of data (Bennison, forthcoming). As Hyland's work on the Anchucaya *khipus* explains, when discrepancies arose about the contributions of an *ayllu* to collective labour events, the details recorded by two authorities in charge of maintaining matching accounts in two separate *khipus* would be discussed 'until an agreement was reached on the correct figures' (Hyland, 2016, p. 493).

17 My translation from the Spanish: 'muchos leyes de la era arcaica' (*The Entablo* f. 19).

18 Guaman Poma used the verb *entablar* when describing how the Inca disseminated the forms of governance he describes in his account (Bennison, 2019).

Figure 9.2 An alguacil (junior-ranking functionary) reads out passages of The Entablo in 2018. Image: Sarah Bennison

As a set of collectively agreed-upon regulations and a community's sacred constitution, *The Entablo* illuminates the finely detailed workings of the Andean community traditional justice system, where the organisation of the *champería* requires the ritual authorities or functionaries [*funcionarios*] to conduct extensive calculations in the ordering and delegation of work parties. The regulations outlined in *The Entablo* are helpful for illustrating the proportional, egalitarian nature of the division of labour in the Casta canal-cleaning ritual. [19]

19 The egalitarian division of labour in Andean canal-cleaning ceremonies has also been noted for Huaquirca, Peru (Gose, 1994, p. 95).

Assisted by community elders, the functionaries had to memorise large data sets and were required to maintain detailed accounts, recording various aspects of participants' performance at points throughout the *champería*. Their work involved recording the agreed obligations to be submitted (including material submissions such as food, drink, skilled crafts, coca leaves, and cigarettes from the participants in addition to their labour contributions), and recording whether these obligations were fulfilled by making entries on the *khipu* board *padrones* [registers]. The regulations for the *champería* are egalitarian in that they are proportional; the obligations to be submitted by the functionaries reflect their respective grade in the hierarchy. The regulations for the first Monday of the *champería* instruct that the functionaries should meet in the morning, with everyone organised and ready for work:

> In this meeting, the functionaries will bring out their obligations for this day. The Sr. Campo will give a pound of coca, a bottle of rum, two packets of cigarettes of any quantity, two starter flares; the Regidor Mayor will give the same obligation. The Regidor Campo will give half a pound of coca, half a bottle of rum, one packet of cigarettes of any quantity, and a flare. The Alguacil Mayor will give the same as the Regidor Campo. (*The Entablo* f. 4r)[20]

The Entablo instructs that the functionaries must file out in hierarchical order at various points during the *champería*.[21] The instructions for the Wednesday describe the solemn moment when the functionaries assemble at the sacred site of Otagaca and kneel down, reciting a prayer geared at ensuring the canal-cleaning work goes well. Following this, the Teniente must recite a speech, while the other functionaries must stand in formation: 'lining up in order with the Alcalde Campo first and next, the Regidor Mayor and so forth with the rest right down to the very last enthusiast' (*The Entablo*, f.9r).

The emphasis on performing a clearly defined hierarchy serves to assert and legitimise the proportional degree of authority conferred to all the respective functionaries. The fact that the functionaries are required to file out according to rank during the canal-cleaning ritual is particularly fitting given that, as I mentioned earlier, *wachu* refers to both a rank file and a furrow for irrigation. The *wachu* system is well-suited for the governance of common resources and associated infrastructural maintenance in that the hierarchical system confers power and obligation proportionately according to rank. Trawick has noted the importance of maintaining proportionality, 'a basic moral principle that clearly defines everyone's rights' (Trawick, 2002, p. 42). He explains that a

20 For a similar but slightly modified presentation of this section of the manuscript, see Bennison forthcoming *c*.

21 Pérez Galán (2008) explores the logics of traditional authorities filing out in order in Pisac, suggesting that through their physical movements, they engage with and symbolise the movements of the sun and the cosmic order. Furthermore, the respective functionaries must perform their rank in relation to that of the other functionaries above and below them (Pérez Galán, 2008).

lack of proportionality concerning duties and rights leads to resentment and conflict and, ultimately, erosion of communal life (Trawick, 2001, p. 14). This characteristic of Andean ritual makes accountancy central for the prevention of dissonance since the regulations for individual responsibilities and contributions in labour and in-kind are publicly agreed and recorded. This is done close to the canals whose maintenance all members have a stake in.

Ritual punishments were also proportional. In *khipus*, the regulations for ritual performance were communicated transparently in public. As the early colonial chronicle of Guaman Poma explains, the Inca-mandated *hordenanzas* [*hordenansas*], or laws, decreed that there should be various *khipu* scribes in each village in order to uphold the royal Inca justice system. These included a public scribe with commandeering duties, a royal or elected accountancy scribe sent from afar and senior accountants in charge of making *khipu* accounts every month and year of all the unfulfilled taxes in the Tawantinsuyu kingdom (Guaman Poma, 1615/1616, p. 185 [187]).

The Inca-era justice system apparently included *khipu*-like signs known as *unañchas*[22] where numerical values were attributed to various kinds of behaviour categorised as moral or immoral (Fernández Osco, 2001, p. 12). These *unañchas* functioned through a decimal system where ten different categories of offences – such as failing to heed the words of the elders – corresponded with a finger on the hand.[23] Legal codes of this nature applied to canal-cleaning rituals in Casta and likely elsewhere; the *khipu* boards introduced by the Mercedarians in the 17th century emulated the Inca use of *khipus* for moral compliance and compliance with material obligations, i.e. taxation (Hyland et al., 2021). The *khipu* boards in the *champería* in Casta performed infrastructural functions associated with *khipus,* whose uses following colonisation appear to have been no less colonial than the hybrid *khipu* boards. Based on the use of hybrid *khipu* devices in the colonial era and beyond, *khipus* were clearly important for structuring and generating the labour that kept water flowing through the canals.

The Entablo explains that the functionaries used *khipu* boards to numerically categorise participants' performance in the canal-cleaning ritual and how individuals were publicly punished if they failed to fulfil their respective obligations (Hyland et al., 2021; Bennison, forthcoming). This practice resembles the similarly *khipu*-like one Hall describes, where the recording of ritual scores by ritual authorities on written *padrones* in Llanchu, Cusco today is taken seriously by participants since their number grade carries significant social repercussions (Hall, 2014). According to Rösing, disagreements and

22 While the Quechua noun *unancha* may refer to a sign (Harrison, 1989, pp. 79–80), the term has legal connotations; Salomon glosses the related form *hunanchasca* as 'law' (Salomon, 1991, p. 71).

23 Fernández Osco's description of *unañchas* draws on a February 1950 article in *El Diario* by Arias, based on chronicles produced by 16th-century friars (Fernández Osco, 2001, p. 12).

Figure 9.3 During the champería in Casta, one of the Michco functionaries whips the water 'so that it does not delay on its way to the village'. Image and caption: Luis Miguel Silva-Novoa Sánchez[23]

unmitigated ritual failings incur a *sacrificial debt*, preventing the ancestors from providing water access (Rösing, 1995). As Fernández Osco explains, if *ayllu* law based on *justicia de acuerdos* – which attributes numerical values to categories of offences – is not applied, moral offences are left unresolved since punishments are not commensurate with the ideological offence. As such, the *pena* [penalty or shame] remains in the community domain (Fernández Osco, 2001, p. 12). According to this logic, elders in early to mid-20th century Andean communities may have seen the abandonment of this quantifiable system to be harmful since failure to apply it could permit the accumulation of shameful penalties, which would materialise in the canals. Ritual penalties are punishable by the mountain deities governing communities who respond by negatively impacting community production and wellbeing, such as withholding water (Allen, 2015, p. 28; Gow and Condori, 1976; Rösing, 1995).[24]

The Entablo's instructions for the Saturday accounts mention that the elders approved punishment number scores at the end of the Casta canal-cleaning. It is likely that the kinds of offences listed on an Inca *unañcha,* such as failing to heed the words of the elders, were punishable offences in Casta's *champería*. Anyone back-chatting or giving excuses would likely have been attributed a rebel number score and be publicly punished. The punishments resembled a blend of Inca moral codes of law and vice-

24 I am grateful to Luis Miguel Silva-Novoa Sánchez for allowing me to use this image.

regal criminal penalties. The regulations describe the final duties of the Camachico authorities, who must assess the moral performance and material obligations of the ritual participants through multiple accounts, including *khipu* board *padrones*. The *notables* (elders) then assess the Camachicos' performance:

> The notables call for the outgoing Camachicos and
> the Camachico commands that that [*sic*] they tie their hands behind
> them and he [they?] gets taken to stand before the notables and receives
> his punishment for having helped certain citizens or having altered their
> mandated duties or obligations. The *notables* order him to go to the
> Council and they take him to the table where the crupper and whip are
> and then one person comes out from among the *notables'* circle to give
> them their correction, taking the scissors and carrying out the ceremony of
> shaving him [them?]. (*The Entablo* f. 15v)[25]

The cutting of hair as a punishment for failing to maintain order during the canal-cleaning ritual served to remind the participants of the Camachico functionary's responsibility for upholding the rank-file system. Haircutting was a colonial punishment used for native rebels alongside lashes and beatings (Spalding, 1984, p. 289; Larson, 2004, p. 190). Haircutting was apparently an established punishment prior to the colonial era; according to Guaman Poma, drunken criminal behaviour was punished severely under the '*buena justicia*' of the Inca: 'those who argue or fight while drunk [got] fifty lashes and were shorn of their hair'[26] (Guaman Poma, 1615/1616, p. 259 [261]). The use of haircutting as a ritual punishment during the *champería* in Casta is likely a legacy of the colonial-era public ridicule and debasement of criminals, which in turn may have emulated Inca punishments for lawless behaviour.

Interlegality and intertextuality: *khipus*, canals, and constitutions

The Entablo emerged from a context of *interlegality*, meaning: 'the use, the co-existence and the transformation of diverse legal systems in one specific social setting, which create a situation of legal porosity'[27] (de la Puente Luna and Honores, 2016, p. 14). Various scholars have described the ways in which colonial-era Andeans appealed to both Spanish and pre-Hispanic Andean legal norms in their construction of the law (Salomon, 1998; Harrison, 2015, p. 141,

25 For a similar but slightly modified presentation of this section of the manuscript, see Bennison forthcoming *c*.

26 My translation from the Spanish: 'Al que rriñe o pelea, estando borracho, cincuenta asotes luego y tresquilado' (Poma, 1615/1616, p. 259 [261]).

27 My translation from the Spanish: 'Por "interlegalidad" entendemos el uso, la coexistencia y la transformación de diversos ordenamientos jurídicos en un espacio social específico, los mismos que configuran una situación de porosidad normativa' (de la Puente Luna and Honores, 2016, p. 14).

Figure 9.4 The annual huayrona settling of accounts in Casta at the sacred site Cuhuay, presided over by the elders and Yachaq ritual expert (seated). The authorities stand between the elders (to their left) and the padrón accounts (to their right). Image: Sarah Bennison

Figure 9.5 The secretario updates the padrón comunal beneath the gaze of the elders, located opposite on a raised platform. In 2018, an elderly collaborator explained that in her youth, the khipu board padrones were displayed here. Image: Sarah Bennison

de la Puente and Honores, 2016, p. 14). Such dualist interlegal approaches have persisted into current times (Drzewieniecki, 1995); according to Seligmann, people in Huanoquite deftly blend new legal codes with principles deriving from their ancient ancestral laws (Seligmann 1997, p. 116).

National legislation had a significant impact on record-keeping in Peruvian Andean communities in the early 20th century. A result of the 1920 national constitution was the formalisation of indigenous communities who, once legally recognised, were obliged to keep records in Spanish of community decisions and legislative affairs (Hall, 2014, p. 15). As García-Sayán has pointed out, throughout the 20th century, during the process of obtaining official recognition from the Peruvian state, some indigenous communities partially codified their traditional laws, and decisions based on them, in separate and secret books when administering justice (Drzewieniecki, 1995, citing Diego García-Sayán, personal communication). It is likely for this reason that the authorities in Casta, like the *ayllu* groups in Tupicocha, Huarochirí, wrote themselves modernist constitutions (Salomon, 2008, p. 299). Salomon writes: 'These were understood as replacements for "customs" such as *khipu*' (Salomon, 2008, p. 300). This appears to be the case for Casta: a collaborator explained that *The Entablo* was produced in the absence of older inscriptive devices such as *khipus* (Bennison, 2019). It is likely that many communities across Peru maintain *khipu*-inspired manuscripts penned from the 1920s onwards. According to García-Sayán, the 'double record' can be observed throughout communities in Cusco (personal communication). There may be commonalities in the ways Andean communities throughout Peru adjusted their internal recording practices over time in accordance with (and often exceeding) national legal infrastructure. *Khipu*-inspired agreements may have been instrumental for maintaining cohesion in that their content, like *khipus*, would have constituted the agreed terms for group membership.

Perhaps the punishments at the October 1921 canal-cleaning ceremony were severe; *The Entablo* was written days afterwards, following a collective agreement.[28] The dictated memories of three highly esteemed elders formed the basis of its content, which began with the following explanation:

> The functionaries are not fulfilling their duties and obligations. In light of the many interventions and disagreements concerning the obligations starting from the Teniente right down to the last functionary, which is the Camachico, they agreed to collectively set down an official record, under [the jurisdiction of] our signatures so that they are obliged to fulfil their duties. They must fulfil them in a punctual manner and cannot give the excuse of taking on their roles without there being a written record and claiming diminished force of law. (*The Entablo*, 1921, f. 3)[29]

28 At the end of each *champería* in Casta, the community assesses the success of the event and elects next year's functionaries (Ráez Retamozo, 2001, p. 3). Prior to the 1920s, these procedures would have likely been documented in *khipus*.

29 Also see Bennison forthcoming *c*.

The Entablo's instructions would serve as an official response to the claims of functionaries who had underperformed and gave the excuse that there was no official written record. It is difficult to ascertain if there were records accessible to the elders of the duties latterly set out in *The Entablo*. Ethnographic evidence from the period indicates that, in the Huarochirí village of Anchucaya, *khipu* use was obligatory until around 1910, when younger community members insisted that the accounts be kept in books and jotters (Hyland, 2016, p. 496, citing Tello, 1935). Tello's collaborator, Mariano Pomajulka, stated that the decline of khipu customs in Anchucaya saw the khipucamayoc, the functionary who had previously been in charge of khipu accounts, be replaced by a scribe (Hyland, 2020, p. 246, citing Tello, 1935). It is possible that in 1921 Casta there was a record of some kind, but some functionaries did not acknowledge its legal status. While the *champería* regulations were described locally as Inca-era laws, the increasing legal presence of the state since the 1920 national constitution in community life evidently led to shifting attitudes regarding what may constitute a valid *constancia* – an official record.

As models of good moral behaviour, the elders played a key role in the administration of punishments within the ritual, and also invigilated the performance of the functionaries charged with promoting compliance with the laws governing work standards. Ritual accounts were conducted in sites associated with *huaca* ancestor beings, suggesting that each community's justice system was tied to specific points in the local landscape that represented the sacred past (Hyland et al., 2021). In this respect, the justice system was inscribed on the land and at points situated along the canal. Could nation-building projects such as the national constitution of 1920 and road building from 1918 onwards have led to the undermining of community ancestral sites' authority? To what extent might the national laws and the allure of labour (Drinot, 2011) have contributed to Lima city coming to represent economic promise and legal power over and above the *huaca* ancestors, whose generosity relied on compliance with the traditional authority system?

A 1926 entry in *The Entablo* suggests that these were real concerns; in it, the elders ruled that participants in the October 1926 *champería* had lost sight of the Inca-era laws in terms of the kinds of alcohol that were consumed. The entry explains that the elders agreed on the Saturday at the sacred site of Cuhuay that bottles of beer and non-local wines remained banned and that in future years, participants must drink only *chicha* (fermented maize beer; *The Entablo* f. 20v). Whereas the sacred ritual *chicha* beer was produced locally using local irrigation water and labour, purchased beers from elsewhere were unsuitable. Bottled beers were also likely antithetical to the ethics of reciprocity, since they are produced through (and so represent) an economic model based on individual accumulation and consumption rather than cooperation and reciprocity. Bottled beers therefore represented individual interests and person-focused economic agency: precisely the kinds of modern interests that threatened social cohesion and the maintenance of the canals.

Conclusions: canals, *khipus,* roads, and rebellion

Inscriptive practices are central for understanding the lived experiences of infrastructures and particularly their temporal dimensions in the Andes. My discussion highlighted the role of *khipus* in the governance of canal maintenance, where these infrastructures collapse time and require adherence with Inca legal codes. Through *khipus*, community members were encouraged to express a sense of community belonging, expressing one's debts to the sacred 'owner-governor' ancestors who would arbitrate whether the group may channel water through the canals they built in the remote past. This context reflects the perspective of infrastructure as relationally and temporally dynamic, and not necessarily associated with modernity (Gupta, 2018; Harvey and Knox, 2015).

Through reconstructing the social dynamics where *khipus* and associated records have legal status in determining the canal-maintenance regulations, my discussion revealed the invisible legal climate Appel (2018) deems conducive for the construction and maintenance of infrastructure. A focus on the *wachu* traditional authority system likewise made visible the intangible infrastructures ideologically knitting *khipus* and canals together, while my discussion of early-20th century social change described the conditions that led to their ideological unravelling.

As icons and ordering indices of the hierarchical *wachu* system, *khipus* likely became objects of conflict in communities where factions of the youth saw the *wachu* system as ideologically opposed to the notion of individual rights and an equitable distribution of power and resources. The prospect of being connected to the nation through the roads-to-be built may therefore have played a part in changing attitudes towards *khipu* infrastructure and the model of governance they symbolised, since new possibilities for the distribution of power and resources became imaginable among those exposed to urban ideologies. As *The Entablo* suggests, these tensions were expressed and negotiated at canal-cleaning rituals.

In Casta, the intergenerational conflicts that led to the youth rebellion phenomenon in other Peruvian communities where the traditional community justice system was abolished were evidently present. Nevertheless, these conflicts were managed through *khipu* logics of justice codified in a format compatible with the modern national laws written on paper in Spanish. Through transcribing *khipu* logics onto a paper-law format an increasingly modernised youth idealised, the makers of *The Entablo* ensured that the laws dictated by the ancestors would be adhered in Casta for years to come. The efforts of the three notable elders whose ritual expertise formed the basis of the agreed regulations ensured that their memories of the past are respected as community law a century later. *The Entablo* is revered as a sacred bible in Casta today, and the leading community authority must study it ahead of the *champería* each year.

The context I have explored, where canal-dwelling ancestors are central figures in the social life of infrastructure, serves as a reminder that infrastructures do not only function to communicate and transport goods or information between people, but also with non-human and/or formerly human actors. This dynamic resembles the way infrastructures mediate with the nation state, evoking de la Cadena's proposal for earth beings' agency in Andean political life to be acknowledged (de la Cadena, 2010).

Canal maintenance in Andean communities relies on the reinforcement of positive, proportionate relationships among community members, including with the founding community ancestors controlling the irrigation system's water. Irrigative infrastructure functions as a temporal intermediary, where hopes for a productive economic future do not lie entirely in the robustness of the material composition of infrastructure, but also in its ideological durability. The Inca authorities were surely aware of this fact when the laws they mandated for canal maintenance exceeded the technical aspects. Maximum adherence was encouraged through making all community members accountable in multiple literal respects.

In the Andes, the social life of irrigative infrastructure is defined by a legal emphasis on cooperation as law. The ability of the canals to keep giving is dependent on continued human engagement with the moral and economic ideals associated with the time the canals – and the lineages that would come to depend on them – came into being. The appeal of integration with the modernist state through roadbuilding and increased articulation with Lima meant that the model of prosperity the canals offered was undermined by that of the roads and the appeal of the material and ideological novelties that could be gained through them.

Having developed a nuanced and relational approach to the evolution of infrastructure over time, I advocate giving greater attention to the many diverse infrastructural forms which intersect, mutually support and, at times, undermine and compete with one another over time. Through this approach, the lesser-studied entanglements bound up in the dynamic and relational social lives of infrastructure may come to the fore, even if the sources on infrastructural social history require contextualisation to be unravelled and understood.

References

Abercrombie, T.A. (1998) *Pathways of Memory and Power. Ethnography and History among an Andean People* (Madison: University of Wisconsin Press).

Alberti, G. (1972) 'Educación y movilización colectiva', in G. Alberti and J. Cotler (eds.), *Aspectos sociales de la educación rural en el Perú* (Lima: Instituto de Estudios Peruanos), pp. 15–28.

Allen, C.J. (2002) *The Hold Life Has: Coca and Cultural Identity in an Andean Community*, 2nd ed. (Washington DC and London: Smithsonian Institution Press).

Allen, C.J. (2015) 'The whole world is watching: new perspectives on Andean animism', in T.L. Bray (ed.), *The Archaeology of Wak'as: Explorations of the Sacred in the Pre-Columbian Andes* (Boulder: University Press of Colorado), pp. 23–46.

Appel, H. (2018) 'Infrastructural time', in N. Anand, A. Gupta, and H. Appel (eds.), *The Promise of Infrastructure* (Durham, NC and London: Duke University Press), pp. 41–61. DOI: 10.2307/j.ctv12101q3.5.

Arguedas, J.M. (2002) 'Puquio: "A culture in the process of change"', in *Yawar Fiesta*, translated by F.H. Barraclough (Long Grove, IL: Waveland Press), pp. 149–92.

Bennison, S. (2016) 'Who are the children of Pariacaca?: exploring identity through narratives of water and landscape in Huarochirí, Peru' (doctoral thesis, University of Newcastle-upon-Tyne).

Bennison, S. (2019) '"Waqay": a word about water and the Andean world in a twentieth-century Spanish manuscript from Huarochirí (Peru)', *Anthropological Linguistics*, 61 (4): 459–90. muse.jhu.edu/article/803828

Bennison, S. (forthcoming) 'Introductory essay: the Entablo manuscript of San Pedro de Casta, Huarochirí', in S Bennison [working title], *The Entablo Manuscript: Water Rituals and Khipu Boards in San Pedro de Casta, Peru* [working title] (Austin: Texas University Press).

Bennison, S. (forthcoming *b*) '¿Quiénes son los hijos de Pariacaca? Agua y medio ambiente como base de la identidad cultural en Huarochirí', in C.I. Rubina and C.T. Zanelli (eds.), conference proceedings: 'Simposio internacional: el manuscrito quechua de Huarochirí, circa 1608', Catholic University, Lima, 2013. (Lima: Instituto Francés de Estudios Andinos).

Bennison, S. (forthcoming *c*) *The Entablo Manuscript: Water Rituals and Khipu Boards in San Pedro de Casta, Peru* [working title] (Austin: University of Texas Press).

CCSPC Comunidad Campesina de San Pedro de Casta (CCSPC) (1921) *Entablo comunal* (Lima: Comunidad Campesina de San Pedro de Casta).

de la Cadena, M. (1989) 'La institucionalización de la cooperación y las necesidades técnicas de la producción', in E. Mayer and M. de la Cadena (eds.), *Cooperación y conflicto en la comunidad andina: zonas de producción y organización social* (Lima: Instituto de Estudios Peruanos), pp. 80–9.

de la Cadena, M. (2010) 'Indigenous cosmopolitics in the Andes: conceptual reflections beyond "politics"', *Cultural Anthropology*, 25: 334–70.

de la Puente Luna, J.C. (2019) 'Calendars in knotted cords: new evidence on how khipus captured time in nineteenth century Cuzco', *Ethnohistory*, 66 (3): 437–64.

de la Puente Luna, J.C. and R. Honores (2016) 'Guardianes de la real justicia: alcaldes de indios y justicia local en los Andes', *Histórica,* 40 (2): 11–48.

de Pedro, R., R. Howard, and L. Andrade Ciudad (2018) 'Translating rights: the Peruvian languages act in Quechua and Aymara', *Amerindia*, 40: 219–45.

Drinot, P. (2011) *The Allure of Labor: Workers, Race, and the Making of the Peruvian State* (Durham, NC and London: Duke University Press).

Drzewieniecki, J. (1995) 'Indigenous people, law, and politics in Peru' (conference paper, Latin American Studies Association, Washington, D.C., September 28–3).

Fernández Osco, M. (2000) *La ley del ayllu: práctica de jach'a justicia y jisk'a justicia (justicia mayor y justicia menor) en las comunidades aymaras* (Bolivia: Programa de Investigación Estratégica en Bolivia).

Fernández Osco, M. (2001) 'La ley del ayllu: justicia de acuerdos', *Tinkazos. Revista Boliviana de Ciencias Sociales*, 9: 11–28.

Fernández Osco, M. (2009) 'El ayllu y la reconstitución del pensamiento aymara' (doctoral thesis, Duke University), <https://hdl.handle.net/10161/1645> (accessed 10 April 2022).

Flora Tristán and Centro de la Mujer Peruana Flora Tristán and Centro de Documentación sobre la Mujer (CENDOC-Mujer) (eds.) (2002) *Hijas de Kavillaca: tradición oral de mujeres de Huarochirí* (Lima: Ediciones Flora Tristán).

Gelles, P.H. (1984) 'Agua, faenas y organización comunal: San Pedro de Casta – Huarochirí', *Anthropológica del Departamento de Ciencias Sociales*, 2 (2): 305–34.

González Holguín, D. (1952) [1608] *Vocabulario de la lengua general de todo el Peru llamada quichua o del inca* (Lima: Ediciones del Instituto de Historia, Imprenta Santa María).

Gose, P. (1994) *Deathly Waters and Hungry Mountains: Agrarian Ritual and Class Formation in an Andean Town* (Toronto: University of Toronto Press).

Gow, R. and B. Condori (1976) *Kay pacha: tradicón oral andina* (Cuzco: Centro Bartolomé de las Casas).

Guaman Poma de Ayala, F. (1615/1616) *El primer nueva corónica y buen gobierno* (Copenhagen, Det Kongelige Bibliotek, GKS 2232 4°, 1615/1616), www5.kb.dk/permalink/2006/poma/info/es/frontpage.htm (accessed 19 April 2022).

Gupta, A. (2018) 'The future in ruins: thoughts on the temporality of Infrastructure', in N. Anand, A. Gupta, and H. Appel (eds.), *The Promise of Infrastructure* (Durham, NC and London: Duke University Press), pp. 62–79.

Hall, I. (2014) 'Compter les journées de travail, classer les individus et ordonner la société dans une communauté des Andes sud-péruviennes', *Ethnologie et mathématiques*, 29, <www.researchgate.net/publication/285574661_Compter_les_journees_de_travail_classer_les_individus_et_ordonner_la_societe_dans_une_communaute_des_Andes_sud-peruviennes> (accessed 10 April 2022).

Harrison, R. (1989) *Signs, Songs, and Memory in the Andes: Translating Quechua Language and Culture* (Austin: University of Texas Press).

Harrison, R. (2015) 'Guaman Poma: law, land, and legacy', in R. Adorno and I. Boserup (eds.), *Unlocking the Doors to the Worlds of Guaman Poma and His Nueva Corónica* (Copenhagen: Royal Library, Museum Tusculanum Press), pp. 141–62.

Harvey, P. and H. Knox (2015) *Roads: An Anthropology of Infrastructure and Expertise* (New York: Cornell University Press).

Huber, L. (2002) *Consumo, cultura y identidad en el mundo globalizado: estudios de caso en los Andes* (Lima: Institito de Estudios Peruanos (Colleción Mínima, 50)).

Hyland, S. (2016) 'How khipus indicated labour contributions in an Andean village: an explanation of colour banding, seriation and ethnocategories', *Journal of Material Culture*, 21 (4): 490–509.

Hyland, S. (2017) 'Writing with twisted cords: the inscriptive capacity of Andean khipus', *Current Anthropology*, 58 (3): 412–19. https://doi.org/10.1086/691682.

Hyland, S. (2020) 'El testimonio del quipucamayos Mariano Pumajulca, transcrito por Sabine Hyland', in M. Setlak, V. Moscovich, S. Hyland, and L. Milillo (eds.), *Quipus y quipucamayoc. Codificación y administración en el antiguo Perú/* (Lima: EY Peru Ernst & Young Peru/Apus Graph Ediciones), pp. 244–51.

Hyland, S. (2021) 'Festival threads: khipu calendars and Mercedarian missions in Rapaz, Peru (c. 1565–1825)', *The Catholic Historical Review,* 107(1): 119–47. DOI: 10.1353/cat.2021.0004.

Hyland, S., S. Bennison, and W.P. Hyland (2021) 'Khipus, khipu boards, and sacred texts: toward a philology of Andean knotted cords', *Latin American Research Review,* 56 (2): 400–16. DOI: http://doi.org/10.25222/larr.1032.

Hyland, S. and C. Lee (2021) 'Indigenous record keeping and hacienda culture in the Andes: modern khipu accounting on the Island of the Sun, Bolivia', *Hispanic American Historical Review*, 101 (3): 409–32. DOI: https://doi.org/10.1215/00182168-9051807.

Hyland, S., G.A. Ware, and M. Clark (2014) 'Knot direction in a khipu/alphabetic text from the Central Andes', *Latin American Antiquity*, 25 (2): 189–97.

Isbell, B.J. (1978) *To Defend Ourselves: Ecology and Ritual in an Andean Village* (Long Grove, IL: Waveland Press).

Lampland, M. and S.L. Star (2009) *Standards and Their Stories: How Quantifying, Classifying, and Formalizing Practices Shape Everyday Life* (Ithaca, NY: Cornell University Press).

Larson, B. (2004) *Trials of Nation Making: Liberalism, Race, and Ethnicity in the Andes, 1810–1910* (Cambridge: Cambridge University Press).

Llanos, P.O. and J.P. Osterling (1982) 'Ritual de la fiesta del agua en San Pedro de Casta, Perú', *Journal of Latin American Lore*, 8: 115–50.

Mayer, E. (1989) 'Zonas de producción', in E. Mayer and M. de la Cadena (eds.), *Cooperación y conflicto en la comunidad andina: zonas de producción y organización social*, 1st ed. (Lima: Instituto de Estudios Peruanos), pp. 15–76.

Mayer, E. (2002) *The Articulated Peasant: Household Economies in the Andes* (Boulder, CO: Westview Press).

Mitchell, W. and D. Guille (eds.) (1994) *Irrigation at High Altitudes: The Social Organization of Water Control Systems in the Andes*, vol. 12 (Washington DC: American Anthropological Association).

Murra, J.V. (1975) 'El control vertical de un máximo de pisos ecológicos en la economía de las sociedades andinas', in J.V. Murra (ed.), *Formaciones económicas y políticas del mundo andino* (Lima: Instituto de Estudios Peruanos), pp. 59–115

Paerregaard, K. (1994) 'Why fight over water? Power, conflict and irrigation in an Andean village', in W.P. Mitchell and D. Guillet (eds.), *Irrigation at High Altitudes: The Social Organization of Water Control Systems in the Andes*, vol 12 (Washington, DC: American Anthropological Association), pp. 189–202.

Pérez Galán, B. (2004) *Somos como Incas: autoridades tradicionales en los Andes* (Madrid: Iberoamericana Vervuert, 2004).

Pérez Galán, B. (2008) 'Alcaldes y kurakas. Origen y significado cultural de la fila de autoridades indígenas en Pisac (Calca, Cuzco)', *Bulletin de l'Institut Français d'Études Andines*, 37 (1): 245–55.

Petrocchi, M.C. and J.C. de la Puente Luna (2013) 'Contar concertando: quipus, piedritas y escritura en los Andes coloniales', in M. Curatola and J.C. de la Puente Luna (eds.), *El quipu colonial. Estudios y materiales* (Lim: Pontificia Universidad Católica del Perú), pp. 193–243.

Pimentel, N. (2014) ¿'De qué y cómo "hablan" los khipu etnográficos aymaras?', in C.A. Hoffman (ed.), *Sistemas de notación inca: quipu y tocapu: actas del simposio internacional, Lima 15–17 de enero de 2009* (Lima: Ministerio de Cultura, Museo Nacional de Arqueología, Antropología e Historia del Perú, 2014), pp. 177–96.

Ráez Retamozo, M.P. (2001) 'Introduction', in M.P. Ráez Retamozo (ed.),*Traditional Music of Peru, Vol. 7: Lima.* Smithsonian Folkways Recordings SFW40450, (Lima: Catholic University of Peru, Centre for Andean Ethnomusicology).

Rösing, I. (1995) 'Paraman purina – going for rain: "mute anthropology" versus "speaking anthropology": lessons from an Andean collective scarcity ritual in the Quechua-speaking Kallawaya and Aymara-speaking Altiplano Region (Andes, Bolivia)', *Anthropos*, 90: 69–88.

Rösing, I. (2003) *Religión cotidiana en los Andes. Los diez géneros de Amarete* (Madrid: Vervuert: Ibero Americana).

Salomon, F. (1991) 'Introductory essay: the Huarochirí Manuscript', in F. Salomon and G.L. Urioste (eds.), *The Huarochiri Manuscript: A Testament of Ancient and Colonial Andean Religion* (University of Texas Press, Austin), pp. 1–38.

Salomon, F. (1998) 'Collquiri's dam: the colonial re-voicing of an appeal to the Archai', in E.H. Boone and T. Cummins (eds.), *Native Traditions in the Postconquest World*, 1st ed. (Washington, DC: Dumbarton Oaks), pp. 265–93.

Salomon, F. (2004) *The Cord Keepers: Khipus and Cultural Life in a Peruvian Village* (Durham, NC and London: Duke University Press).

Salomon, F. (2008) 'Late khipu use', in J. Baines, J. Bennet, and S. Houston (eds.), *The Disappearance of Writing Systems: Perspectives on Literacy and Communication* (London: Equinox), pp. 285–310.

Salomon, F. (2013) 'The twisting paths of recall: khipu (Andean cord notation) as artifact', in K.E. Piquette and R.D. Whitehouse (eds.), *Writing as Material Practice: Substance, Surface and Medium* (London: Ubiquity Press), pp. 15–43.

Salomon, F. and M. Niño-Murcia (2011) *The Lettered Mountain: A Peruvian Village's Way with Writing* (Durham, NC: Duke University Press).

Salomon, F. and G.L. Urioste (1991) *The Huarochirí Manuscript: A Testament of Ancient and Colonial Andean Religion* (Austin: University of Texas Press).

Seligmann, L. (1997) 'La jerarquía político-religiosa actual en la sierra surandina', in H. Urbano (ed.), *Tradición y modernidad en los Andes* (Cusco: Centro de Estudios Regionales Andinos 'Bartolomé de Las Casas'), pp. 111–46.

Sherbondy, J.E. (1998) 'Andean irrigation in history', in R. Boelens and G. Dávila (eds.), *Searching for Equity: Conceptions of Justice and Equity in Peasant Irrigation* (Assen: Van Gorcum), pp. 210–14.

Soler, E. (1958) 'La comunidad de San Pedro de Huancaire', in J.M. Mar (ed.), *Las actuales comunidades indígenas de Huarochirí en 1955* (Lima: UNMSM), pp. 169–257.

Spalding, K. (1974) *De indio a campesino: cambios en la estructura social del Perú colonial* (Lima: Instituto de Estudios Peruanos).

Spalding, K. (1984) *Huarochirí: An Andean Society under Inca and Spanish Rule* (Stanford: Stanford University Press).

Spalding, K. (2012) 'Ensayo preliminar', *El diario histórico de Sebastián Franco de Melo: el levantamiento de Huarochirí de 1750. Preliminary study by Karen Spalding.* (Lima: Centro Peruano de Estudios Culturales), pp. 27–106.

Stevenson, W.B. (1825) *A Historical and Descriptive Narrative of Twenty Years' Residence in South America* (London: Hurst, Robinson and Company).

Taylor, G. and F. Ávila (2008) *Ritos y tradiciones de Huarochirí* (Lima: Instituto Francés de Estudios Andinos).

Tello, J.C. (1935) Archivo Tello (Lima: Centro Cultural de San Marcos, UNMSN).

Tello, J.C. and M. Próspero (1923) 'Wallallo: ceremonias gentílicas realizadas en la región cisandina del Perú Central', *Revista Inca*, 1 (2): 475–549.

Trawick, P.B. (2001) 'Successfully governing the commons: principles of social organization in an Andean irrigation system', *Human Ecology*, 29: 1–25.

Trawick, P.B. (2002) 'Comedy and tragedy in the Andean commons', *Journal of Political Ecology*, 9: 35–68.

Valderrama Fernández, R. and C. Escalante Gutiérrez (1988) *Del tata mallku a la mama pacha: riego, sociedad y ritos en los Andes peruanos* (Lima: Centro de Estudios y Promoción del Desarrollo).

10. The Cuban nuclear dream: the afterlives of the Project of the Century

Nicole Fadellin

In 1953, as part of his defence for his role in the attack on the Moncada Barracks, a young Fidel Castro outlined how the future revolutionary government would address poverty and inequality in Cuba, citing nuclear technology as a means to bring electricity to every corner of the island. It is a small detail in the nearly four-hour speech, yet it marked the beginning of what became known as *el sueño nuclear cubano*. This dream would begin to materialise 20 years later, in 1976, when Cuba and the Soviet Union signed a bilateral agreement to build two nuclear reactors near Cienfuegos. The project required a monumental investment of labour and resources. A generation of Cuban scientists travelled around the world to gain expertise in nuclear engineering while manual labourers from across the island moved to the isolated location to build the nuclear plant and a 'city of the future' from the ground up. The Soviet Union provided materials, expertise, and significant financial support. By the 1990s, however, as the socialist bloc collapsed and Cuba entered a severe economic crisis, Castro explained that the Caribbean nation could not bear the cost of the project alone. With the first reactor nearly 90 per cent complete, construction was halted indefinitely.

For the Cuban state, the Nuclear City would become an uncomfortable reminder of this failed project, since many of the people that were convened to bring the nuclear dream into existence still live among the unfinished structures. Increasingly, the Nuclear City and its inhabitants have been the topic of chronicles, films, and literary texts that seek to shed light upon this forgotten community. This chapter considers two such works: the 2015 film *La obra del siglo,* directed by Carlos Machado Quintela, and *Zona,* a play written by Atilio Caballero and first staged at Teatro de La Fortaleza in 2017. The first centres on a nuclear engineer who lives with his father and son in the abandoned Nuclear City, and the second is an absurdist drama in which six characters discuss the possibility of a toxic leak as they await the arrival of an unidentified group of people who will either interview or interrogate them. Through a comparative

N. Fadellin, 'The Cuban nuclear dream: the afterlives of the Project of the Century' in *The Social and Political Life of Latin American Infrastructures*, ed. J. Alderman and G. Goodwin (London, 2022), pp. 253–269.

reading of these two works, this chapter explores the entanglement of ideas, physical structures, and people that persist in the wake of the Project of the Century. It focuses on how the promise of the Cuban nuclear dream lingers over the unfinished structures, eliciting a range of emotions from the city's inhabitants, including nostalgia, indifference, or even fear.

In his contribution to *The Promise of Infrastructure*, anthropologist Brian Larkin (2018) explains that infrastructure can attract intense emotional investments regardless of whether it is finished or even built. He attributes this paradox to the unique temporality of infrastructure as a 'promising form'. According to Larkin:

> A promise can refer to a vow, or a commitment, but its other meaning refers to the coming to be of a future state of affairs, the idea we have that someone or something holds promise. Its referent is not to the here and now of things but to an uncertain future that infrastructure is to bring about and institutes a temporal deferral that refuses to deliver something in the present. It involves both expectation and desire, frustration and absence. (p. 181)

In this sense, the Project of the Century was expected to usher in a socialist technological utopia that would allow the island nation to escape energy dependence, bring low-cost electricity to all its citizens, and establish a new form of sociality built around collective infrastructures.

Today, the unfinished nuclear plant serves as a reminder of these ambitious promises of a future that never came to pass. This panorama comes into view most clearly through the perspective of the engineers that dedicated their lives to the project. In their study of road construction in Peru, anthropologists Penny Harvey and Hannah Knox (2015) demonstrate that the engineer is simultaneously inside and outside the social and material world that they seek to transform. They show that, contrary to popular belief, engineering is an embodied and relational practice. In different ways, the creative works considered in this chapter reveal the social complexity that surrounds the Cuban nuclear engineer, a subject shown to have an intimate knowledge of the materials, the technical difficulties, and the individual and collective hopes wrapped up with the Project of the Century.

Finally, the secondary characters of these works have a completely different relationship to the abandoned nuclear plant. They find its presence annoying and even overbearing, responding with frustration, derision, or fear. Even though the plant was never operational, and the radioactive material was never delivered, these characters are haunted by the possibility of nuclear contamination, a sensation that is developed through visual and auditory elements within the film and the mysterious illness at the centre of the play.

In the pages that follow, I begin with an outline of the historical context for the Cuban nuclear dream. Then, through a comparative reading of *La obra del siglo* and *Zona,* I explore the atmosphere of the present-day Nuclear City, analyse the portrayal of the Cuban nuclear engineer, and consider how the material properties of radiation influence the uncanny sensation that pervades both works. The chapter closes with a reflection about what is in store for the Nuclear City.

The Cuban nuclear dream

On 26 July 1953, Fidel Castro led a group of young rebels in an attack on the Moncada military barracks in Santiago de Cuba. During the trial that followed, Castro represented himself and delivered a historic four-hour defence. His address, later published under the title *La historia me absolverá* (History will absolve me), justified their attack as a reaction to the extreme inequality that plagued Cuba under the dictatorship of Fulgencio Batista. In his legal-defence-cum-manifesto, he laid out the goals of the future revolutionary government. Nuclear energy is briefly mentioned as a means for taking electricity to every corner of the island and, by extension, providing dignified housing for all Cubans (Castro, 2007 [1953]). The speech marks the beginning of the Cuban nuclear dream. It was also the origin for the 26 July Revolutionary Movement that would succeed in defeating Batista five and a half years later.

In the article 'The revolutionary city: socialist urbanisation and nuclear modernity in Cienfuegos, Cuba', geographer Gustav Cederlöf (2020) traces the evolution of the Cuban nuclear programme throughout the second half of the 20th century. He shows that the Juraguá nuclear plant was part of a multifaceted effort by the revolutionary government to use infrastructure to transform Cuba both socially and economically. The construction of housing complexes and the implementation of a network of ration shops known as *bodegas* 'enabled socialist urban practices' (p. 58). He also documents the expansion of the national electricity system, presenting the thermoelectric plants as a direct precursor for the nuclear programme. Although near total electrification would eventually be achieved through this oil-based network, Cederlöf explains that the shift to nuclear power would have allowed the island to reduce its dependence on fossil fuels and re-export the oil received from the Soviet Union for hard currency (2015, p. 655, 2020, p. 69).

When mutual aid came to an end, all of this fell apart. Rations were cut, thermoelectric plants went dark, and Russia dramatically reduced its financial, technical, and logistical support for the Cuban nuclear programme. Cuba no longer had a reliable source of enriched uranium. Nor did it have access to an international fleet of ships to transport materials. The nail in the coffin of the Project of the Century was the fact that Cuba would now have to come up with hard currency to pay the salaries of the Soviet technicians. As a severe economic crisis took hold throughout the island, Castro travelled to the Juraguá nuclear plant on 2 September 1992, to announce the suspension of the project.

Literary critic Ahmel Echevarría (2016) tackles the emotional and psychological impact of this moment in his essay 'Seis millones de pares de zapatos plásticos' [Six million pairs of plastic shoes].[1] He boils down the almost 40-year period between 1953 and 1992 to a single, dramatic image: 'The parenthesis of the nuclear dream is opened and closed by the same person. The same fiery discourse in the name of a Revolutionary Government for the good of the people.'[2] In both historical moments, the famed orator invokes duty, sacrifice, and the greater good. In the 1953 speech, the greater good involves reducing inequality, eliminating poverty, and increasing access to electricity, healthcare, housing, and education. By 1992, however, it takes on a strangely specific material form. Castro insists that they cannot continue burying money in the project by paying the salaries of the foreign technicians since that same sum could buy enough raw material for 6 million pairs of plastic shoes a year (Castro, 1992).

As part of an implicit socialist social contract, Cuban citizens were expected to relinquish some civil liberties while the revolutionary government would provide basic goods (electricity, housing, foodstuff) and services (education and healthcare) for all. During the extreme economic crisis of the 1990s, known as the Special Period in Times of Peace, the Cuban government was unable to uphold its end of the social contract, yet the same sacrifices were still expected of the Cuban people (de Ferrari, 2015). With the phrase '6 million pairs of plastic shoes', Echevarría underscores the rhetorical manoeuvre that Castro used to recast the social contract within the context of the Nuclear City. In other words, the promise of efficient electricity and national autonomy was replaced by a finite number of plastic shoes. The plant workers were asked to make this final sacrifice for the greater good. According to Echevarría, the nuclear dream began to devolve into a nightmare.

The government proceeded to divert resources to the tourist industry as a stopgap for the extreme economic crisis. The *Contingente Vladimir Ilich Lenin*,[3] the construction brigade summoned for the Project of Century, was transferred to the island's famous keys to build luxury hotels, while many of the scientists and support workers simply stayed in the unfinished Nuclear City. Nuclear engineers, supervisors, security guards, performers, journalists, teachers, spouses, and children would make up the unlikely transnational community in the isolated location across the Cienfuegos harbour.

In *Post-Soviet Social*, historian Stephen Collier (2017) considers the fate of small and medium-sized industrial cities throughout Russia following the collapse of socialism. Just like the Cuban Nuclear City, these 'cities of the future'

1 In this essay, Echevarría identifies a corpus of works that portray the abandoned Nuclear City, including *Zona* and *La obra del siglo,* as well as a documentary film, narrative fiction, and chronicles.

2 Original: 'El paréntesis del sueño energético lo abre y cierra una misma persona. El mismo verbo encendido en nombre de un Gobierno Revolucionario por el bien del pueblo.'

3 The name of the work brigade draws inspiration from Lenin's electrification campaign. See Cederlöf (2015) and Bloom (2015).

had been built as part of an effort to reorganise populations around production and, at the same time, forge new forms of sociality through urban planning. Each city included public spaces, centralised infrastructure, and universal social services while industrial production connected the community to a national distribution network. These industrial cities suffered a total economic collapse following the introduction of economic liberalisation policies in the 1990s, and Collier explains that 'the devastation was as much existential as it was material'. Decaying buildings and obsolete infrastructures served as 'stark reminders of a vision of the future (…) that was now past', a vision that had been forged through decades of hard work and sacrifice by its inhabitants (p. 6).

Interestingly, these same collective infrastructures seemed to hold the communities together. Borrowing a concept from economic geographer Ann Makrusen, Collier explains that 'things were bad but (...) they were also "sticky"' (p. 7). Rather than suffering an exodus or succumbing to abject poverty, these small cities banded together to raise funds for those in need and make political demands to their representatives. To some degree, socialist urban planning had succeeded in shaping social practices. In Russia, these cities would survive the difficult years of the 1990s. The collective infrastructures would even resist, and ultimately shape, the neoliberal reforms of the 2000s.

In the decades following the suspension of the project, the Nuclear City would not become the focus of public policy or spending. It would survive, however, as a community with a distinctive identity and shared history. The film *La obra del siglo* and the play *Zona* explore the daily life of the engineers, labourers, ferry drivers, Russian teachers, opera singers, and scrap metal traders that live on in the wake of the Project of the Century.

The city of the future, 20 years later

La obra del siglo, by director Carlos Machado Quintela (2015), portrays the tense cohabitation of three generations (grandfather, father, and son) who share an apartment in the city that was built for plant workers near the Juraguá nuclear plant. The film is set in the year 2012, exactly 20 years after the project was suspended and the same year that Nuclear City native Robeisy Ramírez won gold at the London Olympics. About halfway through the film, Otto (the grandfather) and Leo (the grandson) chat about Robeisy's win over beers as they sit outside a gas station. Otto notes that the Nuclear City did not even make the news. Instead, the win was attributed to the city of Cienfuegos. The oversight leads Otto to explain to his grandson that the Nuclear City had become a ghost town, an embarrassing reminder of the failed nuclear dream: 'They want us to just disappear out here. They're ashamed that we're still here.'[4]

4 Original: 'Todos quieren que nos perdamos por aquí. Tienen vergüenza que sigamos aquí' (Machado Quintela, 2015: 00:51:30).

The film juxtaposes the black-and-white narrative sequences set in 2012 with archival footage from the 1960s–1990s. At first glance, this strategy seems to suggest a simple contrast between past enthusiasm for a socialist technological utopia and a sombre post-apocalyptic present. Upon closer examination, however, the collage style of the film offers surprising emotional and psychological depth. It draws attention to the social bonds forged through the Project of the Century, while highlighting the shortcomings of some of the values associated with socialism. It does not completely abandon the socialist project, but it does criticise the lack of basic social goods and services in the present.

In the first narrative scene of the film, for example, Otto answers the door of the apartment he shares with his son and grandson, and he is met by a team of fumigators. Later in the film it will be revealed that the fumigation is due to an *Aedes Aegypti* plague and subsequent dengue epidemic triggered by the lack of a functional water supply system. In the present moment of the film, however, Otto chats with the supervisor of the fumigators on the balcony of the apartment. The supervisor begins to reminisce about the space race; he recalls: 'It was a golden era. There was a sense of epic back then. I miss that … The Cold War. A race to see who had the biggest dick. The Russians or the Americans.'[5] As he speaks, the image cuts away to triumphant archival footage of the first Soviet and Cuban cosmonauts to go to space, and once the camera returns to the present moment, the fumigator notes that the pesticide clouds billowing out of the bottom of a nearby building look like a rocket taking off, commenting that he 'would have liked to have gone to space'.[6] The rumbling noise of the foggers increases in volume and a voiceover countdown in Russian completes the illusion.

In the first scene, the space race is presented as part of an epic effort to forge a socialist technological utopia. Later in the film, the idea of the space race as a competition to see who has the biggest manhood will be recast in a disturbing confrontation between the three main characters. As Rafa attempts to entertain a woman in his room, the sexual energy ramps up throughout the apartment. Leo attempts to masturbate in the bathroom, and Otto begins banging on Rafa's door. He accuses his son's date of trying to steal the apartment and begins shaking his semi-erect penis at the door while he yells for her to come out and look at his 'rocket'. This obscene encounter presents a criticism of the hypermasculinity previously celebrated by the fumigator and conveys the fragile social fabric of the abandoned Nuclear City.

This example also illustrates that narrative film has the capacity to create complex and emotionally impactful scenes and develop concepts over time, highlighting the contradictions and multiplicity that shape lived experience.

5 Original: 'Esa era una época gloriosa, una época que tenía épica, yo extraño eso … La guerra fría. Era una carrera para ver cuál la tenía más grande. Si los rusos o los americanos' (00:04:00).

6 Original: 'A mí me hubiera gustado ir al cosmos. ¿A usted no?' (00:05:24).

These same strategies are used to consider the fate of the broader community that came together to build the Project of the Century. A scene set on a ferry provides the emotional anchor for this reflection. The camera follows the perspective of Otto as he identifies each passenger for his grandson Leo. A thin old woman, with deep wrinkles carved into her face and hollowed out cheeks, holds the gaze of the camera as her hair slightly blows in the wind. She operated a crane for 20 years. Then there is the *picapiedras*, a young, black man who stands out from the middle-aged and elderly passengers. Otto explains that the *picapiedras* sneak into the plant at night to dismantle it and sell the parts for profit. Finally, a nuclear engineer looks up from his reading to meet the camera's gaze. His expression and body language are full of tense energy that is difficult to decipher. Otto notes that this person always reminds him of his son Rafa. Other passengers include a security guard, a former television producer, a Russian teacher, and a soprano singer from Moscow. The penetrating darkness, the extended shot of each passenger, the gestures, and the expressions create a series of haunting living portraits.

Despite the unsettling atmosphere, the ferry scene serves as proof of the transnational community that was forged through the Project of the Century. There are scientists and labourers, as well as educators, artists, and journalists that each contributed to the project in their own way. Details about these secondary characters appear throughout the film. Shortly after the ferry scene, archival footage from *TeleNuclear*, the local broadcast station, shows interviews with the *Contingente Vladimir Ilich Lenin*, the construction brigade that attracted thousands of workers representing all 14 provinces. When asked how such a diverse group manages to get along, a welder explains: 'Everyone knows that if help is needed, Camagüey will come, Santa Clara will come. It's like a big family. Cuba is Cuba. We didn't come here for the province; we came here for the country.'[7] This clip is followed by a propaganda video that touts the amenities of the 'city of the future'. A voiceover explains that the Nuclear City will cover all aspects of life for the plant workers: leisure, entertainment, medical care, and education. The narration is accompanied by shots of the apartment complexes, as well as images of people enjoying the beach and busy telegraph operators connecting messages to the 'main cities of Cuba and the Soviet Union'.

Finally, the continued presence of the support workers from the Soviet Union is felt in unexpected ways. The soprano singer from the ferry provides an extra-diegetic transition between scenes with a rendition of *Te odio* by Félix B. Caignet,[8] while Rafa's Russian teacher materialises out of thin air at his bedside

7 Original: 'Se sabe que si se pide un esfuerzo otra provincia, Camagüey viene, Santa clara viene y bueno ... Es una gran familia. Cuba es Cuba. Nosotros no vinimos por la provincia aquí; vinimos por la nación' (00:27:40).

8 The soundtrack sets the ever-shifting mood with a combination of classic boleros, Cuban ballads from the 1990s, and rock music. The lyrics of the songs share a common theme: the

to correct his pronunciation when he attempts to speak Russian to his date. The exchange then prompts his date to reminisce about her former Soviet lover. Although the 'city of the future' was never finished, these snapshots attest to the 'stickiness' of the Project of the Century. Here, the emphasis is not technology or nuclear power, but all the social infrastructures, relationships, and personal trajectories that became intertwined with the process.

While *La obra del siglo* conveys melancholy and other heavy emotions, *Zona* by Atilio Caballero (2017) immerses its audience in chaos and uncertainty. This absurdist drama is modelled upon *Waiting for Godot* by Samuel Beckett. Drama critic Martin Esslin (1965) recalls that in the wake of World War II, works like *Waiting for Godot* shocked audiences and even angered critics because they eschewed almost all accepted theatrical conventions. He explains that there are no well-defined characters. Actors embody archetypes or switch roles halfway through the play. There is no linear plot either. The audience does not observe the resolution of a problem but instead witnesses the unfolding of a 'poetic image' or 'situation' that takes on new meaning and nuance with each scene.

In the opening scene of *Zona*, we encounter six characters wearing *nasobucos* (facemasks) inside a makeshift second-hand clothing store in the Nuclear City. Over the course of nine brief scenes, they talk about the *situación,* a mysterious illness that is plaguing their community. Mostly, however, they wait. They do not know exactly whom or what to expect. Will they be visited by reporters for an interview? By nurses or scientists that can determine the cause of the strange symptoms plaguing the Nuclear City? Or will they be interrogated and quarantined? No answer is provided. The six characters are based on real-life inhabitants of the Nuclear City, and some of these non-actors are also incorporated into the production, delivering a monologue from a small wooden platform at key moments throughout the play. Both the non-actors and their fictional counterparts evoke the transnational community that inhabits the present-day Nuclear City. There is an opera singer from Kazakhstan (Ekaterina), a prostitute (Ofelia), a libidinous woman (Servicity), and a man in charge of water delivery (Omar). Finally, there are not one but two nuclear engineers: *El Ingeniero* and *El Nervio* (an engineer turned handyman).

The characters speculate about the origin of the mysterious 'situation' plaguing the Nuclear City, and their hypotheses all point to tensions between the Cuban state and the inhabitants of the Nuclear City. *El Nervio* proposes that they could be suffering from the highly contagious blight of capitalism from their contact with the used clothing. His comment reflects the official discourse since the 1990s, when the Cuban government doubled down on its effort to resist ideological infiltration from the USA. Ekaterina runs with this idea, suggesting that they are ground zero of a deadly pandemic transmitted

contradictory emotions of a difficult relationship.

through foreign donations. She is relieved, however, that they will at least be guaranteed a well-rounded diet during treatment. This quip refers to the food shortages and insufficient *canasta básica* (ration of basic foodstuffs) that have plagued Cuba since the Special Period. Finally, Omar develops an elaborate theory based on an experiment from the 1960s involving rats and memory. He believes that a protein deficiency has transformed them into *puros esqueletos desmemoriados* [simple absent-minded skeletons], going so far as to suggest that the government is intentionally depriving the inhabitants of the Nuclear City of essential amino acids so that they will 'forget'. These different theories insinuate that the Nuclear City, more than any other place, has remained trapped in the extreme crisis and uncertainty that marked the Special Period. Through the concept of memory, Omar also hints at the government's complicity in erasing the nuclear project from public discourse and all but abandoning the Nuclear City and its inhabitants.

The engineer as subject: from portrait to parody

To describe his inspiration for *La obra del siglo,* director Carlos Machado Quintela has explained that: 'The real failure wasn't the suspension of the electro-nuclear project, but rather that all these workers handed over their youth and were simply forgotten in exchange.'[9] The most affected workers were without a doubt the nuclear engineers. Great lengths were taken to guarantee that Cuban scientists gained the theoretical and practical knowledge needed to carry out a nuclear programme. Over 1,000 Cubans completed advanced studies abroad in radiochemistry, nuclear physics, and nuclear engineering (Castro Díaz-Balart, 2014). They also gained practical experience at nuclear plants throughout the Soviet Union. When the project was suspended, however, they found themselves in a country and a geopolitical context in which their decades of training had become obsolete.

Within the film, Rafa represents this lost generation. He dedicated his life to the Cuban nuclear dream. In 1992 he lost his livelihood, and over the course of two decades he watched as the physical remains of a socialist Cuba crumbled in front of him. Rafa even became an anachronism in his own house. Otto explains to Leo that while neither of them feel an attachment to socialism or the nuclear dream, it was different for Rafa: 'That's how your father grew up … with all that shit they filled his mind with. Poor guy … he suffered more blows than he deserved.'[10]

9 Original: 'El verdadero fracaso no fue la paralización de aquel proyecto electronuclear, sino que todos esos trabajadores que entregaron su juventud solo recibieron a cambio el olvido' (Lechuga, 2019).

10 Original: 'Así creció tu padre … con toda esa mierda en la cabeza que le metieron. Pobre … le dieron más piñazos de lo que merecía' (00:52:22).

Following this conversation, and upon his grandfather's request, Leo takes his father out. In the next scene, the two make the trip out to see the reactor. It is located on an empty concrete plot, housed between some unfinished walls, a few kilometres away from the Nuclear City. The tone is upbeat. The two men climb into the cylinder and play like children, trying to run up the sides of the shaft, hanging from the inserts where the uranium would have been and playing a makeshift game of baseball. When Rafa tires, he takes a break to explain nuclear fission to his son. Then he begins to tell his story.

He remembers his years in Moscow with nostalgia. He delves into detail about the bitter cold, the idiosyncrasies of his teachers, and the academic challenges, emphasising that he was a dedicated student. The tone changes once the story shifts to Cuba. Personal events are contained in brief sentences yet when he narrates his arrival to the Juraguá plant, he draws out each sentence in a gravelly voice: 'I met your mother. You were born. Your mother left … And I came to work here day and night with the hope that this plant would light up the whole island. I missed out on Cienfuegos by day for fifteen years.'[11]

As Rafa speaks, the image cuts away to archival footage from *TeleNuclear* portraying the arrival of the first reactor in 1989. The tone is surprisingly subdued. Much of the footage shows the trailer carrying the reactor as it creeps down the road towards the plant accompanied by the sound of engines rumbling and safety warnings. A small group of engineers, supervisors, and labourers escort the reactor on foot. This footage links Rafa's memories to the practical, *in situ* experience of bringing the Project of the Century into existence. The promise of nuclear energy would dissipate in the official discourse of the revolutionary government, but for the engineers that worked on the project, this promise is wrapped up with memories of the equations and intellectual demands, a tactile memory of the materials, and a sense of duty linked to decades of sacrifice and dedication.

Rafa continues his testimony. As he approaches the definitive moment of his testimony, monumental political events are reduced to brief sentences. As he recalls the fateful 1992 speech, he mimics Castro's dramatic oratory tone and pace:

> And then what happened? The Berlin wall fell. The Soviet bloc collapsed. The Soviet Union dissolved … And one day Fidel showed up here under the pouring rain to tell us that even though nature was crying we mustn't cry. Because if we cry, it should be out of pride, not cowardice. Because we must face our troubles … Well, I was the first to start crying.[12]

11 Original: 'Me casé con tu mamá. Naciste tú. Tu mamá se fue … Y vine a trabajar de sol a sol porque tenía la esperanza de que ese reactor iluminara toda la isla. Y me perdí Cienfuegos de día durante quince años ...' (01:01:26).

12 Original: '¿Y qué pasó? ¿Qué pasó? Se cayó el muro de Berlín. Se cayó el campo socialista. Se desmoronó la Unión Soviética … Y después apareció Fidel aquí bajo aquel torrencial aguacero para decirnos, si la naturaleza llora nosotros no podemos llorar porque si nosotros lloramos

The scene ends with Rafa alone inside the hull of the reactor. He climbs out and walks around the reactor, observing and touching it. Throughout his testimony, these verbal and visual cues reveal the intimate entanglement of ideas, materials, and people from the perspective of the engineer. This scene also marks a turning point for Rafa. After sharing his story with his son, he demonstrates renewed energy and an interest in daily life. Back in the apartment, he and Leo put a fresh coat of paint on the living room walls. While he teaches his son proper stroke technique, Rafa dances to music on the radio. He also invites a date over for dinner. Ultimately, however, this relief is short-lived.

In their 2015 study of civil engineers and road construction in Peru, Penny Harvey and Hannah Knox develop the concept of the engineer-*bricoleur* who combines academic expertise with embodied, practical experience. The image of the Cuban nuclear engineer presented in *La obra del siglo* coincides with this approach; the film goes to great lengths to portray Rafa as a thinking, feeling subject. *Zona*, however, deconstructs this image into two competing characters. *El Ingeniero* comes across as an out-of-touch expert, while *El Nervio* is an engineer turned all-purpose handyman. The juxtaposition stages an encounter between these two forms of knowing and doing, and this conflict is furthermore mapped onto a hierarchy with racist undertones. At one point in the play, someone tries to insult *El Nervio* him by calling him an alchemist and another character responds that she has never seen a black alchemist and suggests that *brujo* or shaman would be a more fitting epithet.

El Nervio is also accused of causing the 'situation', since he repurposes scrap metal from the ruins of the nuclear plant to make bedframes and other necessities. He delivers a lengthy monologue in his defence as the audience accompanies him on his nightly run to the abandoned plant, explaining that all usable materials had disappeared overnight as a bustling slum arose on the outskirts of the city. He insists that the rumours about his bedframes are not true since there was never any hazardous material in there anyway. For safe measure, adds that: 'If there had been, nothing would have been able to make it out of that tomb.'[13] He then describes the procedure for storing nuclear waste, which includes several layers of ceramic, steel, and titanium, a granite tomb, and an indestructible dome. His insistence does not provide reassurance, but rather draws attention to the perception that others have of him.

El Ingeniero visits *El Nervio* in his 'laboratory', i.e. the abandoned plant, and their exchange further accentuates the group's hypocrisy. *El Ingeniero* asks *El Nervio* to build him a radiation detector and within the same breath he shows his contempt for his counterpart's informal methods. He describes the handyman's work as: 'The twisted, the oblique, that which slithers down

... si nosotros lloramos es por orgullo y no por cobardía, porque nosotros debemos enfrentar nuestros problemas ... Pero yo fui el primero que empezó a llorar' (01:02:00).

13 Original: 'Y de haberlo nada hubiese podido escapar de esa sepultura' (Caballero, 2017c, p. 28).

below, strange mechanics, what everyone knows but no one says aloud. I always tried to distance myself from all that, it has nothing to do with the image that others hold of me.'[14] His sanctimonious attitude, exacerbated by the fact that he is asking *El Nervio* for help, calls into question the hierarchies that privilege 'objective' knowledge over embodied experience.

El Ingeniero considers himself a reputable expert within his community, yet he is perceived as pedantic and full of hot air. The other characters call him a demagogue, make jokes, or simply state that he does not know what he is talking about. As the group attempts to determine the cause of the mysterious illness, *El Ingeniero* assures them that nuclear contamination is not the cause since there is a *Sistema de Vigilancia Radiológica* [Radiological Surveillance System] monitoring the area at all times. The other characters ignore these claims or openly tease him. Ofelia tells him that his naivety is endearing and invites him to lay his head on her lap. And last but not least, in the final scene, the other characters egg him on as he struggles to pull-start his homemade radiation detector, which appears to be a boat motor covered in flashing lights:

> SERVICITY. No matter. Try again.
> OMAR. Fail again.
> EKATERINA. Fail better.[15]

The reference to one of Samuel Beckett's most famous lines is a fitting end for the play. Absurdism is much more than a formal exercise for *Zona*. It calls into question the political, scientific, and philosophical tenets that sustained the ambitious nuclear programme. The potpourri style of delivery questions the primacy of one form of knowledge over all others. Scientific explanations are indistinguishable from literary quotations, conspiracy theories, personal testimonies, and even verborrhea. The overall effect is a destabilisation of meaning and an atmosphere of uncertainty.

Finally, the parody of the engineer takes on new meaning in light of the metadramatic elements used throughout the play. Teatro de La Fortaleza, the group responsible for creating *Zona*, has a rigorous creative methodology that involves observation, interviews, historical research, fictional reading assignments, and post-dramatic theatre exercises (Caballero, 2017a). For *Zona*, the group decided to incorporate interventions from the residents that served as inspiration for the characters. The stage notes indicate that a small wooden platform should be placed onstage for these non-actors, similar to Speakers' Corner in Hyde Park. The script includes varying degrees of detail for these

14 Original: 'Lo transversal, lo oblicuo, lo que serpentea por debajo, la mecánica rara, lo que todo el mundo sabe pero no se dice en voz alta. Todo eso de lo cual yo siempre me he alejado, y que nada tiene que ver con la imagen que los demás tienen de mí' (p. 29).

15 Original: 'Dale. Prueba otra vez. Fracasa otra vez. Fracasa mejor' (p. 35). The fragment is a translation of the well-known line from Samuel Beckett's 1983 novella *Worstward Ho*. In the original work, the quotation forms part of a broader wordplay that is darker than the famous soundbite suggests.

monologues. The resident who inspired the pedantic engineer clarifies that he does not like vodka; he does not fantasise about being the anonymous Russian soldier who climbed atop the Reichstag cupola to raise the Soviet flag in 1945, nor does he care much about impressing others. Lucho Medina, who served as the basis for *El Nervio,* simply 'tells his story'.

Together with the video camera facing the actors onstage at all times, and the pretence of the interview/interrogation that never materialises, these monologues draw attention to the act of testimony. Although the long-awaited reporters/nurses/scientists never arrive, it becomes clear that the play itself has allowed the characters and their doubles to tell their stories through all the expressive languages that theatre affords. In this way, perhaps, *Zona* breaks with absurdist form by creating an opportunity for meaningful and potentially fulfilling connection between the residents of the Nuclear City, the actors, and the audience.

The disaster that never happened

> —Otto, have you stopped to think about what would have happened if that monster exploded?
> —Sure, I've thought about it, because of Chernobyl, but for that they would have had to finish it.[16]

In 1986, just three years after construction began on the first reactor at Juraguá, disaster struck at the Chernobyl nuclear plant, located in present-day Ukraine. The horrific events triggered public opposition to nuclear energy throughout the world, and the Cuban government carried out an extensive press campaign to defend the Juraguá project, drawing attention to the difference between the reactor models and the implementation of additional safety measures. Through archival footage, *La obra del siglo* provides a glimpse of some of these press conferences. In the same sequence, the film also includes interviews with Cuban technicians that complain of missing parts, defects, and other setbacks. Finally, an intertext imitating a computer screen from the 1980s scrolls across the screen, concluding that even under optimal conditions these issues would have triggered unpredictable events.

Following this sequence, the camera pans out to show the Nuclear City in the present day. Pesticide clouds hang in the air as a grating, low-frequency alarm sounds in the background. The image cuts away to what appears to be Leo coughing as he smokes with a friend in a vacant, unfinished apartment. Finally, the fumigators from the opening scene reappear. The camera follows the fumigators as they leave the floor, passing the other residents who fill the hallway, biding time as they wait for the smoke to clear. A voiceover begins to describe the different categories of radiation exposure, explicitly linking the visual cues and sound effects to the idea of nuclear disaster. Once again,

16 Machado Quintela, 2015, 00:40:49.

the pesticide clouds evoke what *could have been.* Nostalgia for the space race morphs into the haunting sensation of a disaster that never happened.

Zona, in contrast, portrays contamination in the present-day Nuclear City. The unique material properties of radiation make this impossible situation seem plausible. Radiation is odourless and invisible and, as Rahul Mukherjee (2020) explains in his study of radiant infrastructures in contemporary India, it can silently 'spread through air, water, river and soil' (p. 12). For this reason, Mukherjee notes that 'living next to an atomic test site or nuclear reactor can totally disrupt a human being's sense of time and space' (p. 73). The material properties of radiation increase apprehension and deniability, frequently leading to conflict between communities that live near radiant infrastructures and government officials that negate toxicity. In this faceoff, the bodies of victims and survivors often 'rebel', displaying the physical and emotional traces of 'unwanted intimacies with radiant energies' (p. 14).

In *Zona*, a character named Omar insists, 'Whether you want to see it or not, there is something there, and that something has impacted almost everyone that lives here.'[17] As proof, he points to a series of curious symptoms: a glazed-over expression, a resigned attitude, nervous giggles, an air of sexual arousal, an addiction to telenovelas. Ofelia, the well-read prostitute, suggests that the symptoms are reminiscent of apraxia, a neurological disorder that impairs communication between the brain and the rest of the body, making it impossible to carry out simple tasks or movements. Finally, all the characters note that the population has been undergoing sudden changes in size.

There is no consensus about the cause of these symptoms, but the most common hypothesis is, of course, the nuclear plant. The characters repeatedly mention the possibility of a leak or contaminated materials, and the two engineers attempt to reassure them. *El Ingeniero* declares the idea a malicious rumour. On multiple occasions, he insists that there is a surveillance system monitoring the air, and when this does not convince the rest of the group, he commissions *El Nervio* to build the radiation detector so that he can set the record straight himself. In the final scene, a brief intervention by the two real-life engineers addresses the mechanics of nuclear fission works and the possibility of a leak. Finally, *El Ingeniero* starts his makeshift 'contraption', which looks like a boat motor covered in flashing lights. The machine captures the cacophony of daily life in the Nuclear City: voices, profanity, domino games, telenovelas. As the play ends, the characters realise that no one is coming. The machine starts to emit recognisable, albeit random songs, and *El Nervio* begins

17 Original: 'Lo quieras ver o no, algo hay, y ese algo ha influido sobre casi todos los que viven aquí' (p. 18).

to dance, performing a mix between rhythmic dance and Tai Chi. Slowly, the other characters start to imitate him.

In the end, all their theories boil down to one concern: radiation poisoning. *Zona* develops an uncanny atmosphere of nuclear contamination, even though there was never any radioactive material delivered to the Project of the Century. The material properties of radiation, combined with the overwhelming feeling of being abandoned by the state, triggers anxiety, hypervigilance, and uncertainty. While it becomes clear that their attempts to find answers have been futile, the final dance provides an open ending. Its interpretation depends on the gestures and affect expressed by the actors in the moment.

Conclusion

Both works analysed demonstrate the potential of fiction to express social complexity. They employ diverse representational strategies. *La obra del siglo* makes use of archival footage and extra-diegetic visuals and sounds while *Zona* revels in word play, nonsense, and metadramatic interventions. In both works, the Cuban nuclear engineer is shown to be immersed in the entanglement of ideas, materials, and people that made up the Cuban nuclear dream. Equally important is the representation of the transnational community of support workers and family members that were brought together around the Project of the Century. It is difficult to pinpoint why these secondary characters stayed or what they feel, but both works succeed in conveying a vague, conflicted attachment to place and ambivalence towards the remains of the nuclear plant.

Each work develops a different, yet equally haunted atmosphere. In *La obra del siglo* the mood is lethargic, eerie, and surreal. The pesticide clouds signal a lack of adequate infrastructure in the Nuclear City, while also evoking the utopian *and* dystopian potential of a future that never came to pass. In *Zona,* contamination comes to stand in for the many problems facing the community in the present: lack of livelihood, food, water, health, and information. The characters are plagued by rumours, conspiracy theories, and mysterious symptoms. The most important takeaway from both works is abandonment.

State neglect can have potentially devastating consequences for the future of the Nuclear City. In between the release of *La obra del siglo* and *Zona,* it was announced that the crumbling structure of the Juraguá plant would become a storage facility for hazardous substances. The plant is projected to store waste from national industries, yet there is concern that it will give way to the lucrative business of importing nuclear waste. The director of *Zona*, Atilio Caballero, is one of the people following these developments with great concern. In a series of articles published in an alternative media source, he draws attention to a little-known clause in the 1997 Environmental Law that makes it possible to import radioactive waste when deemed 'socially justified' (Caballero, 2017b). According to Caballero, the inhabitants of the Nuclear City have not been consulted and many are unaware of this significant change. Whether the ruins are used to store local or international waste, the decision is a painful epilogue for Project of the Century. It is a topic that requires more attention as ongoing market-oriented reforms in Cuba open the door for nuclear necropolitics.

References

Bloom, L. (2015) 'Hauntological environmental art: the photographic frame and the nuclear afterlife of Chernobyl in Lina Selander's "Lenin's Lamp"', *Journal of Visual Culture*, 17 (2): 223–37.

Caballero, A. (2017a) 'A history of Teatro de la Plaza', *Interdisciplinary Studies in Literature and the Environment*, 22 (4): 895–900.

Caballero, A. (2017b) 'Sub-zona 1 (I) and Sub-zona 1 (II)' *Hypermedia Magazine*, <www.hypermediamagazine.com/author/atilio/> (accessed 4 January 2021).

Caballero, A. (2017c) *Zona* (Matanzas: Ediciones Matanza).

Castro, F. (1992) 'Discurso pronunciado en el acto por el XXXIX aniversario del asalto al Cuartel Moncada y el XXXV del levantamiento de Cienfuegos, efectuado en Cienfuegos, el 5 de septiembre de 1992', *Portal Cuba*, <www.cuba.cu/gobierno/discursos/> (accessed 14 October 2020).

Castro, F. (2007) *La historia me absolverá*, 5th ed. (Havana: Editorial de Ciencias Sociales).

Castro Díaz-Balart, F. (2014) 'La física nuclear en Cuba: apuntes para una historia', *Nucleus*, 56: 5–16.

Cederlöf, G. (2015) 'Thermodynamics revisited: the political ecology of energy systems in historical perspective', in R.L. Bryan (ed.), *The International Handbook of Political Ecology* (Cheltenham: Edward Elgar): 646–58.

Cederlöf, G. (2020) 'The revolutionary city: socialist urbanisation and nuclear modernity in Cienfuegos, Cuba', *Journal of Latin American Studies*, 52 (1): 53–76.

Collier, S.J. (2017) *Post-Soviet Social: Neoliberalism, Social Modernity, Biopolitics* (Princeton, NJ: Princeton University Press).

de Ferrari, G. (2015) *Community and Culture in Post-Soviet Cuba* (New York: Routledge).

Echevarría, A. (2016) 'Seis millones de pares de zapatos plásticos', *Hypermedia Magazine*, <www.hypermediamagazine.com/arte/cine/ahmel-echevarria-seis-millones-de-pares-de-zapatos-plasticos/> (accessed 14 September 2019).

Esslin, M. (1965) *Absurd Drama* (Harmondsworth: Penguin).

Harvey, P. and H. Knox (2015) *Roads. An Anthropology of Infrastructure and Expertise* (Ithaca, NY: Cornell University Press).

Larkin, B. (2018) 'Promising forms: the political aesthetics of infrastructure', in N. Anand, A. Gupta, and H. Appel (eds.), *The Promise of Infrastructure* (Durham, NC: Duke University Press): 175–208.

Lechuga, C. (2019). 'Sobre cómo fracasar mejor… una conversación con el joven cineasta Carlos Quintela', *Revista El Estornudo,* <www.revistaelestornudo.com/carlos-quintela-cine-cubano/> (accessed 14 October 2020).

Machado Quintela, C. (Dir.) (2015) *La obra del siglo* [The project of the century] (Argentina and Cuba: Rizoma Films/Uranio Films/Raspberry & Cream Films/World Cinema Fund/ICAIC).

Mukherjee, R. (2020) *Radiant Infrastructures: Media, Environment, and Cultures of Uncertainty* (Durham, NC: Duke University Press).

Index

www.ingramcontent.com/pod-product-compliance
Lightning Source LLC
LaVergne TN
LVHW051031210426
836737LV00021B/64

* 9 7 8 1 9 0 8 8 5 7 9 5 8 *